family handyman
MOST REQUESTED PROJECTS

BUILD IT. FIX IT. LIVE IT!

family handyman

MOST REQUESTED
PROJECTS

Most Requested Projects

Project Editor   Mary Flanagan
Cover Photography   Tom Fenenga
Cover Art Direction   George McKeon
Page Layout   Mariah Cates, Jenny Mahoney,
    Andrea Sorensen

Text, photography and illustrations for
Most Requested Projects are based on articles
previously published in *Family Handyman* magazine
(2915 Commers Dr., Suite 700, Eagan, MN 55121,
familyhandyman.com). For information on advertising in
Family Handyman magazine, call (646) 518-4215.

Hardcover: 978-1-62145-484-7
Paperbook: 978-1-62145-450-2

A NOTE TO OUR READERS: All do-it-yourself activities
involve a degree of risk. Skills, materials, tools and site
conditions vary widely. Although the editors have made
every effort to ensure accuracy, the reader remains
responsible for the selection and use of tools, materials
and methods. Always obey local codes and laws, follow
manufacturer instructions and observe safety precautions.

Family Handyman

Chief Content Officer   Nick Grzechowiak
Editor-in-Chief   Gary Wentz
Associate and Contributing Editors   Mike Berner,
    Brad Holden, Travis Larson, Rick Muscoplat, Mark Petersen
Associate Creative Director   Vern Johnson
Design and Production   Mariah Cates, Jenny Mahoney,
    Marcia Roepke, Andrea Sorensen
Illustrations   Steve Björkman, Ron Chamberlain, Ken Clubb,
    Jeff Gorton, John Hartman, Trevor Johnston, Don Mannes,
    Christopher Mills, Frank Rohrbach
Photography   Tom Fenenga
Managing Editor   Donna Bierbach
Set Builder   Josh Risberg
Editorial Services Associate   Peggy McDermott
Production Manager   Leslie Kogan

Trusted Media Brands, Inc.

President & Chief Executive Officer   Bonnie Kintzer

PRINTED IN CHINA

Contents

1 OUTSTANDING OUTDOOR PROJECTS

SHEDS
Dream Shed...6
Yard Shed 16
Compact Shed...28

OUTDOOR FURNITURE
Perfect Patio Chairs 38
Fabulous Fire Table..44
Cedar Potting Bench 54
Simple Timber Bench 60

DECKS
Maintenance-Free Deck 66
Dream Deck...80

PLANTERS
Raised Gardens 92
3-Season Planter 99
Patio Planter 105
Self-Watering Raised Planting Bed...............111

ADD-ONS
Backyard Oasis 116
Space-Saving Tool Holder............................ 124
Garden Closet... 126

INCREDIBLE INDOOR PROJECTS

BOOKCASES
Bookcase with Secret Hiding Places 130
No-Excuses Bookcase 139
Super-Simple Bookcase 144

KITCHEN STORAGE UPGRADES
Kitchen Cabinet Rollouts 150
Cabinet Door Rack 156
Ultimate Container Storage 158

CLOSETS
Small Closet Organizer 163
Triple Your Closet Space 169
Wire Shelving Made Easy 178

INTERIOR TRIM
Interior Trim Simplified 182
Painting Woodwork 195
No Cutting Corners 201

TILE
Ceramic Tile Floor 207
Tile a Shower with Panache 214
Tile a Backsplash 220

ENTRYWAY ENHANCEMENTS
Hide-the-Mess Lockers 224
Entry Organizer 228

3 BIG IMPACT FIXES

Cures for Top 5 Lawn Problems 236
Patio Cover-up 242
Recap Concrete Steps 246
Fixing Cracks in Concrete 249

Recoat a Driveway 256
Seal Attic Air Leaks 260
Replace a Storm Door 266
Replace a Toilet 271

OUR MOST POPULAR WORKBENCHES

Super-Simple Workbench 276
Classic Workbench 280
Best Workbench Upgrades 284

Chapter One

OUTSTANDING OUTDOOR PROJECTS

SHEDS
Dream Shed.. 6
Yard Shed 16
Compact Shed... 28

OUTDOOR FURNITURE
Perfect Patio Chairs....................................... 38
Fire Table 44
Cedar Potting Bench 54
Timber Bench 60

DECKS
Maintenance-Free Deck 66
Dream Deck... 80

PLANTERS
Raised Gardens 92
3-Season Planter 99
Patio Planter 105
Self-Watering Raised Planting Bed............... 111

ADD-ONS
Backyard Oasis... 116
Space-Saving Tool Holder............................. 124
Garden Closet 126

Dream Shed

*Build this masterpiece
designed by a pro*

WHAT IT TAKES

TIME: Three or four weekends

COST: $3,000

SKILL: Intermediate to advanced

TOOLS: Standard hand tools, a
circular saw and a drill. Nice but
not necessary: table saw, miter
saw, nail gun and jigsaw.

In the past couple of decades, we've built a lot of garages and sheds, and at least a half dozen have appeared in this magazine. In that time we've learned how to build sheds quicker and better, and how to make a plain shed look great without spending an arm and a leg.

This shed incorporates many of the building methods we've learned. It includes special features like custom brackets and homemade windows and doors, which set the shed apart from kits you'll find at the home center. And the best part is that you can build this shed knowing that we've worked out the kinks.

Start with a simple shed, then add...

■ Frame-and-panel doors
We made these doors on-site, but they rival expensive factory-made doors in looks and durability.

■ Hand-crafted brackets
Building brackets is the easiest part of this project, but they make a huge impact on the look of the shed.

■ Lots of trim
We used LP Smartside trim and siding. The trim costs much less than knot-free wood, so you can add lots of it without blowing your budget.

■ Planter boxes
These planters are just wooden boxes with simple brackets underneath. But they're the perfect finishing touch.

■ Custom windows
Inexpensive barn sashes are the key to making your own windows. Add decorative trim to complete the custom look.

Here are some of the features that make this shed easy to build, affordable and long lasting:

- The floor rests on a foundation of treated 6x6s and gravel. It's cheap and simple.
- Walls are prebuilt on the floor and covered with siding while they're still lying down.
- The roof is framed with homemade trusses that you also assemble right on the shed floor.
- The siding and trim are long-lasting composite material that comes preprimed and ready to paint.
- Doors and windows are handmade to save money and provide a custom look.

For detailed drawings on framing, siding and trim as well as window and door construction, go to familyhandyman.com/2013shed

MEET THE EXPERT

Before starting work at *Family Handyman*, Jeff spent more than 15 years as a remodeling contractor building additions and garages and doing whole-house renovations as well as kitchen and bathroom remodeling. He used knowledge gained from this experience to design and build the shed you see here.

Figure A
Shed

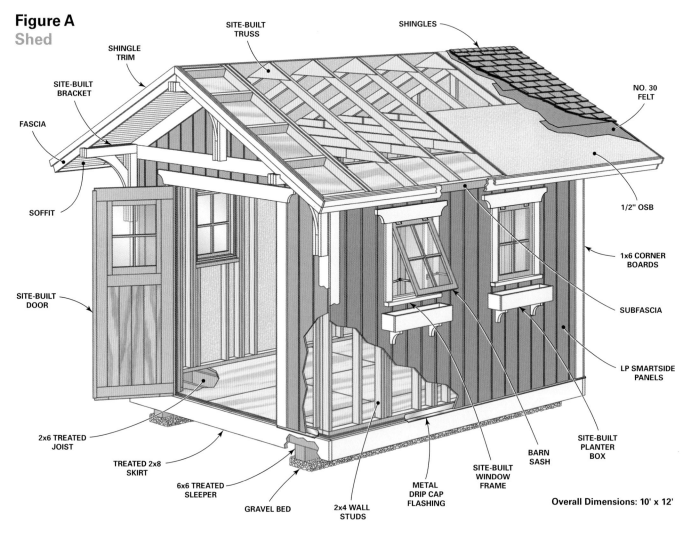

SITE-BUILT TRUSS

SHINGLES

SHINGLE TRIM

SITE-BUILT BRACKET

FASCIA

SOFFIT

NO. 30 FELT

1/2" OSB

1x6 CORNER BOARDS

SITE-BUILT DOOR

SUBFASCIA

LP SMARTSIDE PANELS

2x6 TREATED JOIST

TREATED 2x8 SKIRT

6x6 TREATED SLEEPER

GRAVEL BED

2x4 WALL STUDS

METAL DRIP CAP FLASHING

SITE-BUILT WINDOW FRAME

BARN SASH

SITE-BUILT PLANTER BOX

Overall Dimensions: 10' x 12'

Money, time and tools

You'll find most of the materials to build this shed at home centers or lumberyards. You may have to special-order the LP SmartSide trim. We found the barn sash at a local home center, but if you're not so lucky, go to combinationdoor.com to find a retailer near you. The materials for this shed cost us $3,000.

To build this shed, you'll need standard carpentry tools including a circular saw and drill. A framing nail gun and compressor will speed up the framing. And a power miter saw and table saw would save you time and help you get perfect cuts on the trim pieces. But they aren't necessary. You'll also need a pocket screw jig to build doors like ours.

If you've built a deck or have some carpentry experience, you shouldn't have any trouble building this shed. With a few helpers, you should be able to get the foundation and floor built in a day. The next day you can build the trusses and get a start on the walls. Round up a few strong friends when it's time to stand the walls. If you keep at it, you'll be able to finish building the shed in three or four weekends.

Getting started

In most areas, sheds 120 sq. ft. or smaller do not require a permit to build, but check with your local building department to be sure. Also ask if there are rules about where your shed can be located on the lot.

Take the **Materials List** (you'll find it at familyhandyman.com/2013shed) with you to your favorite lumberyard or home center and go over the list with the salesperson to see what items you may have to order. Then set up a delivery so you'll be ready to build when your help arrives. A few days before you plan to dig, call 811 or visit call811.com for instructions on how to locate buried utility lines.

Build the floor

We chose to build the shed on a wood floor supported by treated 6x6s, but you could also pour a concrete foundation or choose a different method of supporting the joists.

Start by laying out the perimeter of the shed, either with stakes and a string line, or with a rectangle built with 2x4s to represent the outside edges of the

1 LEVEL THE SLEEPERS. Set treated 6x6 sleepers on level beds of gravel. Tamp down the sleepers to level them.

2 SQUARE THE RIM JOISTS. Nail the rim joists together. Make sure diagonal measurements are equal. Then nail or screw the joists to the beams.

TOP OF RAFTERS

3 COMPLETE THE FLOOR. Add the rest of the joists. Then nail treated plywood to the joists, staggering the seams.

4 MARK THE TRUSS PATTERN ON THE SHED FLOOR. Snap chalk lines to make a template for the trusses (see Figure C at familyhandyman.com/2013shed for details). Screw 2x4 blocks to the floor to complete the pattern.

RAFTER

BOTTOM CHORD

GUSSETS   BLOCK

5 BUILD THE TRUSSES. Join the rafters and chords with gussets cut from plywood or OSB. Fasten the gussets with screws and glue.

10 x 12-ft. floor. Now measure in 14-3/4 in. from the long sides and drive stakes to mark the center of the trenches. Dig trenches about 12 in. wide and about 10 in. below where you want the bottom edge of the joists to end up. Pour 4 in. of gravel into the trenches and level it off. Make sure the gravel in both trenches is at the same level. Then cut the 6x6s to 12 ft. long and set them in the trenches. Measure to make sure the 6x6s are parallel. Then measure diagonally from the ends to make sure they're square. The diagonal measurements should be equal. Finally, tamp the 6x6s with a sledge to level them (**Photo 1**).

Now you're ready to build the floor. Start by cutting the 12-ft.-long rim joists for the sides and marking the joist locations 16 in. on center. Assemble the perimeter frame on top of the 6x6s (**Photo 2**, p. 9, and **Figure B** online). Then fill in the remaining joists. When you're done, use a taut string line or sight down the 12-ft. rim joist to make sure it's straight. Then drive toenails through the joists into the 6x6s. Finish up by nailing the 3/4-in. treated plywood to the joists (**Photo 3**).

Assemble the trusses

The shed floor makes a perfect work surface for building the trusses. Use the dimensions from **Figure C** online to lay out the truss pattern and cut the rafters (**Photo 4**). Screw 2x4 blocks to the plywood along the top line to hold the

Labels on image: WINDOW TRIMMER, REGULAR STUD

Label on image: ALIGN PLATE WITH CHALK LINE

6 **MARK THE WALL FRAMING. Cut** the 2x4 plates and set them in place on the floor. Mark the position of studs, windows and doors according to the plan.

7 **BUILD THE WALLS. Arrange the studs, trimmers, cripples and headers between** the top and bottom plates. Line them up with your layout marks and nail through the plates to assemble the wall.

rafters in place while you connect them with the OSB (oriented strand board) gussets (**Photo 5**). Build five regular trusses and two gable end trusses. Remember to cut eight additional rafters to use for the gable-end overhangs. Take your time building the trusses to make sure they're all identical.

Stand the walls

Building and siding the walls while they're lying on the floor saves time and ensures that the walls are perfectly square. But it does require you to move heavy walls around. If you don't have help, then leave the siding off until after the walls are standing.

Start by chalking lines on the floor to indicate the inside edges of the walls. These lines provide a reference for straightening the bottom plate of the walls after the walls are standing. Cut bottom plates from treated 2x4s and top plates from untreated lumber. Arrange the plates along the chalk lines and mark them (**Photo 6**, and **Figures D** and **E** online).

Build the front and back walls first. Before you install the siding, align the bottom plate with the chalk line and tack it with a few 8d nails or screws to hold it straight. Then adjust the top plate until diagonal measurements from the corners of the walls are equal and tack the top corners to the floor to hold the wall square. Position the sheets of siding so the

8 **STAND AND BRACE THE SIDE WALLS. Lift the side walls and support them with** temporary braces. Align the bottom plates with the chalk lines and nail the plates to the floor joists. Next, lift the front and back walls into place.

9 SET THE TRUSSES. Screw a brace to the back wall to support the back truss. Set the front and back trusses. Then stretch a string between the peaks and nail on a truss brace with layout marks to align the remaining trusses. Toenail them to the top plate.

10 ADD THE OVERHANGS. Build the gable-end overhangs. Line the tops up with the roof framing and nail the overhangs to the wall and subfascia.

11 SHEATHE THE ROOF. Nail OSB to the rafters. Stagger the seams by starting with a half sheet on the second row.

bottom edge extends 1 in. beyond the bottom plate and nail it to the studs with 6d galvanized siding nails. Set the front and back walls aside. Then build and stand the side walls (**Photos 7** and **8**).

Finish the wall framing by nailing the corners together and adding a second top plate. Tie the walls together by overlapping the second top plate onto the adjacent wall.

Set the trusses

There are a few setup steps to take before you're ready to set trusses. Start by marking the truss positions on the top plates of the side walls. Then screw a long 2x4 to the center of the end wall so that it extends high enough to support the end truss (**Photo 9**). Lift the end truss onto the walls and center it so there's an equal amount of overhang on both sides. Then nail it to the plate and screw it to the temporary brace.

Next, mark the truss layout, including the overhangs, on a 16-ft.-long 2x4 to use near the top as a temporary brace. This brace will run parallel to the side walls and close to the ridge. Using this brace as support, set the truss on the other end, once again making sure it's centered. The final setup step is to stretch a string line between the peaks of the end trusses. You'll use this line as a reference to center the remaining trusses. Elevate the line slightly so it clears the trusses.

Now you're ready to set trusses. Just lift them up, line them up with your marks, and make sure the peak is aligned with the string line. Toenail the trusses to the plates on the bottom, and support the tops temporarily by driving nails or screws through the long 2x4 brace near the peak (**Photo 9**). You can remove the brace after you've installed most of the roof sheathing.

Add the overhangs

With the trusses done, you can complete the siding on the gable ends. Then finish the roof framing. Start by nailing 2x4 subfascia to the rafter ends. The subfascia should extend 2 ft. on both ends. Sight down the subfascia to make sure it's straight. Correct any waviness by driving shims between the rafter ends and subfascia. Next build the "ladders" that will form the front and back overhangs. **Photo 10** shows how to install them. Then install the roof sheathing (**Photo 11**). Cover the sheathing with roofing paper as soon as you finish the fascia boards. Then if you don't install your shingles right away, you won't have to worry about your shed getting wet.

Finish the soffits and trim

We used beaded plywood for the soffits to simulate beaded-board soffits. To keep the grooves running the same direction, parallel to the sides, cut the soffit pieces for the front and back overhangs across the 4-ft. dimension of the plywood. Remember, the soffit doesn't have to fit tight to the siding. This edge will be covered by 3/4-in.-thick trim.

After the soffit is complete, install the 1x6 trim boards that fit under the soffit on the sides, and run horizontally across the front and back. Then cut the angled trim pieces for the front and back, and finally install the 1x6 corners. We ripped one of the corner boards down to 4-3/4 in. wide and overlapped the 1x6 for the opposite side onto it. This creates a corner that's 5-1/2 in. wide on both sides.

Build and install the brackets

The shed has three decorative brackets on the front. They're assembled from a 2x10 sandwiched between 2x4s. Using **Figure L** online as a guide, cut the 2x10 and draw the curve on it. Use a 1x2 with two holes drilled in it as a giant compass to draw the curve. Cut the curve with a jigsaw and sand it. Paint all of the parts before you assemble the brackets to save time and provide better protection.

Connect the L-shaped 2x4 sections with 5-in.-long construction screws. Then complete the brackets by screwing the parts together (**Photo 13**). **Photo 14** shows how to mount the brackets.

Assemble the windows

We used inexpensive barn sash for the windows. You could also use sash salvaged from an old double-hung window. But if you do, plan ahead so you can adjust the size of the rough openings when you build the walls. Start by measuring the sash and building a 1x4 frame that's 1/4 in. wider and taller than the sash. Cut 1x2 stops to fit in the frame and position them to hold

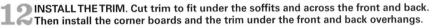

12 INSTALL THE TRIM. Cut trim to fit under the soffits and across the front and back. Then install the corner boards and the trim under the front and back overhangs.

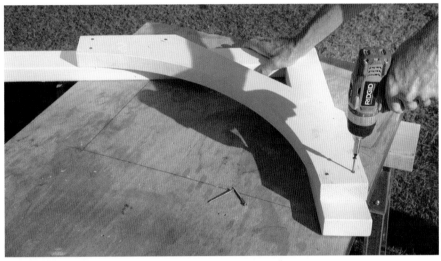

13 BUILD THE BRACKETS. Screw the parts together, sandwiching the curved brace between the 2x4s. Sand and paint all the parts before assembly.

14 MOUNT THE BRACKETS. Screw 2x2 cleats to the shed wall. Then slip the brackets over the cleats and drive screws through the brackets into the cleats to secure them.

16 INSTALL THE WINDOWS. Set the window into the opening. Center it and nail the top corners of the trim. Adjust the frame until there's an even gap around the barn sash and nail the bottom corners. Add a few more nails on the side and top.

15 MOUNT THE SASH IN THE FRAME. Build a 1x4 frame and mount the barn sash to it with galvanized screen door hinges.

17 BUILD THE DOOR FRAMES. Spread waterproof wood glue. Then drive screws though the back frame into the front frame.

1x6 TONGUE-AND-GROOVE

18 ADD THE SASH AND DOOR PANEL. Cut 1x6 tongue-and-groove boards to fit the opening below the window. Attach them with one screw in the center of each board. Mount the barn sash with one screw in each corner.

the sash flush with one edge of the 1x4 frame. Then attach galvanized screen door hinges to the frame, set the sash in place, and screw the hinges to it (**Photo 15**).

Start the window trim by cutting curves on the ends of the 1-in.-thick top casing (**Figure M**, online) and nailing it to the top of the window. Leave 1/4 in. of the 1x4 frame exposed. Next cut the 1x4 side casings with 10-degree bevels on the bottoms. Nail them to the frame. Finish by cutting out the sill with 10-degree bevels on the front and back and screwing it to the side casings. We added Stanley Storm Window Adjuster hardware to the windows to hold them open and as locks.

Installing the windows is simple. Just set them in the opening, making sure they're centered, and nail through the trim to hold them in place. Start by nailing the two top corners. Then adjust the window frame as necessary to create an even space around the sash before nailing the bottom two corners (**Photo 16**).

Build and install the doors

These doors look great, and to buy similar factory-made wood doors would cost a fortune. You can easily make them using the system we show here. Choose the straightest boards you can find for this project. You don't want a warped door!

Start by making the front and back layers (**Figure N**, online). You'll need a pocket hole jig for this. You can buy a pocket hole jig at home centers or online. Search "pocket screw" at familyhandyman.com for information on how to use the jig.

Glue and screw the two layers together to make the door (**Photo 17**). The front panel should extend 1-1/4 in. beyond the back panel on the bottom. This will create a seal on the bottom when the door is hung. If the edges don't line up perfectly, you can plane or sand them later. Finish the doors by adding the 1x6 tongue-and-groove boards and sash (**Photo 18**). We used 1x6s with a beaded pattern running down the center, but you can choose any material you like to fill the panel. The barn sashes are 1 in. thick, so they'll stick out a little on the back.

Install the door trim before you mount the doors. Cut the 1-in.-thick top trim to length and cut curves on the end to match the window trim. Then nail it to the siding, making sure the edge is flush with the framed opening. Cut the trim pieces for the sides and align them flush to the framed opening before nailing them to the wall. Nail 1x2 door stops on the sides and top of the framed opening, 1-1/2 in. back from the face of the door trim.

The trick to mounting the doors easily is to support them on a temporary 2x4 and wedge them into position with shims (**Photo 19**). Attach the doors with your choice of surface-mount hinges. We used black gate hinges. To seal the gap between the doors, nail a 1x2 astragal to the back of the door you want to remain closed most of the time. Then mount surface bolts inside, to the top and bottom of this "stationary" door, to hold it closed. We installed a standard exterior entry lock on the active door and a matching dummy knob on the stationary side.

Finishing up

Before you shingle, install metal drip edge if you plan to use it, then nail a row of starter shingles along the bottom of the roof. Follow the instructions on the shingle package for installing the shingles (**Photo 20**).

We used top-quality acrylic exterior paint for the trim and siding. We protected the window sash, doors and soffit with a coat of Sikkens Cetol SRD translucent finish.

You can add charm with the simple-to-build flower boxes (**Figure P**, online). Inside, add shelves, hooks or cabinets for storage, or build in a workbench for a nice potting shed.

SHIMS

TEMPORARY 2x4 SUPPORT

19 **INSTALL THE DOORS.** Set the doors on a temporary 2x4 ledger. Wedge shims between the doors and the framing to create equal spacing all around the doors. Screw the hinges to the doors and the trim.

20 **SHINGLE THE ROOF.** Snap chalk lines to indicate the top of the shingle courses. For details on fastening the shingles, check the packaging.

Yard Shed

Spacious, attractive and lots of natural light

Who doesn't need a better place to stow all that stuff cluttering up the garage? Wheelbarrows, lawn mowers, bikes, fertilizer spreaders and lawn and garden supplies all steal precious garage space. A yard shed will not only free up your garage but also help you organize and neaten your home and let you park the cars inside the garage again.

We've bent over backward to design a shed that's easy to build yet has lots of useful features. We combined standard 2x4 wall construction with prefabricated roof trusses to make roof framing easy, eliminate tricky soffit (eave overhang) work and simplify trim details. We added an easy-to-build sliding door for wide shed access without the hassles or expense of swinging doors. Additional features include the open portico and wide roof overhangs. They'll shade you from the hot sun and shelter you from the rain so you can work in the open air or just relax.

Here we'll show you the step-by-step process of how to frame and finish this shed. While time-consuming, the process doesn't require any advanced carpentry skills. If you've done some framing and siding and a tad of roofing, you're qualified to tackle this project. We spent about $4,000 (excluding the concrete work) for top-grade materials. The **Materials Lists** tell you what we used, but it's easy to shave off $1,000 or more by excluding some of the cosmetic trim, or substituting a less expensive material for the rough-sawn cedar. If you want to further cut costs, eliminate skylights and use standard shingles in lieu of the architectural-grade shingles.

WHAT IT TAKES

COST: $4,000 (excluding concrete floor)

SKILL: Intermediate to advanced

TOOLS: Circular saw, drill, scaffolding with wheels

Figure A
Framing details

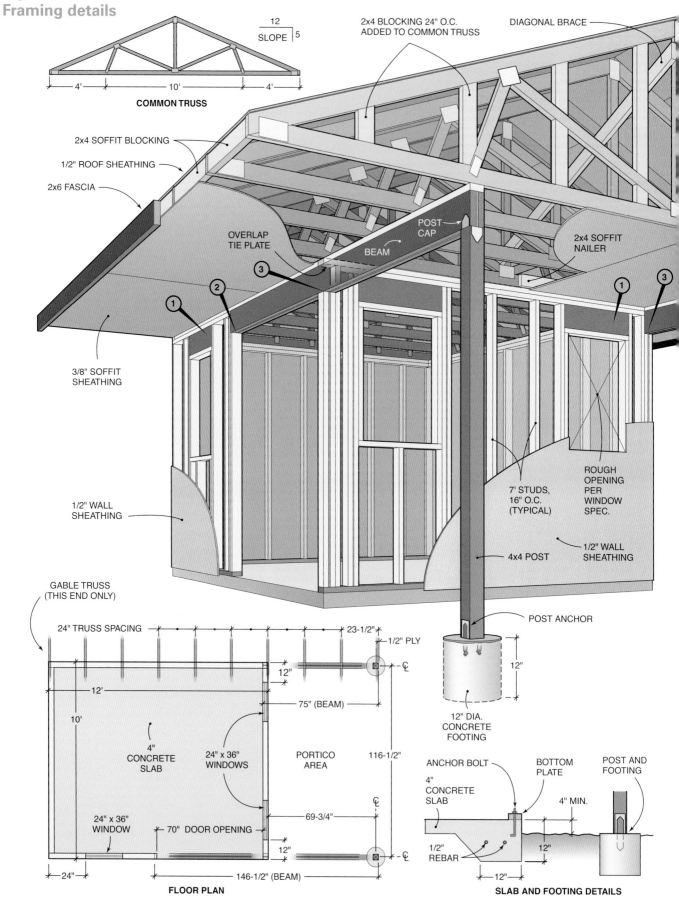

SLOPE $\frac{12}{5}$

COMMON TRUSS

4' — 10' — 4'

2x4 BLOCKING 24" O.C. ADDED TO COMMON TRUSS

DIAGONAL BRACE

2x4 SOFFIT BLOCKING

1/2" ROOF SHEATHING

2x6 FASCIA

OVERLAP TIE PLATE

POST CAP

BEAM

2x4 SOFFIT NAILER

③

②

①

①

③

3/8" SOFFIT SHEATHING

ROUGH OPENING PER WINDOW SPEC.

7' STUDS, 16" O.C. (TYPICAL)

1/2" WALL SHEATHING

1/2" WALL SHEATHING

4x4 POST

POST ANCHOR

GABLE TRUSS (THIS END ONLY)

24" TRUSS SPACING

23-1/2"

1/2" PLY

12"

12"

75" (BEAM)

116-1/2"

12" DIA. CONCRETE FOOTING

12'

12'

10'

4" CONCRETE SLAB

24" x 36" WINDOWS

PORTICO AREA

69-3/4"

24" x 36" WINDOW

70" DOOR OPENING

12"

24"

146-1/2" (BEAM)

FLOOR PLAN

ANCHOR BOLT

BOTTOM PLATE

POST AND FOOTING

4" CONCRETE SLAB

4" MIN.

1/2" REBAR

12"

12"

SLAB AND FOOTING DETAILS

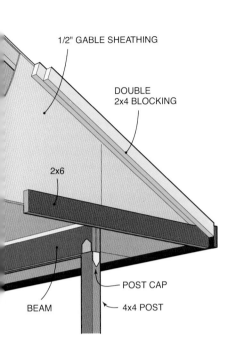

1/2" GABLE SHEATHING

DOUBLE 2x4 BLOCKING

2x6

BEAM

POST CAP

4x4 POST

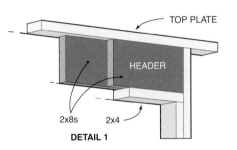

TOP PLATE

HEADER

2x8s

2x4

DETAIL 1

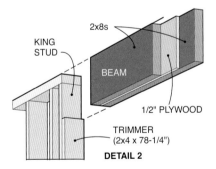

2x8s

KING STUD

BEAM

1/2" PLYWOOD

TRIMMER (2x4 x 78-1/4")

DETAIL 2

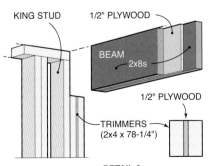

KING STUD

1/2" PLYWOOD

BEAM

2x8s

1/2" PLYWOOD

TRIMMERS (2x4 x 78-1/4")

DETAIL 3

Materials list
Rough framing materials

ITEM	QTY.
Framing materials	
4x4 x 8' treated (portico posts)	2
2x4 x 10' treated (bottom plates)	2
2x4 x 12' treated (bottom plate)	1
2x4 x 8' treated (bottom plate)	1
2x4 x 12' (top and tie plates)	14
2x4 x 7' (studs)	60
2x8 x 14' (door/portico beam)	2
2x8 x 8' (portico beam, window headers)	4
4x8 1/2" plywood sheets (roof and wall sheathing)	25
Roof trusses	
Common trusses	9
Gable end truss	1
Hardware	
16d cement-coated nails (framing nails)	15 lbs
8d cement-coated nails (sheathing nails)	10 lbs.
1-1/2" joist hanger screws (connector fasteners)	1 lb.
Rafter ties (truss anchors)	16
H-clips (plywood joints)	36
Post anchors (post-to-concrete connection)	2
Post caps (post-to-beam connection)	2

Size it to suit

Because we're using standard wall construction and roof trusses, you can build virtually any size shed you wish using these basic construction techniques. The trusses we show are designed to handle the 4-ft. wide soffits. You can also order trusses with shorter soffits or a different roof slope. Our trusses have a 5/12 slope, which means they drop 5 inches for every 12 horizontal inches.

Contact your local building department and ask if a building permit is needed. Be ready to supply the exact location of the shed on your property along with dimensions and building details. Make a copy of **Figure A** and submit that along with a site plan and that'll probably be all you'll need. If you want to wire your shed, you'll need an electrical permit as well.

A few rented tools will save gobs of time

You'll need only an apronful of tools, a circular saw and a screw gun to build this shed, but a couple of rental tools will speed construction. A 6-ft. section of scaffolding, complete with wheels and planks, will simplify roof-related construction. Set it up inside the shed and you'll have a safe platform for setting the trusses. Set it up outside and it'll make sheathing the roof

1 Cut the top and bottom plates to length (see figure a), then mark and drill 5/8-in. Anchor bolt holes in the bottom plates. Tack the pairs together and mark the window, door and stud locations.

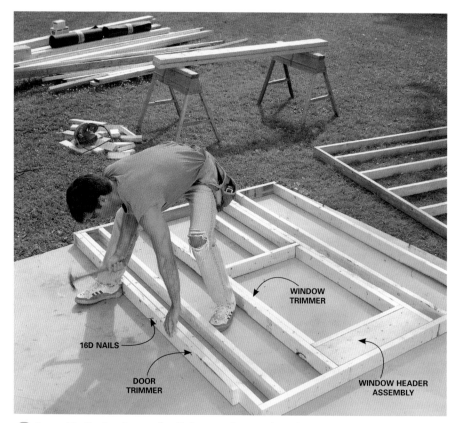

2 Assemble the headers and nail them to the top plates. Then nail the full-length studs to both plates, and finally add the trimmers and other framing for the doors and windows.

Tip

Lay out the wall plates ahead of time, then mark on the forms where you'd like the anchor bolts placed (two on the short walls, three on the back wall) so they won't end up in the doorway or beneath studs.

and installing the fascia boards and the first few rows of shingles much easier. If you're productive, you'll even have rental time left on Sunday afternoon to side the gable ends.

To save time when you're nailing, also consider renting a pneumatic sheathing stapler (**Photo 11**) and a roofing nailer (**Photo 14**).

Pouring the slab

We hired a concrete contractor to pour our floor: a 4-in. thick slab with edges thickened to 12 in. around the perimeter (**Figure A**). It cost us about $1,200. But if you've done concrete work before, you can certainly pour this simple slab yourself for $500 or less. Form it so the top is at least 4 in. above the ground to protect the wood trim and siding from water runoff and splashing. Embed two rows of 1/2-in. rebar in the footings during pouring to strengthen the edges. You'll need to order 4.5 yards of concrete plus any concrete you want for walks, patios or footings outside the structure.

Although we put a paver brick patio in front of the shed and under the portico, you can save time and money by pouring a concrete slab in those areas instead. Just make sure that the concrete outside the shed slopes away so water won't seep in under the walls.

Also dig footings to support the portico posts (**Figure A**). Use string lines to find the post positions, then dig 12-in. diameter, 12-in. deep footings and fill them with concrete to 4 in. below the slab height (to leave room for the finished patio floor). If you extend a concrete patio slab under the posts, increase the thickness of the slab to 8 in. in a 3 x 3-ft. area to support the additional weight. Otherwise, pour 12-in. diameter, 12-in. deep footings and use your string lines to accurately position post brackets in the wet concrete.

3 Stand the walls and drop them over the anchor bolts. Nail the corners together and install the anchor bolt washers and nuts. Then plumb and temporarily brace each corner with a long 2x4 on the inside.

4 Set, plumb and brace the posts. Rest a straight 2x4 on the beam trimmers. Level it and mark both posts for height. Cut off the posts with a circular saw.

Wall and beam construction

Get started on your wall framing by cutting the treated bottom and top plates to length (see **Figure A** for dimensions and **Photo 1**). Mark and drill the 5/8-in. diameter anchor bolt holes, then temporarily tack the plates together with 8d nails and lay out the studs and window and door openings. Note that the bottom plates on each side of the door opening and at the back corner of the portico are longer than the top plates. That's where the trimmers (beam supports) rest on the bottom plates (**Photo 1**) to support the portico and door opening beams.

Assemble each wall and set it aside to use the slab for assembling the other walls (**Photo 2**). After they're built, slip them over the anchor bolts and nail them together at the corners with five 16d nails. Plumb and brace the walls at the corners with the braces on the inside of the shed so they won't interfere with the wall sheathing (**Photo 3**).

Now stand, plumb and brace the posts and assemble and set the beams. Brace the posts back to the building, to each other and to stakes pounded into the ground to keep them plumb and solid for setting the beams (**Photo 5**). Nail the beams, then cap the walls and beams with "tie" plates, overlapping them at the corners (**Photo 6**)

5 Assemble the beams and set them on the posts and trimmers. Nail them to the stud walls and to the post/beam connector.

6 Nail "tie" plates over the top plates, overlapping the corners. Use 16d nails spaced over the studs below. Then nail plywood sheathing to the walls.

Labels in image: GABLE END TRUSS, COMMON TRUSS, PLYWOOD SPACER, BRACE, TEMPORARY 2x4 CLEATS, SCAFFOLDING INSIDE

7 Lay out the truss positions on the top plates. Erect trusses at each end of the roof. Center them, brace them plumb and solidly toenail each to the walls with 16d nails.

Labels in image: PEAK ALIGNMENT STRING LINE, 2x4 RIBBON BOARD

8 Stretch a string between the end trusses and align the intermediate truss peaks with the string. Lay out and tack them to a temporary "ribbon" board to keep them in place and aligned.

9 Screw truss clips to the tops of the walls and to the trusses with special 1-1/2 in. truss screws.

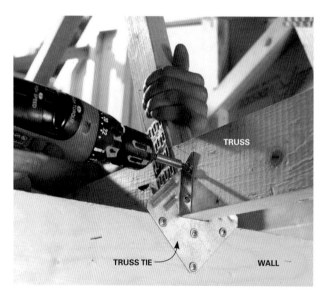

Labels in image: TRUSS, TRUSS TIE, WALL

and over the tops of the beams. Drive two 16d nails at each end and at least one 16d nail every 16 in. Then sheathe the walls with plywood, driving nails or staples every 8 in. along edges and every 12 in. otherwise. After you sheathe the walls, you can remove the bracing, but leave on the post braces until the roof trusses are set and sheathed.

Now go ahead and lay out the truss positions on the tie plates using **Figure A** as a guide. You'll have a fair number of 2x4s left over from the wall construction, but don't worry. You'll need most of them for blocking to support the soffit plywood along the eaves and around the edges of the portico, for siding backers on the end common truss, and for diagonal bracing for the end trusses. Still have leftovers? Use them to build shelving in your new shed!

Ordering and installing roof trusses

Ordering roof trusses from a lumberyard means that the truss manufacturer will engineer the trusses to safely handle the spans that you specify. So you can order trusses to fit any span or width of shed without worrying about strength issues. To make a longer shed, simply order more trusses, one more for every 2 ft. of building length. Bring **Figure A** with you when ordering the trusses and the staff will be able to help you with the order. By the way, you can expand the portico, too. Make it as wide as 8 ft. and as deep as 12 ft. simply by using double 2x10s instead of 2x8s for the beams (but make the door height 2 in. shorter).

You'll be ordering two types of trusses: "common" trusses, the ones that can free-span open spaces, and "gable end" trusses. Gable end trusses have vertical 2x3 studs spaced every 16 in. to simplify siding installation (**Photo 7**). But they aren't designed to span wide-open areas. Since the end truss at the portico doesn't have a wall beneath it, you'll have to install a common truss and add blocking for the sheathing as we show in **Photo 10** and **Figure A**.

Lay out the top plates for truss placement (see **Figure A**), then cluster the trusses toward one end of the building with the tips supported by the scaffolding. That way you'll be able to center, set and

10 Cut and nail blocking spaced every 2 ft. on the end common truss. Then scribe, cut and sheathe both end trusses.

11 Snap a chalk line 48-1/4 in. up from the truss ends and nail down the first row of plywood sheathing. Add plywood clips midway between trusses and nail on the second row of sheathing.

brace the end trusses and then stand each truss in sequence without shuffling trusses around. After standing the gable end trusses, plumb and brace them back to stakes driven into the ground before standing the other trusses. A great way to safely stand the gable end trusses is to use a couple of temporary 2x4 cleats nailed to the wall (**Photo 7**). They'll give you something to anchor the truss to while toe-nailing and adding bracing.

Lay out a nailing 2x4 "ribbon" with the same pattern as with the wall plates (**Photo 8**). Use the ribbon to place and hold each truss in position until you install the roof sheathing (**Photo 11**). String a line at the ridge to help center the middle trusses. Tack each truss in order to the ribbon and toenail each one to the plates (**Photo 8**). The metal clips (truss ties) solidly anchor the trusses to the walls (**Photo 9**). After the trusses are in place, you may need additional diagonal bracing (see **Figure A**). The booklet that comes with your trusses will tell you exactly where to put them.

Nail on the plywood following a chalk line as we show in **Photo 11**. Lay the roof sheathing along the chalk line to keep

12 Nail two layers of 2x4s over the gable sheathing flush with the top of the roof to form small overhangs. If you plan to add skylights to the roof, follow the manufacturer's instructions.

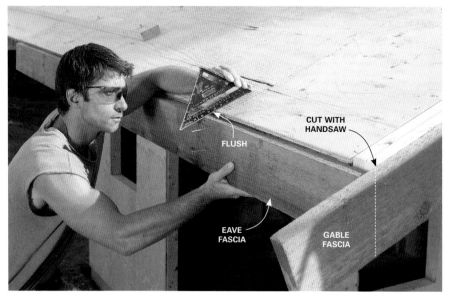

CUT WITH HANDSAW

FLUSH

EAVE FASCIA

GABLE FASCIA

13 Nail the 2x6 gable and eave fascia boards flush with the rooftop. Cut off the gable fascia flush with the eave fascia. Then fit and nail the 1x3 and 1x2 trim in place (Figure B).

Figure B
Exterior cladding details

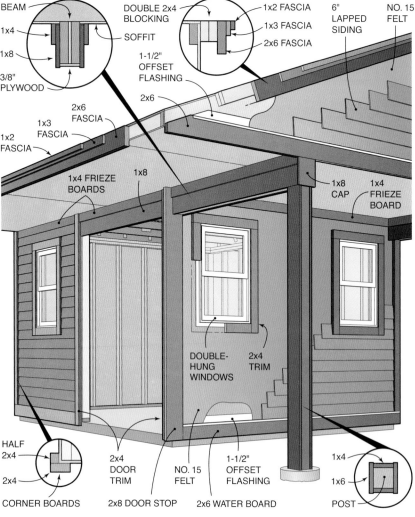

BEAM

1x4

1x8

3/8" PLYWOOD

DOUBLE 2x4 BLOCKING

SOFFIT

1-1/2" OFFSET FLASHING

1x2 FASCIA

1x3 FASCIA

2x6 FASCIA

6" LAPPED SIDING

NO. 15 FELT

2x6

2x6 FASCIA

1x3 FASCIA

1x2 FASCIA

1x4 FRIEZE BOARDS

1x8

1x8 CAP

1x4 FRIEZE BOARD

DOUBLE-HUNG WINDOWS

2x4 TRIM

HALF 2x4

2x4

CORNER BOARDS

2x4 DOOR TRIM

2x8 DOOR STOP

NO. 15 FELT

1-1/2" OFFSET FLASHING

2x6 WATER BOARD

1x4

1x6

POST

Materials list
Exterior cladding materials

ITEM	QTY.
Roofing	
Rolls of No. 15 organic felt	2
Squares of shingles (roofing)	4
Bundle of ridge shingles (ridge cap)	1
Siding and trim (rough-sawn cedar)	
4x8 x 3/8" (soffit plywood)	8
2x6 x 14' (water board)*	1
2x6 x 12' (water board)*	2
2x6 x 8' (water board)*	1
2x6 x 10' (gable bottom boards)*	4
2x6 x 12' (gable fascia)	4
2x6 x 10' (eave fascia)	4
1x3 x 12' (gable fascia)*	4
1x3 x 10' (eave fascia)*	4
1x2 x 12' (gable fascia)*	4
1x2 x 10' (eave fascia)*	4
2x4 x 8' (corner boards)	5
2x4 x 12' (window casing)*	3
2x4 x 8' (door trim)	2
2x8 x 8' (door stop)	1
1x2 x 14' (door track valance)*	1
1x8 x 12' (beam fascia)	1
1x8 x 8' (beam fascia)	3
1x6 x 8' (post casing)	4
1x4 x 8' (post casing)	4
1x4 x 10' (frieze boards)*	1
1x4 x 12' (frieze boards)*	2
1x4 x 8' (frieze boards)*	4
3/4 x 8' (cedar lap siding)	32
3/4 x 12' (cedar lap siding)	42
Hardware and windows	
2" siding nails	10 lbs.
3" siding nails (1-1/2" trim)	5 lbs.
1-1/4" roofing nails (shingles)	10 lbs.
5/16" staples (roofing felt)	1 box
4d galv. box nails (soffit plywood)	1 lb.
1-1/2" x 10' drip cap flashing	8
2' x 3' vinyl double-hung windows*	3
2' x 4' No. 106 Velux fixed skylights*	2
No. 106 skylight flashing kits*	2
*Optional parts	

the first row perfectly straight. We added plywood clips midway between trusses to tie the sheets together. That prevents warping that can show up well after the shingles are on. Offset all plywood butt seams at least one truss space on each row from the one below it.

Siding and trim

Begin the exterior finishing by nailing on the fascia boards. We show a three-part fascia made from a 2x6 and two 1x3 and 1x2 trim boards (**Photo 14**). You can simplify the fascia details by eliminating one or both trim boards. But whatever style you choose, it's easiest to cut and install the gable fascia first, leaving the eave ends long, and then running the eave fascia into it (**Photo 13**). Then cut off the overhanging gable fascia in place with a handsaw. We won't show you shingling details here. Use the directions on the shingle packages for installation procedures. Cut and install the 3/8-in. soffit plywood, adding blocking wherever necessary to secure outer edges that won't be supported by siding trim.

Start cladding the walls by stapling up No. 15 felt, starting at the bottom and overlapping each row by 2 in. Then install the corner boards and 2x6 "water boards" at the bottom (**Photo 16**). Lap the water boards at least 1/2 in. over the edge of the slab to keep water out. Cap the top of the water board with 1-1/2 in. drip cap flashing. Slit the felt and slip the flashing under it.

Then cut and nail on the corner boards. Note that we made the corners from a full 2x4 and half of another one. Nail them together and put them up as a unit.

Since the windows are well protected from weather, you don't have to flash them to keep water out. Simply trim them with 2x4s. Finish the top of the walls with 1x4 frieze boards (see **Photo 16**), and clad the beams and posts with 3x4-in. thick trim as shown. Side the walls, leaving 1/8-in. gaps at the ends of the siding for caulk.

In the opening photo, you'll see decorative brackets. We cut those out of 2x8s with a jigsaw. Use any curve you wish and cut a 60-degree angle on the top and a 30-degree angle on the bottom. Toenail them to the corner boards and soffit with 8d galvanized finish nails.

14 Staple No. 15 roof felt to the roof. Snap chalk lines every other shingle row to keep rows straight. Then nail on the shingles, allowing a 1-in. overhang. Staple more roof felt to the walls and install the windows.

15 Nail blocking between the roof trusses (see Figure A), then cut the soffit plywood to fit and nail it to the blocks and trusses.

FRIEZE BOARDS ⑤

POST TRIM ⑦

OTHER VERTICAL TRIM ③

④ **BEAM TRIM**

① **DOOR TRIM**

⑥ **WINDOW TRIM**

② **WATER BOARD AND FLASHING**

16 Install all of the exterior trim as shown in Figure B, following the numbered sequence in the photo.

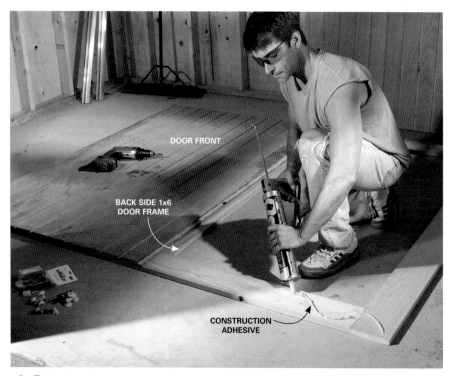

DOOR FRONT

BACK SIDE 1x6 DOOR FRAME

CONSTRUCTION ADHESIVE

18 Cut the door parts using Figure C as a guide. Lay out the 1x6 back-side frame and glue and screw the plywood to it using the edges of plywood to square the door.

LEAVE 1/8" GAPS

SCRIBE CUTS

17 Scribe and cut the siding to fit around openings, then nail it through the sheathing into the studs with siding nails.

Building the sliding door

We chose a sliding door for this shed because it is easy to build, trouble free and best of all, gives a clear 6-ft. opening for wide access. Building a sliding door isn't as tricky as you might think. To build this door, you simply glue, screw and nail the front and back frames to a plywood core. Cut the two sections of plywood to length and width (see **Figure C**), lay them together and use them as a guide for measuring the lengths of the door frame parts.

Assemble the door on the shed floor to keep everything flat and square, and dry-fit the parts before gluing and fastening them (**Photos 18** and **19**).

To hang the door, screw the roller tracks to the soffit (**Photo 21**). You'll need two 6-ft. tracks mounted end to end. You may have to drill additional holes through the track so the screws hit the trusses. Slip the wheel trucks into the track, mount the brackets on the top of the door (**Photo 20**) and then, with a helper, lift the door onto the tracks. The directions that come with the rollers will give you the details.

Finishing touches

If you choose natural wood siding, it's best to protect it with an exterior finish to keep it from graying over time. We coated our siding with two coats of Penofin clear oil finish. Although it's not visible in the photos, we stained the soffit undersides with a moss green opaque stain for added contrast.

Figure C
Sliding door details

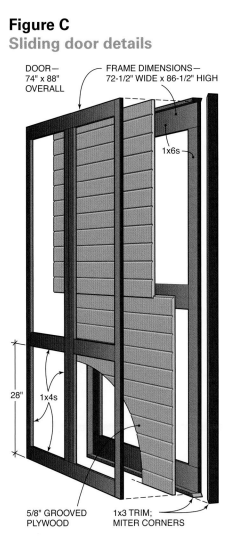

DOOR—
74" x 88"
OVERALL

FRAME DIMENSIONS—
72-1/2" WIDE x 86-1/2" HIGH

1x6s

28"

1x4s

5/8" GROOVED
PLYWOOD

1x3 TRIM;
MITER CORNERS

Materials list
Sliding door materials

ITEM	QTY.
4x8 x 5/8" (grooved fir plywood siding)	2
1x4 x 8' (front door frame)	4
1x4 x 6' (front door frame)	3
1x6 x 8' (back door frame)	2
1x6 x 6' (back door frame)	3
National V13B Gate Latch	1
Johnson pocket door hangers	1 set
Johnson 6' pocket door track www.johnsonhardware.com	2
Door handles	2

1x4
CENTER TRIM

FRONT SIDE 1x4
DOOR FRAME

ALTERNATE
DOOR FRAME JOINTS

19 Glue and nail the front side frame through the plywood and into the back-side frame with 2-in. nails. Space the center trim boards 3/16 in. (a carpenter pencil's width) apart.

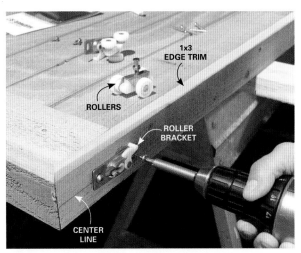

1x3
EDGE TRIM

ROLLERS

ROLLER
BRACKET

CENTER
LINE

20 Cut the 1x3 trim and glue and screw it to the edge of the door. Position and screw the door roller brackets to the top edge.

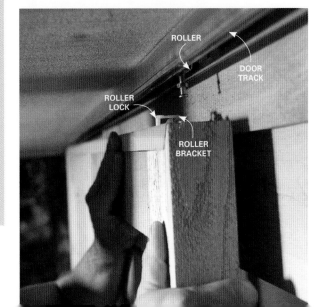

ROLLER

DOOR
TRACK

ROLLER
LOCK

ROLLER
BRACKET

21 Screw the track to the soffit framing (drill new holes as necessary). Slide the rollers into the track, then slip the rollers into the brackets and lock them into place.

Compact Shed

*Pack a lot of yard gear into this small
shed, and do it with style*

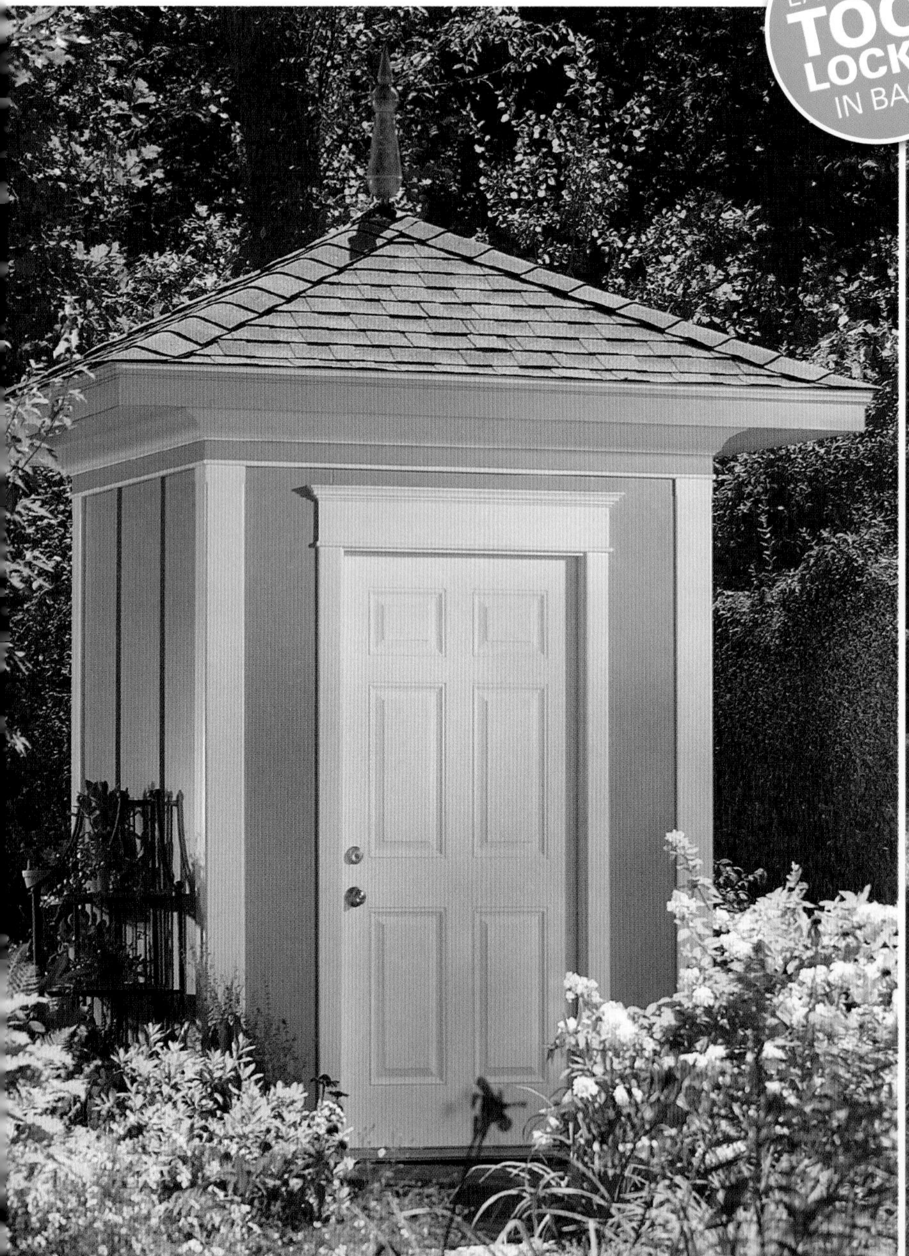

EASY-ACCESS
TOOL
LOCKER
IN BACK!

If you need a home for all your garden tools and supplies but have limited yard space, this small shed is a perfect storage solution. With its 6 x 6-ft. footprint and classic Georgian styling, it fits into tight spots and adds charm to any back yard. The "front room" (53 x 65 in.) provides plenty of space for shelves and even a small potting bench, while the double door on the back of the shed creates a spacious easy-access tool locker. For easy care, we chose low-maintenance siding and trim materials that hold paint and resist rot better than wood.

Tools, time and money

We engineered this shed for easy, modular construction; you can build the major parts in your driveway and assemble them on site. While this isn't a complex project, it does require basic building skills. We'll show you how to assemble the frame, but we won't show you all the finish details like how to hang doors or shingle the roof.

You'll need a drill, a circular saw, a miter saw and a router. Although not absolutely essential, a table saw will make the project go much easier and faster. We also recommend a compressor and an air-powered brad nailer for faster, better trim installation. Plan to spend two weekends building the shed and another day or two painting. The total materials bill for our shed was about $1,300. If you opt for a blank wall on the back of the shed rather than a double door and a tool locker, you'll save about $200.

Preconstruction planning

Call your city building department to find out whether you need a permit to build this 36-sq.-ft. shed. Also ask about any restrictions on where you can place the shed. If you plan to build near the edge of your lot, for example, you may have to hire a surveyor to locate your property lines. You can build this shed on a site that slopes as much as 6 in. over 6 ft. But if your site is steeper, consider building a low retaining wall to create a level site. To find some of the shed materials—especially the fiber cement panels and composite trim boards—you'll probably have to call local lumberyards or special-order through a home center. Special orders can take six weeks to arrive, so choose your materials long before you plan to build.

1 Frame the walls and floor following Figures A and B. Cover the floor with 3/4-in. plywood, the walls with cement panels and the divider wall with pegboard.

(Labels on photo: FRONT WALL, CEMENT PANEL, PEGBOARD WALL, 3/4" PLYWOOD FLOOR)

Frame the whole shed on your driveway

Framing the floor and walls is the fastest part of this project. Before you get started, select your prehung front door so you know the dimensions of the rough opening needed in the front wall. We chose a 36-in. door that required a 38 x 82-1/2-in. rough opening. Your door may require slightly different dimensions. The big opening at the back of the shed will easily accept two 30-in.-wide prehung doors.

Frame the 6 x 6-ft. floor from pressure-treated 2x6s as shown in **Figure A**. Whenever you fasten treated lumber, be sure to use nails or screws that are rated to withstand the corrosive chemicals in the lumber (check the fastener packaging).

2 Cut the truss parts and assemble them with 1/2-in. plywood gussets and 1-1/4-in. screws. Screw 1/2-in. spacers to the bottom chord on the main truss.

(Labels on photo: MAIN TRUSS, SPACER, HALF TRUSS, GUSSET)

Figure A
Shed

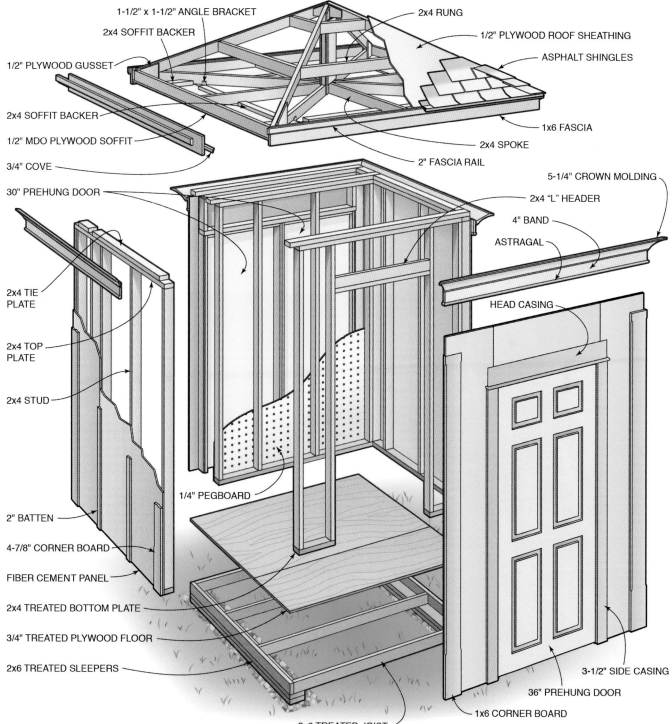

1-1/2" x 1-1/2" ANGLE BRACKET

2x4 SOFFIT BACKER

1/2" PLYWOOD GUSSET

2x4 SOFFIT BACKER

1/2" MDO PLYWOOD SOFFIT

3/4" COVE

30" PREHUNG DOOR

2x4 TIE PLATE

2x4 TOP PLATE

2x4 STUD

2" BATTEN

4-7/8" CORNER BOARD

FIBER CEMENT PANEL

2x4 TREATED BOTTOM PLATE

3/4" TREATED PLYWOOD FLOOR

2x6 TREATED SLEEPERS

1/4" PEGBOARD

2x6 TREATED JOIST

1x6 CORNER BOARD

36" PREHUNG DOOR

3-1/2" SIDE CASING

HEAD CASING

ASTRAGAL

4" BAND

2x4 "L" HEADER

5-1/4" CROWN MOLDING

2x4 RUNG

1/2" PLYWOOD ROOF SHEATHING

ASPHALT SHINGLES

1x6 FASCIA

2x4 SPOKE

2" FASCIA RAIL

HUB GUSSET

MAIN TRUSS

GUSSET

HALF TRUSS

Use pressure-treated 2x4s for the bottom plates of the walls. Cut the plates to the dimensions shown in **Figure B**. Then cut 20 wall studs to 94 in. and assemble the four walls. Also frame the small header wall (14 in. x 65 in.) that fits above the back doors. Before you sheathe the floor and wall frames, take corner-to-corner diagonal measurements to make sure each frame is square. Fasten 3/4-in. treated plywood to the floor frame with 1-5/8-in. screws. Also screw pegboard to the interior pegboard wall. Nail cement panels to the front and sidewalls (**Photo 1**). Position the cement panels flush with the bottom plate, not the top plate (the wall frames are 1 in. taller than the cement panels). The two sidewalls have identical framing, but be sure to attach the sheathing so the right and left sides mirror each other. The cement panels on the front wall overhang the framing by 3 in.

3 Screw half trusses to the main truss and tie them together with 9 x 21-in. hub gussets and 2-1/2-in. screws. Trim the main truss to form a pyramid.

32"

32"

UPPER RUNG

LOWER RUNG

SPOKE

4 Fasten the upper rungs between the trusses with 2-1/2-in. screws. Position the outer edge of the rungs flush with the tops of the trusses.

A complex roof made simple

A typical pyramid roof requires lots of compound angle cuts and endless trips up a ladder to test-fit all the tricky parts. Not this one. There are no compound angles or complex calculations at all. And ground-level construction means faster progress with less strain.

Build the main truss and two half trusses first (**Photo 2**). Choose the straightest 2x4s you can find for these parts. **Figures C** and **D** show the dimensions and angles. Your angle cuts don't have to be perfect; the gussets will make the trusses plenty strong even if the parts don't fit tightly.

Join the three trusses with two hub gussets (**Photo 3**) made from plywood left over from the floor. The "rungs" that fit between the trusses have 45-degree bevel cuts on both ends. You can tilt the shoe of your circular saw to cut bevels or use a miter saw. In order to create a square roof frame, all four lower rungs must be the same length. Cut them to 103-1/8 in., set them all in place to check the fit and then trim them all by the same amount until they fit identically between the trusses.

With the lower rungs in place, insert the spokes (**Photo 4**). One end of each spoke has a double bevel cut; make a 45-degree bevel from one side, then flip the 2x4 over and cut from the other side. This forms a 90-degree point that fits into the corner

5 Dig two trenches 6 in. deep and fill them with pea gravel. Then level treated 2x6 sleepers over the gravel and set the floor on the sleepers.

FLOOR

PEA GRAVEL

SLEEPER

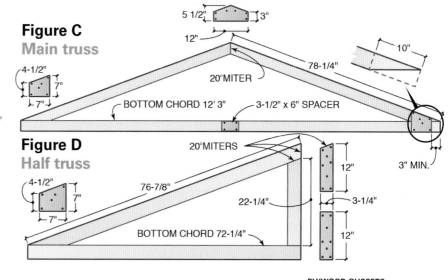

6 Anchor the walls to the floor with 3-in. screws. Start with a sidewall, then add the front wall, followed by the pegboard wall and the other sidewall.

Figure B
Floor plan and wall layout

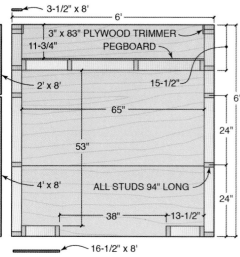

3-1/2" x 8'
6'
3" x 83" PLYWOOD TRIMMER
11-3/4"   PEGBOARD
2' x 8'   15-1/2"
65"
53"   6'
                                   24"
4' x 8'   ALL STUDS 94" LONG
                                   24"
38"   13-1/2"
16-1/2" x 8'

Figure C
Main truss

5 1/2"   3"
12"
4-1/2"   10"
        7"   78-1/4"
   7"   20°MITER
        BOTTOM CHORD 12' 3"   3-1/2" x 6" SPACER

Figure D
Half truss

20°MITERS
4-1/2"   76-7/8"   12"   3" MIN.
        7"   22-1/4"   3-1/4"
   7"
        BOTTOM CHORD 72-1/4"   12"

PLYWOOD GUSSETS
ALL 1/2" THICK.

where the main truss and half truss meet. To complete the roof frame, install the upper rungs (**Photo 4**).

Assemble the shed on site

The shed floor rests on a simple foundation: 2x6 pressure-treated "sleepers" laid on a bed of pea gravel. Dig two parallel trenches about 10 in. wide, 6 in. deep and centered 6 ft. apart. The trenches can run parallel to the sidewalls or the front and back walls of the shed. Fill the trenches with pea gravel. Lay the 6-ft.-long sleepers on the gravel. Using a level, determine which sleeper is higher (**Photo 5**). Level the higher sleeper along its length by adding or removing small amounts of gravel. Then add a little gravel under the other sleeper to make it level with the first. On a sloped site, one end of a sleeper may sit below grade while the other rests above the surrounding soil. You can also screw extra layers of 2x6 over the sleepers to compensate for a sloped site. We added two extra layers to both of our sleepers. That raised the shed and allowed us to slope the surrounding soil away from the shed. Set the floor on the sleepers so that the joists span the space between the

PLYWOOD TRIMMER

REAR HEADER

TIE PLATE

7 Set the rear header on 1/2-in. plywood trimmers and screw it into place from inside. Nail on overlapping tie plates to lock the walls together.

Low-maintenance cement panels

"Fiber cement" siding is basically cement reinforced with cellulose fibers. We chose it because it's durable, affordable and rot-proof, but especially because it holds paint longer than most other exterior materials. Exactly how much longer depends on a variety of factors, but builders have told us of cases where paint on fiber cement lasted twice as long as paint on nearby wood.

Fiber cement is most common in a plank form that's used for lap siding. But it's also available in 4 x 8-ft. sheets (3/16 in. thick) with textured or smooth surfaces (we used the smooth). Some home centers and lumberyards stock the sheet material; others have to special-order it (about $30 per sheet).

Working with fiber cement is a lot like using other sheet materials. Pick up a brochure where you buy the panels or go online to the manufacturer's site for specific instructions. You have to leave 1/8-in. spaces between sheets, for example. When nailing, place nails at least 3/8 in. from edges and 2 in. from corners. Although pros use special blades to cut fiber cement, you can cut it with a standard carbide circular saw blade. Cutting whips up a thick cloud of nasty dust, so a dust mask is mandatory.

Two suppliers of fiber cement siding are certainteed.com and jameshardie.com.

JUST DROPPED IN FROM KRYPTON

SOFFIT BACKERS

8 Screw 16-ft. 2x4s to the shed to form a ramp. Position your stepladders before you slide the roof frame up the ramp and onto the shed. Center the roof frame and fasten the trusses at each corner with a pair of angle brackets. Install 2x4s to provide nailing backers for the soffit.

sleepers. At each corner, drive a 3-in. screw at an angle through the floor frame into the sleepers.

Stand the walls and set the roof

You'll need a helper to carry and stand up the walls. Set one of the sidewalls in place and screw it to the floor every 2 ft. Position the bottom plate (not the cement sheathing) flush with the outer edge of the floor. Use a level to make sure the rear end of the wall is plumb and brace it with a 2x4 (**Photo 6**). Position the front wall and screw it to the floor. Then drive 1-5/8-in. screws through the overhanging front sheathing to tie the front and sidewalls together. Add the pegboard wall next, followed by the other sidewall and finally the rear header wall. Make sure all the walls are plumb, and nail tie plates over the walls (**Photo 7**).

To safely set the 160-lb. roof frame into place, you'll need two helpers, two stepladders and a ramp made from a pair of 16-ft.-long 2x4s. Secure each 2x4 with three 3-in. screws and brace them near the middle with a horizontal 2x4. Then simply slide the roof frame up the ramp and onto the shed (**Photo 8**). Center the roof frame so that all four lower rungs are the same distance (16-1/2 in.) from and parallel to the walls. Fasten the roof frame with metal angle brackets and install soffit backers (**Photo 8**) before you sheathe the roof with 1/2-in. plywood (**Photo 9**).

SUPPORT BLOCK

9 Sheathe the roof with 1/2-in. plywood. Cut each piece 3 in. extra long, nail it in place and cut off the excess. Temporary support blocks help position the plywood as you nail it.

Figure E
Fascia and crown details

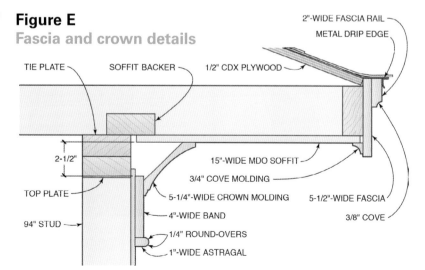

TIE PLATE
SOFFIT BACKER
1/2" CDX PLYWOOD
2"-WIDE FASCIA RAIL
METAL DRIP EDGE
2-1/2"
TOP PLATE
94" STUD
15"-WIDE MDO SOFFIT
3/4" COVE MOLDING
5-1/4"-WIDE CROWN MOLDING
4"-WIDE BAND
1/4" ROUND-OVERS
1"-WIDE ASTRAGAL
5-1/2"-WIDE FASCIA
3/8" COVE

Elegant trim from plain boards

Most of the trim on our shed is made from a "composite" material that stands up to Mother Nature better than wood (see **Editor's Note**, p. 37). We used pine wood moldings only where they're sheltered from sun and rain. The composite boards we used are 5/8 in. thick and come in the same widths as standard wood boards. In a few cases we used these boards "as is." But we dressed up most of the trim parts with a router. The router work adds only a couple of hours to the project and creates a much more elegant look. You'll need three router bits to shape the trim boards: a 1/4-in. round-over, a 3/8-in. round-over and a 3/8-in. cove bit. **Figures E** and **F** provide the specifics. Here are some other details:

- Install the fascia and fascia rails first (**Figure E**). Then shingle the roof. We used asphalt shingles. Be sure to install metal drip edge over the fascia.
- Composite trim must be butted at corners, not mitered, since miter joints often open over time.

Figure F
Corner boards

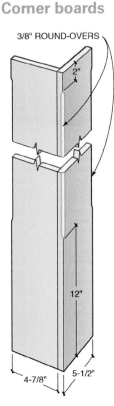

3/8" ROUND-OVERS

2"

12"

4-7/8" 5-1/2"

- For soffit material, we used 1/2-in. MDO (medium density overlay), which is plywood with a tough resin coating. MDO is available at some home centers and lumberyards ($45 per 4 x 8-ft. sheet). You could also use plywood or fiber cement soffit board.
- For the crown molding under the soffits, we used a large (5-1/4-in.) cove profile (**Figure E**). To get molding that wide, you may have to visit a lumberyard or special-order from a home center.
- Corner boards hide nail heads and the edges of the cement panels (**Photo 10**). To hide the cement panel joints and other nails, nail and glue two 2-in.-wide battens over the studs on each sidewall.

Doors and casing

We chose a classic six-panel door for the front of our shed and trimmed it with elaborate casing. To make the side casings, just rip your trim material to 3-1/2 in. wide and rout both edges with a round-over bit. Install the side casings so they project 1/4 in. above the doorjamb opening. Your side

CORNER BOARD

10 Nail and glue the corner boards in place. Install the narrower side first, making sure it's flush with the corner. Then add the full-width piece.

casings may be slightly longer or shorter than the length listed in **Figure G**.

Photo 11 shows how to assemble the head casing that fits over the side casings. The five parts that make up the head casing may also be longer or shorter than the lengths listed in **Figure G**. To determine the correct lengths, measure across the side casings from the outer edge on one to the outer edge of the other. For ours, that measurement was 42-1/2 in. If your measurement is more or less, just add or subtract from the length measurements given in **Figure G**.

For the tool locker on the back of the shed, we bought two simple prehung 30-in. steel doors: a left-hand swing and a right (about $100 each). We pulled the factory-installed trim off the doors and screwed the jambs together to form a double door. To stiffen the assembly, we screwed a 4-in.-wide strip of 1/2-in. plywood across the top of the jambs. Then we installed our double door backward, so it swings out rather than inward (see p. 35).

The corner boards on the back side of the shed act as the door casing, so you can't install them until the doors are in place. Don't round over the edges of these back corner boards. To complete the back-door casing, install a composite 1x6 above the doors.

Primer and caulk for a lasting paint job

Prime the wood and fiber cement with high-quality acrylic primer. The composite trim is factory-primed, but you'll have to prime any exposed cut ends and all the routed profiles. Be sure to prime the bottom ends of the corner boards and battens so they don't absorb moisture. The primer will raise wood fibers in the exposed composite, leaving a rough surface. Remove these "whiskers" by lightly sanding with 100-grit sandpaper.

Careful, thorough caulking is essential for a lasting paint job because it prevents moisture from penetrating the cement panels and trim. Fill all the nail holes and seal any gaps between and along the trim parts with acrylic caulk. Also caulk the two short cement panel joints above the door. After the caulk cures, apply two coats of high-quality acrylic paint.

Editor's Note: Hooked on Composite Trim

One day a few years ago, my local lumberyard did me a huge favor: It ran out of the redwood boards I had always used for trim. The only alternative was a "composite" made from "wood fiber and resin." Saw-dust mixed with glue sounded like a recipe for problems, but I gave it a try and haven't used wood trim boards since.

Composite trim looks better after it's installed and keeps its good looks longer than wood. Every board is straight and free of imperfections like knots or splits. It doesn't chip or splinter when you cut or rout it. It holds paint longer than

wood and resists rot better than most "rot-resistant" woods. As a bonus, composite costs less than good-quality wood boards (about $13 for a 16-ft. 1x6).

Composites aren't perfect; they're heavy and floppy, so they're more difficult to install solo. Cutting or routing churns up a thick, powdery dust cloud, so I always wear a dust mask and do my cutting outdoors. The material is harder than wood and difficult to nail by hand. Manufacturers recommend using a framing nailer or predrilling and hand nailing. Predrilling is slow and framing

nails leave big, ugly nail heads to cover up. So I use a brad nailer along with plenty of exterior-grade construction adhesive. Brads alone don't have enough holding power, but they hold the trim in place until the adhesive sets.

Composite trim is available at lumberyards and some home centers. The composite we chose for this shed is PrimeTrim (gp.com/build). Another widely available product is MiraTec (miratecextira.com).

Materials list

ITEM	QTY.
2x6 x 12' treated	4
2x4 x 8' (2 treated, 28 untreated)	30
2x4 x 10'	6
2x4 x 12'	4
2x4 x 14'	1
2x4 x 16'	2
3/4" treated plywood	2
1/2" CDX plywood	5
MDO plywood	2
1x6 x 16' composite trim	14
4 x 8' fiber cement panels	5
10' metal drip edge	4
30" doors	2
36" door	1
Doorknobs	3
1 square of shingles	
30' of ridge shingles	
Construction adhesive	4 tubes
Acrylic caulk	2 tubes
L-brackets	8
3" exterior screws	1 lb.
2-1/2" exterior screws	1 lb.
1-5/8" exterior screws	1 lb.
1-1/4" exterior screws	1 lb.
8d galvanized nails	5 lbs.
16d galvanized nails	5 lbs.
1" roofing nails	5 lbs.
1-1/4" and 1-3/4" brads	
Pea gravel (50-lb. bags)	10

5-1/4" CROWN

(The lengths of your trim components may differ)

FRIEZE

11 Nail and glue the moldings to the frieze board one at a time. Then fasten the head casing above the door with construction adhesive and brad nails.

Figure G
Door trim

2-3/8" x 46"
1-3/4" x 44-3/4"
1-1/4" x 43-3/4"
FRIEZE 5-1/2" x 42-1/2"

3/8" COVE
3/8" ROUND-OVER
3/8" COVE
1/4" ROUND-OVER

1/4" DOORJAMB REVEAL
3/8" ROUND-OVER
SIDE CASING 3-1/2" x 81"
1" x 43-3/4"

Perfect Patio Chairs

A classic design, reinvented for comfort and easy building

This chair is hard to beat for comfort, economy and ease of building. The design is based on a couple chairs I've had at the family cabin for more than a decade. Being a fiddle-with-it kind of guy, I modified the originals over the years, built others and eventually chose this design.

I think it's about as close to perfect as you can get: It's comfortable to sit in for hours at a time, the arms are wide enough to hold a drink, and you're reclined enough for relaxation, but not so much that you'll groan every time you get up (unlike with most Adirondack chairs). It will accept a common type of outdoor chair cushion, available at any home center, but doesn't require one. It's light enough to move around easily, and you can fit it through a doorway without contortions. Plus, it's inexpensive and easy to build.

Skills, tools & lumber

This is a beginner to intermediate level project. If you have just a little experience with tools, you can do it. You'll need an orbital or a random-orbit sander, a 7/16-in. wrench, six clamps and a drill. You can cut parts with a circular saw and drive nails with a hammer, but you'll get faster, nicer results with a miter saw, an air compressor and an 18-gauge brad nailer.

I've built this design from both pine and cedar. Each pine chair will cost you about $60, cedar about $90. Cedar is a better choice if your chairs are going to spend much time out in the rain. You may find it hard to buy 1x3 cedar, so you may have to rip a 1x6 in half. Also note that rough cedar is usually thicker than 3/4 in., while pine boards come in the standard 3/4-in. thickness. When you're building the seat and back, keep those different thicknesses in mind (see **Photos 2** and **3**).

MEET THE BUILDER

Ken Collier, former editor-in-chief of *Family Handyman* and a longtime cabinetmaker, likes nothing better than sitting in a comfortable chair looking out over his favorite river.

Figure A
Exploded view

Overall Dimensions:
35-1/4" tall x 27" wide x 33-1/4" deep

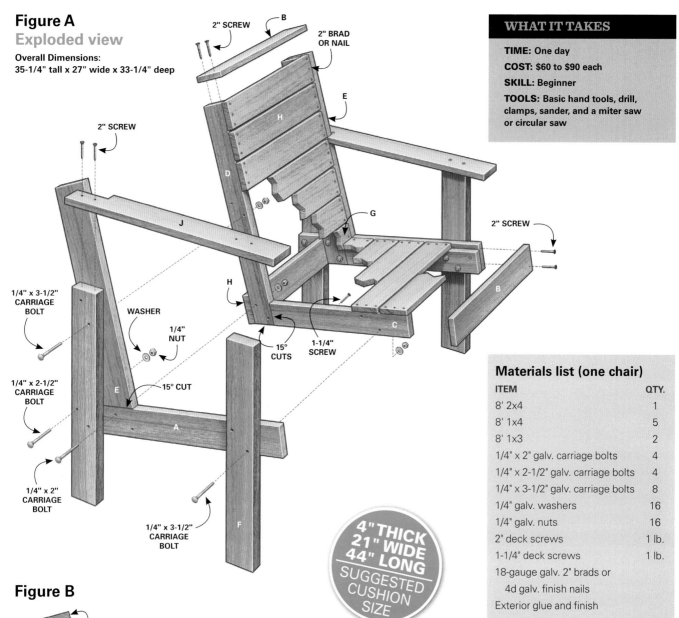

B
2" SCREW
2" BRAD OR NAIL
E
H
2" SCREW
D
J
2" SCREW
G
1/4" x 3-1/2" CARRIAGE BOLT
WASHER
1/4" NUT
H
B
1/4" x 2-1/2" CARRIAGE BOLT
E
15° CUTS
1-1/4" SCREW
15° CUT
C
A
1/4" x 2" CARRIAGE BOLT
F
1/4" x 3-1/2" CARRIAGE BOLT

4" THICK 21" WIDE 44" LONG SUGGESTED CUSHION SIZE

Materials list (one chair)

ITEM	QTY.
8' 2x4	1
8' 1x4	5
8' 1x3	2
1/4" x 2" galv. carriage bolts	4
1/4" x 2-1/2" galv. carriage bolts	4
1/4" x 3-1/2" galv. carriage bolts	8
1/4" galv. washers	16
1/4" galv. nuts	16
2" deck screws	1 lb.
1-1/4" deck screws	1 lb.
18-gauge galv. 2" brads or 4d galv. finish nails	
Exterior glue and finish	

Figure B

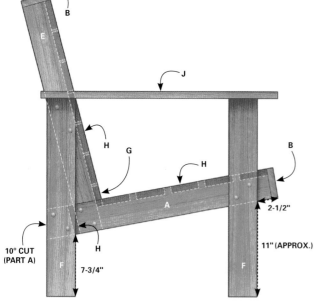

B
E
J
H
G
H
H
A
B
2-1/2"
10° CUT (PART A)
H
F
11" (APPROX.)
7-3/4"
F

Cutting list (one chair)

KEY	QTY.	MATERIAL	LENGTH	NAME
A	2	1x4	28-1/4"	Seat sides (10-degree cut one end)*
B	2	1x4	21-1/2"	Seat front, back top
C	2	1x3	19-1/2"	Seat supports (15-degree cut one end)*
D	2	1x3	27-1/2"	Back supports (15-degree cut one end)*
E	2	1x4	24-1/2"	Back sides (15-degree cut one end)*
F	4	2x4	23-1/2"	Legs
G	1	1x3	19-3/4"	Bottom back slat (cut to fit)
H	12	1x4	19-3/4"	Slats, back brace (cut to fit)
J	2	1x4	29-1/4"	Arms

* Measure to long point on all angled parts

Build a prototype

Over decades of chair building, I've learned this: Every chair is a compromise, and no chair is right for everyone. This chair, for example, is midsized and may not be comfortable for large people. So I strongly recommend that you build a prototype before you settle on this or any other design. Use pine or plywood scrap, and don't bother sanding the parts.

The biggest advantage to a prototype is that you and your family can test it for comfort. You can also shop for cushions and actually try them out on the chair. Thicker cushions change the feel of a chair significantly. A prototype is also a building lesson: Once you've built one chair, you can churn out others faster, better and without mistakes.

First, cut and sand the parts

Begin by cutting all the parts except G and H (**Photo 1**). If you're using cedar that's rough on one side, you need to cut each part so that the smooth side will face out. That means you'll have left and right sides to parts A, D and E. In other words, for each pair of parts, make sure the angled cut goes one direction on one part, the other direction on the other. This will allow you to assemble the chair with the smooth face of the cedar facing out.

As you're cutting, label the parts with masking tape. Parts G and H are cut after

STOP BLOCK

1 CUT THE PARTS. Making more than one chair means cutting a lot of pieces to the same length. A stop block lets you cut a bunch without measuring and marking each board.

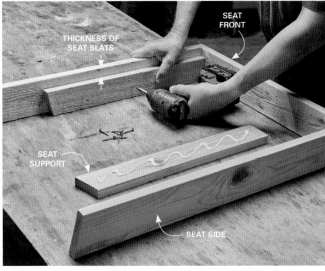

THICKNESS OF SEAT SLATS

SEAT FRONT

SEAT SUPPORT

SEAT SIDE

2 ASSEMBLE THE SEAT BASE. Screw the front to the sides, then glue and screw the seat supports to the sides. If needed, raise or lower the seat supports slightly so that the space above them matches the thickness of the slats.

BACK SUPPORT

BACK SIDE

3 BUILD UP THE BACK SUPPORTS. Screw and glue the back supports to the back sides. Position the back supports to match the thickness of the back slats.

THICKNESS OF BACK SLATS

BACK
SUPPORT

SEAT
SIDE

4 **BOLT ON THE BACK. Attach the back to**
the seat side with galvanized carriage bolts.
Then screw the back brace to the back side supports.

Test the bolts

A heavy buildup of zinc coating on galvanized bolts can make it nearly impossible to thread on the nut. So try a nut on each bolt first. Better to discover a stubborn bolt before you pound it into the hole.

LEVEL
THE
SEAT

PLUMB
THE LEGS

5 **ATTACH THE LEGS. On a flat, level surface, clamp the legs to the seat and back.**
Check the legs for plumb and the seat for level, then bolt on the legs.

END
SLATS

6 **NAIL ON**
THE SLATS.
For both the seat and the back, position the end slats first. Then space the others between them (typically 3/8 in. apart).

the chair is assembled so you can get them to fit perfectly. In cedar, the length is likely to be about 19-3/4 in. instead of 20 in. Once pieces are cut, sand them. Generally, you don't need to sand finer than 120 grit. For cedar parts, sand only the smooth face.

Build the frame

For pieces that are screwed together, you should drill a pilot hole. In pine, you should countersink a little so the screw head doesn't splinter the wood; cedar is so soft that it's better not to.

Build the seat frame on a flat surface so it stays flat (**Photo 2**). Begin by screwing the front (B) to the sides (A), then screw and glue the seat support (C) to the inside surface of A. Now glue and screw the back supports (D) to the back sides (E), keeping the square ends flush (**Photo 3**). The angles at the ends should be parallel. Put the sides in position and tack them on with one screw each at the bottom into the seat sides (A). Screw the back top (B) to the top of the back sides (E). With the back lightly screwed in place, drill two bolt holes each through the seat sides and

Hide the ugly boards

If the seat and back will get covered by cushions, use up knotty or odd-colored stock for the slats. But check the slats before you use them: Big, loose knots can create a weak spot that will crack under stress.

the back supports (see **Figure A**). Install galvanized carriage bolts and tighten the nuts firmly (**Photo 4**).

Attach the legs

Mark two legs (F) at 7-3/4 in. from the end and mark the other two legs at 11 in. Turn the chair assembly on its side and clamp two legs into place (**Figure B**) so one leg is flush to the angled cut on the seat sides (A) and the other is 2-1/2 in. from the front edge of the seat. After clamping the legs to the seat sides and back, turn the chair over and clamp on the other two legs. Turn the chair right side up to adjust the legs (**Photo 5**).

Tweak the position of the chair seat so all four legs are on the work surface, the legs are plumb and the seat is level (assuming your work surface is too). Don't worry if the chair seat is not quite on the leg marks you made earlier. When all is well, drill the bolt holes and attach the bolts. Be careful drilling; your holes must go through the back and seat supports (C and D), well away from the edges where the slats will rest.

Seat slats and arms

Measure the inside width of the chair seat and cut a test slat. If it's a good fit, drill the ends and screw it to the bottom edge of the seat supports, in back (see **Figure A**). Cut part G and the rest of the slats (H).

Divide your slats into good and better, and use the better ones on the back, where they're more visible. Nail on the top slats of the back, the front slat of the seat, and the bottom back slat (G). Then space the other slats out and nail them on (**Photo 6**). It helps to tip the chair over to do the back slats. Follow **Photos 7 – 9** to install the arms.

Sand and finish

Gently round the corners of the arms with a file or sandpaper. Then file a small round-over on all exposed edges, especially on the undersides of the arms, to prevent splinters.

You can cover the screw heads with exterior-grade wood filler or leave them exposed. Lightly sand the entire chair to 120 grit and it'll be ready for finish. I finished our chairs with transparent deck stain.

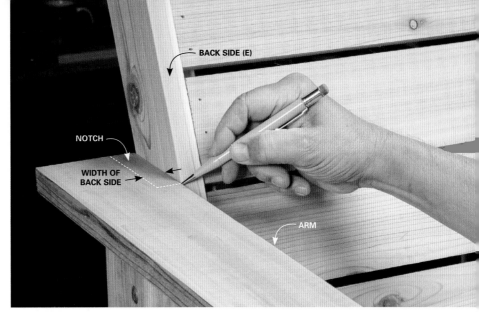

7 MARK THE ARM FOR A NOTCH. Hold the arm in position and mark the angle of the back onto its edge.

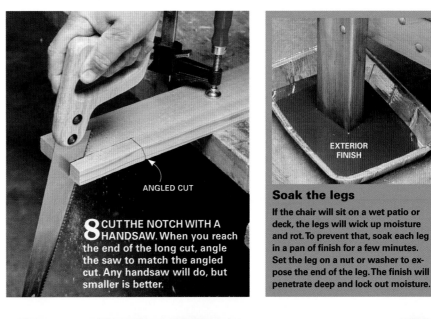

8 CUT THE NOTCH WITH A HANDSAW. When you reach the end of the long cut, angle the saw to match the angled cut. Any handsaw will do, but smaller is better.

Soak the legs

If the chair will sit on a wet patio or deck, the legs will wick up moisture and rot. To prevent that, soak each leg in a pan of finish for a few minutes. Set the leg on a nut or washer to expose the end of the leg. The finish will penetrate deep and lock out moisture.

9 MOUNT THE ARMS. Screw on the arms. Round over corners and sharp edges with a file or sandpaper. Give everything a final sanding and you're ready for finish!

Fabulous Fire Table

Create an outdoor gathering space for family & friends.

WHAT IT TAKES

TIME: Two days

COST: $700 to $825

SKILL: Intermediate

TOOLS: Basic hand tools, drill, table saw, miter saw, trim nailer/ compressor, concrete trowel, large wire cutters or small bolt cutters, and wheelbarrow or mixing tub

A fire table is a beautiful addition to your outdoor living space—and an invitation to gather around, enjoy a drink and shoot the breeze. It's also a stylish centerpiece that gives you a great opportunity to showcase your DIY prowess. And this is a fun build because it entails a variety of skills: woodworking, masonry, metal work and a little mechanical. It does require a few more-advanced tools, and at $825 it's not the cheapest DIY project, but if you shop for one, you could easily spend a couple thousand dollars.

Tools and materials

This table is made from cedar, but you can use pressure-treated wood, which would save you about $30, or whatever exterior-grade lumber is available in your area. The concrete tabletop is formed from Quikrete Countertop Mix. I dyed the top charcoal gray, but many other colors are available. All the materials (besides the burner kit) are available at home centers. The biggest cost by far is the burner kit (see p. 53). You could save about $100 by buying a kit that doesn't have a control panel or a piezo starter.

I built this project with basic hand tools and a miter saw, table saw and trim gun. You could make all the cuts with a circular saw and fasten all the panels with a hammer and trim nails, but it would take a lot longer and the end product probably wouldn't turn out as polished.

How it works

The burner runs on propane and will last six to 12 hours on a 20-lb. tank (that's about $2 to $3 per hour). The fire it produces will warm your hands and take the chill off, but it doesn't throw off enough heat to keep you warm on a cold night the way a bonfire would. The propane tank is stored under the table, but you can bury a line and hook it up to your home's natural gas if you wish.

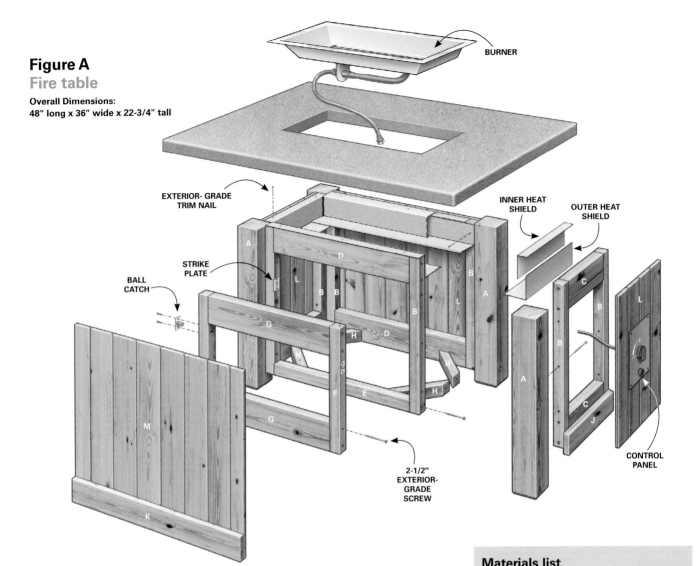

Figure A
Fire table

Overall Dimensions:
48" long x 36" wide x 22-3/4" tall

BURNER

EXTERIOR- GRADE
TRIM NAIL

INNER HEAT
SHIELD

OUTER HEAT
SHIELD

STRIKE
PLATE

BALL
CATCH

2-1/2"
EXTERIOR-
GRADE
SCREW

CONTROL
PANEL

Cutting list

KEY	QTY.	DIMENSIONS	PART
Table box			
A	4	3-1/2" x 3-1/2" x 22"	Corner posts
B	8	1-1/2" x 1-1/2" x 20-1/2"	Frame sides
C	4	1-1/2" x 3-1/2" x 11"	Side frames, top/bottom
D	3	1-1/2" x 3-1/2" x 23"	Front and back frames top and back frame bottom
E	1	1-1/2" x 1-1/2" x 23"	Front frame bottom
F	2	1-1/2" x 1-1/2" x 15"	Door frame sides
G	2	1-1/2" x 3-1/2" x 19-5/8"	Door frame top and bottom
H	4	1-1/2" x 1-1/2" x 9"	Angle braces (45-degree ends)
J	2	3/4" x 2-1/2"	Side trim boards (bevel top, cut to fit)
K	1	3/4" x 2-1/2"	Back and front trim boards (5-degree bevel top, cut to fit)
L	16	1/4" x 3-1/2" x 18-1/4"	Back and side planks
M	8	1/4" x 3-1/2" x 20-3/4"	Door planks
Tabletop Form (cut from a 3/4"-thick 4' x 8' melamine sheet)			
N	1	3/4" x 49" x 56"	Form base
P	2	3/4" x 1-3/4" x 49"	Perimeter side walls
Q	2	3/4" x 1-3/4" x 44"	Perimeter end walls
R	2	3/4" x 1-3/4" x 12"	Interior side walls
S	2	3/4" x 1-3/4" x 22-1/2"	Interior end walls

Materials list

ITEM	QTY.
4x4 x 8' cedar post	1
2x4 x 8' cedar	4
1/4" x 3-1/2" x 96" planks, package of six	1
42" x 84" wire remesh	1
4' x 8' x 3/4" melamine	1
3/4" x 48" wood dowel	1
3-1/2" x 5" x 10' galv. steel dormer flashing	1
3' x 1-1/2" x 8' galv. steel deck ledger flashing	1
Quikrete Countertop Mix, 80-lb. bags	3
2-1/2" exterior-grade screws, 100-pack	1
2" 18-gauge brads, sm. pack	1
1-1/4" ext. trim nails, sm. pack	1
1" 18-gauge brads, sm. pack	1
Construction adhesive	1 tube
Black silicone caulk	1 tube
High-temp RTV silicone	1 tube
Ball catches	2
Exterior-grade wood sealant	1 qt.
Concrete sealer	1 gal.
Burner kit	1

1 TAPER THE FEET. Cut the posts (A) to length on a miter saw (see Cutting List on p. 46). Taper the bottom edges about 1/2 in. up with a miter saw. The tapered edges won't tear out when the table is slid around, and they'll look better when it's sitting on uneven ground.

2 CUT AND ASSEMBLE THE FRAMES. Cut three 8-ft. 2x4s in half to create six 4-footers. Rip down five of the six into 1-1/2-in. x 1-1/2-in. boards. From these, cut the frame sides (B) and the front frame bottom (E). The other frame parts (C and D) are cut from full 2x4s.

Secure the frame sides to the tops and bottoms with two 2-1/2-in. screws. Connect the smaller front frame bottom with one screw in each side. Drill 1/8-in. holes through the frame sides before you install the screws.

3 ATTACH THE SIDE FRAMES TO THE POSTS. Drill three holes through the sides of the side frames. Lay the frames flat on your work surface. Align the frames and posts flush at the top, and secure the frames to the posts with three 2-1/2-in. screws. Take note of the wood grain on the posts and place the most attractive sides facing out.

4 ATTACH THE FRONT AND BACK FRAMES. Set the side frames and posts upside down. Line up the inside corner of the front and back frames with the inside corner of the posts and secure them with three 2-1/2-in. screws driven through predrilled holes.

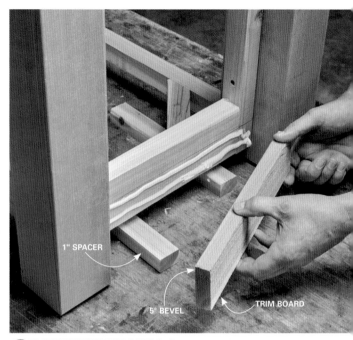

5 INSTALL THE ANGLE BRACES. Cut the angle braces (H) from 1-1/2-in. x 1-1/2-in. stock. The total length (9 in.) is from the long point of the 45-degree angles. Use a framing square to check that all the posts are at right angles from the work surface. Then check that the box itself is square by measuring the diagonal distance from the outside of one corner post to another—the two measurements should be the same.

Once everything is square, install the brackets with a 2-1/2-in. screw on each side through a predrilled hole.

6 FASTEN THE TRIM BOARDS. Set your table saw to a 5-degree angle and rip the 1x4 down to 2-1/2 in. That will create a beveled edge to help shed water. Cut the side trim boards (J) and the back trim board (K) to length, but hold off cutting the front. Apply construction adhesive to the frame and set the trim board on two 1-in. spacers. Drive 2-1/2-in. screws through the frame and into the back side of the trim board. Angle the screws a bit to prevent them from poking through the face of the trim board.

7 FASTEN THE PLANKS. Cut the back and side tongue-and-groove planks (L) to length. On the back, rip 1 in. off the first plank; that way you'll end up cutting about 1 in. off the last one as well. I started the first one by removing the groove side. Apply adhesive, and fasten the planks with 1-in. brads, two at the very top of each plank and two near the bottom. Dry-fit the last two planks on the sides before applying adhesive.

8 BUILD THE DOOR FRAME AND INSTALL THE BALL CATCHES. Cut the door frame sides (F) and door frame top and bottom (G). Assemble the door frame with two 2-1/2-in. screws driven through predrilled holes in the sides into the top and bottom. Dry-fit the door frame in the opening; there should be about a 3/16-in. gap on each side and a 3/8-in. gap above the top.

Predrill a 1/8-in. hole through the sides of the frame 1 in. below the bottom of the top frame board. Using that hole as a guide, drill a 3/4-in. hole (confirm this size with the installation instructions). Either a Forstner or a spade bit will work, but drill in from both sides to avoid a nasty tear-out.

Slide the ball catch into the hole and hold it in place with the retaining plate. The plate can sit on the surface of the wood; no need to cut in a mortise.

9 ATTACH THE STRIKE PLATES. Set the door frame into place with the bottom of it resting on the bottom frame of the table. Mark the top and bottom locations of the strike plate using the ball catch retainer plate on the door frame as a guide. Bore out space with your 3/4-in. bit to make room for the recess in the strike plate.

Install the strike plates backward so the curved part of the plate faces in. If the plate protrudes toward the front, it will bump up against the door planks. Hold the strike plate in place, and mark the screw holes with a pencil.

10 FASTEN THE DOOR PLANKS AND TRIM BOARD. Adjust the ball catches so there's an even gap on both sides. Cut the door planks (M) to length and rip 1-1/8 in. off the first panel. Apply adhesive to the frame and set down 1-in. spacers for the planks to rest on. Start the first plank 1/8 in. short of the corner post, and leave the last plank short 1/8 in. Fasten the planks with two 1-in. brads as low and as high as you can (into the door frame, not the table!). Fasten the trim board with adhesive and 1-in. brads through the back of the door panel.

11 CAULK AND APPLY FINISH. Apply caulk (that matches the finish) on the sides and the back where the tongue-and-groove planks meet the corner posts. Apply caulk to the top side of the trim board on the door. Don't caulk the tops of the other three trim boards. That way, if water does get behind the planks it can escape at the bottom.

A couple coats of an exterior-grade stain/sealer will add some color to your project and protect it from damaging UV rays.

12 INSTALL THE OUTER HEAT SHIELD. Cut the 3-1/2-in. x 5-in. x 10-ft. galvanized steel dormer flashing (available at home centers) to length with tin snips. Install the flashing, keeping the top flush with the top of the box. Secure the pieces with 1-1/4-in. exterior-grade trim nails or small screws. Seal the corners with RTV high-temperature silicone (sometimes called "gasket maker"). **Caution:** The bottom of the pan gets hotter without stones in it, so don't ever run the burner without stones in the pan!

BACK OF FLASHING

FRONT OF FLASHING

13 **INSTALL THE INNER HEAT SHIELD. Cut** the galvanized steel deck ledger flashing (sometimes called "drip edge") to length with tin snips. Pound the bottom lip of the flashing flat with a hammer. Install each side so the bottom of the flashing is facing up, and the lip (that was bent flat) is even with the outside of the box frame but short of the planks. This will create a small air gap between the two pieces of flashing.

Figure B
Tabletop form

Table Dimensions:
48" long x 36" wide x 1-3/4" thick

Hole Dimensions:
24" long x 12" wide

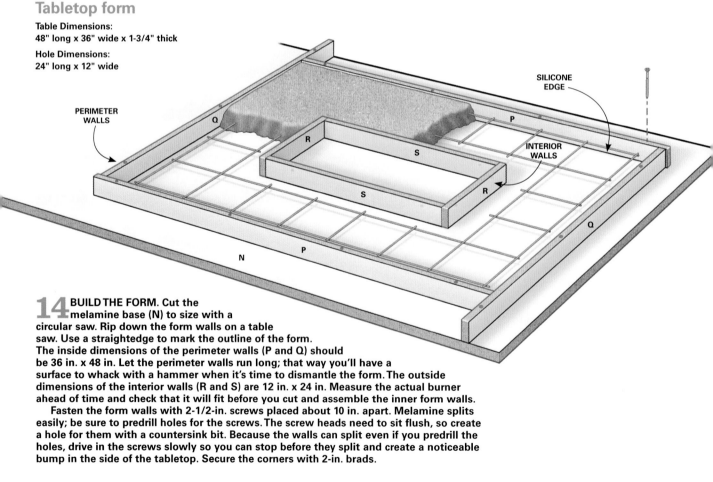

SILICONE EDGE

PERIMETER WALLS

INTERIOR WALLS

Q

P

R

S

S

R

N

P

Q

14 **BUILD THE FORM. Cut the** melamine base (N) to size with a circular saw. Rip down the form walls on a table saw. Use a straightedge to mark the outline of the form. The inside dimensions of the perimeter walls (P and Q) should be 36 in. x 48 in. Let the perimeter walls run long; that way you'll have a surface to whack with a hammer when it's time to dismantle the form. The outside dimensions of the interior walls (R and S) are 12 in. x 24 in. Measure the actual burner ahead of time and check that it will fit before you cut and assemble the inner form walls.

Fasten the form walls with 2-1/2-in. screws placed about 10 in. apart. Melamine splits easily; be sure to predrill holes for the screws. The screw heads need to sit flush, so create a hole for them with a countersink bit. Because the walls can split even if you predrill the holes, drive in the screws slowly so you can stop before they split and create a noticeable bump in the side of the tabletop. Secure the corners with 2-in. brads.

15 CREATE A ROUNDED EDGE WITH SILICONE.

Run a healthy bead of silicone around the perimeter. Tool it into shape using a 3/4-in. dowel with the end cut at 45 degrees. While you're tooling, let the excess spill over onto each side of the bead. After the silicone dries, those two lines can easily be pulled and scraped off. Black silicone works best because you can clearly see any excess that needs to be removed. Don't use silicone on the inside edges. The silicone would make the form walls harder to remove, and those edges will be covered by the burner anyway.

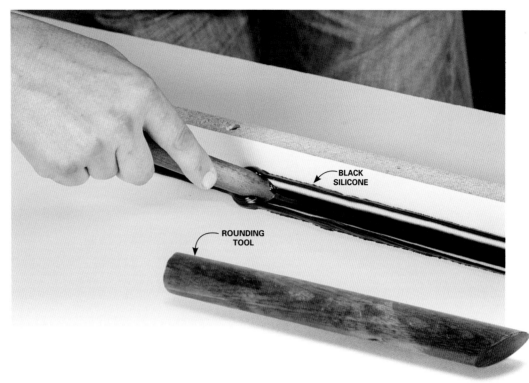

BLACK SILICONE

ROUNDING TOOL

16 MIX THE CONCRETE.

Mix the concrete in a wheelbarrow or mixing tub ($15 at home centers), using a rake or garden hoe. I decided to darken my top by mixing in two bottles of Quikrete Liquid Cement Color dye. It's important to get exactly the same amount of dye into every bag of mix. If you mix each bag individually, stir the dye into some water first, and separate it into three equal amounts, one for each bag.

I used Quikrete Countertop Mix. Some home centers stock it, but most can order it for you. Countertop mix works great because it can be poured a little wetter (like thick pancake batter) but still retain its strength. That helps prevent voids caused by air bubbles. Follow the directions for whatever product you use.

17 FILL THE FORM. Set the form on a few 2x4s resting on sawhorses so you can beat the underside of it with a hammer to remove air bubbles. The form should sit fairly level. Spread out the concrete with a concrete trowel or taping knife. Pour in one of the mixed bags and beat the bottom and sides of the form to remove voids and air bubbles. Repeat the process with the second mixed bag before adding the wire mesh.

18 SET IN THE WIRE MESH. Wire mesh will strengthen the top. I cut down a 42-in. x 84-in. sheet (not roll) of remesh. The grid size worked out perfectly. Whatever size mesh you buy, keep it at least 2 in. away from the edges. I cut mine with a pair of small bolt cutters, but you could also use large wire cutters.

Once the mesh is laid in place, spread the last mixed bag of concrete over the top of it. Tap only the sides with a hammer to remove any voids; do not vibrate the rest of the form. This is very important: Vibrating the form will cause the remesh to sink. You'll get shadow lines if the remesh comes within 1/2 in. of the table's surface.

19 SCREED OFF THE EXCESS CONCRETE. Slide a 2x4 across the surface to scrape off the excess concrete. Wiggle it back and forth as you go, but try not to shake the whole form too much. That could also cause the remesh wire to sink and create shadow lines. Let the concrete harden a bit before you smooth it out with a trowel or taping knife. It doesn't have to be perfectly smooth because nobody will ever see it.

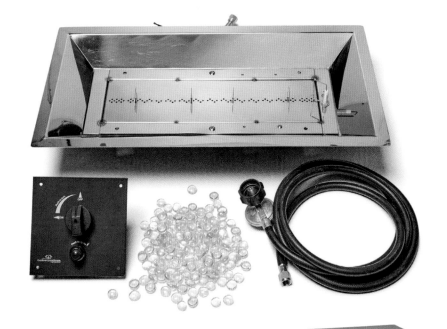

20 THE BURNER KIT. I bought my 12-in. x 24-in. burner kit (No. CF-1224-DIY) at The Outdoor GreatRoom Company (outdoorrooms.com). It cost about $520 and included the gas lines, the control panel, the fire gems and the burner with electronic piezo starter. Hooked to a propane tank, it cranks out about 55,000 Btu set on high. A natural gas orifice is included as well. The burner pan has drain holes, so a little rain won't hurt it, but it should be covered when not in use. And fire is inherently dangerous, so always follow the manufacturer's directions!

21 FINISH UP. Take out the form screws, and remove the form walls with a hammer and a pry bar or sturdy scraper. Have a strong buddy (or two) help you flip the top upside down. Seal the tabletop with an exterior-grade concrete sealer.

Install the control panel (if your kit has one), and set your table base exactly where you want it before setting the top into place. Apply the leftover black and high-temp silicone to the top edge of the table. The top is heavy enough that it shouldn't budge with normal use, but the silicone will create a stronger bond.

Insert the burner and make the gas line connections according to the manufacturer's directions. Fill the burner with the recommended amount of rocks. Too few rocks and the pan will overheat; too many rocks and the flame will sit too high and be blown out by the wind.

All that's left is to invite your friends and family for a relaxing conversation around the fire.

MEET THE EXPERT

Mark Petersen spent 20 years in the construction industry, 10 years as a siding contractor and 10 as a general contractor before he became an editor at *Family Handyman*.

SOLID
NOTCHED
JOINTS

GRATE-COVERED
DIRT CATCHER

BUILT-IN
POTTING SOIL
CONTAINER

REMOVABLE
CONTAINER
COVER

Cedar Potting Bench

Build this handy potting bench in a weekend

Whether you're a spare-time gardener or a hard-core enthusiast, this bench is for you. It has plenty of storage to keep all your plant supplies in one convenient location, and it features a built-in potting soil container and a grate-covered dirt catcher to make messy potting and cleanup a snap.

Here you'll learn how to build this cedar potting bench in a weekend with about $200 worth of materials.

This bench was designed to be strong without complex joints. An experienced woodworker can complete this potting bench in

a day. If you're a beginner, allow two or three days.

You'll need basic carpentry tools like a tape measure, large and small squares, and a chisel. You could make most of the cuts for this potting bench with a circular saw. However, a power miter box will ensure perfectly square end cuts, and a table saw is almost essential for cutting the grate slats. If you don't have a table saw, ask a friend, neighbor or the staff at the lumberyard to cut the pieces for you. You'll also need a drill with the bits mentioned in the story and a jigsaw.

Figure A
Potting bench

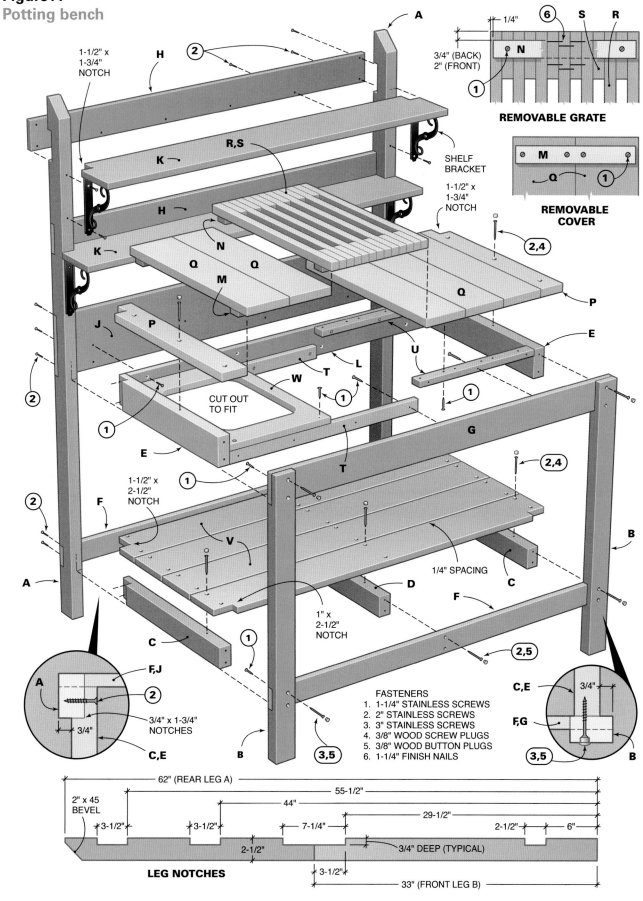

1-1/2" x 1-3/4" NOTCH

H

2

A

1/4"

6

S

R

3/4" (BACK) 2" (FRONT)

N

1

REMOVABLE GRATE

K

R,S

SHELF BRACKET

M

Q

REMOVABLE COVER

1

H

1-1/2" x 1-3/4" NOTCH

K

N

Q

Q

2,4

P

M

J

P

U

E

L

T

W

CUT OUT TO FIT

1

2

1

1

G

E

2

2,4

2

1-1/2" x 2-1/2" NOTCH

F

V

T

1

B

A

1/4" SPACING

C

C

D

F

1" x 2-1/2" NOTCH

C

2,5

1

F,J

A

2

3/4" x 1-3/4" NOTCHES

3/4"

C,E

B

3,5

C,E

3/4"

F,G

B

3,5

B

FASTENERS
1. 1-1/4" STAINLESS SCREWS
2. 2" STAINLESS SCREWS
3. 3" STAINLESS SCREWS
4. 3/8" WOOD SCREW PLUGS
5. 3/8" WOOD BUTTON PLUGS
6. 1-1/4" FINISH NAILS

62" (REAR LEG A)

55-1/2"

44"

29-1/2"

2" x 45 BEVEL

3-1/2"

3-1/2"

7-1/4"

2-1/2"

6"

2-1/2"

3/4" DEEP (TYPICAL)

LEG NOTCHES

3-1/2"

33" (FRONT LEG B)

Materials list

ITEM	QTY.
2x6 x 8' cedar (rip to 2-1/2" for legs)	1
2x4 x 6' cedar (rip to 2-1/2" for lower cross members)	1
2x4 x 4' cedar	1
1x2 x 4' cedar	3
1x3 x 8' cedar	1
1x4 x 8' cedar	2
1x8 x 4' cedar	3
5/4 x 6 x 4' bullnose cedar	9
2' x 2' 3/4" plywood	1

Hardware

1-1/4" stainless steel screws	80
2" stainless steel screws	50
3" stainless steel screws	10
1-1/4" finish nails	1 lb.
3/8" wood screw plugs*	30
3/8" wood buttons*	10
10-oz. tube of construction adhesive	1
Water-resistant wood glue	1
6" x 8" decorative shelf brackets	4
10" x 14" x 18"-deep Rubbermaid wastebasket	1
14" x 20" x 4"-deep litter pan	1
100-grit sandpaper sheets	2

*Wood plugs and buttons are available from home centers and Woodcraft (800-225-1153, or online at woodcraft.com).

Choose straight, nice-looking lumber

Use the **Materials List** below to buy your materials. Shown is cedar, but pine is cheaper. Consider using pressure-treated pine if you'll be leaving the bench outside. All of these are available at home centers and lumberyards.

Make tight-fitting joints for a strong bench

Photos 1 and **2** show how to notch the legs for the horizontal cross members. Notching looks tricky, but it's simple if you follow these key steps: First clamp each pair of legs together, and using dimensions from **Figure A**, mark the lower edge of each notch. Use a square to draw lines across the boards at these marks. Then align the corresponding horizontal board with this line and mark along the opposite edge to get an exact width. Using the boards in this manner to mark the width of the notch is more accurate than measuring. When you saw the notch, cut to the waste side of the pencil line, leaving the line on the board. You can always enlarge the notch or plane the board to fit a notch that's too tight, but you can't shrink a notch that's too wide. Tight-fitting joints strengthen the bench and look better too.

Assembly is quick once the parts are cut

Photos 3 and **4** show how to assemble the leg sections and connect them to form the bench frame. Before you screw the horizontal pieces to the legs, pick the best-looking side of the boards and make sure it's facing the front of the bench. (The best sides are facing down in **Photo 3**.) Drill 5/32-in. clearance holes through the cross

Cutting list

KEY	QTY.	DIMENSIONS	PART
A	2	1-1/2" x 2-1/2" x 62"	Back legs
B	2	1-1/2" x 2-1/2" x 33"	Front legs
C	2	1-1/2" x 2-1/2" x 21"	Lower cross members
D	1	1-1/2" x 2-1/2" x 21"	Middle cross member
E	2	1-1/2" x 3-1/2" x 21"	Upper cross members
F	2	3/4" x 2-1/2" x 47"	Lower rails
G	1	3/4" x 3-1/2" x 47"	Upper rail
H	2	3/4" x 3-1/2" x 47"	Shelf rails
J	1	3/4" x 7-1/4" x 47"	Backsplash
K	2	3/4" x 7-1/4" x 47"	Shelves
L	1	3/4" x 3-1/2" x 42-1/2"	Bench-top support
M	2	3/4" x 1-1/2" x 10-1/2"	Cover cleats
N	2	3/4" x 1-1/2" x 12-1/2"	Grate cleats
P	2	1" x 5-1/2" x 23"	Bench-top ends; cut to fit
Q	5	1" x 5-1/2" x 23"	Bench top
R	7	1" x 1" x 23-1/2"	Slats
S	12	1" x 1" x 4"	Spacers
T	2	3/4" x 1-1/2" x 25-1/2"	Container cleats
U	2	3/4" x 1-1/2" x 16-3/4"	Bench-top cleats
V	4	1" x 5-1/2" x 47"	Lower shelf
W	1	12-3/4" x 20-1/4" x 3/4"	Container support

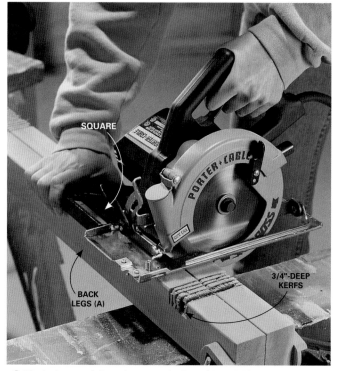

1 Mark the notch locations on the legs (A and B) using the dimensions in Figure A. Make a series of 3/4-in.-deep saw kerfs about 1/4 in. apart to create the notches.

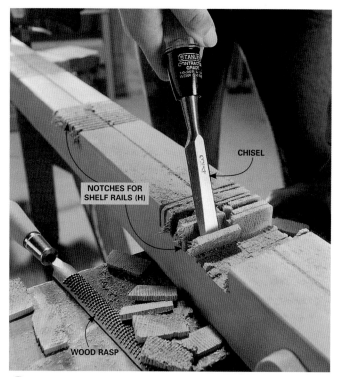

2 Chisel out the waste wood from the notches and smooth the bottom with a wood rasp.

members to avoid splitting them and to allow the screws to draw the boards tight to the legs.

Use only one 1-1/4-in. screw to attach parts F and G to the front legs. Center the screw so it doesn't interfere with the 3-in. screws you'll be installing to secure the leg assembly (**Photo 4**). Use a 3/4-in. spacer block (**Photo 4**) to align the cross members (E) before you drive in the 3-in. screws.

If you'll be leaving your bench outdoors, use stainless steel screws or corrosion-resistant deck screws. For extra strength and durability, put a small dab of construction adhesive on each joint before you screw the pieces together. To hide the 3-in. screws that secure the front legs, use a 3/8-in. brad point drill bit to drill 1/4-in.-deep recesses before you drill the 5/32-in. clearance holes. Then glue 3/8-in. wood buttons into the recesses after you screw the parts together.

Keep a framing square handy as you assemble the leg sections and bench frame and use it to make sure the assemblies are square before you tighten the screws.

Photo 5 shows how to mark and cut the plywood that supports the potting soil container. Shown is a plastic wastebasket, but any container with a lip will work. Trace the shape on a piece of plywood and then cut the hole a little smaller so the plywood supports the lip.

The bench top is made of 1-in.-thick bullnose cedar decking. Join two pieces with cleats to make a removable cover for the dirt catcher (**Photo 7**). Glue 1 x 1-in. slats together with water-resistant wood glue to form the grate (**Photo 6**). Scrape off excess glue before it dries. Then allow the glue to dry overnight before you sand the grate and trim the ends flush. Screw cleats to the bottom of the grate to keep it positioned and allow easy removal.

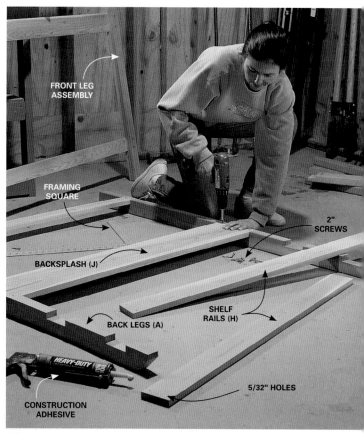

3 Spread a small bead of construction adhesive in each notch and lay the horizontal pieces in place. Use a framing square to make sure the cross members are at right angles to the legs, then drive a pair of 2-in. screws at each joint.

LOWER
RAIL (F)

3"
SCREWS

FRONT LEGS (B)

3/4" SPACER
BLOCK

LOWER CROSS
MEMBERS (C)

UPPER CROSS
MEMBERS (E)

LOWER
RAIL (F)

2" SCREWS

4 Screw the horizontal cross members (C and E) to the back leg assembly. Drill and countersink the front leg assembly and attach it to members C and E with 3-in. screws. Cover the screws with decorative wood buttons.

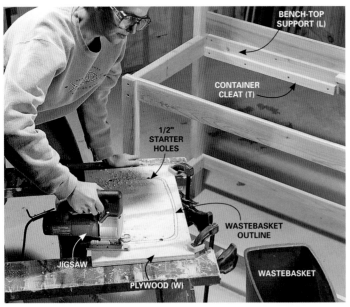

BENCH-TOP
SUPPORT (L)

CONTAINER
CLEAT (T)

1/2"
STARTER
HOLES

JIGSAW

WASTEBASKET
OUTLINE

WASTEBASKET

PLYWOOD (W)

5 Trace the wastebasket onto the 3/4-in. plywood (W). Draw a second line about 1/2 in. inside the traced outline. Drill a 1/2-in. starter hole and cut along the inside line with a jigsaw. Screw the bench-top support (L) and container cleats (T) to the bench and screw the plywood (W) into place.

The width of the end pieces (P) varies, depending on the dimensions of your decking. To determine the width, first center the grate, removable cover and three more boards on the bench top, leaving an equal space on each end. Then measure the distance from the last board to the outside edge of the back leg and cut and notch the end pieces to fit.

Glue 3/8-in. wood plugs into 3/8-in. by 1/4-in.-deep recesses to hide the screws that hold the two end pieces (P) and lower shelf boards in place. Sand them flush after the glue dries.

Complete the potting bench by notching the 1x8 shelves (**Photo 9**) and securing them with 2-in. screws through the horizontal 1x4 shelf rails (H).

Protect your bench with a good finish

Unfinished cedar has some resistance to decay, but the best strategy is to apply a top-quality exterior finish to keep the wood from cracking, splitting and rotting. Penetrating oil–type finishes with a small amount of pigment provide a natural look and reduce fading. Finishes that leave a film provide the best protection. Spar varnish or Sikkens are two examples. Take extra precautions to seal the bottom of the legs to keep them from absorbing moisture from the damp ground.

6 Glue and nail the slats and spacers together to make the grate. Drill 1/16-in. pilot holes for the nails to prevent splitting the wood. Spread water-resistant glue on both surfaces and nail the slats and spacers together with 1-1/4-in. finish nails. Clamp the completed assembly with bar clamps and allow it to dry overnight. Trim the 23-1/2-in. grate to 23 in. with your circular saw or table saw and sand the edge smooth.

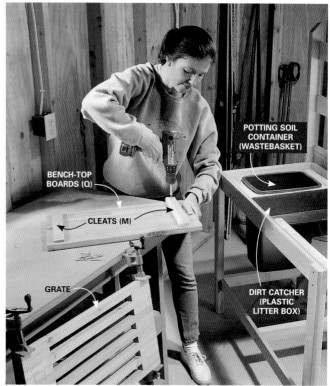

7 Assemble the cover for the dirt container by screwing cleats (M) to the bottom of the 5/4 x 6-in. decking (Q). Screw cleats (N) to the bottom of the completed grate.

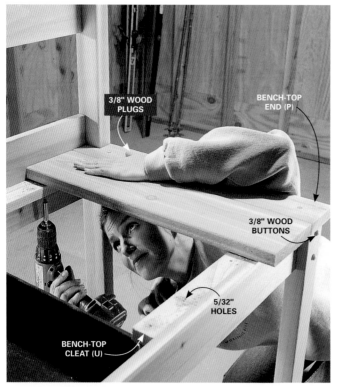

8 Attach the fixed bench-top pieces (Q) with 1-1/4-in. screws driven up through the bench-top cleats (U). Secure the bench-top ends (P) and bottom shelf boards (V) by driving 1-1/4-in. screws through predrilled and countersunk holes. Conceal these screws with wood plugs glued into the recesses. Sand the plugs flush when the glue dries.

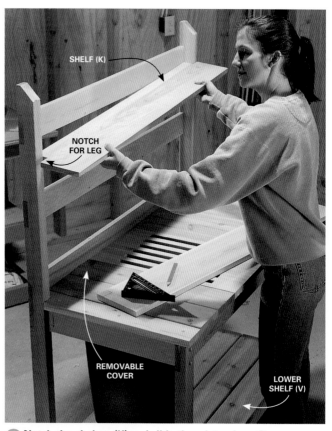

9 Notch the shelves (K) and slide them into place. Screw through the shelf rails (H) into the shelves. Support the front of the shelves with metal brackets.

Simple Timber Bench

We knew what we wanted in a bench, and this one has it all!

✔ *Low cost*
✔ *Stylish design*
✔ *Rock-solid*
✔ *Low maintenance*
✔ *SUPER EASY TO BUILD!*

WHAT IT TAKES

TIME: Half day

COST: $145

SKILL: Beginner

TOOLS: Circular saw, drill/driver, standard hand tools

MEET THE EXPERT

Jason White has 17 years of carpentry and woodworking experience and was an associate editor at *Family Handyman*.

Maybe I'm biased, but I love this simple outdoor bench. It's massive without being clunky, rustic yet modern, well designed (if I do say so myself) and super easy to build. In fact, if you can lift the heavy landscape timbers needed for this project—about 60 lbs. each—you can build this bench! And since the bench is made from treated lumber, it's practically rot-proof, so you'll enjoy it for decades.

Time, tools and materials

Building this bench is surprisingly fast. If you have some experience with power tools, you'll have it built in just a few hours, though staining it may add a couple hours more. You can build it with just a drill/driver, circular saw and basic hand tools, but you'll get faster, better results if you also have a router and a random orbit sander.

All the materials are available at home centers. When you're choosing timbers, take the time to pick through the pile for the straightest ones. They'll twist a little after you build the bench (see "One Year Later" on p. 65), but they need to be nice and straight when you're cutting the joints and assembling the bench.

This bench is made entirely from pressure-treated landscape timbers and a few galvanized lag screws and washers. Add black spray paint and exterior stain and you'll have a beautiful, low-maintenance bench. The hardest part of the project is picking through the pile of heavy landscape timbers at the home center to find the best ones.

3 BASIC PARTS

4x6 TIMBERS

LAG SCREWS

WASHERS

Figure A
Exploded view
Overall Dimensions:
96" long x 19" tall x 18-1/2" deep

BEAM (A)

2" x 5-1/2" NOTCH

12"

3/8" x 6" LAG SCREW

3/8" x 5" LAG SCREW

LEDGER (B)

3/8" x 6" LAG SCREW

LEG (C)

ANY LENGTH YOU LIKE!
Most home centers carry longer 4x6 timbers, so you can make this bench 12 ft. long, 4 ft. long or anything in between!

3-1/2" x 1-1/4" NOTCH

CHEEK

SHOULDER

LEG

Cutting list

KEY	QTY.	DIMENSIONS	NAME
A	3	4x6 x 96"	Beam
B	2	4x6 x 11-1/2"	Ledger
C	4	4x6 x 19"	Leg

Materials list

ITEM	QTY.
4x6 x 8' pressure-treated landscape timbers	5
3/8" x 5" galvanized lag screws	8
3/8" x 6" galvanized lag screws	6
3/8" galvanized washers	14
Exterior stain and black spray paint	

Cut the parts to size

Three of the landscape timbers will become the "beams" for the bench's seat. The timbers are slightly longer than 8 ft. when you buy them, so you'll need to cut a little off each end to make them exactly 96 in. long.

Set each timber on a pair of sawhorses and use a Speed Square to draw a pencil line on all four sides (**Photo 1**). Set your circular saw blade for a full-depth cut. Then, using your square as a guide, make the first cut on one of the wide "faces" of the timber. You won't be able to cut all the way through in one pass; doing three passes works well (**Photo 2**).

When you finish the first cut, flip the timber on edge, start the saw and slip your saw's blade partway into the "kerf" (slit) you just made to align the blade for your second cut. Guide the saw with your square again, finish the second cut, then flip the timber one more time and do the same thing to make the third and final cut. Now cut the rest of the parts to length the same way and use a random orbit sander to remove any saw marks left behind (**Photo 3**).

1 MARK THE LENGTHS OF THE PARTS. For each part, mark where you'll be cutting with a square and pencil. Draw lines on all four sides of the timbers to help align your cuts.

SPEED SQUARE

2 CUT THREE TIMES. A 4x6 timber is too thick to cut in one pass; it's easy to do in three. Guide your circular saw with a square and rotate the timber 90 degrees in between cuts. To align the second cut, slip the saw blade partway into the kerf you made on the first cut. Repeat this for the third and final cut.

3 SAND OFF SAW MARKS. Remove any saw marks left behind with a random orbit sander and 60-grit sandpaper.

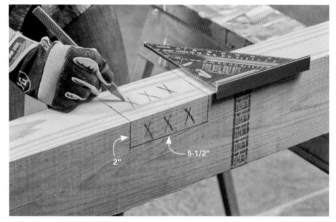

2"   5-1/2"

4 MARK THE NOTCHES. Draw layout lines for the notches in the legs and beams (Figure A). Make Xs to remind yourself where to cut.

SHOULDER CUT

5 MAKE THE SHOULDER CUTS. Guide your saw with the square to make dead-straight "shoulder" cuts that will define the outsides of the notches in the legs and beams (Figure A). The beams get two shoulder cuts per notch. The legs get one shoulder cut per notch.

KERF CUTS

6 MAKE THE KERF CUTS. Cut a series of freehand kerfs between the shoulder cuts you made for the notches in the beams. The legs have only one shoulder cut per notch, so start your kerf cuts at the ends and work toward the shoulder cut.

7 KNOCK AWAY THE SLIVERS, Remove the thin slivers of wood left behind with the claw of a hammer.

8 CHISEL THE NOTCHES SMOOTH. Smooth the "cheek" of each notch (Figure A) with a sharp wood chisel.

Cut the notches

The joinery that connects the legs to the seat beams looks complicated, but it's really simple. The outside beams of the bench's seat are supported by L-shape notches in the legs. U-shape notches are also cut into the seat beams so the leg's faces can sit about 1/4 in. proud of the beams. The notches are all formed the same way using a circular saw, a square and a sharp wood chisel.

Tip each of the outside beams on end and, using a pencil and your square, mark layout lines for the sides and bottoms of the notches (**Photo 4**). Set your circular saw blade to the proper depth and then, using the square as a guide (clamp it down if needed), make a perfectly straight cut on each side of the notch (**Photo 5**). Then make a series of freehand kerf cuts between the two outside cuts you made (**Photo 6**). The notches for the legs are made nearly the same way.

When you're done cutting, knock out the thin slivers of wood with the claw of your hammer (**Photo 7**) and use a sharp wood chisel to smooth and flatten the bottoms of all the notches (**Photo 8**).

Round over the sharp edges

The edges of the seat beams and legs are sharp and can give you splinters, so deal with them now before you assemble the bench. Lay the beams and legs on sawhorses and knock off all the sharp edges with a router and 1/4-in. round-over bit (**Photo 9**). Be sure to go counterclockwise with the router. If you don't have a router, you can do the job with a block plane, a sanding block or a random orbit sander. Don't round over the edges of the notches.

ROUND-OVER BIT

9 ROUND OVER THE EDGES. Remove the sharp edges from the beams and legs with a router and 1/4-in. round-over bit.

Assemble the bench

If you're planning to stain your bench, do it now before you assemble all the parts. You might need to let the wood dry out a bit before staining because pressure-treated lumber is very wet when you buy it. Be sure to read the directions on the can.

Set the outside beams for the seat upside down across your sawhorses with the U-shape notches facing out and fit the L-shape notches of the legs into each of the U-shape notches. The L-shape notches should fit snugly into the U-shape notches and the tops of the legs should be flush with the tops of the seat beams. The faces of the legs will sit a little proud of the seat beams—about 1/4 in. If the joints won't go together by hand, knock them together with a rubber mallet or dead blow hammer. If they still won't go together, you might have to fine-tune the fit of each joint with your chisel.

Set the third beam (the one without notches) between the other two beams, making sure the spaces are even—about 1/2 in. Now set the ledgers between the legs, pull everything together tightly and use long clamps to hold it temporarily. Drill pilot holes through the tops of the legs for lag screws (**Photo 10**)—two through each L-shape notch and one below each notch's shoulder (**Figure A**) and drill one hole in the center of each ledger.

Next, spray-paint the heads of the lag screws and washers and let them dry before driving (**Photo 11**). Once they're dry, drive the lag screws with washers through all the pilot holes you drilled (**Photo 12**). Touch up the tops of the lag screws with more paint if they get scuffed up (spray a little on a disposable brush).

One year later…

My bench sat outside, completely unsheltered, through a hot summer and a hard Minnesota winter and it still looks great! The timbers twisted a little, but that just added to the rustic look. The joints loosened up a bit from wood shrinkage, but that was easily fixed by tightening the lag screws.

10 DRILL PILOT HOLES FOR LAG SCREWS. Temporarily clamp together all the bench parts and drill 5/16-in. pilot holes for lag screws.

LEDGER

11 PAINT THE LAG SCREWS AND WASHERS. Coat the heads of the lag screws and washers with black spray paint. Save the can for future touch-ups.

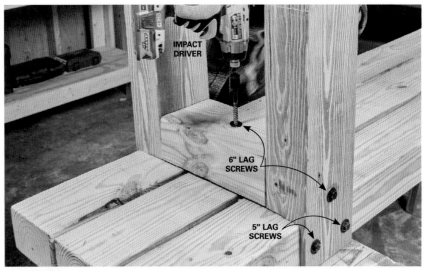

IMPACT DRIVER

6" LAG SCREWS

5" LAG SCREWS

12 DRIVE THE LAG SCREWS. Drive lag screws with washers through the pilot holes you drilled earlier. An impact driver with a socket works great for this, but you can also use a wrench or ratchet. Touch up any scuffs on the lag screws with black paint.

Maintenance-Free Deck

Composite decking, treated wood and special building techniques all add up to a durable, low-maintenance deck

WHAT IT TAKES

SKILL: Advanced

COST: $11,000

TOOLS: Circular saw, drill, posthole digger, level

Who says natural is the only way to go? Occasionally humans invent something that not only lasts longer than Mother Nature's products but is easier to maintain. Here we'll tell you how to use some of these materials to build yourself a deck that will last a long time, look good and be easy to maintain. Here we'll also show you tricks and tips to make the building process simpler and "mistake-tolerant."

Decks are great do-it-yourself projects, and this one, big as it looks, is no exception. Although this multilevel deck looks complex, you can build it using standard tools. A circular saw, tape measure, chalk line, hammer and posthole digger can be adequate for building anything from a simple 12 x 12-ft. deck to an elaborate multilevel structure. But don't think you'll knock this one off in a couple of weekends. This deck took 12 skilled-carpenter days to build, so if you're new to carpentry, add a few days for the learning curve, weather delays, weekend-only work and family obligations. Realistically, a deck this size could turn into a summer-long project.

1 Determine the size of your deck by laying out garden hose to mark its footprint (size and shape) on the yard exactly where it will be built. We used two garden hoses of different colors, one to lay out the deck and the other to lay out the planter boxes. Then pretend it's your finished deck by arranging chairs, tables, barbecue grills or whatever else you expect to keep on it.

The plastic/wood composite decking (the planks you walk on) used for this deck is called Trex and costs about $2.30 per linear foot. Using Trex in lieu of cedar added $400 to the project cost. That sounds like a lot of money, but when you figure that 15 years from now you'll be vacationing in Mexico instead of replacing the old deck, it doesn't seem so bad. For decking material pros and cons, see "**The Case for Composite Decking**" on p. 75.

The key ingredients that'll make your deck last (almost) forever

- **Decking:** The floor bears the brunt of rot on decks. Because deck boards lie flat, water collects in cracks and knots and soaks into the end grain—especially at splices. Because these areas stay wet for long periods of time, they are the most vulnerable to decay. Although we used Trex for the decking, we chose rough-sawn cedar lumber for the privacy wall, planter trim and other exposed wood to give the project a more natural, tactile character. Because these items are largely vertical, they can be made of wood and will last a very long time.
- **Lumber:** The wood for all the above-ground framing is .40-grade pressure-treated lumber, which will last for decades without any maintenance. Posts and planter framing that are underground call for foundation-grade .60-treated lumber (stamped FNDN), the same material

> **Tip**
> Wear gloves when working with treated lumber.

Materials list
(Color indexed with Figure A and B)

ITEM	USE
Lumber	
.60 foundation-grade 2x4	Middle of posts, top and bottom plates, studs and braces for planters
.60 foundation-grade 2x6	Outsides of posts, footing plates for planters
.60 foundation-grade 1/2-in. plywood	Planter liner
.40 treated 2x12s	Stair stringers and deck beams
.40 treated 2x10s	Wall ledgers, deck joists, rim joists and stair plate
.40 treated 1x6s	Ground board for planters
5/4 x 6 Trex	Decking, stair treads
1x10 cedar	Trim that hides joists
1x8 cedar	Stair risers
2x4 cedar	Corner boards on planter, upper and lower rails on privacy wall
2x6 cedar	Center board and top cap on privacy wall panels
2x10 cedar	Planter top caps
2x12 cedar	Dress skirt
2x2 cedar	Privacy wall pickets, top trim for planters
4x4 cedar	Privacy wall posts
Siding	Planter box siding
Pine 1x4s	Batter boards
Hardware	
3-in. stainless nails	Framing nailing
2-1/2 in. stainless ring or spiral-shanked nails	Decking and plywood liner fasteners
2-in. and 3-in. siding nails	Siding and cedar trim
3-in. stainless screws	Planter top cap and privacy fence
3/8 x 4-in. bolts, nuts and washers	Privacy fence posts
Joist hangers with exterior-rated 1-1/2 in. joist hanger nails	Joist attachment to ledger
Rafter tie hangers	Stair stringer to rim connections
3/8 x 4-in. lag screws	Ledger to house
3/8 x 3-in. lag screws	Planter braces and outside corners
1-1/2 in. drip cap	Over ledger, behind house siding
7/8-in. drip cap	Over planter ground board, behind siding
Miscellaneous	
Premixed concrete	1 bag for each posthole
3/4-in. gravel	Planter box fill, planter and stair footings

Figure A
Main deck assembly

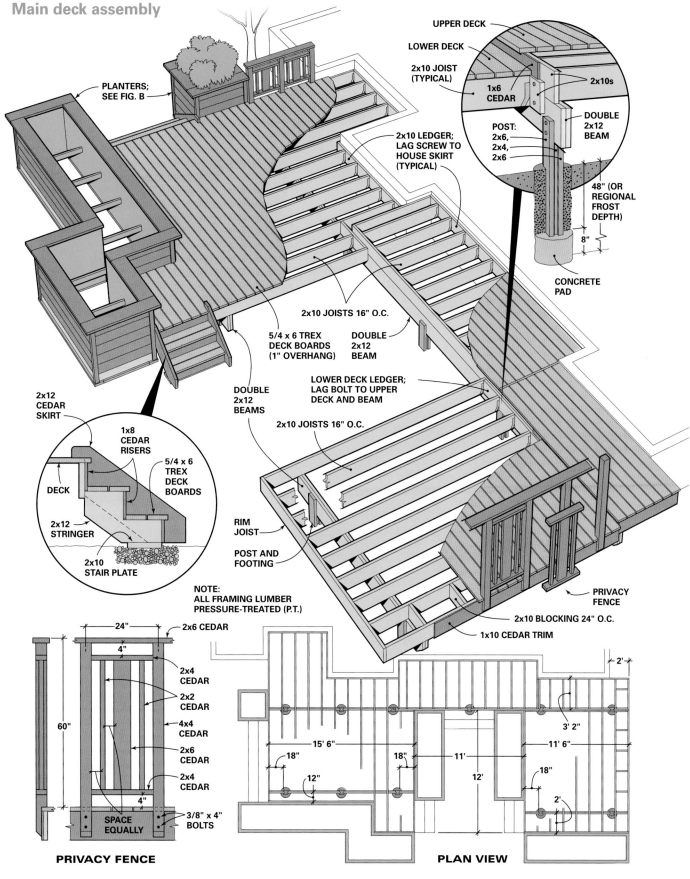

PLANTERS;
SEE FIG. B

UPPER DECK

LOWER DECK

2x10 JOIST
(TYPICAL)

1x6
CEDAR

2x10s

POST:
2x6,
2x4,
2x6

DOUBLE
2x12
BEAM

48" (OR
REGIONAL
FROST
DEPTH)

8"

CONCRETE
PAD

2x10 LEDGER;
LAG SCREW TO
HOUSE SKIRT
(TYPICAL)

2x10 JOISTS 16" O.C.

5/4 x 6 TREX
DECK BOARDS
(1" OVERHANG)

DOUBLE
2x12
BEAM

DOUBLE
2x12
BEAMS

LOWER DECK LEDGER;
LAG BOLT TO UPPER
DECK AND BEAM

2x10 JOISTS 16" O.C.

2x12
CEDAR
SKIRT

1x8
CEDAR
RISERS

5/4 x 6
TREX
DECK
BOARDS

DECK

2x12
STRINGER

2x10
STAIR PLATE

RIM
JOIST

POST AND
FOOTING

NOTE:
ALL FRAMING LUMBER
PRESSURE-TREATED (P.T.)

PRIVACY
FENCE

2x10 BLOCKING 24" O.C.

1x10 CEDAR TRIM

PRIVACY FENCE

24"

4"

2x6 CEDAR

2x4
CEDAR

2x2
CEDAR

4x4
CEDAR

2x6
CEDAR

2x4
CEDAR

60"

4"

SPACE
EQUALLY

3/8" x 4"
BOLTS

PLAN VIEW

2'

3' 2"

15' 6"

18"

18"

11'

11' 6"

12"

12'

18"

2'

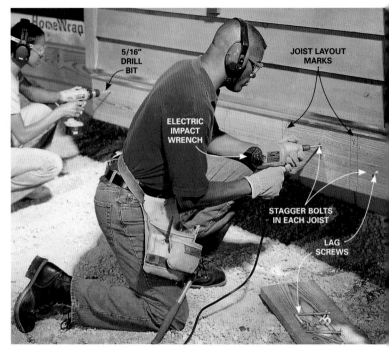

2 Cut out the siding with a circular saw to create a space for the deck ledger to attach to the house. Leave space for the decking to slide under the siding. Tuck drip cap under the siding. Level and tack the ledger to the rim of the house with 16d galvanized nails.

3 Draw joist layout marks every 16 in. on the ledger board. Drill a pilot hole, then install a 3/8-in. x 4-in. lag screw between each floor joist. (Screw length may vary, but the screws should extend through the house sheathing and the rim joist of the house.) Stagger the lag screws in every other joist space to prevent the ledger from splitting.

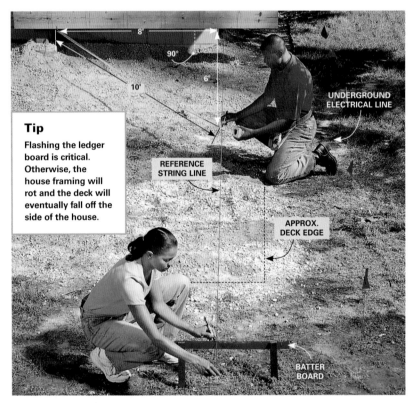

Tip

Flashing the ledger board is critical. Otherwise, the house framing will rot and the deck will eventually fall off the side of the house.

4 Install batter boards outside the perimeter of each corner of the deck so that the center of the batter boards is "eyeball" square to the left and right ends of the ledger board. Stretch a string line at right angles to the ledger board at each end using the 3-4-5 triangle squaring method (6-8-10 in this instance for more accuracy). Pound a small nail into the batter board where the string crosses it and tie the string to the nail. The string is a square reference guide parallel to the edge of the deck for laying out the rest of the framing.

used for wood foundations. FNDN material may be a special-order item in your part of the country, but most lumberyards can get it for you.

- **Hardware:** Plan on spending a few extra dollars to get quality hardware designed for outside use. That means using double-hot-dipped galvanized nails or, better yet, stainless steel nails for all nailing and exterior-rated joist hanger nails. Install drip cap above the ledger and behind the siding (**Photo 2**). Don't scrimp on hardware; remember that for the first time ever, the deck's structure could outlast the hardware.

- **Design:** Take pains to plan your deck for the long term. Think far into the future to get the size and shape right. Think in terms of a room addition more than a deck. We hired an architect for a site visit, a couple of preliminary drawings and final plans. He had numerous suggestions and ideas we wouldn't have thought of. With the design fee only 6 percent of the total project, it was a bargain.

- **Footings:** Make sure your footings are deep and wide enough for your climate. When you take your plans in to get a building permit, your inspector will let you know about the local requirements. In the upper Midwest, that means 42-in. deep footings, but we went 48 in. to

BEAM CANTILEVER

STRING IS OUTSIDE EDGE OF BEAM

DECK CANTILEVER

ADJUST TO MARK CENTER OF HOLE

POSTS ARE APPROX. 24" FROM INSIDE EDGE OF DECK

.60 FNDN GRADE 2x6, 2x4, 2x6 SANDWICH POSTS

24"

FUTURE DECK JOISTS

END POSTS ARE APPROX. 18" FROM INSIDE OF DECK

Tip

Using deck joists as straightedges will help keep the posts in line, assist in layout and hold the posts steady while backfilling.

5 Measure from the deck ledger to position batter boards and strings for the beams that run parallel to the house. Mark the outside edge of the beam locations with the strings. Drive stakes into the ground to mark the center of each posthole (remember that the string marks the outside edge of the beam, not the middle).

Tip

If you cantilever the beams, your posts can be off by a mile, and you can still fudge your way to a square, true deck.

6 Assemble the posts from FNDN 2x4s and 2x6s, nailing them below their future cut-off level—see Photos 8 and 9. Drop them into their holes and align them with the string line. Lay temporary 2x10s (joist material) alongside the posts to help position them. Plumb the posts both ways and tack them into the floor joists. Fill the holes, packing the dirt as you fill.

Figure B
Planter

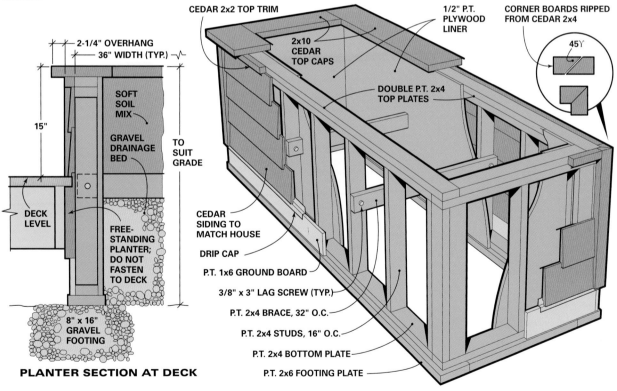

CEDAR 2x2 TOP TRIM

1/2" P.T. PLYWOOD LINER

CORNER BOARDS RIPPED FROM CEDAR 2x4

2x10 CEDAR TOP CAPS

45°

DOUBLE P.T. 2x4 TOP PLATES

2-1/4" OVERHANG
36" WIDTH (TYP.)

SOFT SOIL MIX

GRAVEL DRAINAGE BED

15"

TO SUIT GRADE

DECK LEVEL

FREE-STANDING PLANTER; DO NOT FASTEN TO DECK

CEDAR SIDING TO MATCH HOUSE

DRIP CAP

P.T. 1x6 GROUND BOARD

3/8" x 3" LAG SCREW (TYP.)

P.T. 2x4 BRACE, 32" O.C.

P.T. 2x4 STUDS, 16" O.C.

P.T. 2x4 BOTTOM PLATE

P.T. 2x6 FOOTING PLATE

8" x 16" GRAVEL FOOTING

PLANTER SECTION AT DECK

Digging postholes with fewer blisters

The soil at our site was a combination of loose sand, rocks and hard clay, so we ended up using a power auger, a steel bar to loosen rocks and a clamshell-style posthole digger to extract the rock and clean out loose soil at the bottom of the hole. A drain tile shovel is great for loosening the clay at the bottom of the hole and for dislodging rocks.

Power augers cost about $90 per day to rent, and they don't always make posthole digging a quick, easy chore. They take two strong people to run, and they bog down in heavy soil and skip over the top of any rocks bigger than a tangerine. They are, however, worth their weight in gold if you have lots of holes to dig—especially if you're digging in sandy soil. The corkscrew end on the auger will extract the dirt more efficiently than the clamshell digger because sand falls through the end of the clamshell blades when you're lifting the tool out of the hole. The pros usually end up hand-digging about 40 percent of the holes even if they do have a power auger at their disposal. If you choose to rent an auger, remember to hand-dig a pilot hole a few inches deep before firing up the machine. Otherwise the auger has a tendency to wander at startup and your hole might shift several inches off your layout.

POWER POSTHOLE DIGGER

12" AUGER

STEEL BAR

CLAMSHELL POSTHOLE DIGGER

DRAIN-TILE SHOVEL

7 Set aside the beam strings and dig 12-in.- dia. postholes the correct depth for your area. Solidly pack the loose soil at the bottom of the holes with the end of a 2x4 and pour a 60-lb. bag of premixed concrete into the holes to form an 8-in. thick footing pad.

STRAIGHT 2x4

TOP OF BEAM

BEAM WIDTH

BOTTOM OF BEAM

8 Level from the deck ledger to each post with a straight board. Measure down from the ledger level the depth of your beams to establish cut-off lines.

CUT THIS 2x6 TO TOP OF BEAM

2x4

NO NAILS ABOVE CUT-OFF LEVEL

CUT TO BOTTOM OF BEAM

STAMP FOR FOUNDATION-GRADE WOOD

12"

THREE 16D NAILS

DOUBLE 2x12

FOUR 16D NAILS

9 Cut off one 2x6 and the middle 2x4 with a circular saw. If your posts will show, you may want to cut off the 2x6 away from the house. Complete the cut with a handsaw. Cut off the longer 2x6 even with the top of the ledger.

10 Set the double 2x12 beam on the posts and fasten it to the long 2x6 with 16d galvanized box nails. Nail the 2x12s to each other with three nails every 12 in., one close to each edge and one in the middle. Be sure the beam projects several inches past the edge of the deck for later trimming.

ensure that the deck would be able to handle our frigid winters.

■ **Structure:** Build with shorter spans, narrower spacing and heavier materials than you would for a normal, wood deck. Our deck spans called for 2x10 beams and 2x8 joists, but we supersized the structural members to 2x12 beams and 2x10 joists to give a more beefy, permanent feel to what we expect will be an often-used outside living room.

Plan your deck with a garden hose

Spend some time walking around on your "hose deck" (**Photo 1**) to get a feel for the adequacy of its size and shape. We decided to split our deck into three distinct areas. There's a small boardwalk next to the house for accessing the two lower decks, one of which is for lounging and the other, for a dining table and chairs.

Although a deck with different levels is more interesting visually, it also entails more complicated construction and shrinks usable space. If you're just planning on a 12 x 12 postage stamp–sized deck, you probably don't need any professional design work, but if you envision a large, elaborate, multilevel deck, consider hiring a professional designer to help with the plans. The pro's final design will have the correct

Tip
When you nail up the joists, you see your deck take shape for the first time.

6" STEP

END JOIST (A)

90°

TOENAIL

BEAM

2x10 JOISTS

TOENAIL

11 Nail the first end joist (A) into the end of the ledger and square it to the ledger with the 6-8-10 triangle technique (Photo 4). Mark the beam even with the outside edge of the end joist, slide the joist away from the cut mark, draw a square cut-off line and cut off the end of the beam. Toenail the joist into the beam and measure from the joist to make 16-in. layout marks on the top of the beam for joist placement. Use the joist layout marks on the ledger as a guide to transfer marks to the beam for setting the joists. Install the remaining joists, toenailing them into the rim and beam. After you're satisfied with the joist placement, secure them to the ledger with joist hangers.

CARPENTER'S SQUARE

END JOIST (B)

DEPTH OF DECK FRAMING MINUS 1-1/2" FOR RIM END

CHALK LINE

Tip

If you're installing a rail, use a 2-ft. level to mark end cuts to get a perfectly plumb, true rim joist and a straight rail.

12 Set end joist (B) parallel with end joist (A), mark for beam cut-off, slide the joist away and cut off the beam end.

13 Measure from the rim joist the depth of the deck, mark the end joists and snap a line for cutting off the ends of the joists. (When measuring, don't forget to subtract for the 1-1/2 in. thickness for the rim joist.) Draw cut-off lines with a carpenter's square and cut off the ends with a circular saw. If you're installing a rail, use a 2-ft. level to mark end cuts to get a perfectly plumb, true rim joist and a straight rail.

END JOIST (B)

RAISE OR LOWER RIM JOIST TO ALIGN TOP EDGE

RIM JOIST

END JOIST

Tip

If you select the straightest 2x10s for rims, this step will be pain-free.

14 Nail the end rim joist onto end joist (A) and have your partner raise and lower the rim joist to make the top edge of the rim flush with the top edge of the joists. Nail each joist, working your way from end joist (A) to end joist (B). Cut the end of the rim off flush with the end of the last deck joist.

structural details to make your deck strong and safe. Whether you do the drawing yourself or hire it done, you'll need drawings to get the building permit and order materials. If you draw your own plans, a helpful lumberyard or building inspector will assist in sizing and spacing all the important structural members of your deck.

Use construction-friendly building methods

Follow the photo series for step-by-step building techniques and keep these labor-saving tips in mind.

- We employed cantilevers (beams hanging over posts, and joists hanging over beams) in our design because they make layout and construction much easier. They also give the deck a floating appearance by moving the main structural supports in from the deck's perimeter. Cantilevering also helps by providing "fudge factors" throughout construction. They allow you to fine-tune the dimensions of the deck as you build. Non-cantilevered decks require exact placement of posts at each corner from the moment you dig your first posthole. Unfortunately, all too often you discover only after setting the posts that footing and

The case for composite decking

No splinters!
You can walk on this composite deck in your bare feet.

Decks used to be built solely of redwood, cedar or cypress because of their inherent wood preservatives. But as some of us have learned the hard way, all wood eventually rots—especially in shady, moist locations.

For the last 20 years or so, preservative-treated (green) lumber has been the accepted material for a long-lasting, rot-resistant deck. But treated wood has its downsides too. Besides not being particularly attractive, it has a tendency to split, warp and twist (and those treated splinters embedded in the bottom of your feet are no picnic either).

There are now alternatives to conventional treated and natural wood. Various manufacturers are now distributing their versions of plastic or composite plastic/wood decking. You'll find everything from simple Trex clones to elaborate space-frame vinyl and fiberglass extrusions with, of course, elaborate prices. These products are not available in all areas. You'll need to visit the lumberyards in your area to see what your choices are.

We chose Trex for this deck because of its wide availability and reasonable

price. It's a 50/50 mix of surplus wood fibers and polymers (plastics) that is molded into various shapes and sizes. The decking material we used is the classic 1-1/4 x 5-1/2 in. shape of conventional wood decking. In addition to decking, Trex comes in a variety of non-structural dimensions such as 2x6s and 2x4s, which you can use for benches, rails or privacy screens. But Trex can't be used for posts, beams, joists or any other load-bearing purpose. Trex decking is limited to 16-in. spans, so the joists need to be spaced every 16 in. instead of the more common 24 in. used for full 2x6s.

Although Trex comes in several attractive colors (tan, dark brown and gray), it does have a bit of an artificial look. Gone are wood's subtle grain, color variegation and knots. In short, you sacrifice the natural character of real wood.

Trex is also denser and heavier than wood. Consequently, it's harder to haul around and a bit harder to drive fasteners into. The good news is that its monolithic nature means Trex won't split, warp, twist, cup or crack— ever. Its surface is skid-resistant even when wet, and you'll get that warm, fuzzy feeling knowing that fewer trees gave their lives for your deck.

Use conventional woodworking tools and techniques with Trex

All of the woodworking techniques you've learned over the years apply to Trex as well. Conventional saw blades, router bits, drills and fasteners work with Trex the same as they do with wood. Trex will also receive wood stains and paints like the real thing. Just remember before applying a finish that it will add that maintenance factor you're attempting to avoid. Except for cosmetic reasons, paint and stain are unnecessary. Trex achieves its final weather-adjusted color in 6 to 12 weeks and will be somewhat lighter than the installed shade. If you're planning to apply a finish, you'll need to wait until the fading is complete.

DISTANCE A

CEDAR FASCIA BOARD

DISTANCE B

2"

Tip

If you only have help for a short time, tack the decking and final-nail later.

15 Nail off the decking with ring-shanked 10d stainless steel nails, working from the outside of the deck toward the house using 16d nails for spacers. Let the decking hang over the end joists at least 2-1/2 in. Measure from the house side of the deck every five or six boards to confirm that the decking is running parallel to the house (distances A and B) and make small spacing adjustments as necessary. Leave off the last piece of decking because the house will block the last cut made by the circular saw.

16 Measure 2 in. from the end joists and mark the decking for cut-off by snapping a line. The 2-in. overhang allows for the 7/8-in.-thick cedar face board and a 1-1/8 in. overhang.

LEAVE OFF LAST DECK BOARD AND CUT BEFORE INSTALLING

CHALK LINE

DOG EARS

SPLICE BOARD

1-1/4"

1-1/8"

17 Cut off the excess decking. Measure the final cut lengths of the deck boards and cut the last deck board to length, rip it to width if necessary, and install it.

18 Cut notches in a piece of decking so that it protrudes above the joists 1-1/4 in. (flush with the top of the decking), away from the deck edge and even with the decking overhang.

TOENAIL SECOND JOIST AGAINST SPLICE

16D NAIL SPACER

19 Nail the notched piece to the side of the joist. Nail a second joist against it and toe-nail the joist into the rims. Nail the decking, leaving a gap between the splice board and the end of the decking.

2x10 "BEATER" BOARD

LEVEL THESE THREE USING PLATE NEAR DECK

2x6 FOOTING PLATE

20 Dig trenches 6 in. deep and 12 in. wide and fill with gravel. Measure down from the deck to keep gravel levels within 1/2 in. of desired height. Lay down .60 foundation-grade lumber for footing plates a few inches longer than the intended planter length and width. To set the footing plates, measure down from the deck and pound on them with a heavy board. Use a 4-ft. level, working off the first plate when setting the plates that don't adjoin the deck.

post placement are off by several inches. You're then faced with living with an out-of-square deck or making some very time-consuming fixes.

- Begin construction by installing the ledger board. (Don't forget the drip cap!) Use the ledger for laying out the rest of the deck, including posthole placement.

- Don't cut anything until you have to. If possible, install members before cutting them to length to give you the opportunity to make minor adjustments in the structure as you build. That means installing posts longer than they have to be, running beams longer than the deck is wide and attaching joists to the ledger before cutting them to their finished length.

- Make your deck at least 6 in. smaller than the standard 2-ft. increments of lumber. We made our 12-ft. section of deck 11 ft. 6 in. and our 16-ft. section 15 ft. 6 in. This lets you trim bad ends on deck boards, maintain a 1-in. overhang along the edges and install cedar trim boards to hide the treated lumber framing.

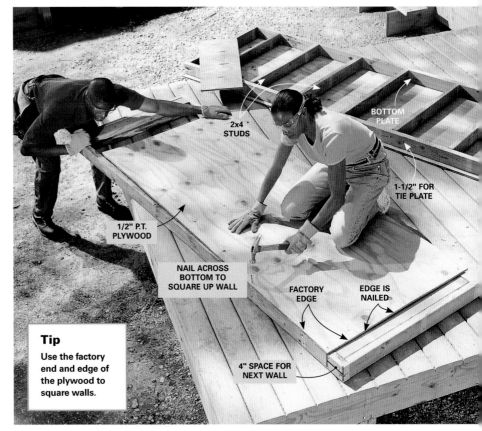

2x4 STUDS

BOTTOM PLATE

1-1/2" FOR TIE PLATE

1/2" P.T. PLYWOOD

NAIL ACROSS BOTTOM TO SQUARE UP WALL

FACTORY EDGE

EDGE IS NAILED

4" SPACE FOR NEXT WALL

Tip

Use the factory end and edge of the plywood to square walls.

21 Lay out all pairs of plates on walls that face each other so that the braces are square when you attach them to the studs. Nail the studs to the top and bottom plates and nail on the plywood after first fastening it to an end stud. Then square the wall by working the plywood up and down to align the bottom of the plywood with the bottom of the plate, nailing across the bottom from the fastened end toward the other end. Finish nailing the plywood to the studs and the top plate every 8 in.

Splice decking with a single seam

The typical way to handle a deck that is wider than the deck boards is to randomly butt the ends together and split them over a deck joist. Cutting and fitting all these joints takes a lot of time and forces you to butt two boards tightly together to share the 1-1/2 in. thickness of a floor joist. Nailing close to the ends makes wood split and rot prematurely because moisture gets into the splice and doesn't dry out for long periods of time.

A more elegant, longer-lasting way is to create a single seam with a dogeared length of decking perpendicular to the deck itself. Then toe-nail in another floor joist for nailing the ends of the next section. Having a full 1-1/2 in. of joist for nailing each deck board allows for a space between the end of the decking board and the splice board for drying, and helps keep nails away from the splitting zone.

PLANTER WALLS AGAINST DECK HAVE 2x4s INSTALLED BEFORE STANDING

1/2 HEIGHT OF WALL

2x4 BRACES

1/2" .60 PRESSURE TREATED WOOD

Tip
Measure studs in opposite planter walls to line up for 2x4 braces.

22 Cut 1-5/8 in. x 3-5/8 in. holes for the 2x4 braces halfway up the wall every 32 in. Cut 2x4 braces the same length as the width of the wall, slip them through the walls and lag-screw them to the sides of the studs before standing them against the deck (they may be inaccessible later, depending on the height of your deck and planters).

3" LAG SCREWS

CAULK GAPS

TIE PLATES TIE TOGETHER WALLS

LAP OF FOOTING PLATES OPPOSITE OF WALL LAPS

23 Tack the corners together with 16d nails. Fasten the ends of the walls with three equally spaced 3-in. lag screws to tie the corners together, and one 3-in. lag screw through each wall brace. Cut and nail tie plates so that the tie plates overlap adjoining walls. Nail with two 16d nails over each stud.

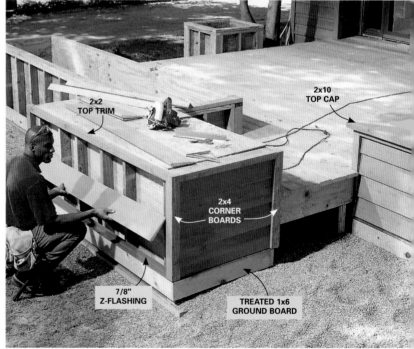

2x2 TOP TRIM

2x10 TOP CAP

2x4 CORNER BOARDS

7/8" Z-FLASHING

TREATED 1x6 GROUND BOARD

24 Install treated 1x6 boards at grade to protect cedar from ground contact, then top with 7/8-in. Z-flashing to keep water from getting behind the siding. Nail 2x4 corner boards, positioning the tops flush with the top of the framing and install 2x2 horizontal trim boards between the corners. Side the walls and cap with 2x10s.

PREFABRICATED PANELS

4" SPACER BLOCK

4x4 NOTCHED INTO DECK

2x2, 2x6, 2x4 RAILS

9" LONG x 2" DEEP NOTCH CUT INTO POST

1" COUNTERSINK HOLES FOR 3/8" x 4" BOLTS WITH NUTS

25 Notch 4x4s and decking and cut 4x4s to length (4-ft. 10-1/2 in. above deck). Plumb posts with a 4-ft. level and bolt to rim of deck after predrilling 1-in. countersink hole and boring a 3/8-in. hole through the post, cedar trim and end joist. Nail on a 2x6 top cap and install premade panel assemblies by toe-screwing into the side of the posts.

COSMETIC STRINGERS

2x10 FOOTING PLATE

RAFTER TIE HANGER

GRAVEL FOOTING

STAIR STRINGER

26 Cut stair stringers and use them for positioning 2x10 footing plate for stairs to rest on. Tack stringers onto rim joist and install rafter tie joist hangers to permanently attach stringers. Nail stair risers to face of stringers and install treads.

Think through rail, planter and stair details or they'll trip you up later

Most building codes call for 36-in. high guardrails on any deck that's more than 30 in. above ground and any set of stairs that has more than three risers. Our deck had only one side higher than 30 in., so we decided to handle that area with a 5-ft. privacy wall (**Photo 25**) to provide a safety rail and to screen the deck from a nearby road.

For the rest of the deck perimeter, we built planter boxes in lieu of railings (**Photos 20–24**) because we didn't want our lake view obstructed. We also liked the idea of being surrounded by a deck-level flower garden. Frame the planters like a conventional stud wall made of foundation-grade lumber and rest them on a gravel footing. It's important to make the planters freestanding. The lack of a frost footing means they'll rise and fall with frost movement and will lift the deck if they're attached to it. Don't consider them as legal guardrails but as a passive barrier to keep people from accidentally stepping off the edge. They were designed so the tops were 15 in. above the deck to double as casual seating.

We added some cosmetic side stringers (**Photo 26**) to dress the stair sides and decked the treads with Trex. Rest the steps on a gravel footing topped with a treated 2x10 (**Photo 26**) using the same setting methods demonstrated for the planters (**Photo 20**).

Dream Deck

Cantilevered bays, overhead lattice, custom rails and cascading stairs make this deck unique and highly functional

This deck isn't huge—about 16 ft. wide x 18 ft. deep plus bays and stairs—but it's big on features. The upper deck is just the right size for entertaining small groups—spacious but intimate. It has cantilevered nooks on both sides that provide space for seating and barbecue storage. The pergola shades the upper deck and the home's interior from the sun, and it offers a space for hanging or climbing plants. The lower deck is a great place to hang out in the sun, while the cascading stairs flow into the yard and provide lots of space for planters and pots.

This deck has some out-of-the-ordinary construction details that contribute to its unique look. For starters, the deck joists run parallel to the house and overhang the beams to form the cantilevered bays on both sides. Rather than a bolted-on ledger board, special "long-tail" joist hangers support the deck at the house. The deck material is a low-maintenance composite material with a tongue-and-groove shape that allows you to hide the fasteners by driving them through the tongues.

1 Set stakes at the house and drive nails to indicate the beam centers. Stake out batter boards about 1 ft. beyond the perimeter. Stretch a string between the boards parallel to the house. Use the 6-8-10 triangle method to stretch strings perpendicular to the house. Measure diagonally to check for square.

BEAM CENTER — 6' — 8' — 10' — 90 DEGREES — BATTER BOARDS

2 Dig the footing holes. Mix two 80-lb. bags of concrete for each footing hole and shovel it in. Nail a 6-in. 2x4 to the bottom of a longer 2x4 and use this to tamp and flatten the top of the footings.

TAMPER — 42" DEEP FOOTING HOLES — CONCRETE

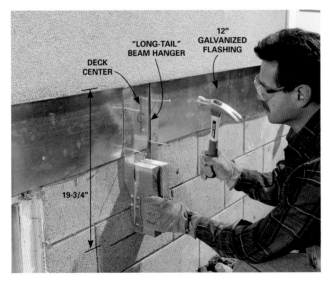

3 Remove the siding from the level of your finished deck on down. Slide No. 30 building paper and galvanized flashing under the siding and nail it with galvanized roofing nails. Position the beam hangers and nail them to the house framing.

DECK CENTER — "LONG-TAIL" BEAM HANGER — 12" GALVANIZED FLASHING — 19-3/4"

The rail system combines horizontal boards for privacy and an open design of copper plumbing tubes at the top, allowing you to see out easily. These unusual details make the deck a bit harder to build, so you'll have to follow the photos and drawings carefully to get everything to fit. If you have some carpentry experience, you shouldn't have any trouble building this deck. It's a big project, though, and will probably take you and a helper about two solid weeks to complete. You don't need any special tools, although a power miter saw speeds up the work.

Plan ahead—you may have to special-order a few items

You'll find treated lumber, cedar boards and many of the metal fasteners at your local home center or full-service lumberyard. You'll probably have to special-order the Geodeck decking, the 6x6 QuattroPosts (flwinternational.com) and the special "long-tail" beam hangers. You can substitute other hanger brands, but use joist hangers labeled G-185. These have extra zinc coating to prevent corrosion caused by the chemicals in treated wood. Expect to spend about $7,000 on materials for this deck.

Before you order materials, submit a deck plan to your local building department. Include details for the footings, attachment to the house, steps and handrails, and brand of composite decking. Some of the details we show may not be acceptable in your area. A few days before you plan to dig the footings, call 811 or visit call811.com to have underground utilities located and marked. Then follow **Photos 1–21** and **Figures A–F** to build the deck, rail and trellis.

Locate the footing holes accurately with string lines

Start by driving two stakes along the house, centered on the outside beams. Drive nails into these stakes to mark the center of the beams. Next stake out two sets of batter boards about 1 ft. outside

Figure A
Deck

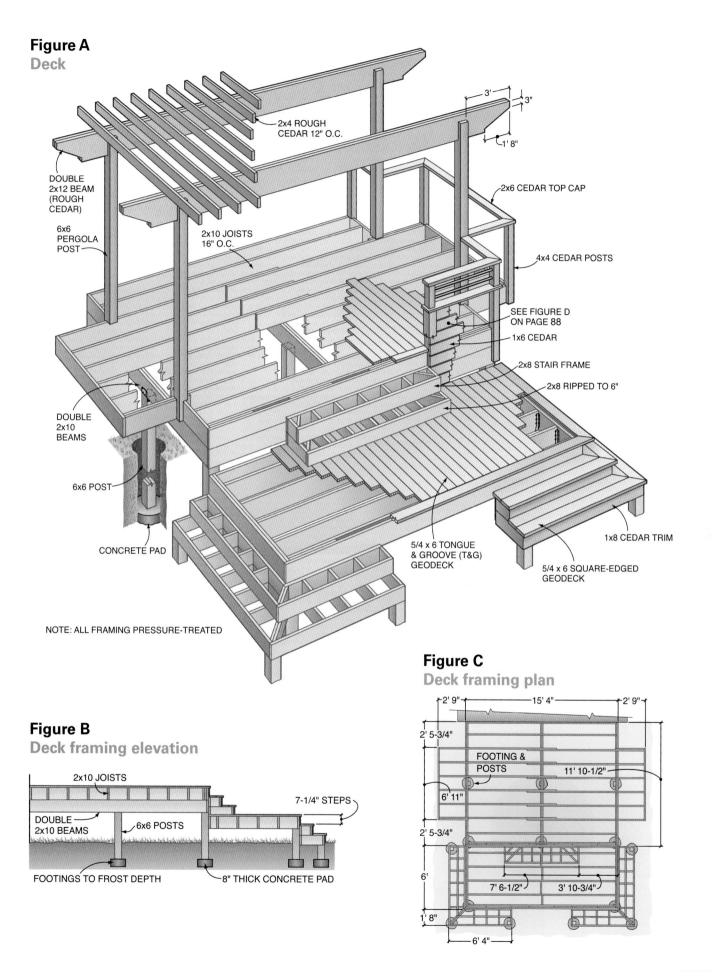

2x4 ROUGH CEDAR 12" O.C.

3'

3"

1' 8"

2x6 CEDAR TOP CAP

DOUBLE 2x12 BEAM (ROUGH CEDAR)

6x6 PERGOLA POST

2x10 JOISTS 16" O.C.

4x4 CEDAR POSTS

SEE FIGURE D ON PAGE 88

1x6 CEDAR

2x8 STAIR FRAME

2x8 RIPPED TO 6"

DOUBLE 2x10 BEAMS

6x6 POST

CONCRETE PAD

5/4 x 6 TONGUE & GROOVE (T&G) GEODECK

1x8 CEDAR TRIM

5/4 x 6 SQUARE-EDGED GEODECK

NOTE: ALL FRAMING PRESSURE-TREATED

Figure B
Deck framing elevation

2x10 JOISTS

7-1/4" STEPS

DOUBLE 2x10 BEAMS

6x6 POSTS

FOOTINGS TO FROST DEPTH

8" THICK CONCRETE PAD

Figure C
Deck framing plan

2' 9"

15' 4"

2' 9"

2' 5-3/4"

FOOTING & POSTS

11' 10-1/2"

6' 11"

2' 5-3/4"

6'

7' 6-1/2"

3' 10-3/4"

1' 8"

6' 4"

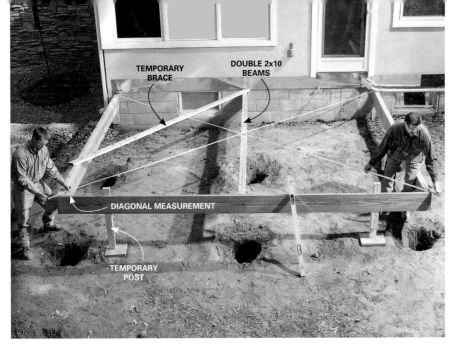

TEMPORARY BRACE **DOUBLE 2x10 BEAMS**

DIAGONAL MEASUREMENT

TEMPORARY POST

4 Cut and nail together 2x10s for the three double beams. Rest the beams on the beam hangers and nail a 2x10 across the front. Prop the beams so they slope about 2 in. down from the house. Adjust the beam assembly until the diagonal measurements are equal. Then nail on a diagonal brace.

CENTER BEAM **MARK POST**

5 Mark the 6x6 posts to fit under the beams and cut them to length. Then position the posts with their outside edges flush with the beams (Figure C) and attach them with metal post-to-beam anchors (Photo 7).

CANTILEVERED JOISTS **HURRICANE ANCHORS** **OVERLAP JOISTS**

EXTRA BLOCKING

6 Cut the 2x10 joists and position them according to the dimensions in Figure C. Attach them to the beams with hurricane anchors. Overlap the cantilevered joists in the middle.

the perimeter of the deck (**Photo 1**). The top of the horizontal boards should be close to level with the top of the stakes near the house. Finally, stretch strings between the stakes and batter boards and square them to the house.

Use the 6-8-10 triangle method to establish lines that are perpendicular to the house (**Photo 1**). Measure 6 ft. along the house then 8 ft. out from the house and mark the string. Then measure between the 6-ft. and 8-ft. marks and move the end of the string line along the batter board until the distance is exactly 10 ft. (**Photo 1**). Double-check your entire string setup by measuring diagonally from corner to corner as in **Photo 4**. Adjust the lines until the diagonal measurements are equal.

After marking the footing locations, dig the holes to the depth required. Make the holes at least 12 in. in diameter to allow room for slightly adjusting the position of the 6x6 treated posts. After your building inspector has approved the excavation, pour an 8-in. deep concrete pad in the bottom of each hole (**Photo 2**).

You don't need a bolted-on ledger board for this deck

The beams are supported by 6x6 posts and are connected to the house by special "long-tail" beam hangers (**Photo 3**). The details of installing flashing and attaching these hangers to your house may differ from what we show, but a successful installation hinges on two key points. After you cut away the siding, slide the flashing under the siding and the existing building paper to make sure it sheds water. And second, nail the hangers into solid wood or consult your building inspector for the correct way to fasten the hangers to concrete, brick or block if necessary. Use 16d common hot-dipped galvanized or stainless steel nails to attach the hanger to the house and to the beams. Measure carefully to make sure the hangers are the correct distance down from the top of the deck surface and that they're level with each other (**Photo 3**).

After the beam hangers have been attached to the house, the next step is to construct the beams and install them on temporary supports. Since the tongue-and-groove decking boards fit tight together, without space for water to run through, slope the deck about 2 in. away from the house for drainage. Do this by leveling the beams and marking the temporary 2x4 supports. Then measure down 2 in. and make another set of marks. Line up the beams with the lower marks. Tie all three beams together with a 2x10 across the front. Then square and brace the beams (**Photo 4**).

With the beams in place, it's easy to measure for the posts. Just cut them a little

POST CAP ANCHOR

INVERTED FLANGE HANGER

JOIST HANGER

SPACER BLOCK

ALIGN TOPS FLUSH

7 Attach the beams for the lower deck section to the two outside posts with special inverted flange joist hangers. Cut and attach the corner posts and square the assembly as shown in Photos 4 and 5. Nail joist hangers to the beams. Use a 2x10 scrap to aid in positioning.

EXTRA JOIST

BLOCKING

RIM JOIST

BLOCKING

STACK RIM JOIST FLUSH WITH BEAM

8 Cut the joists to length, drop them into their hangers and nail them with galvanized hanger nails. Cut and nail blocking between the joists at the midpoint.

9 Set a full-length deck board to overhang the joists by 1-1/2 in. and screw temporary blocks behind it. Cut six deck boards for the cantilevered section and press the tongues and grooves together. Measure the overhang (it should be 1-1/2 in.) and nail the first board into place. Unscrew the blocks and slide the decking back.

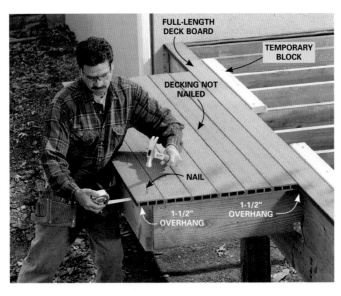

FULL-LENGTH DECK BOARD

TEMPORARY BLOCK

DECKING NOT NAILED

NAIL

1-1/2" OVERHANG

1-1/2" OVERHANG

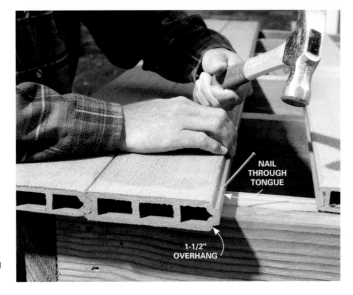

10 Slide the tongues and grooves together and line up the ends. Then nail through the tongue into each joist at the angle shown. Use 10d stainless steel ring shank nails.

NAIL THROUGH TONGUE

1-1/2" OVERHANG

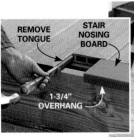

REMOVE TONGUE

STAIR NOSING BOARD

1-3/4" OVERHANG

11 Run the edge of your saw bed against the straightedge to cut a straight line for the recessed stair nosing board. Remove the tongue at one end with a chisel to allow a tight fit. Nail on the stair nosing board.

STRAIGHTEDGE

SCREWS

long and drop them into the holes (**Photo 5**). Place the uncut factory end of the post down for the best rot resistance. Then mark the post at the bottom of the joist and cut each post at the marks. Connect the posts to the beams with metal post-to-beam anchors (**Photo 7**). Double-check that the beam assembly is square. Then fill the holes with the soil you removed, packing it as you go.

Adding joists is a snap

Prepare for installing the joists by marking their positions on the top of the beams. Study **Figures A** and **C** for help in positioning the joists that overhang the beams. They overlap in the center and require additional blocking at the overhang to line up correctly. Cut the joists and tack them to the beams. Check that the overhanging sections are square to the main deck. Also sight down the front joist and outside joists of the overhanging sections to make sure they're straight. When you're confident everything's square and straight, fasten the joists to the beams with hurricane ties (**Photo 6**).

The joists for the lower deck section fit inside the beams, rather than run overtop. Build the beams and support them on posts just as you did for the upper section (**Photo 7**). Then cut the joists to fit inside and attach them with metal joist hangers and galvanized joist hanger nails (**Photo 8**). Add a row of blocking down the center to increase stiffness. The extra joists and blocking on the front of both the upper and the lower sections are needed to support the deck board that forms the stair nosing (**Photo 8** and **Figure C**).

We designed this deck to use all full-width and continuous-length deck boards

To avoid having to rip the deck boards lengthwise and expose the hollow inside, we planned the deck framing to accommodate full-width boards. Adjust your framing dimensions if you use a different-width deck board. With careful planning, you'll have 1-1/2 in. overhangs.

The horizontal 1x6s in the railing cover the hollow ends of the deck boards. We left a 1/2-in. space between the deck boards and rail to allow water and debris to escape.

Photo 9 shows how to get started installing the decking. Precutting and laying out the boards without nailing them gives you a chance to double-check your framing and make sure the first 12-ft. long deck board is straight and has the proper overhang. You'll have to drive nails through the top face of the first board (**Photo 9**). Nail the remaining deck boards through their tongues into each joist (**Photo 10**). We used 2-1/2 in. stainless steel ring-shank siding nails, but 2-1/2 in. hot-dipped galvanized nails will also work.

Sight down the first full-length board to make sure it's perfectly straight. It's difficult to correct problems later. Leave the ends of the boards long and use a straight board as a guide to cut them later (**Photo 11**).

Along the edge of the lower platform and at the stairs, use square-edged rather than tongue-and-groove decking (**Photo 11** inset and **Photo 19**). **Photo 19** shows how to cut and nail the stair nosings and border pieces. Face-nail these boards.

Take your time crafting the posts; they're full of tricky details

The rail system starts with posts that are notched 1-1/2 in. to fit around the joists and drilled to accept the 1-in. copper tubing. The trickiest part about making the posts is keeping track of the orientation of the notches and holes. **Here's a tip:** cut the posts to length and distribute them to their locations on the deck. Move from one to the next, marking the notches and

CORNER POST
CLEAN UP CORNER
END POST

12 Mark the 1-1/2 in. notches for the six 4x4 corner posts to fit over the joists and decking. First, cut them with your circular saw. Pry out the cutout piece and clean up the notch with a sharp chisel. Notch four 4x4 posts for the ends. Drill 1-1/8 in. holes 3/4 in. deep for the copper railings (Figure D).

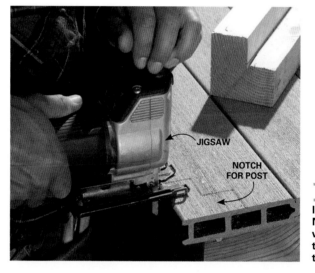

JIGSAW
NOTCH FOR POST

13 Mark the corners and end post locations on the decking. Notch out the decking with a jigsaw to allow the posts to fit tight to the joists.

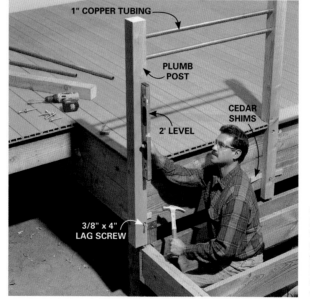

1" COPPER TUBING
PLUMB POST
CEDAR SHIMS
2' LEVEL
3/8" x 4" LAG SCREW

14 Drill 1-in. countersink holes and 3/8-in. clearance holes in the posts for the lag screws. Cut the copper tubes and set them in their holes. Plumb the posts with shims and attach them with lag screws.

15 Cut a test piece from a 6x6 scrap and use it to check the deck notching and as a guide for laying notches on the 6x6 pergola posts. Mark the waste with a scribbled line to avoid confusion. Use a circular saw to cut the notches and finish them with a handsaw.

NOTCH FOR BEAM
6x6 POST
12"
3"
3"
TEST PIECE
SCRIBBLE WASTE
SPACE FOR 2x4 BACKERS

holes. Then move them to your sawhorses for cutting and drilling (**Photo 12**).

We used manufactured 6x6 posts for the trellis (QuattroPost brand). They won't split and twist like regular 6x6s and are almost perfectly straight. The hollow interior makes it easier to cut and notch these posts. Standard 6x6s will also work, but they're likely to crack. Double-check measurements before cutting. You don't want to goof up on these expensive posts.

Notch the decking for the posts (**Photo 12**). Then drive 3/8-in. x 4-in. lag screws through predrilled 3/8-in. clearance holes

Figure D
Pergola post

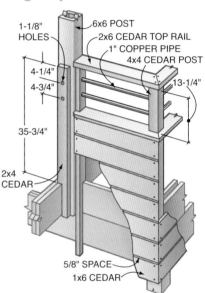

1-1/8" HOLES
6x6 POST
2x6 CEDAR TOP RAIL
1" COPPER PIPE
4x4 CEDAR POST
4-1/4"
4-3/4"
13-1/4"
35-3/4"
2x4 CEDAR
5/8" SPACE
1x6 CEDAR

16 Cut the lower rail caps to fit (see "Marking and Cutting the Lower Rail Cap," below). Butt a 3-3/4 in. block against the copper tube and clamp it in place. Predrill holes. Then drive 2-in. deck screws to support the 1x6 caps. Cut, fit and nail the 2x6 top rail into place.

"WEATHERED" COPPER TUBING
3-3/4" BLOCK
POST
2" DECK SCREWS

Marking and cutting the lower rail cap

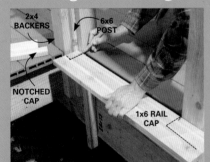

2x4 BACKERS
6x6 POST
NOTCHED CAP
1x6 RAIL CAP

1 Cut the 1x6 lower rail caps, allowing extra length. Mark the post locations. Then use a Speed square to mark the 3-1/2 in. deep notches at these locations. Saw out the notches for the posts.

NOTCHED CAP
MARK INTERSECTION
MARK INTERSECTION

2 Mark the intersection of the two tails. Make another mark on each cap where they intersect at the post. Connect the marks and cut the angle with a power miter saw or circular saw.

MARK FOR MITER

3 Lap the cut piece overtop and mark the angle on the lower piece. Cut this angle and check the fit.

Figure E
Deck railing

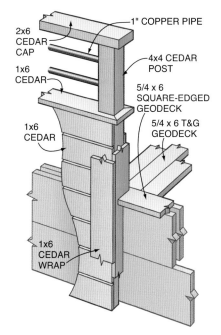

- 2x6 CEDAR CAP
- 1" COPPER PIPE
- 1x6 CEDAR
- 4x4 CEDAR POST
- 5/4 x 6 SQUARE-EDGED GEODECK
- 1x6 CEDAR
- 5/4 x 6 T&G GEODECK
- 1x6 CEDAR WRAP

TOP 2x6 CAP

MITER

1x6 LOWER RAIL CAP

WRAP POST

NOTCH TO FIT

17 Space the horizontal 1x6s with 5/8-in. thick blocks and nail them to the posts. Rip and notch boards to wrap the end posts. See Figure E, left.

18 Rip 2x8s for the lower stair and build the stair platforms. Stack and level them. Nail the platforms to the deck and to each other. Dig footings and pour concrete pads for the bottom stairs. Cut 6x6 posts to support them.

2x8 STEP PLATFORMS

MARK POSTS

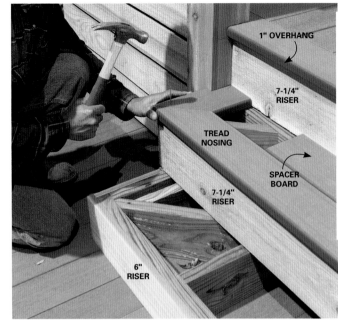

19 Cover the framing with 1x8 cedar riser boards ripped to fit. Then cut and nail on the treads. Use square-edged Geodeck for the treads. Miter the corners of the outside treads to conceal the hollow interior of the deck boards.

Labels on photo: 1" OVERHANG · 7-1/4" RISER · TREAD NOSING · SPACER BOARD · 7-1/4" RISER · 6" RISER

Figure F
Stair elevation

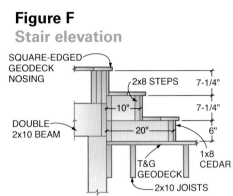

Labels: SQUARE-EDGED GEODECK NOSING · 2x8 STEPS · 7-1/4" · 10" · 7-1/4" · DOUBLE 2x10 BEAM · 20" · 6" · 1x8 CEDAR · T&G GEODECK · 2x10 JOISTS

Materials list

ITEM	QTY.
Foundation	
1x3 pine (batter boards and stakes)	24 lin. ft.
Bagged concrete mix	28 bags
6x6 x 8' .60 treated lumber	7
Beams and joists	
2x10 x 12' .40 treated lumber (joists and beams)	24
2x10 x 16' .40 treated lumber (joists and beams)	14
Stair frame	
2x8 x 8' .40 treated lumber	30
Decking	
5/4 x 6 t&g Geodeck, 12' lengths	52
5/4 x 6 t&g Geodeck, 14' lengths	7
5/4 x 6 square-edged Geodeck, 16' lengths	12
Railing	
4x4 x 10' cedar (rail posts)	3
4x4 x 8' cedar (rail post)	2
1x6 x 12' cedar boards (rails and post wrap)	20
1x6 x 14' cedar boards	8
2x4 x 12' cedar (rail backing)	4
2x6 x 8' cedar (rail cap)	3
2x6 x 12' cedar (rail cap)	2
1" copper plumbing, 10' lengths	10
Stair risers and trim	
1x8 x 8' cedar boards	10
1x8 x 10' cedar boards	6

ITEM	QTY.
Pergola	
6x6 x 10' QuattroPost	4
2x4 x 12' rough cedar	18
2x12 x 16' rough cedar (beams)	6
Hardware	
12" galvanized metal flashing	18 lin. ft.
3-1/8" x 22-1/4" adjustable strap hanger "long-tail" (Kant-Sag MSH222-2)	3
6x6 post cap (Kant-Sag PB66-6)	11
Hurricane ties (Kant-Sag RT 7)	20
Double 2x10 inverted flange hangers (Kant-Sag HD210-21F)	2
Single 2x10 joist hangers (Kant-Sag HD210)	12
3/8" x 4" galvanized lag screws (rail posts)	36
3/8" washers (for lag screws)	36
16d common double-dipped galvanized nails	10 lbs.
8d stainless steel ring-shank siding nails (decking)	10 lbs.
1" galvanized roofing nails	1 lbs.
Galvanized joist hanger nails	5 lbs.
8d galvanized casing nails	2 lbs.
16d galvanized casing nails	2 lbs.
2" deck screws	1 lb.
2-1/2" deck screws	2 lbs.

to secure the posts. Use a tubing cutter to cut the copper tubing and install it along with the posts. Don't forget to cut, drill and center the two short pieces of 2x4 cedar that support the top railing and copper tubes on each cantilevered section (opening photo).

Fitting the 1x6 lower rail cap is challenging, since it's notched around each post and mitered at the corners. The key is to mark boards in place whenever possible. See "Marking and Cutting the Lower Rail Cap," p. 88. Even though the cap fits between the posts at about 21 in. above the deck, mark the notches at deck level. This will ensure that the posts will be parallel to each other when the caps are screwed in.

Install the horizontal 1x6s

Start at the top and work down, using 5/8-in. blocks to maintain even spaces between boards. Cut the end of the 1x6 square and overlap them at the outside corners. Plan the overlaps so the butt ends of the boards are facing the sides of the deck where they're less conspicuous. Measure down to the decking at opposite ends before nailing each row to keep the boards parallel to the decking. The lower boards hide the treated framing. Cover the ends of the boards near the stairs by wrapping the boards and 4x4 posts with 1x6s (**Photo 17** and **Figure E**). You'll have to rip and notch the 1x6 boards to fit.

You don't need to cut complicated stringers for these stairs

Rather than notch 2x12s to make traditional stair stringers, we chose to build and stack platforms. This method requires more lumber but eliminates complicated layout work. If the top surface of your deck is 42-1/2 in. above the ground, you can build the two sets of steps exactly as shown in **Figure A**. Otherwise you'll have to adjust the rise or change the number of steps to fit your situation. To simplify the design process, draw the entire stair system actual size on a large piece of cardboard (**Figure F**). It takes an hour or so but helps prevent mistakes. Codes vary slightly, so check with your building inspector before constructing the stairs. In general, plan for a rise (distance from the top of one tread to the top of the next tread) of between 6 and 7-1/2 in. and a tread about 10 in. (11 in. with the nosing). Finish the stairs with 1x8 riser boards, ripped to fit, and treads (**Photo 19**). On sloping lots, you can regrade the lawn a little to make the lowest rise more consistent.

Set beams on the notched 6x6 posts and add 2x4s to complete the pergola

To avoid having to special-order 22-ft. long beam material, simply splice shorter pieces as we show (**Photos 20** and **21**). A single 2x12 has enough strength. The second 2x12 simply improves the appearance. Start by arranging the 16-ft. 2x12s for the best grain and color match at the splices. Then lay out and cut one tail (**Figure A**) and use it as a pattern to mark and cut the three remaining tails. Use 2-1/2 in. deck screws to connect the beams to the notched 6x6 posts. Install the first layer (**Photo 20**). Then nail the second layer to the first with 2-1/2 in. galvanized casing nails. Complete the lattice by screwing the 12-ft. 2x4s to the beams (**Photo 21**).

Finish the wood parts of your deck to protect and preserve them

We applied Cabot's clear finish for the most natural look. The drawbacks to clear finishes like this is that they don't protect against graying as well as finishes with more pigment and they must be reapplied annually. In general, the more pigment, or color, a deck finish has, the greater protection it offers.

SPLICE AT POST

SCREW TO POST

20 Cut decorative ends and splice the front 2x12s over the center of the posts. Attach them with 2-1/2 in. deck screws. Nail a second 2x12 to the first to create a beam. Splice the second 2x12 in the center.

ANGLED 2-1/2" DECK SCREW

MARKS FOR 2x4S

21 Mark the top of the 2x12s for the 2x4 lattice boards. Cut the 2x4s to length and mark the beam locations on them. Align the marks and screw them together with 2-1/2 in. deck screws.

Raised Gardens

A fresh way to grow a bumper crop

WHAT IT TAKES

TIME: One day

COST: $200

SKILL: Beginner

TOOLS: Miter saw or circular saw, drill/driver, metal shears, stapler, level

CPVC ARCH

WINDOW SCREEN

PVC SLEEVE

① ② ③

Accessorize it! Easy add-on options:

1 SCREEN OUT CRITTERS. Simple arched ribs made from CPVC pipe let you protect your crop from hungry birds and beasts, especially deer!

2 EXTEND THE SEASON. Those same ribs can support plastic sheathing. This creates a "cold frame," allowing you to start plants earlier in spring and protect them against frost in autumn.

3 WATER ONCE A MONTH. Fill a buried reservoir that keeps soil moist for weeks. For details on how to add this feature to any raised planter, search for "self watering" at familyhandyman.com.

1 BUILD THE END FRAMES. Clamp the parts to a flat surface with the best-looking sides face up. Join the parts with screws as detailed in Figure A. The bottom rails (C) require a 2-in.-deep countersink hole drilled with a 5/8-in. spade bit.

ome gardeners prefer traditional ground-level gardening, but not the ones we've been hearing from in recent years. Those who've made the switch love raised garden planters and won't go back.

The list of reasons is long, but these are the main advantages:

- Tending raised plants is a lot easier on the back and knees.
- You can fill planters with top-quality soil for more productivity in a smaller space.
- Raised beds curtail creeping weeds and drifting seeds.
- The height discourages pests, especially rabbits.

To build on these advantages, we designed our own raised planter. On the outside, it looks a lot like others. But we engineered ours for longevity and simple construction. And we added some optional improvements to make an even better home for your vegetables.

Gathering materials

Everything you need is available at home centers for about $200 per planter. We chose pressure-treated lumber that's cedar tone rather than green. Take the time to select straight, good-looking lumber. When you get it home, cover it with plastic to slow its drying. Pressure-treated lumber tends to warp badly as it dries; much better to let it dry after assembly when the parts are fastened together.

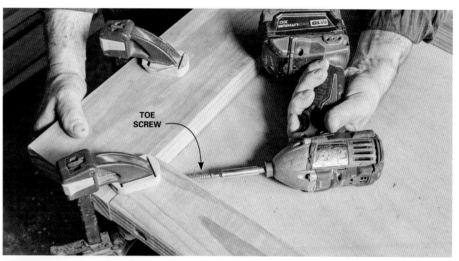

2 BUILD THE SIDE FRAMES. Fasten the side frame parts with "toe screws" (screws driven at an angle). If any of the screw heads don't sink into the wood, drill a shallow countersink hole sized to match the screw head. See Figure A for details.

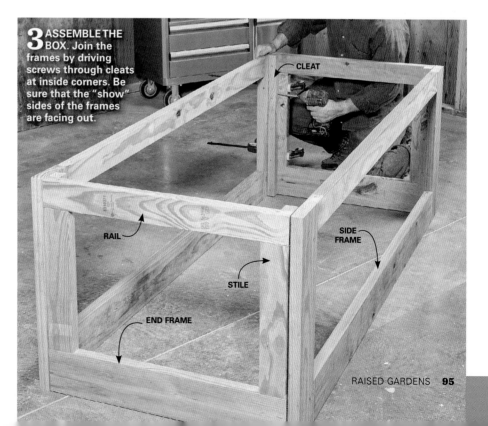

3 ASSEMBLE THE BOX. Join the frames by driving screws through cleats at inside corners. Be sure that the "show" sides of the frames are facing out.

MEET THE EXPERT

Tom Dvorak is an engineer and carpenter who is also a contributor to *Family Handyman*.

METAL SHEARS

4 CUT THE METAL. First, slip on gloves—those metal edges are sharp! Then cut the panels to length with metal shears. Standard 26-in.-wide metal panels don't require cutting to width.

5 INSTALL THE METAL. Screw the panels to the frames, placing screws every 8 in. along the top and bottom edges. Along the side edges, drive a screw at every second rib.

TREATED PLYWOOD

2x4 BLOCK

6 ADD PLYWOOD BACKING. Reinforce light-gauge corrugated metal by screwing plywood over the metal. Set the plywood on 2x4 blocks to help position it.

Home centers typically carry light-gauge corrugated metal, which is fine for this project as long as you reinforce it with plywood (see **Photo 6**). Our metal is 30 gauge. When looking at gauges of metal, remember that a higher number means thinner material. Also, make sure all the screws you choose are rated for use with treated lumber.

Building tips

- Start by cutting the parts according to the **Cutting List**. Cut shorter parts from your imperfect boards and save your straightest material for the long parts (E, G, M).
- To avoid assembly mix-ups, note that the rails fit between the stiles on the side frames. On the end frames, the stiles fit between the rails.
- We didn't use a finish on our planters. If you do, note that it will be much easier to apply before you install the metal panels.
- If you're tempted to miter the corners of the rim, reconsider. Outdoor miters look better than square-cut butt joints at first, but they inevitably develop ugly gaps as the wood absorbs and releases moisture.
- Here's how to install the planter: Set it into position, then slice into the soil around it, marking its footprint. Move the planter aside and dig a shallow perimeter trench, just a couple inches deep. Set the planter in place again and check it for level in both directions. Add soil or deepen the trench to level the planter.
- When the planter is in place, cut a couple large slits in the bottom of the plastic liner so excess water can drain into the soil below—unless you plan to install a self-watering system. That requires a watertight liner.
- Filling this planter requires a lot of soil, almost a cubic yard. But there are ways to fill the lower half of the planter with less effort and expense. One common filler is plastic milk jugs (with caps screwed on tight). Another trick is to set plastic buckets in place upside down.

Figure A
Raised garden planter

Overall Dimensions:
84" long x 36" wide x 28-1/4" tall

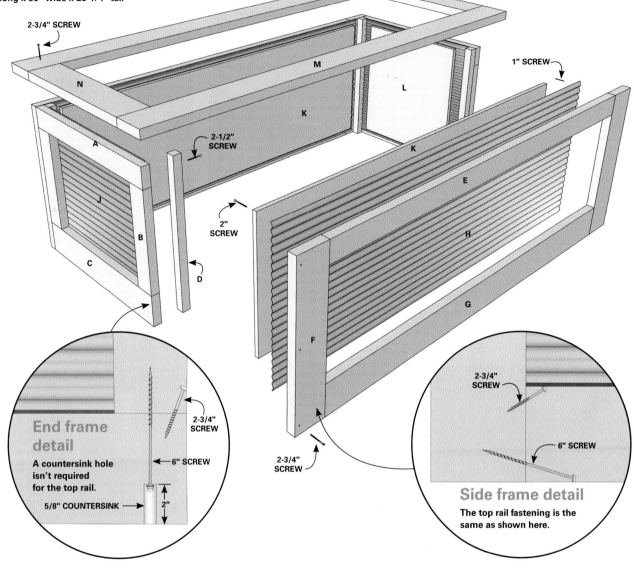

2-3/4" SCREW

1" SCREW

2-1/2" SCREW

2" SCREW

End frame detail
A countersink hole isn't required for the top rail.

5/8" COUNTERSINK

2-3/4" SCREW

6" SCREW

2"

2-3/4" SCREW

Side frame detail
The top rail fastening is the same as shown here.

2-3/4" SCREW

6" SCREW

Cutting list

KEY	QTY.	DIMENSIONS	NAME
A	2	2x4 x 31"	End frame top rails*
B	4	2x4 x 17-3/4"	End frame stiles*
C	2	2x6 x 31"	End frame bottom rails
D	4	1-1/2" x 1-1/2" x 26-3/4"	Cleats
E	2	2x4 x 71"	Side frame top rails
F	4	2x6 x 26-3/4"	Side frame stiles
G	2	2x6 x 71"	Side frame bottom rails
H	2	26" x 75-1/2"	Metal side panels
J	2	26" x 27-3/4"	Metal end panels
K	2	3/4" x 24" x 73-1/4"	Plywood side panels
L	2	3/4" x 24" x 22-3/4"	Plywood end panels
M	2	2x6 x 84"	Top side rims
N	2	2x6 x 25"	Top end rims

Materials list

ITEM	QTY.
2x6 x 10' treated lumber	5
2x4 x 8' treated lumber	4
2x2 x 8' treated lumber	2
3/4" x 4' x 8' treated plywood	1
26" x 10' corrugated metal panel	2
1/4" x 6" coated construction screws	1 lb.
1" sheet metal screws with washers	1 lb.
2" coated deck screws	1 lb.
2-1/2" coated deck screws	1 lb.
2-3/4" small-head deck screws	1 lb.
6-mil plastic, 9' x 12'	1
1/4" stainless steel staples	1 pkg.

***Stiles** are the vertical parts of a frame.

***Rails** are the horizontal parts. These terms are most often applied to cabinet doors and face frames.

6-MIL POLY

7 LINE THE BOX. Staple plastic sheeting to the inside of the box, then trim off the excess with a utility knife. A plastic liner helps to keep the wood dry and the soil moist.

TOE SCREW

RIM

8 TRIM THE BOX. Top off the planter with a 2x6 rim. If necessary, add toe screws to the joints to hold parts flush.

Easy arches for pest or frost protection

Arches can support screen or mesh to stop pests, or poly sheeting to keep plants frost-free overnight. The three arches are simply 5-ft. sections of 1/2-in. CPVC pipe that you can bend and slip into 12-in. sleeves made from 1-in. PVC pipe. A 4-ft. x 25-ft. roll of fiberglass window screen costs about $20.

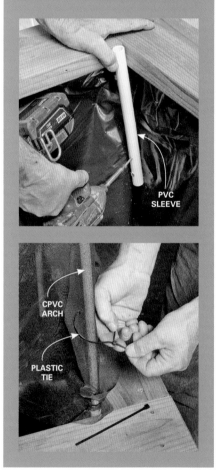

PVC SLEEVE

CPVC ARCH

PLASTIC TIE

3-Season Planter

This planter has a secret inside

It's lined with an ordinary plastic planter box, the kind you can get at any home or garden center. That means you can lift out one plastic box and drop in another, instantly swapping plants. You might, for example, start the growing season with spring bloomers in your planter while the other plants grow elsewhere. When the spring plants are past their prime, you can drop in the next set of plants.

The inner plastic box has practical advantages too. It separates damp soil from the wooden planter, which protects the wood from moisture problems like rot and peeling paint. And since this planter is really just a decorative container for the plastic pot, it's much easier to build than a typical planter.

If you use cedar lumber, this project will cost you about $100. Built from pressure-treated or untreated pine, it will cost about $80.

Customize it!

This planter is basically a plywood box with legs that fit over each corner. That simple structure allows you to easily change the size, shape or look while following the same building steps. For example, you can cover the box with siding or wood shingles. You can coat your planter with paint, stain or a clear finish. The plans for the two examples shown here are on pp. 103 and 104.

WHAT IT TAKES

TIME: One weekend

COST: $100 or less

SKILL: Beginner

TOOLS: Basic hand tools, drill, table saw

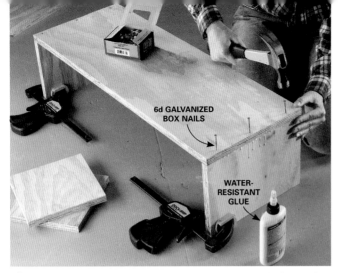

1 BUILD THE BOX. Cut the plywood sides to size and glue and nail the sides together. Use clamps to hold the sides upright.

2 ADD THE BRACES. Predrill screw clearance holes through the planter sides and screw in a plywood brace at each end. Center the brace.

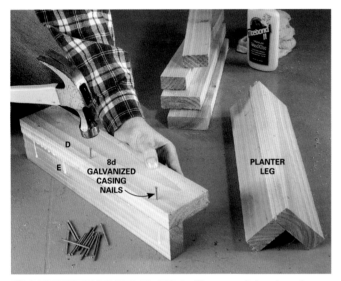

3 ASSEMBLE THE LEGS. Rip 5/4 decking material and cut it to length for the legs. Glue and nail a 3-in. piece to a 2-in. piece. Buy your plastic planter boxes first and adjust the planter dimensions if necessary.

4 ATTACH THE LEGS. Set the plywood box on a flat surface and screw the leg assemblies to it. Make sure the legs are flush with the top of the planter box.

The core of this planter is a box made from 3/4-in. CDX or BC plywood. Most home centers and lumberyards will sell you a partial sheet of plywood and cut it into manageable sizes for you to haul home. Cut plywood pieces to final size with a table saw, or clamp a straightedge to the plywood and cut it with your circular saw. Assemble the box with water-resistant wood glue and 6d galvanized box nails or exterior-grade screws (**Photo 1**). Add plywood braces inside the long planter to square the box and hold the long sides straight. We centered our braces, but you can shift them down if they obstruct the liner (**Photo 2**). The other two planters don't need braces if you make sure they're square after you assemble them. Check

with a framing square and add braces if they're needed.

We used 5/4x6 (1-in. x 5-1/2-in. actual dimensions) cedar decking for the legs, but you can substitute other 5/4 decking. First rip the deck boards to 5-1/4 in. to remove the rounded corners on one edge. Then run the squared edge against the table saw fence when you rip the 3-in.- and 2-in.-wide leg pieces. Cut the pieces to length and then glue and nail them together with 8d galvanized casing nails (**Photo 3**). Sand the saw marks from the board edges before you screw the assembled legs to the box (**Photo 4**).

Ripping the bevel on the 2x4 top cap (**Photo 5**) may require you to remove the blade guard as we did. If so, use extreme

Plastic planters are perfect

Plastic planters or liners keep wet dirt away from wooden parts. And because plastic containers come in various shapes and sizes, you have a lot of freedom in designing your planter.

Figure A
Beadboard planter

Overall dimensions:
36" long x 13-1/2" deep x 16-1/2" tall

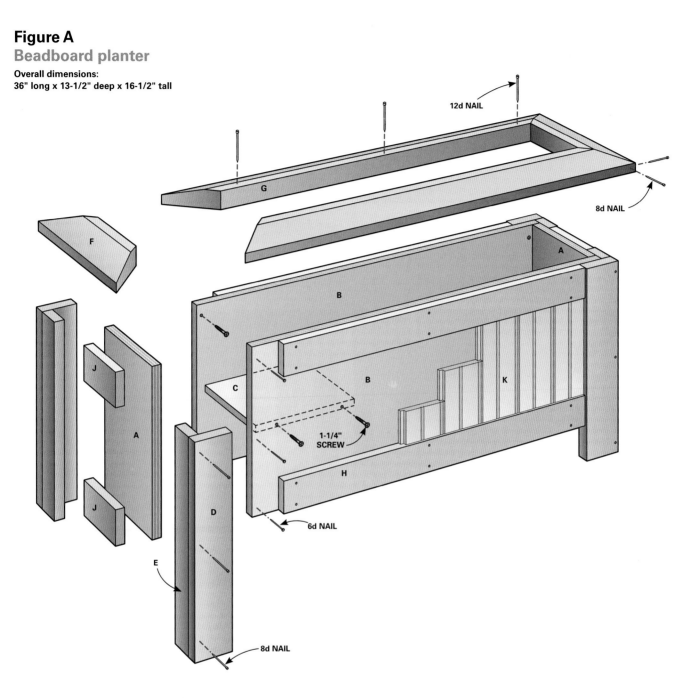

12d NAIL

8d NAIL

G

F

A

B

1-1/4"
SCREW

C

B

K

J

A

J

H

D

6d NAIL

E

8d NAIL

Materials list

ITEM	QTY.
2' x 4' 3/4" CDX plywood	1
5/4x6 x 6' deck board	1
2x4 x 6' cedar or pine	2
1x3 x 6' cedar or pine	2
5/8" x 3-1/2" beaded tongue-and-groove	14'
Water-resistant glue	
4d, 8d and 12d galvanized casing nails	
6d galvanized box nails	
1-1/4" deck screws	
Plastic planter (to fit 6-1/2" x 29" opening)	

Cutting list

KEY	QTY.	DIMENSIONS	NAME
A	2	3/4" x 8" x 11-7/8"	Plywood ends
B	2	3/4" x 32" x 11-7/8"	Plywood sides
C	2	3/4" x 8" x 7-3/4"	Plywood braces
D	4	1" x 3" x 15"	Legs
E	4	1" x 2" x 15"	Legs
F	2	1-1/2" x 3-1/2" x 13-1/2"	Beveled cap
G	2	1-1/2" x 3-1/2" x 36"	Beveled cap
H	4	3/4" x 2-1/2" x 28-1/2"	Top trim (cut to fit)
J	4	3/4" x 2-1/2" x 6"	Trim (cut to fit)
K	22	5/8" x 3-1/4" x 6-7/8"	Lengths of beadboard

FEATHERBOARD

20°
BEVEL

5 BEVEL THE CAP BOARDS. Rip a 20-degree bevel on the 2x4 caps with a table saw. Use a featherboard and push stick for extra safety.

CAUTION
You may have to remove the blade guard for this cut. Saw carefully.

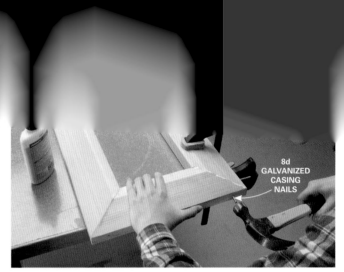

8d
GALVANIZED
CASING
NAILS

6 ASSEMBLE THE CAP. Cut the cap pieces to length with 45-degree miters on the ends. Drill pilot holes for the nails. Then glue and nail the miters together.

12d
GALVANIZED
CASING
NAILS

5/32"
DRILL BIT

7 ATTACH THE CAP. Drill pilot holes and glue and nail the cap to the planter box. Measure to make sure the overhang is even on all sides.

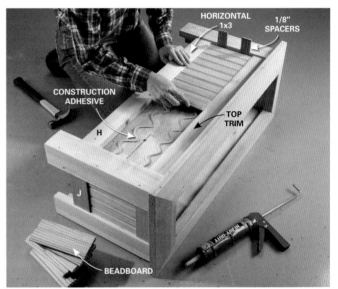

HORIZONTAL
1x3

1/8"
SPACERS

CONSTRUCTION
ADHESIVE

TOP
TRIM

H

J

BEADBOARD

8 COVER THE BOX. Cut the trim pieces H and J to length and nail them to the top and bottom edges of the box. Cut beadboard to fit and glue the pieces onto the plywood with construction adhesive.

caution to keep your fingers well away from the blade. Make sure the blade is tilted away from the fence as shown in the photo. Mount a featherboard and use push sticks to complete the cut. Start the cut by pushing with your back hand while holding the board down with a push stick in your front hand. Keep a second push stick within easy reach. When your back hand gets to the rear edge of the table saw, pick up the second push stick and use it along with the front push stick to push the board clear past the saw blade. Keep your attention focused on the saw blade at all times. Shut off the saw and wait for the blade to stop before retrieving the beveled board.

Photo 6 shows how to assemble the top cap pieces into a frame that's easy to attach to the box. Start by gluing the miters and clamping one long side as shown. Then drill 1/8-in. pilot holes for the nails. Drive a pair of 8d galvanized casing nails from opposite sides at each corner to pin the miters together. Offset the nails slightly so they don't hit each other.

Mount the frame to the box by centering it with an even overhang all around and nailing it down with 12d galvanized casing nails (**Photo 7**). Measure and drill 5/32-in. pilot holes for the nails, making sure they're centered on the top edges of the plywood.

Add siding to complete the planter

Beadboard is great for a traditional-looking painted planter. For the best-looking planter, plan ahead and cut the first and last boards to equal width. Start by nailing the top trim (H) to the plywood box with 4d galvanized casing nails. Use a precut length of beadboard as a spacer to position the bottom board precisely. When you glue in the beadboards, be sure to leave a 1/8-in. space at each end to allow room for expansion (**Photo 8**). Fill the space with caulk before painting.

We sided the tall box with 1/2-in. x 3-1/2-in. cedar lap siding. Simply cut the siding to fit between the legs. Rip a 1-in. strip off the thin edge of a siding piece for a starter. (Rip the leftover to fit at the top later.)

Nail the starter strips along the bottom of the plywood (under the first row of siding) to hold the first piece of siding at the correct angle. Predrill 1/16-in. holes 3/4 in. from the end and 5/8 in. from the bottom of each piece to prevent splitting. Then nail on the siding with 4d galvanized box nails. The top cap on this planter fits flush to the inside edge of the plywood box, which may cause the nails protruding through the inside to interfere with the plastic planter. If so, bend them flat or clip them off. You'll save measuring time by making a simple spacing jig as shown below. We finished this planter with transparent deck stain.

Materials list

ITEM	QTY.
4' x 8' x 3/4" CDX plywood	1
5/4x6 x 6' deck board	2
2x4 x 8' cedar or pine	1
1/2" x 3-1/2" lap siding	36'
Water-resistant glue	
4d, 8d and 12d galvanized casing nails	
6d galvanized box nails	
1-1/4" deck screws	
Plastic planter (to fit 12" x 12" opening)	

Cutting list

KEY	QTY.	DIMENSIONS	NAME
A	2	3/4" x 12" x 29"	Plywood ends
B	2	3/4" 13-1/2" x 29"	Plywood sides
C	4	1" x 3" x 32"	Legs
D	4	1" x 2" x 32"	Legs
E	4	1-1/2" x 3-1/2" x 19"	Beveled cap
F	40	1/2" x 3-1/2" x 9-3/4"	Siding (cut to fit)

Figure B
Lap siding planter
Overall dimensions: 19" long x 19" deep x 33-1/2" tall

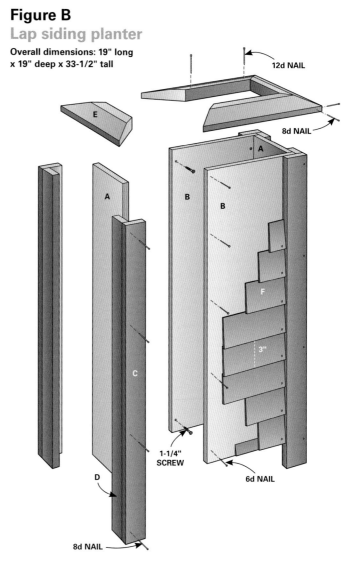

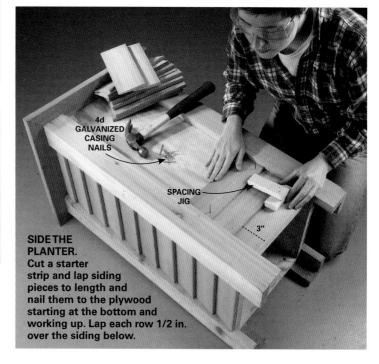

SIDE THE PLANTER. Cut a starter strip and lap siding pieces to length and nail them to the plywood starting at the bottom and working up. Lap each row 1/2 in. over the siding below.

Wood shingles are perfect for a rustic-looking box. And finishing the planter is a snap if you use deck stain like we did. The only drawback to shingles is that you may have to buy a whole bundle, many more than you'll need to side one planter.

The butt end of shingles is a little too thick for the proportions of this planter. So before cutting the shingles to their final length, trim off about 4 in. from the thick end (assuming your shingles are about 16 in. long). Then cut and install them as shown.

Start with a double thickness of shingle on the first row. Then offset the joints by at least 1-1/2 in. from one row to the next. Also stagger the shingles up and down if you like the "shaggy" look. Nail the shingles to the plywood box with 3d galvanized box nails. Position the nails so the next row will cover them. The nails will stick through the inside of the box but won't interfere with the plastic planter box.

Figure C
Cedar shingle planter
Overall dimensions: 20" long
x 20" deep x 20-1/2" tall

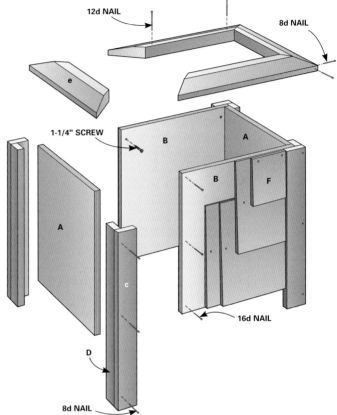

Materials list

ITEM	QTY.
16" x 62" x 3/4" CDX plywood	1
5/4x6 x 8' deck board	1
2x4 x 8' cedar or pine	1
Bundle of cedar shingles (50 or 60)	1
Water-resistant glue	
8d and 12d galvanized casing nails	
3d and 6d galvanized box nails	
1-1/4" deck screws	
Plastic planter (to fit 13" x 13" opening)	

Cutting list

KEY	QTY.	DIMENSIONS	NAME
A	2	3/4" x 16" x 14-1/2"	Plywood ends
B	2	3/4" x 16" x 16"	Plywood sides
C	4	1" x 3" x 19"	Legs
D	4	1" x 2" x 19"	Legs
E	4	1-1/2" x 3-1/2" x 20"	Beveled cap
F	50–60	12"	Cedar shingles (cut to fit)

SHINGLE THE PLANTER. Cut 4 in. off the thick end of all 16-in. shingles to reduce their length to 12 in. Then cut them to fit and nail them to the plywood, starting at the bottom. Stagger the slots between shingles.

Patio Planter

*A mini garden with
fresh veggies—steps
from your kitchen*

9 advantages of a raised garden bed

- Tend your crop without straining your knees or back.
- Pick fresh herbs or veggies a few steps from your kitchen.
- Soil quality is easy to control; just fill your planter with a quality potting mix.
- Creeping weeds can't sneak into your plot.
- Fewer weed seeds blow in.
- Its height foils rabbits and other non-climbing critters.
- Placed near your house, it discourages shy wildlife.
- Plant diseases are less likely.
- When frost threatens, covering tender plants is easy.

A raised planter "beets" traditional gardening in a bunch of ways. And our planter is tops for easy construction, sturdiness and convenience. Plus, the curves and trim make it a pretty addition to your deck or patio. You'll get about 8 sq. ft. of planting area. If you need more, you could make a larger planter, but consider building two instead: A bigger planter filled with soil is tough to move.

A better design

1. The optional trellis supports climbing plants like tomatoes and peas.
2. Side tables are convenient work surfaces and handles when you need to move the planter.
3. Boards protrude at ends or corners. Those "reveals" hide mistakes. If your measurements or cuts are a little off, no one will notice.
4. Notched joinery is super sturdy and easy enough for a beginner.
5. Lower shelf provides about 8 sq. ft. of storage space.

WHAT IT TAKES

TIME: One day
COST: $175
SKILL: Beginner
TOOLS: Framing square, drill, standard woodworking tools, jigsaw, circular saw

1 CUT THE LOWER LEG NOTCHES. Set your saw depth to 1-1/4 in., then make a series of cuts no more than 1/2 in. apart. Drive a chisel into the cuts and pry; the little fingers will shear off. Flatten the remaining nubs with a chisel. Grab a 2x4 scrap and make sure it fits into the notch.

2 CUT THE UPPER LEG NOTCHES. Set your saw depth to 2 in. and make a series of cuts near the end of the notch. Break out the fingers as shown in Photo 1. To complete the notch, make the long cut. Your saw won't cut completely through the leg, so you'll have to flip the leg over and cut from the other side.

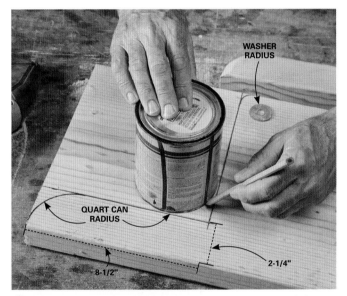

WASHER RADIUS

QUART CAN RADIUS

8-1/2"   2-1/4"

3 MARK THE SHELF SUPPORTS. Cut the long box sides (B) to length, then use a square, a paint can and a washer to mark the shelf supports. Make the straight cuts with a circular saw and the curves with a jigsaw. Soften the cut edges with sandpaper or a router and round-over bit.

4 ASSEMBLE THE BOX. Join the sides to the ends with 3-in. exterior screws. Drill pilot holes and drive the screws until the heads are slightly sunk into the wood. You can cover the heads with exterior wood filler or leave them exposed.

Skills and materials

All of the materials are available at any home center. The legs and planter box are made from treated dimensional lumber. The extension tables, bottom shelf and trim boards are made from what's commonly known as "5/4 decking material" or just "deck boards."

Note: Treated lumber is more variable in width and thickness than standard dimensional lumber. We found 2x12s ranging from 11-1/8 in. to 11-3/4 in. wide at our home center. And we found two types and thicknesses of treated decking material: The "premium" stuff was almost 1-1/4 in. thick while

Is treated lumber safe for veggies?

You may read that it isn't safe to grow edible plants in containers made of treated lumber. But read closer, and you'll see that they're talking about wood treated with arsenic (CCA), which was banned for residential use back in 2003. The treated lumber you can buy today contains no arsenic and is considered safe for food contact and growing food. Some common types of treated lumber are ACQ, CA and MCQ.

Round-over bits: The key to a pro look

To make almost any project, including this one, look more polished, eliminate all the sharp edges with a router and round-over bit. The softer edges look nicer, prevent splinters and hold finishes better. We used a 1/4-in. round-over bit on this project. A 1/2-in. bit is shown here.

the standard was barely 1 in. Keep this in mind as you build—and adjust your measurements accordingly.

Let's build this thing

Cut the four legs (A) to length, then mark the positions of the upper and lower notches. Create the lower notches by making a series of 1-1/4-in.-deep cuts as shown in **Photo 1**, prying the fingers away with a chisel, then smoothing the bottoms with a chisel. Create the upper notches by making a series of 2-in.-deep kerf cuts (to create a square bottom) and long circular saw rips (to remove the bulk of the material) as shown in **Photo 2**. **Note:** Your notches should be as long as your 2x4s and 2x12s are wide.

Figure A
Patio planter

Overall Dimensions:
70-1/2" long x 30-3/4" wide
x 33" tall (72" tall with trellis)

Figure B
Side and leg details

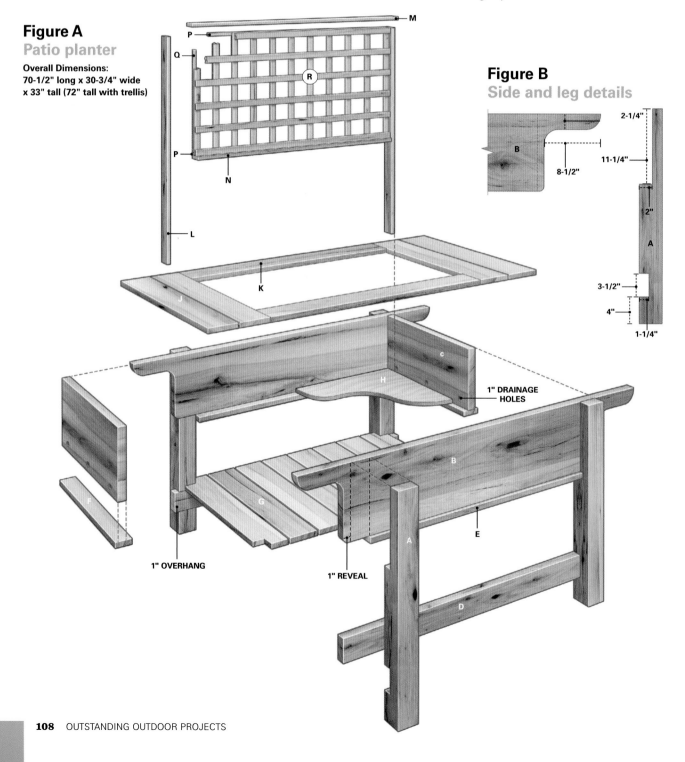

2-1/4"

11-1/4"

8-1/2"

2"

A

3-1/2"

4"

1-1/4"

1" DRAINAGE HOLES

1" OVERHANG

1" REVEAL

5 ADD THE LEGS. Mark the leg locations 1 in. from the ends of the sides using a framing square. Position the legs and fasten them to the box side with 3-in. screws.

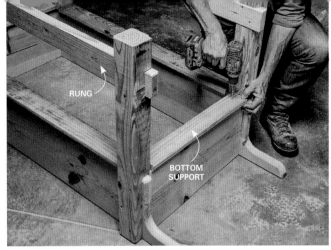

6 INSTALL THE RUNGS AND SUPPORTS. Place the rungs in the leg notches and secure them with 3-in. screws. Position the bottom supports (E, F) so they extend about 5/8 in. inside the box and screw them in place.

7 INSTALL THE SHELF SLATS AND BOTTOM. Space the shelf slats (G) evenly and screw them into place. Notch the end slats to fit around the legs. Then install the planter bottom.

8 BUILD THE LATTICE PANEL TRELLIS. Build the panel support frame as shown, then install the stops and lattice panel. Secure the frame to the planter by driving screws through the panel legs into the planter box.

Cutting list

Treated lumber can vary greatly in width; adjust measurements accordingly.

KEY	QTY.	MATERIAL	DIMENSIONS	NAME	KEY	QTY.	MATERIAL	DIMENSIONS	NAME
A	4	4x4 treated pine	3-1/2" x 3-1/2" x 32"	Leg	K	2	5/4 treated pine decking*	1" x 3-1/2" x 48"	Long shelf slats
B	2	2x12 treated pine	1-1/2" x 11-1/4" x 70"	Long box side	L	2	5/4 treated pine decking**	1" x 2-3/4" x 48"	Lattice panel sides
C	2	2x12 treated pine	1-1/2" x 11-1/4" x 24"	Short box side	M	1	5/4 treated pine decking**	1" x 2-3/4" x 50"	Lattice panel top
D	2	1x4 treated pine	1-1/2" x 3-1/2" x 53"	Rungs	N	1	5/4 treated pine decking**	1" x 2-3/4" x 46"	Lattice panel bottom
E	2	5/4 treated pine decking	1" x 3-1/2" x 44"	Long bottom supports	P	2	5/4 treated pine	1" x 1" x 46"	Long lattice stops
F	2	5/4 treated pine decking*	1" x 3-1/2" x 23"	Short bottom supports	Q	2	5/4 treated pine***	1" x 1" x 22"	Short lattice stops
G	8	5/4 treated pine decking	1" x 5-1/2" x 27-1/2"	Bottom shelf slats	R	1	Treated pine lattice	1" x 24" x 46"	Lattice panel
H	1	Treated plywood	3/4" x 24" x 48"	Box bottom					
J	4	5/4 treated pine decking	1" x 5-1/2" x 30-3/4"	Top shelf slats					

* If 4"-wide material is unavailable, rip it from 6" material

** 5/4x6 material ripped in half

*** 5/4 material ripped into strips

9 CAP OFF THE PLANTER. Screw shelf boards to the shelf supports; the inner ones should extend just a little past the inside edge of the box. Install the side trim, letting those edges extend slightly inward, too.

MEET THE EXPERT

Spike Carlsen is a former editor at *Family Handyman* and the author of several books, including *Woodworking FAQ: The Workshop Companion*.

Cut the box sides to length, then use a quart paint can and washer to create the curved corners (**Photo 3**). We used a 1-1/4-in. washer, but any large washer will do. Cut these out using a circular saw and jigsaw. Assemble the box as shown in **Photo 4**, then lay the box on its side to install the legs (**Photo 5**). Install the 2x4 rungs in the lower notches, letting the ends extend an inch past the legs.

Flip the planter upside down and install the bottom support boards as shown in **Photo 6**. These support the plywood bottom and provide a decorative touch. The overhang should be the same on both sides.

Position the planter upright and install the slats for the bottom shelves (**Photo 7**). Space them about 1/4 in. apart and notch the corners of the outer slats as needed. Drill three or four 1-in. drainage holes about 1/2 in. up from the bottom of each end board. Plop the 3/4-in. plywood

bottom into place and secure it with a few 1-1/4-in. screws.

Install the top shelf slats, letting the inner slats slightly extend over the lip of the planter box (**Photo 9**). Then install the long trim boards on each side.

The trellis and finishing touches

The lattice panel trellis is an optional but great feature for those wishing to grow plants requiring support.

Begin by ripping a 5/4x6 x 10-ft. board in two. Construct the panel frame (L, M, N) as shown in **Photo 8**, then rip 5/4 x 5/4 stops (P, Q) out of scrap material and secure them to the frame. Cut the lattice to size, set it into the frame and nail it to the stops using 3d nails. Secure the lattice panel to the back of the planter with screws.

We applied a coat of exterior stain to the planter. You can also leave the wood natural and let it mellow to a soft gray.

To prevent soil from seeping out the drainage holes, line the bottom of the planter box with landscape fabric, letting it extend a few inches up each side. Fill the planter with soil or other growing medium and get digging.

Materials list

ITEM	QTY.
4x4 x 6' treated lumber	2
2x12 x 8' treated lumber	2
2x4 x 10' treated lumber	1
5/4x4 x 8' treated decking	3
5/4x6 x 10' treated decking	5
3/4" x 2' x 4' treated plywood	1
1" x 2' x 4' treated lattice	1
3" deck screws	5 lbs.
1-1/4" screws	1 lb.
2-1/2" screws	1 lb.
3d galvanized nails	1 lb.
Exterior finish	1 gallon

Self-Watering Raised Planting Bed

Build a raised planting bed and have tonight's salad at your fingertips!

Growing veggies during high summer means daily watering, which becomes a problem if you go away for vacation. You could hire the neighbor kid—and maybe he'll remember or maybe you'll come home to withered veggies.

Solution: Self-watering veggie planters that you can leave for a week without watering. The planter boxes themselves are gorgeous, they keep rabbits and other critters from munching on the greens, and you can be gone for weeks on end without having to water. We watered three times all summer long (no kidding), and had garden-fresh salads until frost. Here we'll show you how to build one for yourself. The secret is in the perforated drain pipe.

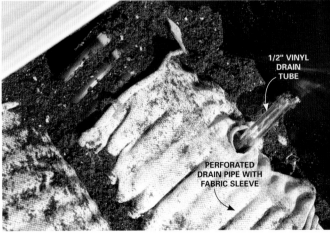

1/2" VINYL DRAIN TUBE

PERFORATED DRAIN PIPE WITH FABRIC SLEEVE

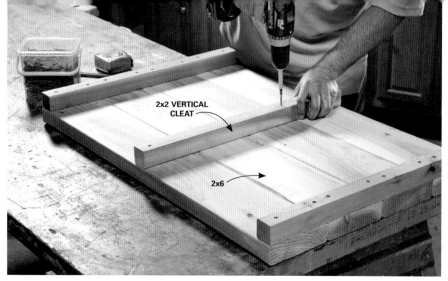

1 SCREW THE BOX ENDS TOGETHER. Pick the straightest 2x2s for the corner cleats. Align the parts with the corner of your worktable to keep the assembly square.

2x2 VERTICAL CLEAT

2x6

2 CONSTRUCT THE BOX SIDES. Straighten bowed boards with a clamp. The top boards need to be straight so the cap will go on straight and tight.

3 SCREW THE BOX TOGETHER. Clamp the edges together and press firmly with the other hand when screwing each plank so everything comes together tightly.

Self-watering planters are sometimes called "sub-irrigated planters" or SIPs, because your plants get to "sip" water whenever they want. Our version uses inexpensive perforated drain pipe with a fabric sleeve in the bottom of the planter. Once you fill the drain pipe reservoirs, they allow air to circulate and water to wick up to your plants' roots whenever they need it.

When plants are watered from below, the roots stay consistently moist, there's less evaporation and you don't need to water as much. The vinyl tubing allows any overflow water to drain. There are many commercial self-watering planters available—the EarthBox is one (earthbox.com). But you can easily make your own.

Build your planting box

Photos 1–6 show you how to build a handsome wood planter box. We used cedar (you can save money by using treated wood) and a thick EPDM pond liner (thinner versions at home centers are a lot less). To give the box a nice finished look, we routed the boards and sanded the faces and cap. We left the cedar unfinished, but you could seal yours. After we built the basic box, we moved the planter to its final position and then added the self-watering system, soil and plants. Even without the soil and plants, this planter is heavy!

Figure A
Self-watering planter
Overall dimensions:
3' long x 6' deep x 23-1/2" tall

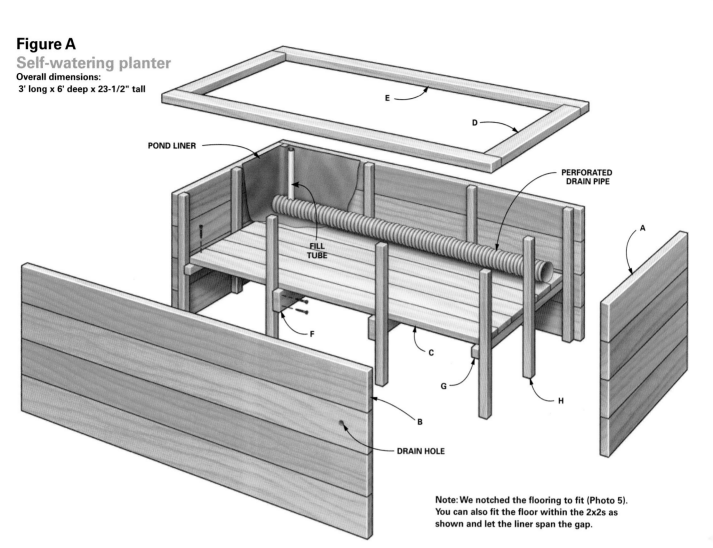

POND LINER

PERFORATED DRAIN PIPE

FILL TUBE

A

F

C

G

H

B

DRAIN HOLE

E

D

Note: We notched the flooring to fit (Photo 5). You can also fit the floor within the 2x2s as shown and let the liner span the gap.

Cutting list

KEY	QTY.	DIMENSIONS	NAME
A	8	1-1/2" x 5-1/2" x 33"	Ends
B	8	1-1/2" x 5-1/2" x 72"	Sides
C	6	1" x 5-1/2", cut to fit	Floor
D	2	1-1/2" x 3-1/2" x 30"	End cap
E	2	1-1/2" x 3-1/2" x 73"	Side cap
F	2	1-1/2" x 3-1/2" x 33"	Joists
G	2	1-1/2" x 1-1/2" x 33"	Horizontal cleats
H	10	1-1/2" x 1-1/2" x 22"	Vertical cleats

Materials list

ITEM	QTY.
12' cedar 2x6s (sides and ends)	6
12' cedar deck boards (planter floor)	3
10' 2x4s (top cap)	2
8' 2x4 (joists)	1
8' 2x2s (cleats)	4
24' of 4"-diameter perforated drain pipe with sleeve	
Pond liner (rubber or poly)	
Exterior screws	
Soilless potting mix	
1/2" vinyl tubing (drainage)	
1" CPVC (fill tube)	

Good choices for containers

VEGETABLES AND HERBS	SOIL DEPTH
Chives, lettuce, radishes, salad greens, basil and coriander	4–5"
Bush beans, garlic, onions, Asian greens, peas, mint and thyme	6–7"
Pole beans, carrots, chard, cucumbers, fennel, leeks, peppers, spinach, parsley and rosemary	8–9"
Beets, broccoli, potatoes, tomatoes, summer squash and dill	10–12"

FLOORING DEPTH GUIDE

TOP OF DECKING JOIST

4 MARK FOR THE DECKING JOISTS. Determine the floor depth (see "Building Tips," p. 115), and cut a block that length to mark the locations of the horizontal cleats and joists.

2x2 HORIZONTAL CLEAT

2x4 JOISTS

5 ATTACH THE JOISTS AND LAY THE FLOOR. Screw the horizontal end cleats in place first and then the center joists. Notch your deck boards to fit around the vertical supports.

6 STAPLE THE RUBBER MEMBRANE IN PLACE. Fold it at the corners and staple it around the perimeter. Trim the excess.

9 advantages of a raised garden bed

- Choose a spot that gets at least six hours of sun. If your planter is against a wall, you can get by with less sun because of the reflected heat.

- A 4-ft.-wide planter is ideal for harvesting from both sides. Keep it to 3 ft. wide if you're placing your planter against a wall or fence.

- Line your planter with a "fish-safe" rubber membrane/pond liner. It will prolong the life of the wood without leaching chemicals into the soil (and your food). You can buy fish-safe pond liners in different thicknesses and materials at home centers, garden centers and online retailers.

- Don't use garden soil or a heavy potting soil in your raised garden. Use a light, fluffy "soilless" blend that will retain moisture without compacting or becoming water-logged. You can also buy potting soil specifically formulated for self-watering planters.

- Mulch your containers to keep weeds down and to slow evaporation.

- For more great ideas for building sub-irrigated planters (SIPs), visit insideurbangreen.org.

Photos **7** and **8** show you how to construct the self-watering system. Once you're ready to plant, add a soilless mix to just below the top of the planter.

Once your plants are in, fill the drain pipe reservoirs through the fill tube until water runs out the drainage hole (this can take a while). The water will slowly wick out of the perforated pipes into the potting mix packed around it and eventually up into the potting mix and plant roots above.

You'll have to experiment to see how long your planter will stay moist. Fill the drain pipes whenever the soil feels dry 2 or 3 in. down. When we set up this planter, we filled the drain pipes and gave the plants an initial surface watering and then mulched around them. After that, and despite a record hot summer, we refilled the pipes only three times over the summer and had herbs and greens growing until the first frost!

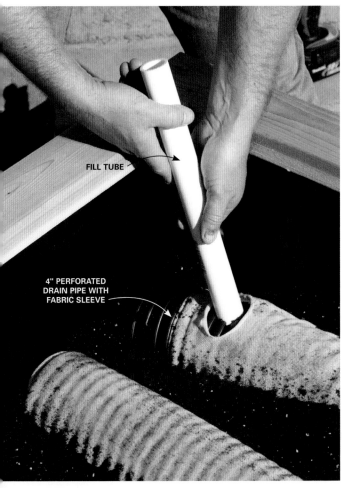

FILL TUBE

4" PERFORATED DRAIN PIPE WITH FABRIC SLEEVE

1/2" VINYL TUBE

7 POSITION THE DRAIN PIPE AND THE FILL TUBE. Space the drain pipes evenly along the deck floor, wedging the ends tightly against the short sides of the planter. Pack potting mix around the pipes to keep them straight. Stick a fill tube in the top end of one of the outside drain pipes.

8 DRILL A DRAIN HOLE AND FIT THE TUBING. In the end of the planter opposite your fill tube, drill a drainage hole just above the height of the pipe. Run vinyl tubing from the drain pipe to the drainage hole.

Building tips

- When assembling the box ends (**Photo 1**) and sides (**Photo 2**), leave gaps between the planks to allow for expansion and contraction. We used 1/16-in. washers as spacers.
- To determine where to put your planter floor (**Photo 4**), add together your soil depth, the flooring thickness and the height of the drain pipe and add an inch to that so the soil level will sit an inch below the top of the box.
- For greater strength, use 2x2 horizontal cleats (33 in. long for our planter) for each end and 2x4s for the center two joists.
- Don't miter the top cap—miter joints open with changes in humidity. Butt joints will look neater than miter joints over time.

- Cut the perforated drain pipe into 6-ft. lengths and lay them in rows across the bottom of the planter. Wedging them in place against the sides will prevent potting mix from getting into the pipes, so you don't need to cap the ends.
- Wedge the CPVC fill tube tightly into the top of the drain pipe. It should be long enough to poke out of the top of your soil once your container is planted (**Photo 7**). You only need one fill tube in the planter because the water will flow through the perforations of the pipe section with the fill tube and then into the surrounding soilless potting mix and through the perforations of all the other drain pipes.
- You can buy perforated drain pipe with an attached sleeve at home centers and landscape centers.

Backyard Oasis

A shaded retreat that's surprisingly easy to build

1 Position the post footings using a layout frame as a template. Square, brace and level the frame. Then mark the post locations and dig the holes.

If you treasure your time outdoors, this simple shelter is the perfect retreat for you. It's open and airy, yet it'll shade you from that hot afternoon sun as well as keep you dry when it rains.

We designed it so you can easily connect it to your existing deck. Or you could build it freestanding in your yard. In either case, it'll quickly become your favorite destination!

Here we'll show you how to assemble this structure step by step. Don't be intimidated by the "post and beam" design. It's not difficult to build, and we'll walk you through the key details. We've simplified the difficult steps with goof-proof techniques—like positioning the posts with a 2x4 frame and shaping the ends of beams with a circular saw. If you've tackled jobs like basic deck building or wall framing, you can build this shelter.

You'll need a miter saw and a table saw to make the angle cuts on the walls. A brad nailer will save you time but isn't absolutely necessary. You'll need at least three full weekends and occasional help from a friend to complete the job.

Planning your shelter

The floor can stand as little as 14 in. above ground to about 8 ft. above ground. But if you build it more than 4 ft. above ground,

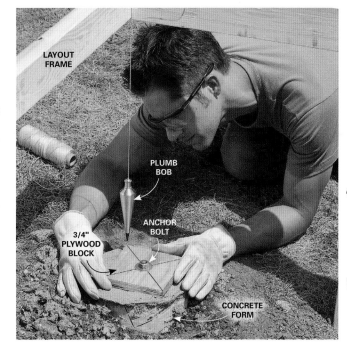

2 Fill the footings with concrete. Position the anchor bolts using 5-1/2-in.-square "bolt blocks." When the concrete hardens, remove the blocks and bolt on the post bases.

you'll have to add diagonal "knee braces" between the posts and the floor (consult a structural engineer on this detail). The floor can be level with the deck or stand higher or lower and include stairs.

When you apply for a building permit, ask your inspector about local requirements, including how deep to dig the footings. Be sure to include bridge plans. For a bridge more than 4 ft. long or 4 ft. wide, your inspector may require that

you strengthen the deck itself. A few days before you dig the footing holes, visit call811.com or call 811 to have utility lines marked.

Most home centers carry 6x6s only as treated lumber. If you want a different wood, you may have to special-order it.

Position posts perfectly with a layout frame

A layout frame makes positioning footings and posts foolproof (**Photo 1**). Later, it

Figure A
Deck shelter details

Footprint: 8' x 8'

Floor to roof peak: 141" (approx.)

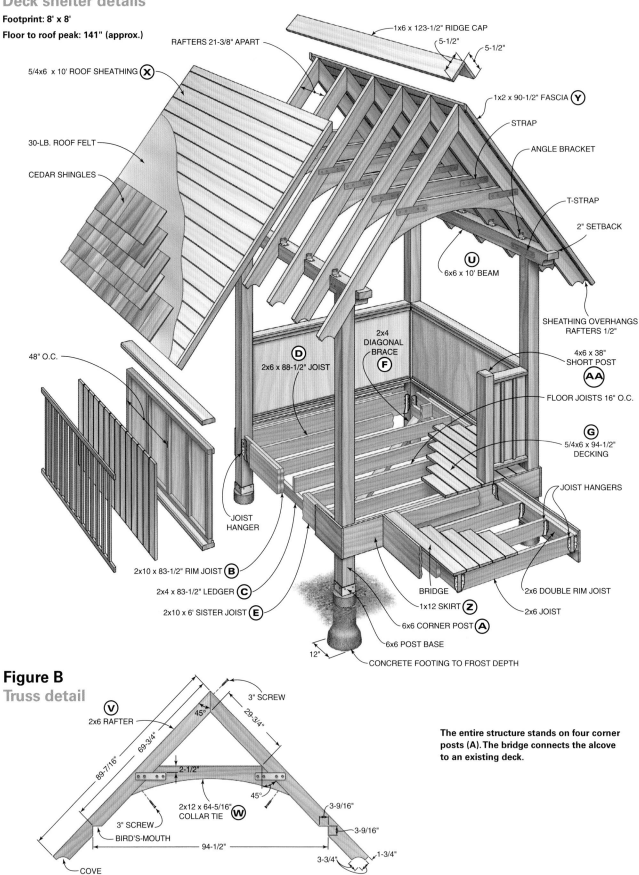

RAFTERS 21-3/8" APART

1x6 x 123-1/2" RIDGE CAP

5-1/2"

5-1/2"

5/4x6 x 10' ROOF SHEATHING (X)

1x2 x 90-1/2" FASCIA (Y)

STRAP

30-LB. ROOF FELT

ANGLE BRACKET

CEDAR SHINGLES

T-STRAP

2" SETBACK

6x6 x 10' BEAM (U)

SHEATHING OVERHANGS RAFTERS 1/2"

48" O.C.

2x4 DIAGONAL BRACE (F)

4x6 x 38" SHORT POST (AA)

2x6 x 88-1/2" JOIST (D)

FLOOR JOISTS 16" O.C.

5/4x6 x 94-1/2" DECKING (G)

JOIST HANGERS

JOIST HANGER

2x10 x 83-1/2" RIM JOIST (B)

2x4 x 83-1/2" LEDGER (C)

2x10 x 6' SISTER JOIST (E)

BRIDGE

1x12 SKIRT (Z)

6x6 CORNER POST (A)

6x6 POST BASE

2x6 DOUBLE RIM JOIST

2x6 JOIST

12"

CONCRETE FOOTING TO FROST DEPTH

Figure B
Truss detail

3" SCREW

2x6 RAFTER (V)

45°

29-3/4"

89-7/16"

69-3/4"

2-1/2"

2x12 x 64-5/16" COLLAR TIE (W)

45°

3-9/16"

3" SCREW

BIRD'S-MOUTH

94-1/2"

3-9/16"

3-3/4"

1-3/4"

COVE

The entire structure stands on four corner posts (A). The bridge connects the alcove to an existing deck.

FIRST 6x6 POST

DIAGONAL BRACE

LAYOUT FRAME

7'

POST BASE

FOOTING

3 Cut the posts (A) to length and screw the first post to its base and to the frame. Add stakes and braces to hold it plumb. Set the other posts and plumb each of them.

helps you determine post heights and position the floor framing (**Photo 4**).

Screw two 2x4s (94-1/2 in. long) between 14-ft. 2x4s to form a square with inside dimensions of 94-1/2 x 94-1/2 in. Square the frame by taking diagonal measurements and add a diagonal brace (**Photo 1**). Rest the frame's "legs" on the deck, position the frame and make sure it's parallel to the deck. Then clamp or screw the legs to the deck. Support the other end

with upright 2x4s. Roughly level the frame.

Hang a plumb bob from each corner of the frame to locate footings (similar to **Photo 2**). The plumb bob locates the outer corner of each post, not the center. Mark the footings using spray paint.

Slide the frame out of your way so you can dig the holes. But first, trace around the frame's legs on the deck with a pencil to mark their exact positions. When the holes are complete, move the frame back

into position. Double-check to make sure the frame is square, perfectly positioned and level. Add extra vertical supports so the long 2x4s won't sag.

Pour the footings and set the posts

Pour 12 in. of concrete into each hole, set the tube forms into place, backfill around them and fill them with concrete. To position the anchor bolts perfectly, cut four

Figure C
Wall detail

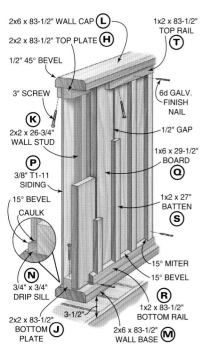

2x6 x 83-1/2" WALL CAP **L**

2x2 x 83-1/2" TOP PLATE **H**

1/2" 45° BEVEL

3" SCREW **K**

2x2 x 26-3/4" WALL STUD **P**

3/8" T1-11 SIDING

15° BEVEL

CAULK **N**

3/4" x 3/4" DRIP SILL

2x2 x 83-1/2" BOTTOM PLATE **J**

3-1/2"

2x6 x 83-1/2" WALL BASE **M**

1x2 x 83-1/2" TOP RAIL **T**

6d GALV. FINISH NAIL

1/2" GAP

1x6 x 29-1/2" BOARD **Q**

1x2 x 27" BATTEN **S**

15° MITER

15° BEVEL

1x2 x 83-1/2" BOTTOM RAIL **R**

Materials list

This list doesn't include materials for roofing, bridge or railings.

ITEM	QTY.	ITEM	QTY.
6x6 cedar (corner posts; lengths vary)	4	2x4 x 8' (frame, bracing, stakes; see Photo 3)	6
6x6 x 10' cedar (beams)	2	Hardware, etc.	
4x6 x 8' cedar (short wall posts)	1	Anchor bolts, washers and nuts	4
2x6 x 8' cedar (wall bases and caps, rafters)	19	Joist hangers (for 2x10s)	8
2x12 x 12' cedar (collar ties)	3	Post bases	4
5/4x6 x 10' cedar (decking, roof sheathing)	49	Angle brackets	12
1x12 x 8' cedar (skirt)	4	Straps	24
1x6 x 10' cedar (wall boards)	12	T-straps	8
1x2 x 8' cedar (rails, battens, fascia)	30	5/8" x 2" lag screws	48
2x10 x 8' pressure-treated (rim joists)	4	5/8" x 2-1/2" bolts and nuts	48
2x10 x 12' sister joists)	2	8" tube forms	4
2x4 x 8' (joist ledgers)	2	3" galvanized nails, 2" deck screws, joist hanger nails, 10d galv. nails, 6d galv. finish nails	
2x6 x 8' (floor joists)	5		
2x4 x 12' (diagonal brace)	1	Concrete mix	
2x2 x 8' (wall plates and studs)	13	Construction adhesive	
4' x 8' T1-11 plywood (wall sheathing)	3		
2x4 x 14' (frame; see Photo 1)	3		

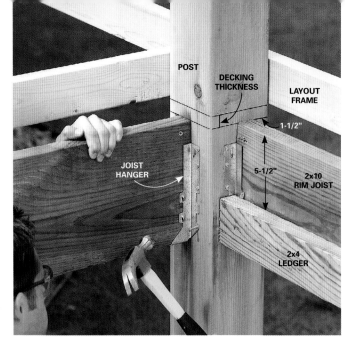

4 Mark the thickness of the decking below the layout frame. Install 2x10 rim joists at that height using joist hangers. Nail 2x4 ledgers to two rim joists. Remove the layout frame.

POST

DECKING THICKNESS

LAYOUT FRAME

1-1/2"

JOIST HANGER

5-1/2"

2x10 RIM JOIST

2x4 LEDGER

5 Nail 2x6 floor joists into place. Drive in shims to straighten a bowed rim joist. Nail additional 2x10 "sister" joists (see Figure A) alongside each rim joist, then install the decking.

2x6 FLOOR JOIST

2x4 LEDGER

2x10 RIM JOIST

6 Frame the sidewalls as detailed in Figure C. Cover the insides of the walls with plywood siding and the outsides with boards and battens.

1x6 BOARDS

T1-11 PLYWOOD SIDING

1x2 BOTTOM RAIL

1x2 BATTEN

2x6 WALL BASE

5-1/2 x 5-1/2-in. "bolt blocks" from plywood (**Photo 2**). Drill a 5/8-in. hole at the center of each block, insert the anchor bolt and add the nut. Set each bolt into the wet concrete. Then stand up and eyeball the block to make sure it's parallel to the layout frame. The blocks leave impressions in the concrete. When the concrete hardens, use those impressions to position the post bases.

Next, cut the posts to length. To determine the length of each post, measure from the post base to the layout frame. Then add 7 ft. to that measurement. A 7-1/4-in. circular saw won't cut through a 6x6, so cut from all four sides and finish with a handsaw.

Recheck the position of the layout frame. Set one of the back posts first. Add braces to hold it plumb. Set the other posts (**Photo 3**), then check each one with a level. If a post is out of plumb, don't simply shove it into position—the layout frame will push the others out of plumb. Instead, slip a wrench inside the post base and loosen the nut on the anchor bolt. The oversized bolt hole in the base lets you move the base slightly and plumb the post. Don't forget to retighten the nut.

Frame a sturdy floor—fast

Measure down from the layout frame to mark the position of the floor framing on each post (**Photo 4**). Toe-screw each rim joist (B) into place and add the joist hangers. Be sure to inset the rim joists 1-1/2 in. from the outer edges of the posts. Remove the layout frame, but leave the post braces in place until you install the sidewalls.

To support the floor joists, add ledgers (C) to two of the rim joists (**Figure A**), driving 10d nails every 4 in. Using ledgers is easier and faster than using joist hangers. Set the floor joists (D) on the ledgers and nail them into place (**Photo 5**). Then add the sister joists (E). Nail the diagonal brace (F) to the undersides of joists. Lay the deck boards as you would on any deck, flush with the sister joists.

Stiffen the structure with solid sidewalls

The walls that surround the alcove aren't just for looks; they also stiffen the structure and make it safer.

Build the sidewalls (**Photo 6**), but leave the rear wall off until the roof trusses are in place. **Figure C** shows all the details. To start, install the 2x2 wall framing (H, J, K). Chamfer the wall cap (L) and base (M) by tilting your table saw blade to 45 degrees. Check the posts for plumb before you nail on the plywood siding (P). Next, nail on the 1x6 boards (Q). Then tilt your table saw blade to 15 degrees and bevel the 1x2 bottom rails (R) so they'll shed rainwater. Add the top rails (T) after all the battens (S) are in place. To install the wall caps (L), apply construction adhesive to the inner and outer top rails. Then predrill and drive screws up through the rails and into the cap. To avoid dents from dropped tools, we left the caps off until later.

Cut perfect coves and set the beams

Coved ends give the beams (U) a more graceful look than square-cut ends. And there's a fast way to do it using a circular saw (**Photo 7**). We first tried a 7-1/4-in. saw, but found that a slightly larger cove cut with an 8-1/4-in. saw looked better and was well worth the rental fee.

Before you cut coves, determine the position of the stop block. We clamped our block 5-5/8 in. from the ends of each beam, but that measurement will differ with a different saw. Clamp your stop block to a 6x6 scrap left over from the posts. Cut until the saw bumps against the block, then measure the length and depth of the cut. Adjust the stop block until the length and depth are equal. Measure the position of the block and use that measurement to position the block on the beams. When you cut the coves, hold the saw flat against the beam; if you tip down the back of the saw, you'll cut too deep.

Set the beams on the posts (**Photo 8**) and fasten them to the posts with T-straps. We spray-painted the heads of our lag screws black before installing them and touched them up with an artist's brush after.

Build fancy roof trusses with basic skills

Building the six trusses is simple but time consuming. So consider building them in your garage before you break ground for this project. **Figure B** shows all the details.

First, mark an arc on the 2x12 collar ties

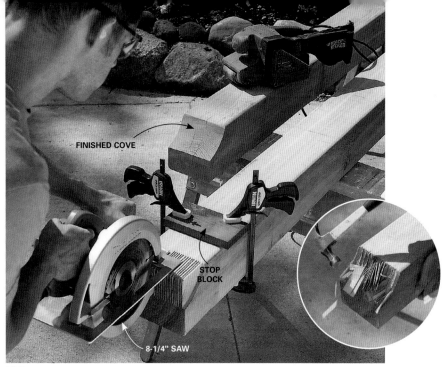

FINISHED COVE

STOP BLOCK

8-1/4" SAW

7 Cove the beams with an 8-1/4-in. circular saw, using a stop block to ensure uniform cuts. Break out the chips and smooth the cove with a 100-grit sanding belt.

STOP BLOCK

T-STRAP

BEAM

T-STRAP

8 Lag-screw T-straps outside each post and set the beams. Then add the inside straps. Clamp stop blocks to the posts so the beam can't fall off while you position it.

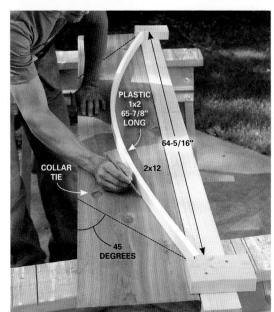

PLASTIC 1x2 65-7/8" LONG

64-5/16"

2x12

COLLAR TIE

45 DEGREES

9 Trace arcs on collar ties using a flexible arc jig. Cut the arcs with a jigsaw and smooth them with a belt sander. Cut the 45-degree ends with a circular saw.

10 Cut the rafters as shown in Figure B and assemble the trusses on a 2x4 crib. Drill perpendicular bolt holes using a simple 1x4 drill guide.

RAFTER

COLLAR TIE

CRIB

5/8" BIT

DRILL GUIDE

BOLT HOLE

RIDGE BRACE

FIRST TRUSS

TRUSS BRACE

STRAP

11 Set the first truss, level it and brace it to the deck. Set the second truss, then screw on a temporary ridge brace to hold the trusses upright.

(W; **Photo 9**). Screw blocks to a 2x4 and bend a "spring stick" between them. Plastic molding makes a perfect spring stick. Slide the jig to the left or right to avoid knots in the 2x12 and select the most attractive part of the board.

Next, cut the rafters (V). To assemble the trusses quickly and consistently, build a simple 2x4 crib that will hold the truss parts in position (**Photo 10**). Join the parts with 3-in. screws. Then line up the straps using a 4-ft. level. Mark the bolt-hole locations by drilling shallow holes. Then set the strap aside and finish the holes, using a guide to hold the drill bit perfectly vertical so the holes match up on both sides (see **Photo 10**, right inset). The guide is simply two square blocks screwed together. Bolt on the straps.

Set the trusses and sheathe the roof

Mark the truss locations on top of both beams. Set the front truss first, fastening it with angle brackets (**Figure A**). Then set and brace the remaining trusses (**Photo 11**).

The bird's-mouths may fit so tightly over the beams that it's difficult to set the trusses. Here's how to solve that problem: After the first truss, fasten only one side of each remaining truss. That way you can tug the beams inward as you set each truss. (To allow this, you must build the back wall only after the trusses are installed.) Fasten the loose side of each truss and build the back wall before you sheathe the roof with deck boards (X). Start at the bottom of the rafters, overhanging the first board by 1/2 in. and spacing the boards 1/4 in. apart. These boards will be visible from below, so be sure to lay the best side face down. Cover the ends of the roof sheathing with fascia trim (Y; **Photo 12**). Whatever type of roofing you choose, be sure to use short roofing nails that won't pop through the underside of the roof sheathing.

> **Tip**
> Sand and stain the truss parts and roof sheathing before you assemble them.

CAUTION
The roof is too steep to stand or kneel on. At the very least, you'll need roof jacks and a 2x10 plank (see Photo 12). Scaffolding makes the job easier and safer.

The bridge and railings

The bridge is basically a small deck (see **Figure A**). After you frame and deck the bridge, add the 1x12 skirt boards (Z).

The front walls are just shorter versions of the walls shown in **Figure B**. If you can't find 4x6s for the front wall posts (AA), you can cut them from 6x6s using a 10-in. table saw. To extend the deck railing, you'll have to cut out a section of the existing railing and add two new railing posts, copying the existing ones. Then install the new railing, again copying the existing design. We finished all the exposed wood with transparent deck stain.

FASCIA

12 Sheathe the roof with 5/4-in. deck boards. Nail 1x2 fascia trim to the sheathing at the front and back, then shingle the roof. Take safety precautions on the steep roof.

Cut the cost in half

We spent about $3,000 on materials. But we could have built a nearly identical structure for about half that. Here's how:

- We used cedar for the exposed parts. Using treated lumber instead would save on lumber costs.
- We chose cedar shingles for the roof. Using asphalt shingles would save several hundred dollars.
- The 32 metal straps and T-straps (plus fasteners) amounted to about a fifth of the total cost. You could use half as many straps, placing them on one side of each post and truss, instead of on both sides. (The connections will still be strong enough.) Or you could use inexpensive galvanized hardware and spray-paint it black.

Space-Saving Tool Holder

Organize your gardening tools in an afternoon

If you are constantly contending with backyard-tool clutter, this handy holder is just the ticket. It's a great way to organize your rakes, shovels and other long-handled tools.

The versatile design fits a variety of long-handled garden and yard tools, including those with "D-shaped" handles. Before getting started, measure your tool handles—especially the D-shaped ones—to make sure they'll fit the dimensions shown in the plan at far right. If not, you can easily adjust the grid measurements to fit your own tools.

Step-by-step instructions

1. Rip the sides and ends for the top and bottom frames from the 1-in. x 8-in. pine board according to the board layout in **Figure B**.

2. Assemble the top and bottom sections by fastening the sides to the ends with 2-in. finishing nails. Be sure to square the corners as you nail. (When nailing close to the end of a board as you are here, it's best to predrill the nail holes using the same size finishing nail as a drill bit.)

3. Cut four 26-in. lengths from the 2x2s. Set these pieces (labeled G in **Figure A**) aside.

4. Rip a second 1-in. x 8-in. board into 1-in. strips following the board layout in **Figure B**. These pieces will form the grid that holds your long-handled tools.

The larger openings will provide a 4-1/2-in. space for holding D-handled tools. Measure your tool handles to be sure this space will accommodate them. Adjust the size of the grid as needed.

Shopping list
- 12' of 1" x 8" No. 2 pine board
- Two 8' 2x2s
- 2", 1-1/2" and 1-1/4" finishing nails
- 1-5/8" deck screws

Recommended tools
- Table saw
- Combination square

Figure A
Tool holder

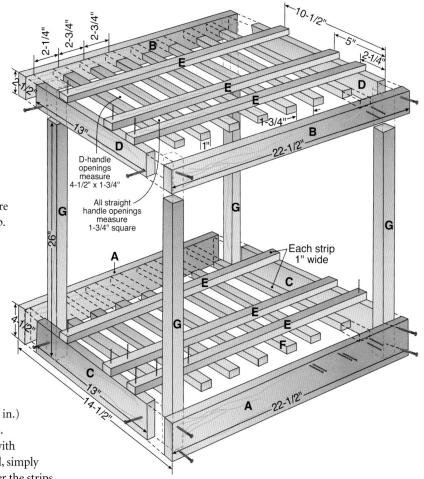

5. It's time to sharpen your measuring skills. Starting from either end of the 22-1/2-in. side of one of the frames, measure 2-1/4 in. from the inside edge of the frame (mark this measurement on the top edge of the frame on both sides).

6. Place one of the 13-in. strips inside the frame so it's centered on the two marks you made and flush with the top of the frame with the 1-in. side facing up. Using the first marks as a starting point, position the remaining six strips 2-3/4 in. apart on center (see **Figure A**).

7. Nail the strips in place with 1-1/2-in. finishing nails. Before you do, make sure your measurements are accurate. There should be 1-3/4 in. between each strip. Repeat this process for the other frame, which will be identical in spacing.

8. Nail the 1-in. x 22-1/2-in. strips perpendicular and on top of the 13-in. strips you just attached.

To position them, start from either end of the 14-1/2 in. side of one of the frames and measure 2-1/4, 5 and 10-1/2 in. from the inside edge (again, mark these measurements on the opposite end of the frame, too). Center three of the 22-1/2-in.-long strips on those marks and check your measurements (all the spaces will be 1-3/4-in. square, except for the D-handled ones, which will measure 4-1/2 in. x 1-3/4 in.) and nail them into place with 1-1/2-in. finishing nails.

9. Every intersection of the grid should be secured with 1-1/4-in. finishing nails. To provide support as you nail, simply cut the end of a scrap piece of 2x4 so it fits snugly under the strips. Repeat this process for the other frame.

10. Use the four 26-in. 2x2 uprights which you cut in step 3 to attach the top and bottom frames to one another. Fasten these pieces with 1-5/8-in. deck screws to the corners of the bottom frame (drive screws through both the sides and the ends for added strength). Attach the top in the same manner, but first double check that the spaces in the top grid align with the spaces in the bottom grid.

Your project's complete! Now the only thing left to do is pick up those tools off the garage or shed floor and fill your handy new organizer.

Figure B
Board layout

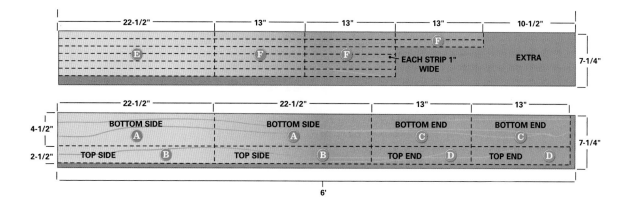

Garden Closet

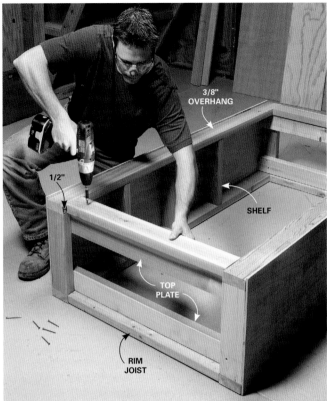

1 Frame and sheathe the walls, then join them with plates and joists. Use the best pieces of lumber in the front where they'll show.

If you don't have room in your yard for a large, free-standing shed, you can still create plenty of space for garden tools with a shed attached to the back or side of the house. If you're an experienced builder, you can build this shed in a couple of weekends. Ours cost about $400, but you could save about $75 by using treated lumber, pine, and asphalt shingles instead of cedar.

Frame the walls and roof

Nail together the side walls, then square them with the plywood side panels. Overhang the panels 3/8 in. at the front—this will hide the gap at the corner when you hang the doors.

Join the two sides with the top and bottom plates and rim joists. The sides, top and bottom are all mirror images of each other except for the top front rim joist, which is set down 1/2 in. from the top so it stops the doors (**Photo 1**). Use screws to fasten the framework together except in the front where fasteners will be visible—use 2-1/2-in. casing nails there.

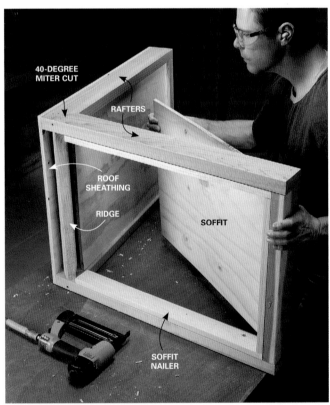

2 Build the roof on your workbench. Start with an L-shaped 2x4 frame, then add the nailers, soffit, sheathing and trim. Shingle with cedar or asphalt shingles.

Figure A
Garden closet construction details

Overall dimensions:

86" tall x 38-3/8" wide x 24" deep

The shed is made from three components—the roof, the walls and the doors, with edges covered by trim boards.

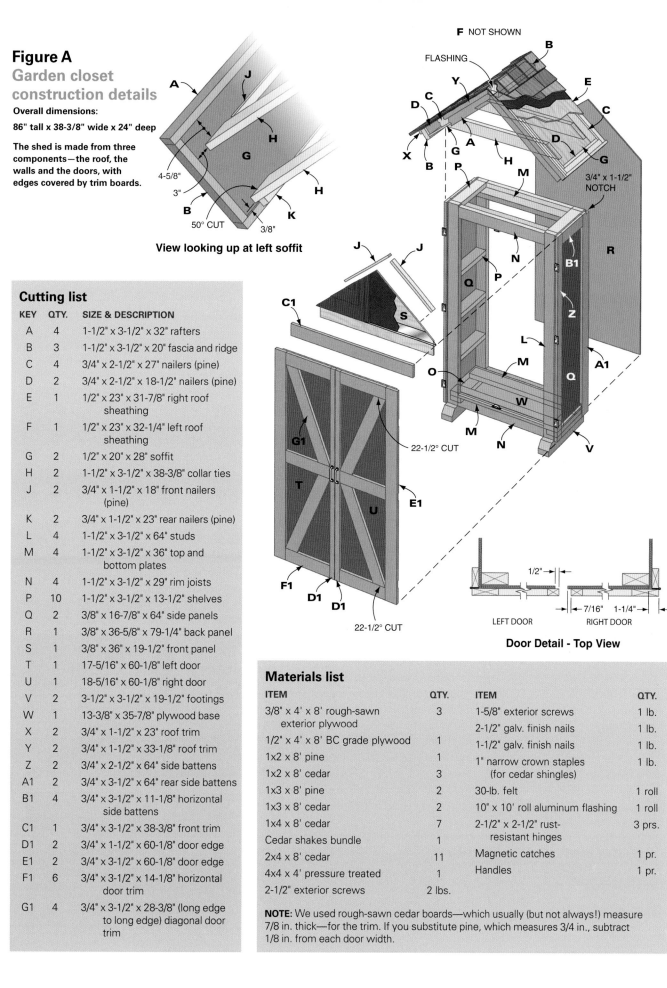

View looking up at left soffit

F NOT SHOWN

FLASHING

3/4" x 1-1/2" NOTCH

22-1/2° CUT

22-1/2° CUT

Cutting list

KEY	QTY.	SIZE & DESCRIPTION
A	4	1-1/2" x 3-1/2" x 32" rafters
B	3	1-1/2" x 3-1/2" x 20" fascia and ridge
C	4	3/4" x 2-1/2" x 27" nailers (pine)
D	2	3/4" x 2-1/2" x 18-1/2" nailers (pine)
E	1	1/2" x 23" x 31-7/8" right roof sheathing
F	1	1/2" x 23" x 32-1/4" left roof sheathing
G	2	1/2" x 20" x 28" soffit
H	2	1-1/2" x 3-1/2" x 38-3/8" collar ties
J	2	3/4" x 1-1/2" x 18" front nailers (pine)
K	2	3/4" x 1-1/2" x 23" rear nailers (pine)
L	4	1-1/2" x 3-1/2" x 64" studs
M	4	1-1/2" x 3-1/2" x 36" top and bottom plates
N	4	1-1/2" x 3-1/2" x 29" rim joists
P	10	1-1/2" x 3-1/2" x 13-1/2" shelves
Q	2	3/8" x 16-7/8" x 64" side panels
R	1	3/8" x 36-5/8" x 79-1/4" back panel
S	1	3/8" x 36" x 19-1/2" front panel
T	1	17-5/16" x 60-1/8" left door
U	1	18-5/16" x 60-1/8" right door
V	2	3-1/2" x 3-1/2" x 19-1/2" footings
W	1	13-3/8" x 35-7/8" plywood base
X	2	3/4" x 1-1/2" x 23" roof trim
Y	2	3/4" x 1-1/2" x 33-1/8" roof trim
Z	2	3/4" x 2-1/2" x 64" side battens
A1	2	3/4" x 3-1/2" x 64" rear side battens
B1	4	3/4" x 3-1/2" x 11-1/8" horizontal side battens
C1	1	3/4" x 3-1/2" x 38-3/8" front trim
D1	2	3/4" x 1-1/2" x 60-1/8" door edge
E1	2	3/4" x 3-1/2" x 60-1/8" door edge
F1	6	3/4" x 3-1/2" x 14-1/8" horizontal door trim
G1	4	3/4" x 3-1/2" x 28-3/8" (long edge to long edge) diagonal door trim

Door Detail - Top View

1/2"

7/16" 1-1/4"

LEFT DOOR

RIGHT DOOR

Materials list

ITEM	QTY.	ITEM	QTY.
3/8" x 4' x 8' rough-sawn exterior plywood	3	1-5/8" exterior screws	1 lb.
		2-1/2" galv. finish nails	1 lb.
1/2" x 4' x 8' BC grade plywood	1	1-1/2" galv. finish nails	1 lb.
1x2 x 8' pine	1	1" narrow crown staples (for cedar shingles)	1 lb.
1x2 x 8' cedar	3		
1x3 x 8' pine	2	30-lb. felt	1 roll
1x3 x 8' cedar	2	10" x 10' roll aluminum flashing	1 roll
1x4 x 8' cedar	7	2-1/2" x 2-1/2" rust-resistant hinges	3 prs.
Cedar shakes bundle	1		
2x4 x 8' cedar	11	Magnetic catches	1 pr.
4x4 x 4' pressure treated	1	Handles	1 pr.
2-1/2" exterior screws	2 lbs.		

NOTE: We used rough-sawn cedar boards—which usually (but not always!) measure 7/8 in. thick—for the trim. If you substitute pine, which measures 3/4 in., subtract 1/8 in. from each door width.

3 Set the completed roof on the shed base. Screw on the front and back panels to join the roof and the base.

ROOFING FELT

1" MINIMUM OVERLAP

FLASHING

4 Cover the front panel with roofing felt and shingles. Place metal flashing over the trim so water won't seep behind it.

Screw the 4x4 footings to the bottom plates, then nail on the plywood base. Cut and screw together the two pairs of rafters, then nail on the fascia and ridge boards. Nail on the roof sheathing and the soffit, butting the corners together (**Photo 2**). Screw on the collar ties at the points shown in **Figure A**, then screw on the front and rear nailers. Nail the roof trim on, staple on a layer of roofing felt, then shingle the roof. If you use cedar shingles, fasten them with narrow crown staples or siding nails. Leave 1/8-in. to 1/4-in. gaps between cedar shingles for expansion, and nail a strip of aluminum flashing across the ridge under the cap shingles.

Tip the shed upright, then set the roof on, aligning the front collar tie with the front rim joist and centering it side to side (**Photo 3**). Nail the cedar trim to the sides, aligning the 1x3s on the sides with the overhanging edge of plywood along the front edge. Glue and screw on the back and front siding panels to join the roof and base together. Use the back panel to square the structure and make it rigid.

Nail on the front trim piece, aligning it with the horizontal side battens. Attach flashing and felt to the front panel, then cover it with cedar shakes (**Photo 4**).

Hang the doors

Finally, construct the doors (see **Figure A**, detail), cut the hinge mortises (see below) and hang the doors. Leave a 1/8-in. gap between the doors and trim along the top. Paint or stain if desired, then set the shed against the house on several inches of gravel. Add or take away gravel under the footings until the shed is tight against the siding and the gap above the doors is even. Screw the shed to the studs in the wall to keep it from tipping. Drill two 1/2-in. holes for the screws through the plywood near the rim joists, then loosely fasten the shed to the wall with 2-1/2-in. screws and large fender washers so the shed can move up and down if the ground freezes and thaws.

How to mortise a hinge

Mark the hinge locations on the doorjamb, then on the door, less 1/8 in. for clearance at the top of the door. Separate the hinge leaves, then align the edge of the leaf with the edge of the door or jamb. Predrill and fasten the leaf, then cut along all three edges with a razor knife to about the same depth as the hinge leaf (**Photo 1**).

Remove the hinge and make a series of angled cuts to establish the depth of the mortise (**Photo 2**). Turn the chisel over and clean out the chips using light hammer taps.

Holding the chisel with the beveled front edge against the wood, chip out the 1/4-in. sections. Check the fit of the hinge leaf and chisel out additional wood until the leaf sits flush.

If the hinges don't fit back together perfectly when you hang the door, tap the leaves up or down (gently) with a hammer.

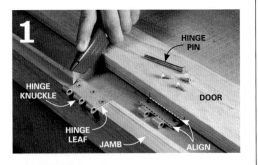

1

HINGE PIN

HINGE KNUCKLE

DOOR

HINGE LEAF

JAMB

ALIGN

2

DEPTH OF HINGE LEAF

Chapter Two

INCREDIBLE INDOOR PROJECTS

BOOKCASES

Bookcase with Secret Hiding Places 130
No-Excuses Bookcase 138
Super-Simple Bookcase 144

KITCHEN STORAGE UPGRADES

Kitchen Cabinet Rollouts 150
Cabinet Door Rack 156
Ultimate Container Storage 158

CLOSETS

Small-Closet Organizer 163
Triple Your Closet Space 169
Wire Shelving Made Easy 178

INTERIOR TRIM

Interior Trim Simplified 182
Painting Trim 195
Tips for Tight Miters 201

TILE

Ceramic Tile Floor 207
Tile a Shower with Panache 214
Tile a Backsplash 220

ENTRYWAY ENHANCEMENTS

Hide-the-Mess Lockers 224
Entry Organizer 228

Bookcase with Secret Hiding Places

High style, tons of storage—and clever hidden compartments

Can you keep a secret? This bookcase contains more than meets the eye. Behind the magnificent Arts and Crafts styling, there are 10 hidden compartments. Some are big, some are small, but they're all easy to build, and most of them don't reduce regular storage space at all.

I splurged on the wood and built this bookcase with rift-sawn red oak for a total materials cost of $700. The straight-grain lines of rift-sawn oak give furniture an authentic Arts and Crafts look. But you could use rotary-cut plywood and plain-sawn solid oak and cut your costs by about $225. Either way, it's a bargain price for an heirloom like this—even if you don't have anything to hide.

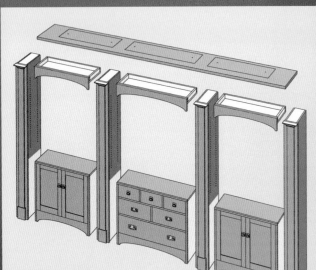

11 easy pieces

It may look complicated, but this bookcase is mostly a collection of plywood boxes dressed up with solid wood: drawer boxes, cabinet boxes...even the columns are nothing more than tall, skinny boxes with decorative faces. The bridges, too, are just shallow boxes with arched fronts. If you can build boxes, you can build this bookcase.

All of the components are separate units, so you can easily disassemble the whole bookcase in a few minutes—that's great for finishing, even better for moving the bookcase into the house.

Secret Spaces

Five types of secret compartments are shown here. To find the sixth, take a long look at **Figure C** on p. 136. Stumped? See p. 137 and all will be revealed.

Hidden hole

Remove the bottom drawer and lift off the panel to reveal the hiding place.

Overhead hiding place

Each of the top lift-off panels covers a shallow box. You'll need a ladder, so they're best for long-term storage.

Column compartment

The column face is held in place by magnets. Give it a hard tug for instant access. Build just one column this way—or all four.

False-bottom drawer

Flip the drawer over, remove a few screws and slide out the bottom panel.

Drawer nook

A shortened drawer box leaves space behind the drawer. Add a removable panel to hide a concealed cubby.

Build 10 boxes out of plywood

Start with the column box sides (A and B). Rough-cut two sheets of plywood to 80-1/4 in. with a circular saw. Then trim them to their final length of 80 in. using a straightedge and a router fitted with a flush-trim bit. This will give you a perfect edge. Mark the dado locations on the plywood and cut them (**Photo 1**). **Note:** You'll have to add your own bearing to the plywood bit. Repeat the procedure for the cabinet sides (C), cutting the plywood to 30-in. lengths first. You can get the four sides for the door cabinets from a single width of plywood. **Note:** The bottom dado on the drawer cabinet is lower than on the door cabinets in order to create the hidden compartment below the lower drawer. With the column and cabinet sides cut and machined, the next step is to lay out and drill the adjustable shelf holes.

Cut the shelf parts for the columns (S and T) and cabinets (F and G) and cut the dadoes and rabbets as shown. Hold off on the cabinet tops (D and E). You want to assemble the cabinet first to finalize the top dimensions. Dry-fit all the parts to make sure everything goes together right. I prefinished the interior parts of the door cabinets before assembly. Tape off the dadoes to keep them free of stain and varnish.

Make sure the cabinets are square before you drive any screws. The drawer cabinet is assembled from the inside out, starting with the shelves and dividers. With the cabinets assembled, you can determine the final measurements for the tops and the upper compartment bottoms (D and E).

You'll likely have to adjust the sizes given in the **Cutting List**, p. 138. Tiny differences in plywood thickness and dado depth can add up to a cabinet that's a little narrower or wider than the listed dimensions. It's essential that the tops fit perfectly flush to the cabinet sides. **Note:** The bridge bottoms (D and E) are the same size as the cabinet tops and should be cut at the same time. With the tops cut to final sizes, lay out and cut the dadoes on the underside

Mighty Mini Magnets

Rare earth magnets are puny but powerful. So they make great, invisible fasteners for unusual projects like hidden compartments. Three of our six secret spaces rely on rare earth magnets.

2 ASSEMBLE THE COLUMNS. Screws and a little glue are fine for most of the assembly; screw heads will be covered up later. But use clamps rather than screws on the outer sides of both end columns.

1 CUT FOUR DADOES IN ONE PASS. For the column and cabinet sides, dado the plywood first. Then rip the plywood to width. This saves setup time and guarantees that the dadoes will match up.

3 FINGER CLAMP THE CROWNS. Glue and your fingers are the best way to assemble the small parts of the column crowns. Hold them together for a few seconds, then leave them undisturbed while the glue sets. Any wood glue will work, but molding glue bonds faster and won't run all over the place.

Figure A
Drawer cabinet details

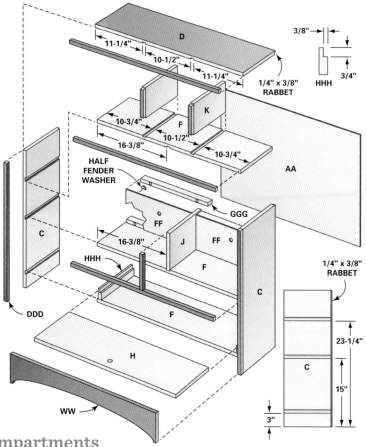

of the drawer cabinet top. Assemble the cabinets and columns with glue and screws (**Photo 2**). Glue and clamp the tops to the cabinets.

OK, seven boxes down; there are just three to go. Time to build the bridge boxes that do double duty as secret compartments. It's critical to build the bridge boxes so they're exactly the same width and length as the cabinet tops below. Fortunately, that's easy to do since the cabinet tops and the compartment bottoms are identical. Simply add the sides (P, Q and R) to the compartment bottoms. Double-check your work by setting the bridge boxes on top of the assembled cabinets. They should line up perfectly with the cabinet tops.

Add compartments to the cabinets

To build the secret compartment below the bottom drawer, simply cut and rout the compartment sides (HHH) and install them at the bottom of the drawer cabinet with screws. Cut the lid to the compartment (H) and drill a 1-in. finger hole. Ease the edges of the hole with a 1/8-in. round-over bit.

To build the compartments behind the middle drawers: Cut the false backs (FF) and spacers (GGG). Drill a pair of holes for the rare earth magnets toward the end and on the edge of each spacer. Secure the magnets with epoxy. Install the spacers at the back of the cabinet (one reason to leave the cabinet backs off for now). Epoxy four washers on the back of the false back

Figure B
Bookcase overview

Overall dimensions:
120" wide x 16" deep x 81-1/4" tall

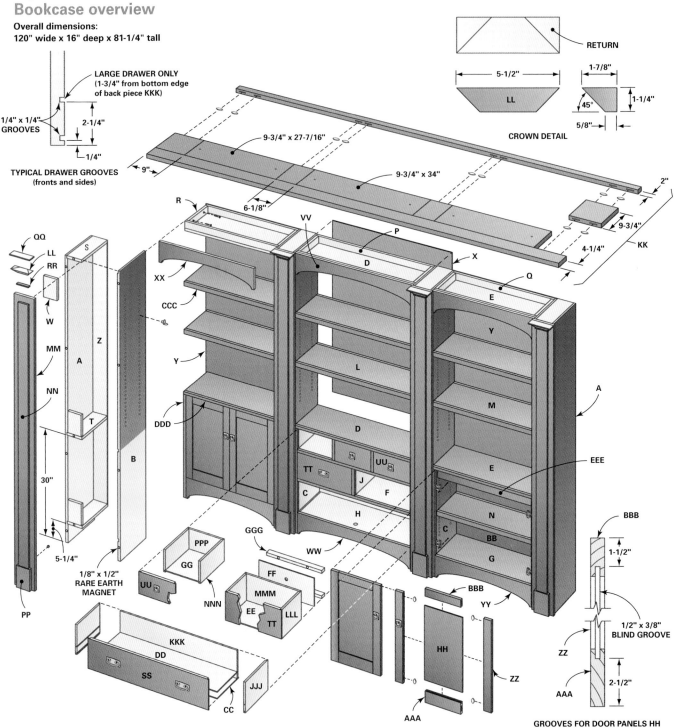

RETURN

5-1/2"

LL

1-7/8"

45°

1-1/4"

5/8"

CROWN DETAIL

LARGE DRAWER ONLY
(1-3/4" from bottom edge of back piece KKK)

1/4" x 1/4"
GROOVES

2-1/4"

1/4"

TYPICAL DRAWER GROOVES
(fronts and sides)

9-3/4" x 27-7/16"

9"

6-1/8"

9-3/4" x 34"

2"

9-3/4"

4-1/4"

KK

R

QQ

LL

RR

S

W

MM

NN

30"

Z

A

T

B

5-1/4"

1/8" x 1/2"
RARE EARTH MAGNET

PP

XX

CCC

Y

DDD

VV

P

D

X

Q

E

Y

L

M

D

TT

UU

J

C

F

H

C

BB

G

N

E

A

EEE

BBB

1-1/2"

UU

GGG

WW

YY

ZZ

ZZ

1/2" x 3/8"
BLIND GROOVE

AAA

2-1/2"

GROOVES FOR DOOR PANELS HH

PPP

GG

FF

MMM

EE

LLL

TT

NNN

KKK

DD

SS

CC

JJJ

AAA

HH

BBB

---

where the magnets make contact. Add a finger hole and you've got two more hiding places.

Cut the two false rails (EEE) that hide the drop-down boxes in the door cabinets and glue the drop-down box lip (FFF) centered on the lower edge on the back. Position the false fronts in the cabinet to act as a stop for the doors (don't forget to consider the

thickness of a felt or cork bumper). Fasten with glue and screws.

Build the drop-down boxes (U, V, JJ) from scrap plywood. Embed two rare earth magnets in the top of the back edge. After the epoxy has set, grab some leftover paint and goop up the magnet faces. Set the box in place and push up on the back edge to mark the corresponding holes in

the underside of the top. Drill and epoxy in the magnets under the top. Cut and fit the backs for the columns and the cabinets. Prefinish the backs of the two door cabinets before installing them.

To complete the cabinets, cut and fit the hardwood trim (DDD) for the cabinets. Use glue and a brad nailer to fasten the trim. Sand the hardwood flush and smooth.

4 SET THE COLUMN BLOCKS. Clamp the column face to the box, then reach in from behind to position and nail the blocks. Add screws to lock them in place. These blocks automatically position and support the removable column face to the column box.

BRIDGE

5 ASSEMBLE THE WHOLE THING. Screw through the cabinet boxes into the columns. To install each bridge, clamp it in place and then add screws.

6 GLUE UP THE TOP. Clamp up the top using the access panels as spacers between the blocks. Old business cards work great as spacers around the access panels. Be careful not to glue the panels in place.

PANEL

BLOCK

Complete the columns

Cut the column backers (MM), columns (NN) and column bases (PP). Leave the columns (NN) a little long. Machine the crown (LL); see **Figure B**. Assemble the crowns with glue (**Photo 3**). Machine the stock for the crown cap (QQ) and base (RR) and cut to size. You'll want to sand the individual parts to 180-grit before assembly.

Lay out all the column face parts on the column backer. Adjust the final length of the column so all the parts fit perfectly on the backer. Screw the columns and bases to the backer through the back of the column backers. Nail and glue the crown base to the top of the column. Attach the crown with screws from behind and nail the cap in place. You should have four very nice-looking column faces that are ready to mount on the column boxes (**Photo 4**).

Now it's time to add the magnets. For maximum grip, I used pairs of magnets that stuck to each other rather than magnets paired with metal plates. Drill a series of holes for 1/2-in. rare earth magnets in the edge of the column box. It's best to do this on a drill press with a Forstner bit so the holes are flat and perpendicular, allowing the magnets to lie perfectly flush with the surface. I spaced four magnets along each edge of the column box and one in the middle of each shelf for a total of 11 magnets. Epoxy the magnets into their holes. Use the paint trick mentioned on p.134 to mark the location for the magnets in the column backer. Set the column on the box and the paint will leave marks where the other magnets go. Drill magnet holes and epoxy in the magnets, taking care to orient the magnets correctly so they grab the magnets in the column boxes and don't repel them. There, now you've got some super-safe hiding places.

If you don't want a secret compartment in a column, simply glue the columns to the column boxes. Position the columns so they

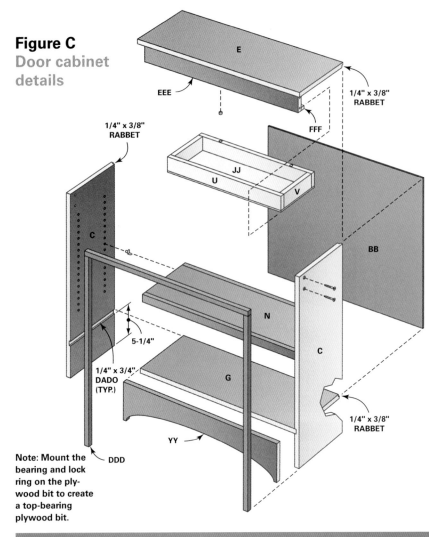

Figure C
Door cabinet details

E

EEE

1/4" x 3/8"
RABBET

FFF

1/4" x 3/8"
RABBET

JJ

U

V

C

BB

N

C

5-1/4"

1/4" x 3/4"
DADO
(TYP.)

G

YY

DDD

1/4" x 3/8"
RABBET

Note: Mount the bearing and lock ring on the plywood bit to create a top-bearing plywood bit.

overhang the edges of the boxes by 1/4 in. on the sides. Secure with a few brad nails and clamp.

When the columns are complete, join them to the cabinets (**Photo 5**), stand back and admire your work. Then get back to work and install the backs that cover the space between the columns above the cabinets.

Make perfect-fitting top panels

I went all out on the top and made it out of glued-up 1-1/4-in. solid oak (KK). First, glue up the boards to make one solid top. To create tight-fitting access panels with an uninterrupted grain pattern, start with a glued-up blank. Make the blank about an inch oversize in length and 1/2-in. extra in width. Next, rip a 2-in. strip off the back edge and a 4-1/4-in. strip off the front and set them aside. Take the middle section and crosscut the panels and blocks in sequence (see **Figure B**, p. 134). Reassemble the top using the panel cutouts as spacers (**Photo 6**).

After the glue has set, you can remove the panels and trim the edges for a clean fit. The result is a top with access panels that fit perfectly without a lot of fussy fitting. The grain pattern is uninterrupted, which helps keep the panel visibility low.

You could build up 3/4-in. and 1/2-in. plywood to make the top. It's a little more work,

Making elliptical arches

An ellipse is a type of arch that curves gently in the middle and more sharply near the ends. It's a complex shape, but I have a simple trick for marking out perfect ellipses. First, you'll need 3/4 x 3/4-in. marking sticks that are half the length of each ellipse: 17-1/4 in. (for part VV), 16-1/2 in. (WW), 14-1/4 in. (XX) and 13-1/2 in. (YY). Cut a 1/2-in. notch in the end of each stick and drive a nail 3 in. from the notch. Next, cut 6-in.-wide MDF template blanks, one for each of the four different elliptical rails. It's best if the templates are a few inches longer than the rails. Mark a square line across the center of each template and clamp a guide along the mark.

To mark each ellipse, hold the marking stick edge against the guide stick edge that's clamped to your center mark. With the nail against the template, swing the marker away from the guide

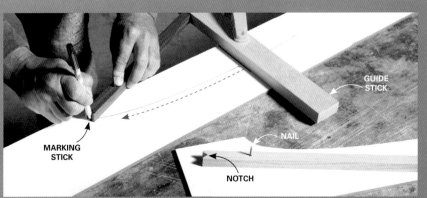

GUIDE STICK

MARKING STICK

NAIL

NOTCH

while the other end of the stick slides along the guide stick edge and the nail slides along the template. The result will be a perfect half ellipse. Reposition the guide stick on the other side of the center mark and repeat for the other half of the ellipse. Carefully cut the ellipse template with a jigsaw or band saw and smooth it with a file and sandpaper.

Use the completed template to mark the rail. Rough-cut the arches, then

clamp the template to the rough-cut rail and run a flush-trim router bit along the template to perfect the arch.

You might be tempted to skip the templates and mark the ellipse right on the rails. But trust me, templates are the way to go. It's much easier to perfect the shape of the arch on 1/4-in. MDF than to do it with solid wood. And once the perfect template is made, you'll get perfect finished parts every time.

Mystery solved

Here's the mystery bookcase compartment not shown on p. 132.

Hang-up box
The cabinet false rail hides a drop-down box that's supported by magnets.

but it will save you some money. To get the 10-ft. length out of 8-ft. plywood, you need to stagger the joints between the 3/4-in. plywood and the 1/2-in. plywood. Cut one length of each to 6 ft. and the other to 4 ft. and butt-joint them end-to-end with biscuits and glue. Glue the 1/2-in. plywood to the 3/4-in. plywood with the butt joints staggered so the 4-ft. length of 1/2-in. falls under the 6-ft. length of 3/4-in plywood. Use screws to clamp the two pieces together, taking care not to leave any screw heads exposed where the top overhangs the cabinets (use clamps in these areas). Rip and cut the access panels in the same manner as with the hardwood top, then add hardwood trim to cover the plywood edges.

> **The label is wrong**
>
> Plywood that's labeled "3/4-inch" is actually a hair thinner than that. A "plywood" router bit is made slightly undersize for a better fit when cutting dadoes.

Build the drawers and doors

Cut the door parts (HH, ZZ, AAA and BBB) and assemble with biscuits. Plywood works fine for the panels, although I think you get a better look with real hardwood panels. The drawers are put together with simple rabbet joints. Assemble the drawers and doors with glue and a brad nailer. I recommend reinforcing the drawer joints with a few trim head screws. The screws guarantee the joints won't pull apart, and the trim heads aren't much bigger than a

finish nail hole. The **Cutting List** for the doors and drawers will give you an exact fit in a perfectly executed cabinet. Measure the openings and adjust your cuts accordingly. Shoot for an exact fit; then plane the door edges for a final fit.

The bottom drawer has a false bottom that hides the last of our secret compartments. There's nothing special about the construction of this drawer other than the fixed false bottom and the extra grooves cut to house it.

The drawer bottoms are sized to stick out past the back of each drawer by 1/4 in. The protruding bottom acts as a drawer stop against the back of the cabinet. This also allows you to easily fine-tune the fit. Simply plane the plywood edge to adjust how far back the drawer sits in the cabinet.

Finish

Take the bookcase apart. Finish-sand everything to 180 grit. I used a Mission Oak stain and topcoated with a wipe-on gel varnish. No need to finish the areas that cover each other such as the outsides of the lower cabinets and the lower parts of the columns.

Enjoy your bookcase and try not to tell everyone about the secret compartments. It's our little secret.

Figure D
Cutting diagram

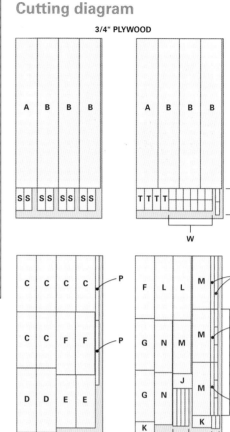

3/4" PLYWOOD

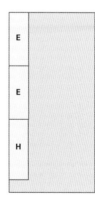

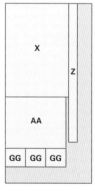

1/4" PLYWOOD

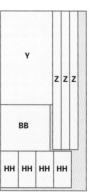

MEET THE EXPERT

Dave Munkittrick is an airline pilot who gave up the sky to become a full-time furniture maker (and a master of secret compartments). It's rumored that his clients include James Bond and Austin Powers. When questioned about this, Dave coldly responds: "If I tell you, I'll have to kill you." So we've stopped asking.

Cutting list

KEY	QTY.	DIMENSIONS	NAME
3/4" plywood			
A	2	12" x 80"	Outside column side
B	6	11-3/4" x 80"	Column side
C	6	11" x 30"	Cabinet side
D	2	11" x 34-1/2"	Drawer cabinet top and center compartment bottom
E	4	11" x 28-1/2"	Door cabinet top and side compartment bottom
F	3	10-3/4" x 33-1/2"	Drawer cabinet shelves
G	2	10-3/4" x 27-1/2"	Door cabinet bottom
H	1	10-3/4" x 32-1/4"	Drawer cabinet compartment lid
J	1	10-3/4" x 8"	Middle drawer divider
K	2	10-3/4" x 6-1/2"	Upper drawer divider
L	2	10-1/8" x 34-3/8"	Adjustable shelf center
M	4	10-1/8" x 28-3/8"	Adjustable shelf side
N	2	2-1/4" x 80"	Adjustable shelf door cabinet
P	2	2" x 34-1/2"	Center compartment front/back
Q	4	2" x 28-1/2"	Side compartment front/back
R	6	2" x 9-1/2"	Compartment side
S	8	4-1/2" x 12"	Column top/bottom shelf
T	4	4-1/2" x 11-3/4"	Column middle shelf
U	4	2-1/4" x 20"	Drop-down box front/back
V	4	2-1/4" x 7"	Drop-down box side
W	6	4" x 6"	Column hangers (3 per false compartment)
1/4" plywood			
X	1	35-1/4" x 50"	Center back
Y	2	29-1/4" x 50"	Side back
Z	4	4-3/4" x 74"	Column back
AA	1	33-3/4" x 27-3/8"	Drawer cabinet back
BB	2	27-3/4" x 34-3/4"	Door cabinet back
CC	1	10-1/2" x 32-1/2"	Lower drawer bottom
DD	2	1-1/2" x 1-3/4"	Center cabinet base side trim
EE	2	9" x 15-5/8"	Middle drawer bottom
FF	1	7-1/2" x 16-1/8"	False back*
GG	3	10-1/2" x 10"	Small drawer bottom
HH	4	9-7/8" x 19-5/8"	Door panel
JJ	2	8-1/2" x 20"	Drop-down box bottom

KEY	QTY.	DIMENSIONS	NAME
1-1/4" oak			
KK	1	16" x 120"	Top (overhangs back by 1/4")
LL	1	2" x 48"	Crown**
3/4" oak			
MM	4	6" x 80"	Column backer (trim bottom for easy removal)
NN	4	1/2" x 3" x 72-1/4"	Column
PP	4	4" x 6"	Column base
QQ	4	1/4" x 2" x 6"	Crown cap
RR	4	1/4" x 3/4" x 3-1/2"	Crown base
SS	1	9" x 33"	Drawer front*
TT	2	7-1/2" x 16-1/8"	Drawer front*
UU	3	6" x 10-1/2"	Drawer front*
VV	1	6" x 34-1/2"	Middle rail top
WW	1	6" x 33"	Middle rail bottom
XX	2	6" x 28-1/2"	Side rails top
YY	2	6" x 27"	Side rails bottom
ZZ	8	2-1/8" x 24"	Door stile
AAA	4	3" x 9-1/4"	Door rail
BBB	4	2" x 9-1/4"	Door rail
CCC	1	1-1/4" x 32"	Shelf edging**
DDD	1	3/4" x 33"	Cabinet edging**
EEE	2	3" x 27"	False rail
FFF	2	1/2" x 3/4" x 20"	Drop-down box lip
GGG	2	1-1/2" x 16-1/8"	False back spacer
HHH	2	2-1/4" x 10-3/4"	Drawer cabinet compartment side
1/2" wood			
JJJ	2	9" x 11"	Bottom drawer sides***
KKK	1	8-1/2" x 32-1/2"	Bottom drawer back***
LLL	4	7-1/2" x 9-1/4"	Drawer sides***
MMM	2	7" x 15-5/8"	Drawer back***
NNN	6	6" x 11"	Drawer sides***
PPP	3	5-1/2" x 10-1/2"	Drawer back***

*Trim to fit

**Cut to fit

***Trim top edge to fit

No-Excuses Bookcase

Think you can't build it? Think again!

There are lots of reasons why a DIYer might not tackle a project like this one. So before building this bookcase, I made a list of them and eliminated each one as I streamlined, simplified and economized the design. The result is a bookcase with the look of a masterpiece, but without the complications. If you've done smaller woodworking projects, you're ready to tackle this one.

Excuses eliminated

Don't have the skills?
The hardest parts of furniture making have been eliminated from this bookcase. There are no miter cuts and no complicated joinery.

Don't have the money?
The total materials bill is about $500. That's about one-third of what you would pay for a store-bought bookcase of similar size and quality.

Don't have the time?
Depending on how fast you work, you can build it in a weekend or two. Add a few hours of finishing work and you're done.

Don't have the tools?
If you have basic woodworking tools, you're ready to build this bookcase. You don't need any exotic or pro-grade equipment.

Don't have the shop space?
This big bookcase consists of three smaller sections that can be assembled in even the smallest shop. You'll need an 8 x 8-ft. area of open floor space to preassemble the sections, but you can do that anywhere (even on your driveway) and then disassemble them to complete the project.

Crown molding

Adjustable shelves

WHAT IT TAKES

TIME:	Two weekends
COST:	$500
SKILL:	Intermediate
TOOLS:	Table saw, drill, miter saw, router or router table

Bur

1 SLICE UP THE PLYWOOD. A circular saw guided by a straight-edge works almost as well as a table saw. For a straightedge, use the factory-cut edge from a sheet of plywood. For clean cuts, use a fresh blade with a tooth count of at least 40.

FACTORY EDGE

2 DRILL SHELF SUPPORT HOLES. Bore the holes using peg-board as a guide. A stop block—simply a wood scrap with a hole drilled through it—prevents drilling too deep. If your pegboard is short, reposition it using a pair of router bits to align and lock the pegboard into holes you've already drilled.

ROUTER BITS

Build the cabinets

First, cut all your 3/4-in. plywood parts (A – K) to size. If shop space doesn't allow you to slice up plywood on a table saw, you can do a fine job with a circular saw and a straightedge (**Photo 1**). Cut rabbets along the back edges of the sides (A and B). These rabbets create a recess so the edges of the backs aren't visible from the sides. I cut the rabbets using a router and a rabbeting bit that makes a 1/4-in. cut. Set the bit to a depth of 3/8 in. Next, drill holes in the bookcase sides (A and B) for the adjustable shelves (**Photo 2**).

With the plywood parts cut and drilled, it's time to assemble the bookcase. All you need is a drill to drive screws. There's no glue to mess with. Most of the screw holes in this bookcase are covered by adjoining pieces. The exposed screws are in the tops and invisible from floor level. If the top of your bookcase will be seen from above (from a staircase, for example), fill the screw holes after final assembly and paint the filler black to match.

Make a couple of I-beam spacers to hold the sides in position while you attach the subtops and subbases (E and J). Build the spacers out of scrap. Be sure the final length of the I-beam holds the sides at the correct outside dimension.

Simply screw the subtops and subbases to the sides (**Photo 3**). The tops and bases (C, D and H) are then positioned and screwed into place. On the smaller side cabinets, remember to keep the tops and bases flush with the cabinet sides where they butt up against the larger center cabinet. The tops and bases overhang the subtops and subbases by 1/4 in. at the back. This creates a rabbet to house the back. Next, cut and fit the backs (L and M).

Trim the tops and bases

I trimmed the parts C, D, E, H and J using one of my favorite tricks: Glue on the raw, square trim first, then shape it with a router. This approach has two advantages: Square stock is easier to cut and clamp than a fancy trim profile, and you don't have to miter the corners.

There are a few steps to take before you glue on and rout the trim. First, fire up your table saw and cut 3/4 x 3/4-in. stock (you'll need about 50 linear ft.). Lay the cabinets on their backs and clamp them together. Fit the corner blocks where the side cabinets meet the center cabinet (see **Photo 4**). These corner blocks allow you to butt the trim into the blocks at inside corners and eliminate the need for miters.

Here's the process: Start with the bases.

Cut and fit the corner blocks (FF and GG) on the bottom of the side cabinets first. Lay them in position. No glue yet. Measure and cut your center cabinet side trim (DD and EE) so it butts up tight to the corner blocks and is flush with the front edge of the plywood (**Photo 4**).

Disassemble the bookcase and attach the trim. Go slow here. Rather than take everything apart at once, take one of the side bookcase tops off and glue and add the trim. Do the same with the other side top, then the subtops and base assemblies. Note that the side trim on parts E and J runs past the back edges by 1/4 in. to hide the backs (L and M).

With the molding stock square, it's easy to lose track of which side is up and what router profile gets put on which piece. I recommend making two piles: one for the ogee profile (subtops and subbases) and one for the simple chamfer (tops and bases). Also, clearly mark which side of the trim gets routed. The underside of the top parts and the top side of the base parts are routed. When you're sure you know which trim gets what cut on which face, go ahead and rout your profiles (**Photo 5**). Use any 45-degree chamfer bit that will cut at least 5/8 in. deep. For the ogee, I used a Bosch No. 85586M. Although you can use a

Figure A
Bookcase overview

Overall Dimensions:
105" wide x 87" tall x
13-3/4" deep

Figure B
Cutting diagram

3/4" birch plywood

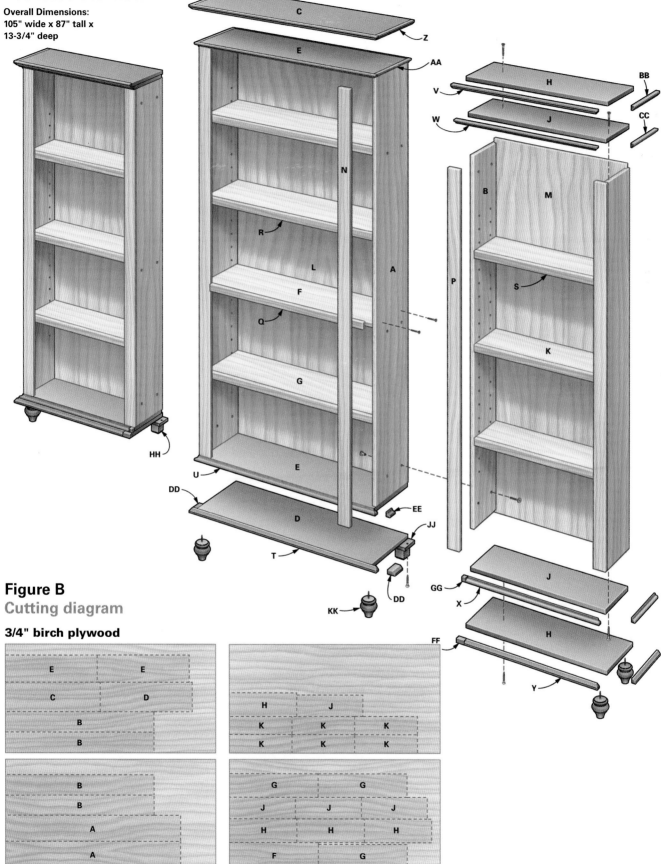

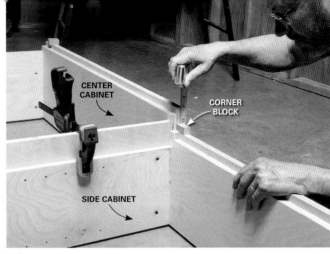

3 **ASSEMBLE THE SHELF BOXES.** Screw the subtops and sub-bases to the sides. A plywood beam spacer takes only a few minutes to make and holds the sides in perfect alignment.

Labels: I-BEAM SPACER, SUBTOP, SIDE

4 **POSITION THE CORNER BLOCKS.** Lay the shelf units on their backs and clamp them together. Place the corner blocks where the side cabinets meet the center cabinet. The blocks allow the trim to meet at inside corners without miters.

Labels: CENTER CABINET, CORNER BLOCK, SIDE CABINET

5 **EDGE THE PLYWOOD, THEN ROUT.** Glue square trim to the plywood, then shape it with a router or router table. This creates perfect outside corners without cutting miters. A backer board prevents splintering at the end of the cut.

Labels: BACKER BOARD, TRIM

6 **DRILL THE FEET.** Bore holes for the dowel screws using a guide to steer the drill bit straight into the foot. The guide is simply two wood scraps glued together to form an "L."

Labels: GUIDE

Materials list

ITEM	QTY.
4' x 8' x 3/4" birch plywood	4
4' x 8' x 1/4" birch plywood	3
1x6 birch boards	40 ft.
Bun feet*	6
3/8" x 3" dowel screws	6
Connector bolts and cap nuts	12
Adjustable shelf supports	
Wood glue	
1-5/8" screws	
Finishing supplies	

*The bun feet (No. 4045) are available at osbornewood.com for $5 each (plus shipping).

handheld router, a router table makes it all easier. To see how to build an inexpensive table, search for "router table" at familyhandyman.com.

With all the trim attached and routed, reassemble the cabinets. It may seem like a pain, but it's the best way to make sure you've done everything right before you finish. Also, having the tops and bases on the cabinets will automatically position the stiles on the cabinets. This is a good time to drill holes and join the side cabinets to the center cabinets with connector bolts.

Separate the three cabinets and glue on the stiles (N and P). While the glue sets, go ahead and drill and mount the feet (**Photo 6**). Be sure the feet are set so the

sides bear down directly onto the feet.

Finish and final assembly

Disassemble the cabinets one last time and sand all parts to 180-grit. Sanding and finishing a collection of flat parts is a breeze compared to working with an assembled bookcase. Prime and paint the upper and lower parts. Satin black spray paint works great. With the finish complete, you're ready to reassemble the bookcase in place. Again, the beauty of this design is that you can take the individual parts to where the bookcase will reside and assemble it there (**Photo 7**).

There, you're done. No excuses.

7 ASSEMBLE IT IN PLACE. You can move the bookcase to its new home in three sections. Or you can make moving it even easier by disassembling each section into small, easy-to-handle parts. Join the sections with connector bolts.

CONNECTOR BOLTS

An easy finish for problem woods

Some types of wood—pine, maple, birch and others—absorb stain unevenly, creating an ugly, blotchy finish. To sidestep that problem, I skipped the initial staining step and used a "glaze" finish instead.

Here's how: First, I brushed on two light coats of gloss polyurethane, sanding lightly after each coat. Then I applied a glaze. The glazing process is just like staining: Brush it on and wipe off the excess. Then add two more coats of polyurethane over the glaze. This process is no more difficult than staining but avoids blotchiness and gives the wood a deeper, richer glow.

Cutting list

KEY	QTY.	DIMENSIONS	NAME
3/4" birch plywood (4 sheets)			
A	2	11-1/2" x 80"	Center cabinet sides
B	4	9" x 68"	Side cabinet sides
C	1	12-15/16" x 43-3/8"	Center cabinet top
D	1	12-15/16" x 42"	Center cabinet base
E	2	12" x 42"	Center cabinet subtop/subbase
F	1	11-1/4" x 40-1/2"	Center cabinet fixed shelf
G	3	10-7/16" x 40-3/8"	Center cabinet adjustable shelves
H	4	10-7/16" x 30-11/16"	Side cabinet tops/bases
J	4	9-1/2" x 30"	Side cabinet subtops/subbases
K	6	8" x 28-1/2"	Side cabinet adjustable shelves
1/4" birch plywood (3 sheets)			
L	1	41-1/4" x 81-1/2"	Center cabinet back
M	2	29-1/4" x 69-1/2"	Side cabinet backs
3/4" birch hardwood			
N	2	2-1/4" x 80"	Center cabinet stiles
P	4	2" x 68"	Side cabinet stiles
Q	1	1-1/2" x 37-1/2"	Center cabinet rail
R	3	1-1/2" x 40-3/8"	Center cabinet adjustable shelf trim
S	6	1-1/4" x 28-1/2"	Side cabinet adjustable shelf trim
T	2	3/4" x 45"	Center cabinet top/base front trim
U	2	3/4" x 43-1/2"	Center subtop/subbase front trim
V	2	3/4" x 31-1/2"	Side cabinet top front trim
W	2	3/4" x 30-3/4"	Side cabinet subtop front trim
X	2	3/4" x 30"	Side cabinet subbase front trim
Y	2	3/4" x 29-7/8"	Side cabinet base front trim
Z	2	3/4" x 13-3/4"	Center cabinet top side trim
AA	2	3/4" x 13"	Center cabinet subtop side trim
BB	4	3/4" x 10-1/2"	Side cabinet top/base side trim
CC	4	3/4" x 9-3/4"	Side cabinet subtop/subbase side trim
DD	2	1-1/2" x 1-3/4"	Center cabinet base side trim
EE	2	3/4" x 1-3/4"	Center cabinet subbase side trim
FF	2	3/4" x 1-1/2"	Side cabinet base corner block
GG	2	3/4" x 3/4"	Side cabinet subbase corner block
2" birch			
HH	2	2-3/4" x 2-3/4" x 3-1/4"	Back feet
JJ	2	4" x 6"	Back feet plates
Soft maple			
KK	6	3-1/4" x 4"	Bun feet

Super-Simple Bookcase

A veteran woodworker and a beginner team up to re-create a classic

Build it yourself and save $151,900!

This bookcase is inspired by a Gustav Stickley model that sold for $12 in 1910. One of the original Stickley models recently sold for $152,000, but you can build ours for about $100.

WHAT IT TAKES

TIME: 12 hours
This is a great weekend project. Our building time was about eight hours, plus a few hours more for final sanding and finishing.

COST: $100
That includes wood, glue, screws and finishes. We used oak boards and plywood. If you choose another species, such as cherry or maple, expect to spend at least $40 more.

SKILL: Beginner

WOODWORKER
This is a great project for anyone who's done some woodworking and is ready to tackle their first real furniture project.

My neighbor, CT, asked me to help him build a bookcase he found in an old Stickley furniture catalog. I love Craftsman furniture and CT is a great neighbor. How could I refuse? We sat down to do a little research and figure out the details. CT wanted a slightly larger bookcase, so we stretched the width from 22 in. to 36.

I told CT we could build it in his garage with nothing more than a table saw, a drill and a pocket hole jig. If you don't own a pocket hole jig, you owe it to yourself to buy one. Pocket screws aren't as strong as most other types of joinery, but they are plenty strong for this bookcase, and you can't beat their speed and simplicity. CT agreed, especially when he found out that for $40 he could buy a complete pocket hole system. For tips on using pocket screws, go to familyhandyman.com and search for "pocket screws." You'll also need at least four pipe clamps for this project, which will cost about $60 altogether.

Wood selection matters

At the home center, we took our time picking through the oak boards. We wanted straight, flat boards, of course, but we also looked closely at grain pattern. Novice woodworkers usually skip this tedious process, but they shouldn't. It has a big impact on the final look of the project. For the legs, we examined the end grain and chose boards with grain that ran diagonally across the ends (see **Photo 4**). This "rift sawn" wood has straight grain on both the face and the edge of the board. ("Plain sawn" boards typically have wilder grain on the face.) Straight grain will give the legs a look that suits the Stickley style.

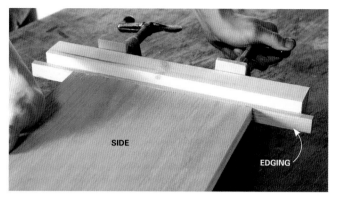

SIDE

EDGING

1 ADD EDGING TO THE SIDES. Cut the plywood box parts to size, then glue strips of wood to the bottom edges of the box sides. This edging keeps the plywood veneer from chipping. Trim off the excess edging with a handsaw and sand it flush with the plywood. Take care not to sand through the thin veneer.

JIG

POCKET HOLES

2 DRILL POCKET HOLES. Pocket hole jigs are super easy to use: Place the jig where you want the holes; clamp and drill. The stepped bit bores a pocket hole and a pilot hole at the same time. The holes on the ends are for attaching the top to the sides. The holes along the front and back are used to attach the box to the face frame.

STEPPED BIT

3 ASSEMBLE THE BOX. Drive in the pocket screws with a drill. To avoid stripping the screws in plywood and softwoods, switch to a screwdriver for the final tightening. Long clamps make assembly easier, but they aren't absolutely necessary.

Figure A
Bookcase

Overall Dimensions:

36" wide, 16" deep, 42" tall

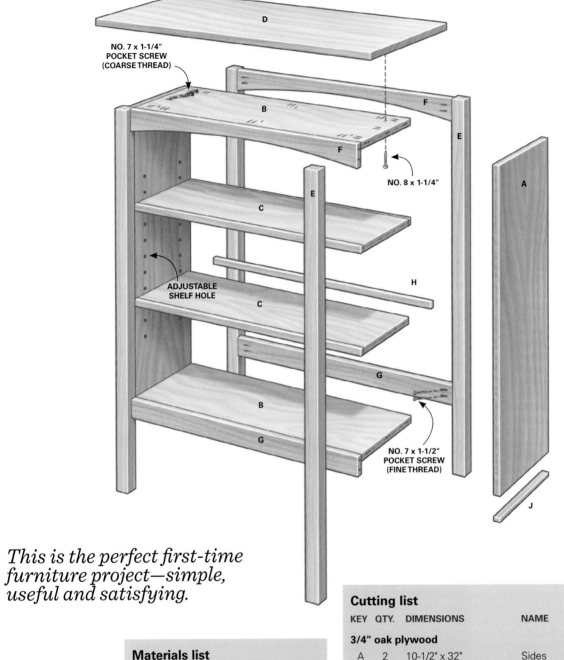

NO. 7 x 1-1/4"
POCKET SCREW
(COARSE THREAD)

NO. 8 x 1-1/4"

ADJUSTABLE
SHELF HOLE

NO. 7 x 1-1/2"
POCKET SCREW
(FINE THREAD)

This is the perfect first-time furniture project—simple, useful and satisfying.

Materials list

ITEM	QTY.
3/4" oak plywood	4' x 8'
1x4 solid oak	24'
1x10 solid oak	6'
Wood glue	
Pocket screws	
Stain	
Polyurethane	
Adjustable shelf supports	

Cutting list

KEY	QTY.	DIMENSIONS	NAME
3/4" oak plywood			
A	2	10-1/2" x 32"	Sides
B	2	10-1/2" x 29-3/4"	Top and bottom
C	2	9-1/2" x 29-5/8"	Adjustable shelves
3/4" oak			
D	1	16" x 36"	Top
E	4	1-1/2" x 1-1/2" x 41-1/4"	Legs (double up 3/4" stock
F	2	2-1/2" x 29"	Arched rails
G	2	2" x 29"	Bottom rails
H	4	1/2" x 29-5/8"	Edging for adjustable shelves
J	2	3/8" x 10-1/2"	Bottom edge sides

4 GLUE UP THE LEG BLANKS. Sandwich two 1x4s together and later cut the legs from this stock. Use scrap wood "cauls" to distribute clamping pressure evenly.

CAUL

LEG BLANK

ARCHED RAIL

5 MARK THE ARCHES. Make an "arch bow" — simply a 3/16-in.-thick strip of wood with slots cut into both ends. Hook a knotted string in one slot, tighten the string to bend the bow and tie off the other end.

Also, glue joints disappear in straight grain wood, so the legs—which are made from sandwiched boards—look better. For that same reason, we chose boards with straight grain along the edges to form the bookcase top (see **Photo 11**).

Build a box and add face frames

After cutting the plywood box parts to size (see the **Cutting List**), we added the 3/8-in.-thick edging (J) to protect the bottom of the cabinet sides (A; **Photo 1**). We applied the same edging (H) to the plywood shelves (C). Then we drilled the pocket holes in the box top and bottom (B; **Photo 2**). After that, we drilled holes for adjustable shelf supports in the plywood sides and—finally—we assembled the box (**Photo 3**).

With the box assembled, we turned our attention to building two identical face frames. (Since the bookcase has no back, it needed two face frames.) Unlike a standard face frame, which has vertical stiles, our face frame has legs (E) made from two layers of 3/4-in.-thick boards. We glued up the leg blanks (**Photo 4**), ripped both blanks into two legs and sanded out the saw marks.

Like many other beginning woodworkers, CT figured that curves were complicated, so he was a little intimidated by the arched upper rails (F). But I showed

6 CUT THE ARCHES. For a smooth cut, use a fine-tooth blade and move slowly, putting only light forward pressure on the saw. If your saw is variable speed, cut at full speed. If the saw has orbital action, switch it off.

7 SAND THE ARCHES. Smooth the arches with an orbital sander. Keep the sander moving so you don't sand too deep in one spot and create a wave in the curve.

8 **ASSEMBLE THE FACE FRAME.** Clamp the face frame together and drive in pocket screws. Pocket screws rarely strip out in hardwood, so you can skip the screwdriver and use only a drill.

9 **DRY-FIT THE FACE FRAMES.** Align the face frames, pocket-screw them to the box and check the fit. If your alignment is a bit off, you can drill new pocket holes and reattach the frames. If the fit is right, you're ready to remove the face frames and add glue.

FACE FRAME

10 **GLUE ON THE FACE FRAMES.** Apply a light bead of glue over the box edges and screw on the face frames as before. There are no screws fastening the legs to the box sides, so you'll need to clamp them.

him a neat trick for marking out a shallow arch (**Photo 5**). His curved cut (**Photo 6**) wasn't perfect, but a little sanding smoothed it out (**Photo 7**).

With the rails and legs complete, we were ready to drill pocket holes in the rails and assemble the face frames (**Photo 8**). It's easy to make mistakes during face frame assembly, so—before driving any screws—we clamped the frames together, then set them on the box to make sure everything was aligned correctly. We used similar caution when we finally attached the face frames to the box: We dry-fitted the face frames (**Photo 9**) before we glued and clamped them into place (**Photo 10**).

Top it off and finish up

CT figured that making the top (D) was a simple matter of edge-gluing two boards together (**Photo 11**). That's mostly true, but there are a few tricks that make it easier. First, always do a complete dry run by clamping up the boards without glue. That will alert you to any clamping or alignment problems before it's too late. Second, start with boards that are an inch or so longer than the final top. It's much easier to trim the boards later than to fuss with edge alignment during glue-up. Finally, to ensure that the tops of the boards meet flat and flush, use pocket screws on the underside of the top. A couple of pocket screws won't provide enough pressure to substitute for clamps, but they will hold the board flush while you crank on the clamps.

When the top was trimmed to size and sanded, CT drilled elongated holes (**Photo 12**) and screwed on the top (**Photo 13**). When I asked him to remove the top, he gave me a look that said, "What's the point of that?" I had two answers: Finishing is always easier when furniture is disassembled, and more important, both sides of the top need to be finished. Wood absorbs and releases moisture as humidity changes. Wood finishes slow that process. So wood with a finish on only one side will end up with differing moisture levels in the finished and unfinished sides. That leads to warping.

So we finished both sides of the top (and the rest of the bookcase) with a coat of General Finishes Mission stain followed by polyurethane. That's it. Not bad for a weekend of woodworking. I wonder how much CT's bookcase will be worth in a hundred years….

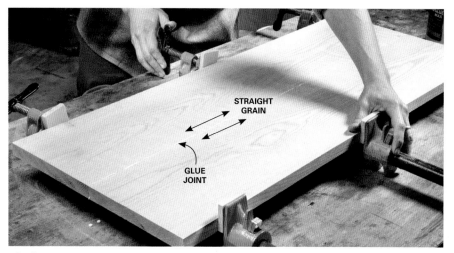

11 GLUE UP THE TOP. Edge-glue the boards together to form the top. Choose boards that have straight grain lines along one edge and place those edges together. A glue joint with straight grain on both sides is almost invisible.

12 DRILL SLOTTED SCREW HOLES. Drill screw holes in the shelf box to fasten the bookcase top. Rock the bit back and forth to bore enlonged slots that will allow the top to swell with changes in humidity.

13 SCREW ON THE TOP FROM BELOW. Drive the screws snug, but not so tight that they won't allow for seasonal wood movement. Remove the top for sanding and finishing.

Kitchen Cabinet Rollouts

Base cabinets have the least convenient storage space in the entire kitchen. Rollouts solve that problem. They make organizing and accessing your cabinet contents back-friendly and frustration free.

Here's how to retrofit nearly any base cabinet with rollouts that'll work as well as or better than any factory-built units.

It's really very easy. Once you take measurements, you can build the rollout drawer (**Photos 2–6**), its "carrier" (**Photos 7–9**),

and attach the drawer slides (**Photos 6** and **7**), all in your shop. Mounting the unit in the cabinet is simple (**Photos 10–12**). You'll also learn how to construct a special rollout for recycling or trash (**Photos 14** and **15**).

The project will go faster if you have a table saw and miter saw to cut out all the pieces. A circular saw and cutting guide will work too; it'll just take a little longer. You can build a pair of rollouts in a Saturday morning.

What wood products to buy

These rollout drawers are made entirely of 1/2-in. Baltic birch plywood. Baltic birch is favored by cabinetmakers because it's "void free," meaning that the thin veneers of the plywood core are solid wood. Therefore sanded edges will look smooth and attractive. If your local home center doesn't stock Baltic birch, find it at any hardwood specialty store.

If you choose, you can make the sides of the rollout drawers from any 1x4 solid wood that matches your cabinets and then finish to match (use plywood for the bases). But if you use 3/4-in. material for the sides, subtract 3 in. from the opening to size the rollout (not 2-1/2 in., as described in **Photo 2** and **Figure A**).

The drawer carriers (**Figure A**) are made from pine 1x4s for the sides (**Photo 7**) and 1/4-in. MDF (medium-density fiberboard) for the bottoms (**Photo 9**). The MDF keeps the drawer bottom spaced properly while you shim and attach it to the cabinet sides. It can be removed and reused for other carriers after installation. If MDF isn't available, substitute any other 1/4-in. hardboard or plywood.

Side-mounted slides are the best choice among drawer slide options. Their ball-bearing mechanisms and precise fit make for smooth-operating drawers that hold 90 lbs. or more. Shown here are 22-in. full-extension side-mount drawer slides that have a 90-lb. weight rating. That means they'll be sturdy enough even for a drawer full of canned goods. Full-extension slides allow the rollout to extend completely past the cabinet front so you can access all the contents. You can find slides at any home center or well-stocked hardware store.

Measure carefully before you build

Nearly all standard base cabinets are 23-1/4 in. deep from the inside of the face frame (**Photo 1**) to the back of the cabinet. So in most cases, 22-in.-long rollout drawer and carrier sides will clear with room to spare. Check your cabinets to make sure that 22-in. rollouts will work. If you have shallower cabinets, subtract whatever is necessary when you build your rollouts and their carriers (see **Figure A**).

Then measure the cabinet width. The drawer has to clear the narrowest part of the opening (**Photo 1**). When taking this measurement, include hinges that protrude into the opening, the edge of the door attached to the hinges, and even the doors that won't open completely because they hit nearby appliances or other

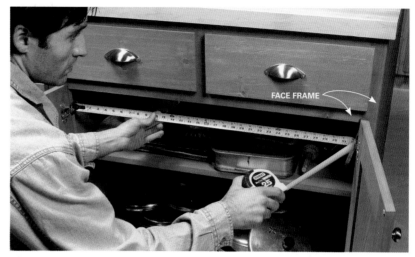

1 Open the cabinet doors to their widest point and measure the narrowest part of the cabinet opening (usually at the hinges).

Figure A
Standard rollout

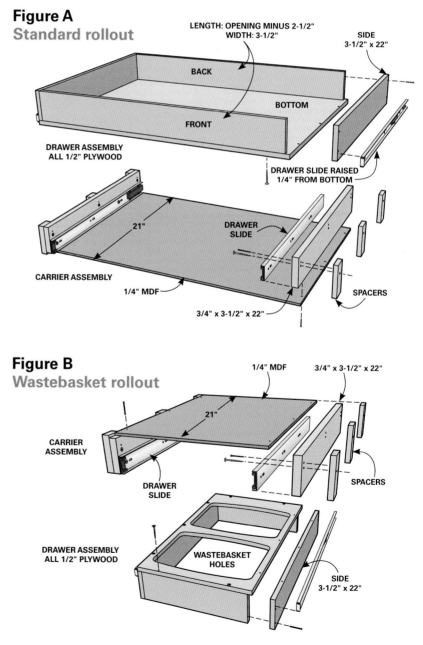

Figure B
Wastebasket rollout

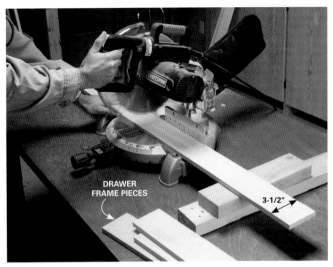

2 Rip 1/2-in. plywood down to 3-1/2 in. wide and cut two 22-in. lengths (drawer sides) and two more to the measured width minus 2-1/2 in. (drawer front and back; Figure A).

DRAWER FRAME PIECES

3-1/2"

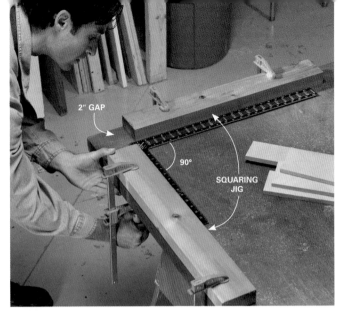

3 Clamp or screw two straight 24-in. 2x4s to the corner of a flat surface to use as a squaring jig. Use a carpenter's square to ensure squareness. Leave a 2-in. gap at the corner.

2" GAP

90°

SQUARING JIG

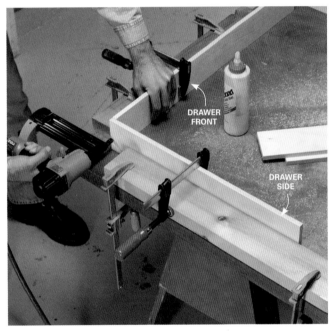

4 Spread wood glue on the ends and clamp a drawer side and front in place, then pin the corner together with three 1-1/4-in. brads. Repeat for the other three corners.

DRAWER FRONT

DRAWER SIDE

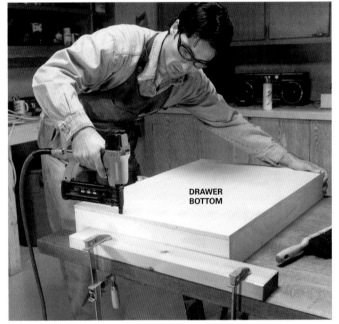

5 Cut a 1/2-in. plywood bottom to size. Apply a thin bead of glue to the bottom edges, and nail one edge of the plywood flush with a side, spacing nails every 4 in. Then push the frame against the jig to square it and nail the other three edges.

DRAWER BOTTOM

cabinets. Plan on making the drawer front and rear parts 2-1/2 in. shorter than the opening (**Figure A**).

Shown here are drawers with 3-1/2-in.-high sides, but you can customize your own. Plan on higher sides for lightweight plastic storage containers or other tall or tippy items, and lower sides for stable, heavier items like small appliances.

Drawer slides aren't as confusing as they may seem

At first glance, drawer slides are pretty hard to figure out, but after you install one set, you'll be an expert. They're sold in pairs and each of the pairs has two parts. The "drawer part" attaches to the rollout while the "cabinet part" attaches to the carrier. To separate them for mounting, slide them out to full length and then push, pull or depress a plastic release to separate the two parts. The cabinet part, which always encloses the drawer part, is the larger of the two, and the mounting screw hole locations will be shown in the directions. (Screws are included with the drawer slides.) The oversized holes allow for some adjustment, but if you follow the instructions, you shouldn't have to fuss with fine-tuning later. When mounting the slides, you should make sure to hold them flush with the front of the rollout drawer and carrier sides (**Photos 6** and **7**). The front of the drawer part usually has a bent metal stop that faces the front of the drawer.

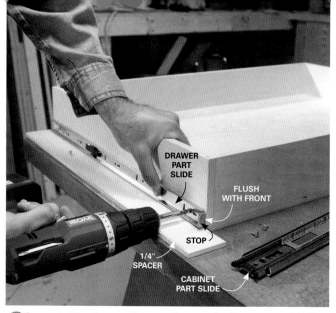

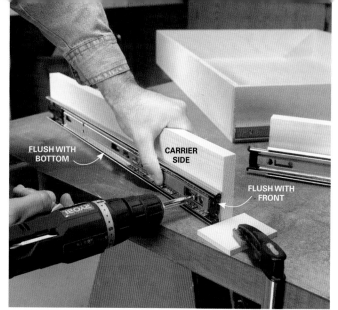

6 Separate the drawer slides and space the drawer part 1/4 in. up from the bottom. Hold it flush to the front and screw it to the rollout side.

7 Mount the carrier part of the drawer slide flush with the bottom and front of the carrier sides.

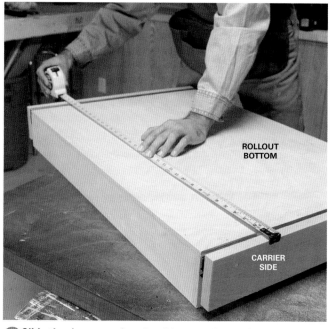

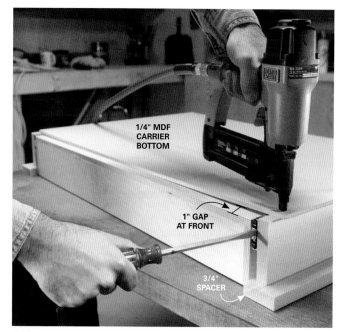

8 Slide the drawer and carrier sides together and measure the carrier width. Cut 1/4-in. MDF to that width and 1 in. less than the carrier depth (usually 21 in.).

9 Rest the carrier assembly on 3/4-in.-thick spacers, pull the carrier sides slightly away from the drawer, then nail on the carrier bottom (no glue).

Assembling parts and finishing the rollouts

It's important to build the rollout drawers perfectly square for them to operate properly. **Photos 3** and **4** show a simple squaring jig that you can clamp to a corner of any workbench to help. Use the jig to nail the frame together, but even more important, to hold the frame square when you nail on the bottom panel. If it hangs over the sides even a little, the drawer slides won't work smoothly.

Use 1-1/4-in. brads for all of the assembly. Glue the drawer parts together but not the bottom of the carrier. It only serves as a temporary spacer for mounting. (After mounting the carrier

and drawer, you can remove it if it catches items on underlying drawers or even reuse it for other carriers.) If you'd like to finish the rollout for a richer look and easier cleaning, sand the edges with 120-grit paper and apply a couple of coats of water-based polyurethane before mounting the slides.

To figure the spacer thickness, rest the lower carrier on the bottom of the shelf, push it against one side of the cabinet and measure the gap on the other (**Photo 10**). Rip spacers to half that measurement and cut six of them to 3-1/2 in. long. Slip the spacers between both sides of the carrier to check the fit. They should slide in snugly but not tightly. Recut new spacers if needed. In out-of-square cabinets, you may have to custom-cut

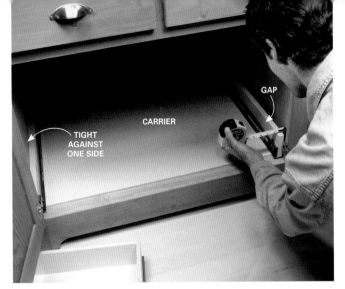

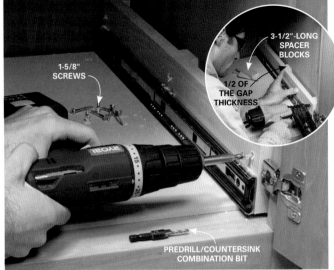

10 Remove the drawer, tip the carrier into the cabinet and push the carrier against one side. Measure the gap and rip six 3-1/2-in.-long spacers to half of the thickness.

11 Nail the spacers to the center and each end of the carrier sides (not into the cabinet; see inset photo). Then predrill and screw the carrier sides to the cabinet in the center of each shim. Slide the drawer back into place.

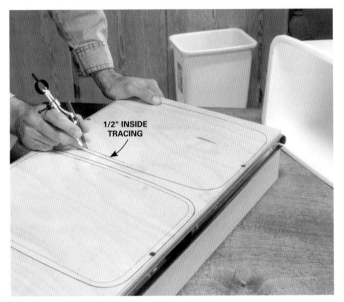

12 Cut plywood spacers to temporarily support the upper rollout and set them onto the carrier below. Rest the second carrier on the spacers and install it as shown in Photo 11.

13 Build an upside-down version of the carrier and rollouts for the wastebasket drawer (Figure B). Center and trace around the rim of the wastebasket(s). Use a compass to mark the opening 1/2 in. smaller.

spacers for each of the three pairs of spacers, so check each of the three spacer positions. It's easiest to tack the spacers to the rollouts to hold them in place before predrilling 1/8-in. holes and running the screws through the rollout frames and spacers and into the cabinet sides (**Photo 11**).

Slip the rollout into its carrier and check for smooth operation. If you followed the process, it should work perfectly. If it binds, it's probably because the spacers are too wide or narrow. Pull out the carrier, remove the spacers and start the spacer process all over again.

The best way to level and fasten the upper rollout is to support it on temporary plywood spacers (**Photo 12**). The photo shows pieces of plywood cut 7 in. high. In reality, the exact height is up to you. If, for example, you want to store tall boxes of cereal on the bottom rollout and shorter items on the top, space the

top rollout higher. You can even build and install three or more rollouts in one cabinet for mega storage of short items like cans, cutlery or beverages. (Those now-obsolete shelves you're replacing with rollouts are good stock to use for your spacers.) Again, pin the spacers in place with a brad or two to hold them while you're predrilling and screwing the carriers to the cabinet sides. Be sure to select screw lengths that won't penetrate exposed cabinet sides! In most cases, 1-5/8-in. screws are the best choice. Strive for 1/2-in. penetration into the cabinet sides. Countersink the heads as far as necessary to get the proper penetration.

Building wastebasket rollouts

Wastebasket rollouts are just upside-down versions of standard rollouts. That is, the carrier is mounted on the top rather than the bottom of the rollout and the slides are positioned at the bottom

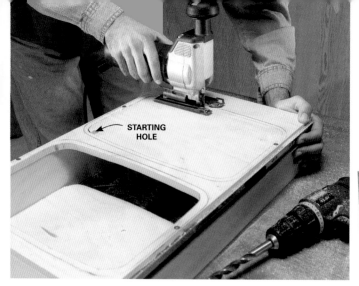

14 Drill 1/2-in. starting holes and cut the openings with a jigsaw.

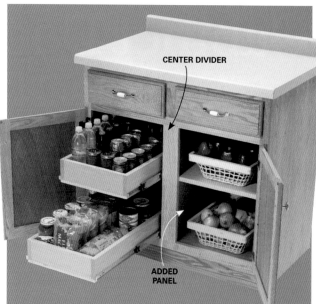

15 Mount the wastebasket carrier and drawer as shown in Photos 10 and 11.

edge of the carrier sides. That lets the wastebasket lip clear the MDF. Follow **Figure B** on p. 151 for the details.

This wastebasket rollout is built inside an 18-in.-wide cabinet, so it fits two plastic containers back to back. If you only have a 15-in. cabinet to work with, you may be limited to one container mounted sideways. Buy your containers ahead of time to fit your opening.

With some wastebasket rollouts, you may need to knock the MDF free from the carriers after mounting so the wastebasket lips will clear. That's OK; it won't affect operation.

It may not always work to center rollout assemblies in all openings with equal spacers on each side. That's especially true with narrow single cabinets that only have one pair of hinges. It's best to test things before permanent mounting. But if you make a mistake, it's a simple matter to unscrew the assembly, adjust the shims and remount everything.

Building rollouts in cabinets with center dividers

Many two-door cabinets have a center divider (photo above), which calls for a slightly different strategy. You can still build rollouts, but they'll be narrower versions on each side of the divider. (Check to be sure they won't be so narrow that they're impractical.) The key is to install a 3/4-in. plywood, particleboard or MDF panel between the center divider and the cabinet back to support the carriers.

Cut the panel to fit loosely between the divider and the cabinet back and high enough to support the top rollout position. Center the panel on the back side and middle of the divider and screw it into place with 1-in. angle brackets (they're completely out of sight). Use a carpenter's square to position the panel perfectly centered and vertical on the cabinet back and anchor it there, again using angle brackets. Measure, build and install the rollouts as shown here.

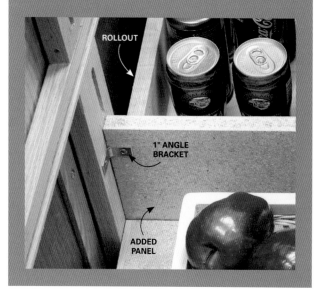

Cabinet Door Rack

A super-simple solution for cabinet chaos

S ome people think black holes exist only in outer space. Not true. There's probably one under your kitchen sink. Place detergent, cleaners or sponges under there and they disappear forever—or at least become really, really hard to find.

Here's a simple project to bring order to the chaos: a door-mounted storage rack. You can modify this basic idea to organize other cabinets too.

WHAT IT TAKES

TIME: 2 hours
COST: $10 to $20
SKILL: Beginner
TOOLS: Circular saw, drill, miter saw or jigsaw

Planning and materials

As you plan your rack, consider building multiple racks. Building two or three doesn't take much more time than building one. Also think about (and measure!) the items you want your rack to hold. You may want to mount the upper shelf a little higher or lower than we did.

Most home centers carry everything you'll need, including 1/4-in.-thick wood strips in species like pine, oak and poplar. If you don't find thin material alongside the other lumber, look for "mull strip" or "mullion" in the millwork aisle. The wood quantities on our **Materials List** will yield a rack sized for most cabinet doors, but you may need a little more or a little less.

How to do it

Begin by looking inside your cabinet. With the door closed, this rack will project 3-3/4 in. into the interior. Make sure the installed rack won't bump into your sink, pipes, garbage disposal or other fixed object.

Measure the cabinet door and opening to determine the measurements of the sides and shelves (**Photo 1**). Mark the position of the upper shelf on the sides: We positioned ours 12 in. from the bottom, but you can adjust the location based on your needs. Secure the shelves to the sides using 2-in. screws and finish washers (**Photo 2**). Drill holes in the four cross slats 3/8 in. from the ends and fasten them to the sides with 3/4-in. screws.

With the rack assembled, we gave it two coats of lacquer. Lacquer is a durable finish, dries in minutes and comes in spray cans for quick, no-mess application.

After the finish dries, screw the four L-brackets to the sides of the racks, making sure to position them so they won't interfere with the door hinges. Clamp the rack to the door, predrill mounting holes using the L-brackets as guides, and secure the rack to the door (**Photo 3**). Put a strip of tape on the floor of the cabinet, 4 in. back from the door, to indicate a "No Parking" zone for items stored inside.

Figure A
Door rack

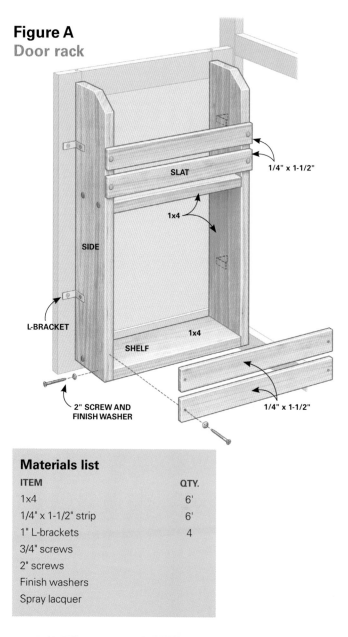

SLAT

1/4" x 1-1/2"

SIDE

1x4

L-BRACKET

1x4

SHELF

2" SCREW AND
FINISH WASHER

1/4" x 1-1/2"

Materials list

ITEM	QTY.
1x4	6'
1/4" x 1-1/2" strip	6'
1" L-brackets	4
3/4" screws	
2" screws	
Finish washers	
Spray lacquer	

1 MEASURE TO SIZE THE RACK. Measure the width of the door and cut the rack shelves 4-1/2 in. shorter than that measurement. Measure the height of the cabinet opening and cut the rack sides 1 in. shorter.

2 BUILD THE RACK. Mark the location of the top shelf on the sides. Drill screw holes and fasten the sides to the shelves using 2-in. screws and finish washers. Add the slats, apply a finish and screw brackets to the rack.

3 MOUNT THE RACK. Center the rack on the door and drill screw holes. Wrap tape around the drill bit to act as a depth guide so you don't drill through the door. Clamps aren't absolutely necessary for this step, but they're a big help.

Ultimate
Container Storage

No more digging for the right lid!

It's always a challenge to find matching containers and lids. This rollout solves the problem by keeping them all neatly organized and easily accessible. The full-extension drawer slides are the key.

To simplify tricky drawer slide installation, we've designed an ingenious carrier system that allows you to mount the slides and make sure everything is working smoothly before the unit is mounted in the cabinet.

Tools and materials

Our 24-in. base cabinet required a 4 x 4-ft. sheet of 1/2-in.-thick plywood for the rollout, plus a 2 x 3-ft. scrap of 3/4-in. plywood for the carrier. Yours may require more or less. We found high-quality birch plywood at a home center for this project. If you have trouble finding nice plywood, consider ordering Baltic birch or ApplePly plywood from a home center or local lumberyard. The carrier fits under the rollout and isn't very conspicuous, so almost any flat piece of 3/4-in. plywood will work for that.

In addition to the lumber, you'll need a pair of 22-in. full-extension ball-bearing slides (about $22 at home centers or woodworking supply stores) and a 1/4-in. aluminum rod.

We used a table saw to cut the plywood parts, but if you're careful to make accurate cuts, a circular saw will work. You'll need a jigsaw with a plywood-cutting blade to cut the curves on the sides and dividers. We used a finish nail gun and 1-1/4-in.-long brad nails to connect the parts, but you could substitute trim-head screws if you don't mind the larger holes they leave.

Measure the base cabinet

Most base cabinets are about 23 in. deep and will accommodate this rollout, but measure yours to be sure. If the measurement from the back of the face frame to the back of the cabinet is less than 22 in., you'll have to build a shallower rollout and use shorter drawer slides.

The other critical measurement is the width. Measure the clear opening width; that is, the width from any protruding hinge or door parts to the opposite side of the cabinet opening (**Photo 1**). Subtract 3 in. from this measurement to determine the width of parts B, C, D and E.

WHAT IT TAKES

TIME: 1 day

COST: $65

SKILL: Beginner to intermediate

TOOLS: Table or circular saw, jigsaw, drill and 1/4-in. bit, hand tools. A brad nail gun simplifies the construction.

1 MEASURE THE OPENING. Measure from any protruding hinges or door parts to the opposite side to find the opening width. Also check to make sure the cabinet is at least 22 in. deep.

2 CUT THE SIDE PANELS. Cut each panel to size. Then cut the notch to form the L-shape. Start with a table saw or circular saw for the straight cuts. Finish the inside corner with a jigsaw.

3 CUT THE CURVES. Mark the curves on the side panels by tracing along a gallon paint can. Mark the dividers using a quart-size paint can. Then cut with a jigsaw.

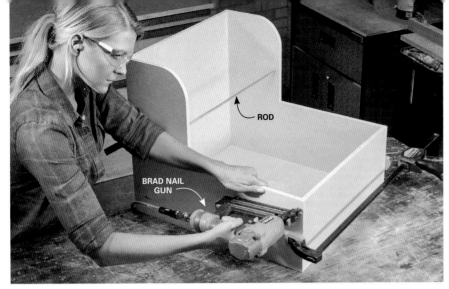

4 ASSEMBLE THE ROLLOUT. Glue and clamp the parts together. Don't forget to install the rod. Align the edges by tapping on the panels with your hand or a hammer. Then nail the parts together.

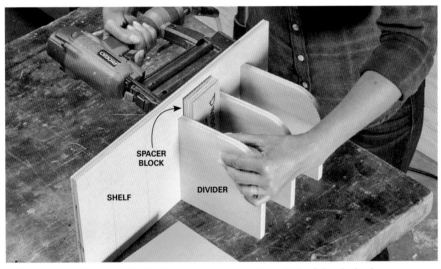

5 NAIL THE DIVIDERS TO THE SHELF. Cut a spacer the width of the desired space between dividers and use it to position the dividers as you nail them to the shelf.

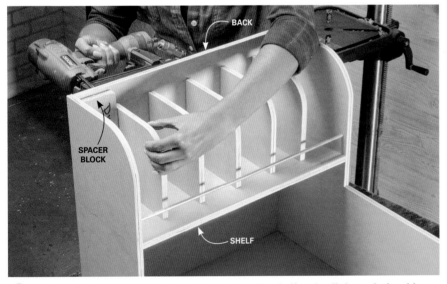

6 NAIL THE DIVIDERS TO THE ROLLOUT. Position the shelf and nail through the sides into the shelf. Then use the spacer block to align the dividers and nail through the back.

Cut out the parts

After adjusting the size of parts B, C, D and E for the cabinet width, you can cut out all the parts except the carrier bottom. If you're using a table saw, make partial cuts to form the L-shaped sides. But remember, you can't see how far the blade is cutting on the underside, so be sure to stop short of your inside corner marks by at least an inch. **Photo 2** shows how to complete the cut with a jigsaw.

Trace along the edge of a 1-gallon paint can to draw the radius for the curve on the side panels. Trace along a quart-size can to draw the radius on the dividers. Cut the curves on the sides and dividers with a jigsaw (**Photo 3**). Smooth the curved cuts with 100-grit sandpaper.

Build the rollout

Mark the location of the 1/4-in. rod on the side panels using **Figure A** as a guide. Wrap tape around a 1/4-in. drill bit 1/4 in. from the end to use as a depth guide while drilling. Drill 1/4-in.-deep holes at the marks. Use a hacksaw to cut an aluminum rod 1/2 in. longer than the width of the bottom.

Apply wood glue to all edges that meet, and arrange the sides, bottom, front and back on a workbench and clamp them together. Work the aluminum rod into the holes. Tap the parts with a hammer to align the edges perfectly before connecting them with brad nails (**Photo 4**). Take your time aiming the nail gun to avoid nail blowouts.

Finish the rollout by adding the dividers. First decide how many dividers you want and calculate the width of the space between the dividers. Cut a spacer block to that dimension and use it as a guide to install the dividers. Attach the dividers to the shelf (**Photo 5**). Then measure down 7-1/2 in. from the top and make marks to indicate the top edge of the divider shelf. Line up the divider assembly with these marks and nail it in. Draw divider center lines on the back of the rollout as a nailing guide. Then attach the dividers (**Photo 6**).

Drawer slides require 1/2-in. clearance on each side, so making the carrier exactly 1 in. wider than the rollout will result in a perfect fit. Measure the width of the completed rollout and add exactly 1 in. to

Cutting list

KEY	QTY.	MATERIAL	DIMENSIONS	PART
A	2	1/2" plywood	1/2" x 22" x 18"	Sides
B	1	1/2" plywood	1/2" x 7-1/2" x 18"	Front
C	1	1/2" plywood	1/2" x 22" x 18"	Bottom
D	1	1/2" plywood	1/2" x 17-1/2" x 18"	Back
E	1	1/2" plywood	1/2" x 7-1/2" x 18"	Shelf
F	5*	1/2" plywood	1/2" x 6" x 6"	Dividers
G	1	3/4" plywood	3/4" x 20" x 22"	Carrier bottom
H	2	3/4" plywood	3/4" x 2-3/4" x 22"	Carrier sides

Note: These sizes are for a 24-in.-wide base cabinet. To fit your cabinet, adjust the sizes according to the instructions in the article.

Materials list

ITEM	QTY.
1/2" x 4' x 4' plywood	1
3/4" x 2' x 3' plywood	1
Pair of 22" full-extension slides	1
36" x 1/4" aluminum rod	1
Small package of 1-1/4" brad nails	1

determine the width of the carrier bottom. Cut the carrier bottom from 3/4-in. plywood. Then screw the carrier sides to the carrier bottom to prepare the carrier for mounting the drawer slides.

Mount the slides

Follow the instructions included with your drawer slides to separate the slides into two parts: a channel and a rail. Usually, pressing down on a plastic lever releases the parts and allows you to separate them. Screw the rails to the drawer (**Photo 7**) and the channels to the carrier sides (**Photo 8**).

When you're done installing the slides, check the fit by carefully aligning the rails with the channels and sliding them together. The rollout should glide easily on the ball-bearing slides. If the slides seem too tight, you can adjust the fit by removing one of the carrier sides and slipping a thin cardboard shim between the carrier side and carrier bottom before reassembling them.

Mount the rollout in the cabinet

Photo 9 shows fitting the carrier assembly into the cabinet. There will be a little side-to-side play, so you can adjust the position to clear the hinge and door. This will probably require you to offset the carrier slightly away from the hinge side. Screw the carrier to the bottom of the cabinet and you're ready to install the rollout (**Photo 10**). Since you've already checked the fit, it should operate perfectly. Now load it up with containers and lids and enjoy your neatly organized container rollout.

Figure A
Rollout

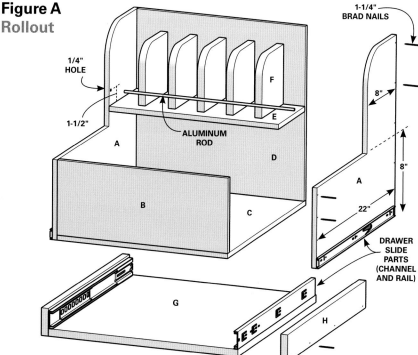

7 SCREW THE DRAWER SLIDE TO THE ROLLOUT. Separate the drawer slides and attach the rail to the rollout. Align the rail flush to the bottom and flush to the front before driving the screws.

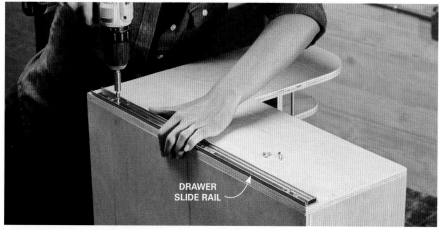

CARRIER

DRAWER SLIDE
CHANNEL

8 SCREW THE DRAWER SLIDE CHANNEL TO THE CARRIER. Rest the drawer slide channel on the carrier and align the front flush to the front of the carrier side.

9 INSTALL THE CARRIER. Position the carrier so that the rollout will clear any hinge or door parts. Drive screws through the carrier bottom into the cabinet.

10 INSTALL THE ROLLOUT. Line up the rails and channels and slide the rollout into the cabinet. Slide it back and forth a few times to make sure it rolls smoothly.

Small-Closet Organizer

Store more in your tiny closet

Most bedroom closets suffer from lack of organization—stuff on the floor; a long, overloaded closet rod; and a precariously stacked, sagging shelf. The simple shelving system shown here cleans up that clutter. It provides a home for shoes; several cubbies for loose clothing, folded shirts, sweaters or small items; and a deeper (16-in.-wide) top shelf to house the stuff that keeps falling off the narrow shelf. Besides the storage space it provides, the center tower stiffens the shelf above it as well as the clothes rod, since it uses two shorter rods rather than a long one.

You can cut and assemble this entire shelving system from a single sheet of plywood (for a 6-ft.-long closet). Birch plywood is used because it's relatively inexpensive yet takes a nice finish. The edges are faced with 1x2 maple for strength and a more attractive appearance. The bottom shelves roll out for easier access.

The key tool for this project is a circular saw with a cutting guide for cutting the plywood into nice straight pieces (**Photo 1**). An air-powered brad nailer or finish nailer makes the assembly go much faster, and a miter saw helps produce clean cuts. But neither is absolutely necessary.

Cut the birch plywood to size

Rip the plywood into three 15-3/4-in. by 8-ft. pieces (**Photo 1**), then cut the sides and shelves from these with a shorter cutting guide. For an average-size closet—6 ft. wide with a 5-1/2-ft.-high top shelf—cut all the sides and shelves from one piece of 3/4-in. plywood. Making the shelving wider means settling for fewer shelves/trays or buying additional plywood. Be sure to support

BEFORE   AFTER

the plywood so the pieces won't fall after completing a cut, and use a guide to keep the cuts perfectly straight. Use a plywood blade in a circular saw to minimize splintering. Cut slowly on the crosscuts, and make sure the good side of the plywood is down—the plywood blade makes a big difference, but the thin veneer will splinter if you rush the cut.

Mark and cut the baseboard profile on the plywood sides, using a profile gauge (**Photo 2**) or a trim scrap to transfer the shape, or remove the baseboard rather than cutting the plywood and reinstalling it later. Either method works fine.

1/2" PARTICLE-BOARD GUIDE

2x4 SUPPORTS

BEST SIDE FACING DOWN

1 Cut the sheet of plywood into three equal widths using a saw guide. Then crosscut the sections into the pieces shown in Figure A, p. 165, using a shorter guide.

Figure A
Small-closet organizer

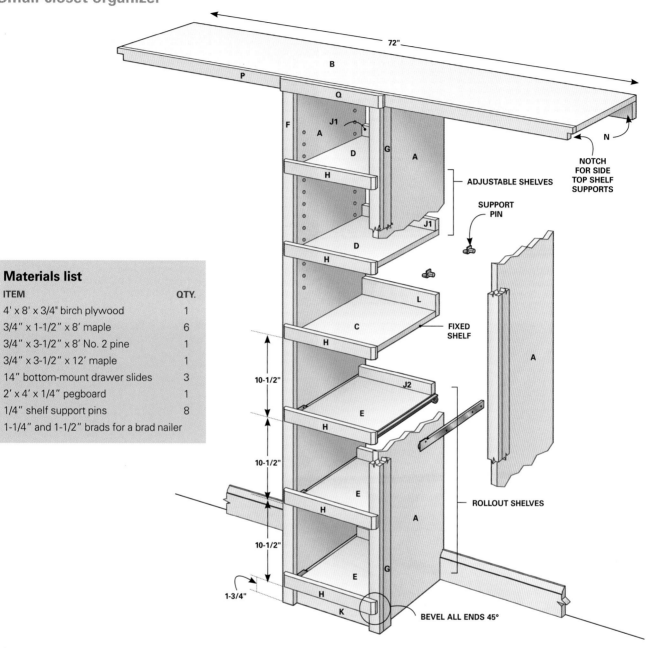

72"

B
P
Q
J1
F
A
D
G
A
H
N

NOTCH
FOR SIDE
TOP SHELF
SUPPORTS

ADJUSTABLE SHELVES

SUPPORT
PIN

D
H

L
C

FIXED
SHELF

A

10-1/2"

H

J2

E
H

ROLLOUT SHELVES

10-1/2"

E
H
A

10-1/2"

E
G
H

1-3/4"

K

BEVEL ALL ENDS 45°

Materials list

ITEM	QTY.
4' x 8' x 3/4" birch plywood	1
3/4" x 1-1/2" x 8' maple	6
3/4" x 3-1/2" x 8' No. 2 pine	1
3/4" x 3-1/2" x 12' maple	1
14" bottom-mount drawer slides	3
2' x 4' x 1/4" pegboard	1
1/4" shelf support pins	8
1-1/4" and 1-1/2" brads for a brad nailer	

Cutting list

KEY	QTY.	DIMENSIONS	NAME	KEY	QTY.	DIMENSIONS	NAME
A	2	15-3/4" x 65-1/4" plywood	Sides	J2	3	3/4" x 1-1/2" x 11" maple	Rollout shelf backs
B	1	15-3/4" x 72" plywood	Top shelf	K	1	3/4" x 1-1/2" x 12" maple	Base
C	1	15-3/4" x 12" plywood	Fixed shelf	L	5	3/4" x 3-1/2" x 12" pine	Bracing
D	2	15-3/4" x 11-7/8" plywood	Adjustable shelves	M	2	3/4" x 3-1/2" x 24" maple	Side top shelf supports—not shown
E	3	15-3/4" x 11" plywood	Rollout shelves	N	2	3/4" x 3-1/2" x 29-1/4" maple	Rear top shelf supports
F	2	3/4" x 1-1/2" x 64-1/2" maple	Vertical front trim				
G	2	3/4" x 1-1/2" x 65-1/4" maple	Vertical side trim	P	1	3/4" x 1-1/2" x 72" maple	Top shelf edge
H	6	3/4" x 1-1/2" x 14-1/2" maple	Shelf fronts	Q	1	3/4" x 1-1/2" x 15-3/4" maple	Top trim
J1	2	3/4" x 1-1/2" x 11-7/8" maple	Shelf backs				

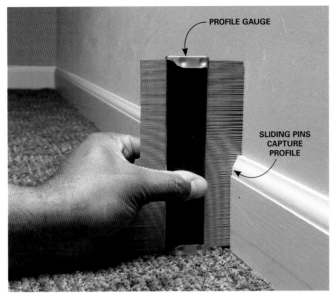

2 Make an outline of the baseboard with a profile gauge and, using a jigsaw, cut out the pattern on the lower back side of the two shelving sides. (See Figure A and Photo 4.)

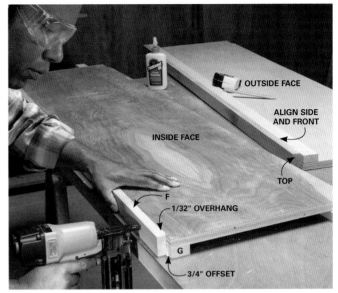

3 Cut the 1x2s to length. Then glue and nail them to the plywood sides (Figure A) with 1-1/4-in. brads. Note the slight (1/32-in.) overhang along the inside.

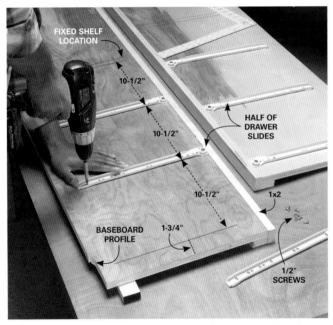

4 Mark the center and rollout shelf locations using a framing square. Then mount half of each of the two-piece drawer slides even with the 1x2 on each side.

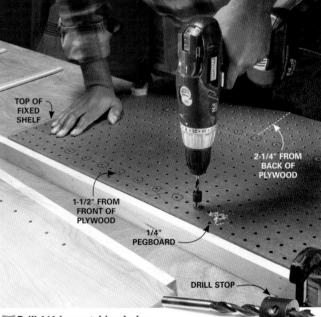

5 Drill 1/4-in. matching holes 3/8 in. deep for the adjustable shelf pins using a pegboard template. Flip the pegboard when switching sides.

Attach the maple edges

Glue and nail the side 1x2s (G) to the best-looking side of the plywood (so it faces out), holding them flush with the front edge (**Photo 3**). Be sure to use 1-1/4-in. brads here so the nails don't go completely through the side. Use 1-1/2-in. brads everywhere else.

Then attach the front 1x2s (F). These 1x2s should be flush with the bottom of the sides, but

Tip

Hold the brad nailer perpendicular to the grain whenever possible so the rectangular nailheads will run with the grain instead of cutting across it. This makes them less prominent.

3/4 in. short of the top. The 1x2s will overlap the edge slightly because 3/4-in. plywood is slightly less than a full 3/4 in. thick. Keep the overlap to the inside.

Lay out the locations for the drawer slides and the fixed center shelf before assembling the cabinet—the 12-in. width is a tight fit for a drill. Use the dimensions in **Photo 4** and **Figure A** for spacing. Vary any of these measurements to better fit shoes or other items. Then take the drawer slides apart and mount them on the tower sides (**Photo 4**). Remember that one side of each pair is a mirror image of the other.

To position the shelf support pins for the two adjustable

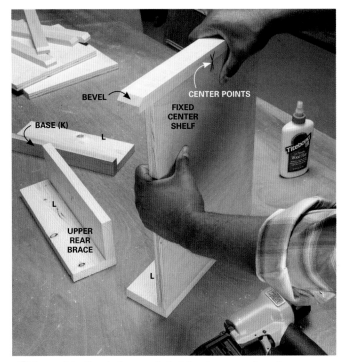

Labels on image 3: BEVEL, CENTER POINTS, FIXED CENTER SHELF, BASE (K), L, L, UPPER REAR BRACE, L, L

6 Assemble the shelves and shelving braces using glue and 1-1/2-in. brads. Align the centers of each piece for accurate positioning.

Labels on image 4: FRONT 1x2

7 Attach the other halves of the slides to the rollout shelves with 1/2-in. screws. Butt them against the front 1x2.

shelves, align the bottom of the 1/4-in. pegboard with the fixed shelf location, then drill mirror-image holes on the two sides (**Photo 5**). Mark the holes to be used on the pegboard—it's all too easy to lose track when flipping the pegboard over to the second side. Use a brad point drill bit to prevent splintering, and place a bit stop or a piece of tape for a 5/8-in. hole depth (1/4-in. pegboard plus 3/8 in. deep in the plywood). Most support pins require a 1/4-in.-diameter hole, but measure to make sure.

> **Tip**
> Make sure the pegboard has square sides.

Cut the bevels and assemble the shelves

Cut the bevels in all the 1x2 shelf fronts, then glue and nail them to the plywood shelves, keeping the bottoms flush (**Photo 6**). Nail 1x2 backs (J1 and J2) onto the adjustable and rollout shelves. Next, nail together the bracing (L) and the base piece (K), which join the cabinet. Then add the slides to the rollout shelves (**Photo 7**).

Assembling the shelving tower is straightforward (**Photo 8**). Position the L-shaped bracing at the top and braces at the bottom, add glue to the joints, then clamp and nail. Because of the slight lip where the 1x2 front trim (F) overlaps the plywood, it requires chiseling out a 1/32-in.-deep x 3/4-in.-wide notch so the fixed shelf will fit tightly (**Photo 9**).

Set the cabinet in the closet

Remove the old closet shelving and position the new cabinet. If there's carpeting, it's best to cut it out under the cabinet for easier carpet replacement in the future (**Photo 10**). For the cleanest look, pull the carpet back from the closet wall, cut out the padding and tack strip that fall under the cabinet, and nail new tack strips around the cabinet position. Then reposition the cabinet, push the

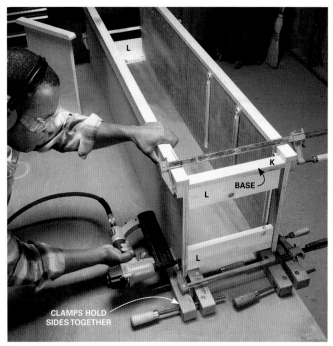

Labels on image 1: L, L, K, BASE, L, CLAMPS HOLD SIDES TOGETHER

8 Set the sides on edge, glue and clamp the braces (I) in place and nail the assembly together with 1-1/2-in. brads. Make sure the braces are square to the sides.

carpet back against it and cut the carpet. Or, simply cut out the carpet and tack strip under the cabinet and tack the loose carpet edges to the floor (but it won't look as nice).

Plumb and level the cabinet, then screw it to the wall. Use hollow wall anchors if the studs are hard to find. The cabinet will be firmly anchored by the upper shelf anyway.

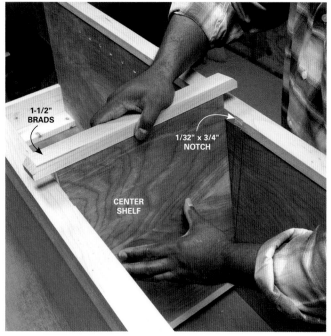

9 Chisel shallow slots in the 1x2 overhang, then slide the center shelf into place. Nail at the front, back and sides.

1-1/2" BRADS

1/32" x 3/4" NOTCH

CENTER SHELF

10 Center the cabinet in the closet against the back wall, mark its position and cut the carpet out around it. Tack the loose edges of carpet to the floor.

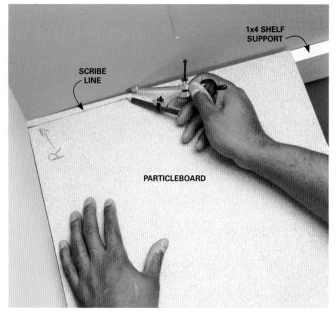

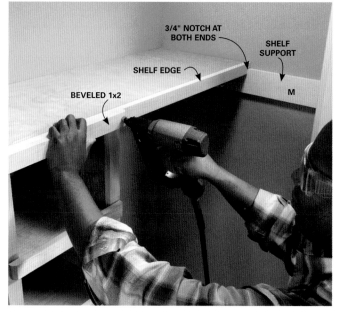

11 Shove a 16 x 24-in. sheet of particleboard into the shelf corners and scribe a line. Cut along the scribe line and use the particleboard as a pattern. Nail the shelf to the supports and cabinet top.

1x4 SHELF SUPPORT

SCRIBE LINE

PARTICLEBOARD

12 Notch the 1x2 shelf edge over the end supports and nail it into place. Then trim the top of the cabinet with a beveled 1x2.

3/4" NOTCH AT BOTH ENDS

SHELF SUPPORT

SHELF EDGE

BEVELED 1x2

M

Scribe the top shelf for a tight fit

Closet shelves are tough to fit because the corners of the walls are rarely square. To cut the shelf accurately, scribe a leftover 16-in.-wide piece of particleboard or plywood in both corners (**Photo 11**) and use it for a template for cutting the ends of the shelf. Then the shelf will drop right into place and rest on 1x4 supports nailed to the side walls and back wall. Make sure the front of the shelf is flush with the front of the tower and nail it to the top. If the back wall is wavy, scribe the back of the shelf to the wall and trim it to make the front flush. Then cut and notch the front 1x2 and nail it to the shelf (**Photo 12**).

Lightly sand all the wood and apply a clear finish. When it's dry, mix several shades of putty to get an exact match to your wood and fill the nail holes. Add another coat of finish and let it dry. Screw on the clothes rod brackets, aligning them with the bottom of the 1x4. Then pile on the clothes.

Triple Your Closet Space

Add extra clothes storage space to any room with these attractive cabinets

It seems like no matter how much closet space you have, there's never quite enough. But building attractive clothes cabinets like these allows you to expand storage into your bedroom or a spare room and gain the extra space you need. You can build one storage tower or connect several together. Each tower consists of a drawer base, a wall cabinet with doors, and two side panels with holes for adjustable shelves. We'll show you how to build the cabinets and assemble the towers. And we'll also include details for adding a clothes hamper drawer, a pullout pants-hanging rack and shoe storage between the two towers.

Even though the style is simple, building these cabinets requires close attention to detail and accurate cuts. If you can cut plywood precisely and have the patience to carefully assemble the parts, you shouldn't have any trouble building this project.

We used 3/4-in. maple plywood for everything but the drawers and the backs of the cabinets. For these we used good-quality shop-grade plywood. You could substitute less expensive plywood for the cabinet boxes to save a little money.

Tons of storage for all your clothes

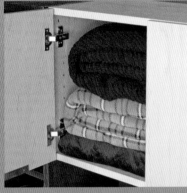

The large, deep drawers hold sweaters and other bulky items. Full-extension ball-bearing slides allow easy access.

The wall cabinet has space for extra bedding or off-season clothes.

The shoe shelves can store shoes, purses and hats, or small baskets for socks and underwear.

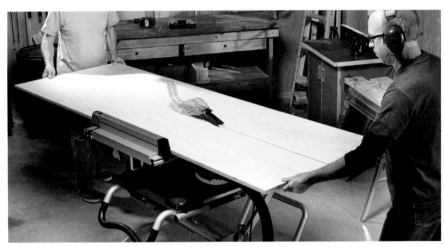

1 **RIP THE PLYWOOD.** Round up a helper and rip the plywood sheets into strips according to Figure E on p. 177. Choose the best-looking plywood for the tall end panels because these are the most visible.

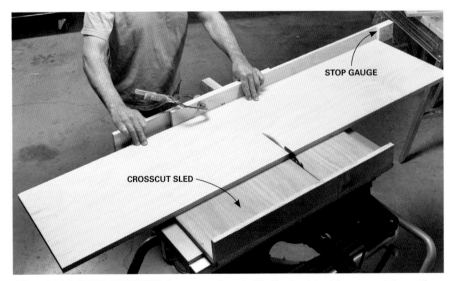

STOP GAUGE

CROSSCUT SLED

2 **CROSSCUT THE PLYWOOD.** A crosscutting sled is the best tool for accurately cutting the plywood strips to length. Take the time to build a sled if you don't have one. Clamp a stop to the crosscutting sled to cut same-size parts accurately.

Cut and prepare the plywood

The most important step in the building process is cutting the parts accurately. Use the **Cutting List** and **Figure E** (p. 177) as a guide. Our plywood was a full 3/4 in. thick, and the sizes shown are for 3/4-in. plywood. If yours is slightly thinner, cut the shelves, doors and drawer parts after you've assembled the cabinet boxes so you can adjust the fit.

A stationary table saw with an accurate fence and outfeed tables would be ideal for this job. But you can get great results with a portable saw too. You'll need a top-quality blade designed to crosscut plywood. We splurged on a 90-tooth 10-in. blade and were amazed at the glass-smooth, splinter-free cuts we got.

After all the parts are cut, separate out the uprights and shelves that receive solid wood nosing. Then cover the raw plywood edges of the remaining 3/4-in. plywood parts with edge-banding veneer. For the cabinet boxes, you only need to cover the front edges. On the doors and drawer fronts, you'll want to cover all four edges.

WHAT IT TAKES

TIME: Two or three weekends

SKILL LEVEL: Intermediate to advanced

TOOLS: Standarad carpentry tools plus a table saw, miter saw, compressor and pin nailer, and a 35-mm Forstner bit

3 COVER THE RAW PLYWOOD EDGES. Finish the edges of the cabinet parts and the shoe shelves with edge banding. We're using self-adhesive edge banding, but iron-on edge banding works well too. Center the edge banding and press or iron it on according to the manufacturer's instructions.

4 TRIM THE ENDS. Place the banded edge down on the work surface and use a sharp utility knife to trim the ends flush.

5 TRIM THE EDGES. Use a veneer edge trimmer to slice off the excess edge banding along the sides. A double-edge trimmer like this one trims both edges at once. Single-edge trimmers cost about half as much and work well. They just take a little longer. Use sandpaper to remove any overhanging edge banding to create a perfectly flush edge.

Build the cabinet boxes

The cabinets are simple plywood boxes with drawers or doors added. The key to accuracy is to make sure that the edges of the plywood remain perfectly aligned as you assemble the boxes and that the cabinet box is square. **Photos 6–8** show how.

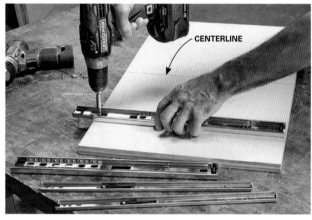

CENTERLINE

6 INSTALL THE SLIDES FIRST. It's easier to attach slides to the cabinet sides before the cabinet is assembled. Draw lines to indicate the center of the slides. Then center the screw holes on the line and attach the slide with the included screws.

7 NAIL, THEN SCREW PARTS. To prevent the plywood from sliding around when you're drilling pilot holes, tack the parts first with a brad nailer. Then drill countersink pilot holes and connect the parts with screws.

8 ATTACH THE BACK. If you're careful to cut the back perfectly square, you can use it to square the cabinet. Apply a bead of glue and set the back onto the cabinet. Make sure one edge of the back is flush with one side of the cabinet box and fasten it with 1-in. nails. Adjust the cabinet box until the other sides align, then partially drive a nail to hold it. Check the cabinet for square, then finish nailing on the back.

Figure A
Clothes storage tower

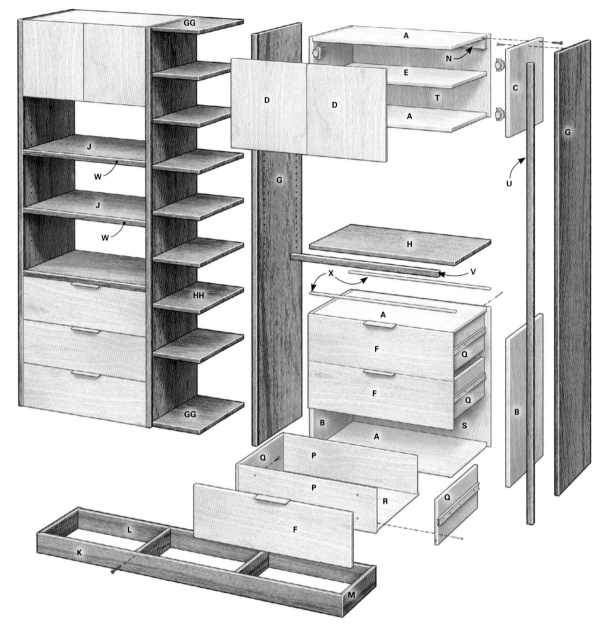

9 GROOVE THE DRAWER PARTS. Set your table saw fence at 1/2 in. and raise the blade 1/4 in. above the table. Cut a groove in the drawer sides and fronts. Move the fence away from the blade about 1/16 in. and make a second pass to widen the groove. Check the fit of the drawer bottom plywood. It should be snug but not too tight. You may need a third pass. After the grooves are cut, rip the backs to width.

Build the drawers

The most critical part of the drawer-building process is to make sure the finished drawer is between 1 in. and 1-1/16 in. narrower than the inside dimensions of the cabinet to allow for the drawer slides. To determine the exact dimensions of the front and back of the drawers (parts P), measure between the cabinet sides and subtract twice the thickness of the drawer plywood. Then subtract another 1-1/16 in. **Photos 9–14** show how to build and install the drawers.

10 BUILD THE DRAWER BOXES. Glue and nail the sides to the front and back. Use glue sparingly to avoid squeeze-out mess. Use 1-1/4-in. nails and aim carefully to prevent them from shooting out the sides. Make sure the grooves line up—it's easy to get a part upside down.

11 SLIDE IN THE BOTTOM. Check the fit of the drawer bottom and trim the width a little if needed. Don't force the plywood or it may push the drawer sides apart.

12 NAIL THE DRAWER BOTTOM. Measure diagonally to make sure the drawer is square. Then drive 1-in. nails through the drawer bottom into the drawer back to hold it in place.

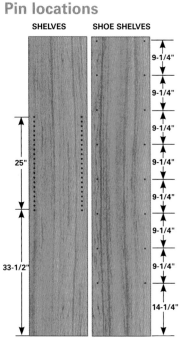

13 ATTACH THE DRAWER SLIDE. Draw a line 3-3/4 in. from the top edge of the drawer. Center the drawer slide on the line, keeping the front edge lined up with the front of the drawer. Attach it with two screws. Add the remaining screws later to secure the drawer slide in place after making any adjustment.

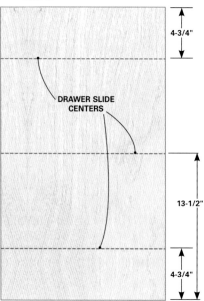

14 INSTALL THE DRAWER FRONTS. Mount each drawer front with hot glue, then pull it out and secure it with four screws driven from inside the drawer. Set the bottom door flush with the bottom of the cabinet. Then use two stacks of two pennies as spacers between the drawer fronts. The top drawer should be 1/8 in. below the top of the cabinet.

Figure B
Pin locations

SHELVES   SHOE SHELVES

9-1/4"
9-1/4"
9-1/4"
9-1/4"
9-1/4"
9-1/4"
9-1/4"
14-1/4"

25"
33-1/2"

Figure C
Super-size drawer or pants rack

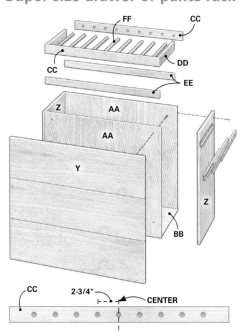

FF
CC
CC
DD
EE
Z AA
AA
Y
Z
BB
CC
2-3/4"
CENTER

Figure D
Drawer slide centers

PART B

4-3/4"
DRAWER SLIDE CENTERS
13-1/2"
4-3/4"

Hang the doors with Euro hinges

This type of cabinet construction is perfect for Euro-style hinges. You simply mount a plate to the cabinet and drill a 35-mm (1-3/8-in.) recess in the door to accept the hinge. The Blum 120-degree clip hinges we're using are adjustable up and down, in and out, and side to side, making final door fitting a breeze. **Photos 15–21** show how to install the hinges and hang the doors.

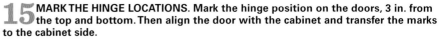

15 MARK THE HINGE LOCATIONS. Mark the hinge position on the doors, 3 in. from the top and bottom. Then align the door with the cabinet and transfer the marks to the cabinet side.

16 START THE HINGE HOLES. We built this plywood jig as a guide for starting the hinge holes. You can also buy a jig, or simply mark the center of the hinge and use a center punch to create a starting hole. For these Blum hinges, the center of the hole is 7/8 in. from the edge of the door. Start drilling the hole with the 35-mm (or 1-3/8-in.) Forstner-style bit.

17 COMPLETE THE HINGE HOLE. Remove the guide so you can judge how deep to drill. With most bits you can drill until the top of the bit is flush with the surface. The recess should be 1/2 in. deep. Drill a hole in a scrap first to check the depth before drilling a door.

18 MOUNT THE HINGE. Press the hinge into the recess and align it with a square. Use a self-centering bit to drill pilot holes for the hinge screws. Then attach the hinge with the screws provided.

19 MARK FOR THE HINGE PLATES. Draw lines 1-7/16 in. from the front of the cabinet to locate the center of the hinge plates. If you're using a different hinge, check the instructions to find the correct distance.

20 ATTACH THE HINGE PLATES. Center the hinge plates on the marks and line up the center of the screw holes with the second mark. Drill pilot holes with a self-centering bit and attach the plates with the screws.

21 HANG THE DOOR. Clip the hinges to the plates to hang the doors. Don't bother to adjust the hinges until after the cabinet is mounted to the wall.

Build the side panels

The side panels have 1-in.-wide solid wood edging on one side and shelf-pin holes on one face. If you'll be adding shoe shelves between two towers as shown in the photo on page 169, then drill holes for these shelf pins too. Be careful to attach the nosing to the correct edge of each panel. Since the shelf-pin holes are not an equal distance from top and bottom, the two sides are not interchangeable, but are mirror images.

22 DRILL THE SHELF-PIN HOLES. We are using a store-bought jig, but you can also use a length of 1/4-in. pegboard as a template for drilling the holes. Mount a stop on your 1/4-in. drill bit to drill the holes 3/8 in. deep.

23 GLUE AND NAIL THE NOSING. Spread a bead of glue along the plywood edge. Align the wood edging flush to the inside edge of the panel and attach it with 1-1/4-in. nails.

Super-size drawer

Replacing three drawers with one huge drawer allows you to hang pants or store two clothes hampers. The big drawer is just a deeper version of the small drawers. But to keep it from sagging, we mounted the drawer on file-cabinet drawer slides instead. To simulate three drawers, we grooved a single sheet of plywood by running it through the table saw with the blade raised 1/4 in., and used this for the drawer front. To convert the drawer for pants storage, just build the dowel rack and rest it on cleats.

Super-size laundry drawer

Figure C shows the parts for the deep drawer. Center the cabinet part of the file-drawer slide 4-3/4 in. from the top of the cabinet, and the drawer part of the slide 1 in. down from the top of the drawer. Finish by mounting the grooved drawer front.

Pullout pants rack

Use **Figure C** as a guide to build this rack from 2-in. strips of plywood and 5/8-in. dowels. Screw cleats to the front and back of the drawer, 2-1/4 in. from the top, to support the rack.

Install the cabinets in your room

After all the cabinets and side panels are built, you'll want to stain and varnish or paint them before installing them in your room. Remove all the drawers, doors and hardware to make finishing easier. Carefully sand all the parts. We used a random orbital sander and 120-grit sandpaper. Then we stained the side panel and shelves and finally brushed two coats of polyurethane on all the parts. After the finish dries, reinstall the hardware and carry the cabinets, side panels and base into your room. Mark the studs in the location where you'll install the cabinets. **Photos 24–27** show the installation steps.

24 **LEVEL THE BASE.** Installing the towers is easier if you start out with a level base. If your floor isn't level, slide shims under the base to level it. Then screw it to the studs. Cut off the shims and cover the gap with molding if necessary. You can make your own molding by ripping 3/8-in.-wide strips from 3/4-in. maple, or buy base-shoe molding.

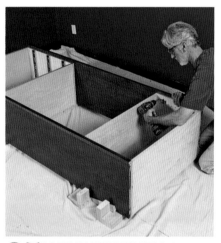

25 **ASSEMBLE THE TOWERS.** Arrange the cabinets and side panels on the floor. We built simple 2x4 supports to hold the cabinets and side panels in place while we screwed them together. Drill holes through the cabinet sides a few inches from each corner. Then carefully line up the panels so the tops and bottoms are flush with the cabinets, and attach them with 1-1/4-in. screws.

26 **ATTACH THE TOWERS TO THE WALL.** Transfer the stud locations to the inside of the cabinet and drive 2-1/2-in. screws into the studs to secure the towers. Use the 12-in.-wide shoe shelves as spacers at the top and bottom to position the second tower.

27 **FINISH UP BY ADDING THE TOPS, DOORS, DRAWERS AND SHELVES.** Tilt the top into place and attach it with 1-1/2-in. screws from inside the base cabinet. Then clip the doors onto the hinge plates and slide the drawers into the drawer slides to finish the job.

Materials list

ITEM	QTY.	ITEM	QTY.
4' x 8' x 3/4" maple plywood	3*	Blum frameless 0mm screw-on mounting plates	4
4' x 8' x 1/2" shop-grade plywood	1	1/4" shelf pins	12
4' x 8' x 1/4" shop-grade plywood	1	Screws, nails, wood glue, drawer and door pulls,	
3/4" x 5-1/2" x 8' maple board	1	finishing supplies	
13/16" maple veneer edge banding	75 ln. ft.	Optional 6" file drawer slide for super-size drawer	1
16" full-extension drawer slides	3 pairs	Optional hamper for super-size drawer	2
Blum 120-degree clip-top hinges	4		

* Leftover materials can be used to make a drawer front for the super-size laundry drawer and the shoe shelves.
The Blum hardware and the file drawer slide are available at woodworking stores and online.

Cutting list

KEY	QTY.	DIMENSIONS	NAME
3/4" MAPLE PLYWOOD			
A	4	15-7/8" x 30-1/2"	Cabinet tops and bottoms
B	2	15-7/8" x 27"	Lower cabinet sides
C	2	15-7/8" x 16"	Upper cabinet sides
D	2	15-3/4" x 15-7/8"	Upper cabinet doors
E	1	15-7/8" x 30-3/8"	Upper cabinet shelf
F	3	8-7/8" x 31-3/4"	Lower cabinet drawer fronts
G	2	16-1/8" x 79-3/4"	Side panels
H	1	16-1/8" x 32"	Lower cabinet top
J	2	15-1/4" x 31-7/8"	Shelves
K	1	4" x 30-1/2"	Base front (extend as needed for two towers)
L	1	4" x 29"	Base back
M	2	4" x 13-1/2"	Base sides
N	1	2" x 30-1/2"	Upper cabinet hanging strip
1/2" SHOP-GRADE PLYWOOD			
P	6*	7-1/2" x 28-1/2"	Drawer fronts and backs (cut backs to fit)
Q	6	7-1/2" x 15-3/4"	Drawer sides
1/4" SHOP-GRADE PLYWOOD			
R	3	15-1/2" x 29"	Drawer bottoms
S	1	27" x 32"	Lower cabinet back
T	1	16" x 32"	Upper cabinet back
3/4" SOLID MAPLE			
U	2	1" x 79-3/4"	Side panel edging
V	1	1" x 32"	Lower cabinet top edging
W	2	1" x 31-7/8"	Shelf edging
X	2	1/4" x 32"	Spacers

Optional Large Drawer
KEY	QTY.	DIMENSIONS	NAME
3/4" MAPLE PLYWOOD			
Y	1	26-7/8" x 31-3/4"	Grooved drawer front
1/2" SHOP-GRADE PLYWOOD			
Z	2	15-3/4" x 25"	Drawer sides
AA	2	28-1/2" x 25"*	Drawer front and back (cut back to fit)

*Adjust size to compensate for plywood thickness

KEY	QTY.	DIMENSIONS	NAME
1/4" SHOP-GRADE PLYWOOD			
BB	1	15-1/2" x 29"	Drawer bottom

Optional Pants Rack
KEY	QTY.	DIMENSIONS	NAME
3/4" MAPLE PLYWOOD			
CC	2	2" x 28-3/8"	Front and back
DD	2	2" x 13-1/8"	Sides
EE	2	1-1/2" x 28-1/2"	Cleats
5/8" DOWELS			
FF	9	13-7/8"	Dowels

Optional Shoe Shelves
KEY	QTY.	DIMENSIONS	NAME
GG	2	16" x 12"	Top and bottom shelves
HH	7	16" x 11-7/8"	Middle shelves

Figure E
Plywood cutting diagrams

1/4" PLYWOOD

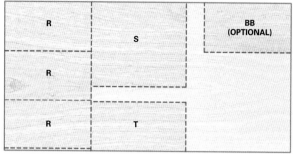

3/4" PLYWOOD

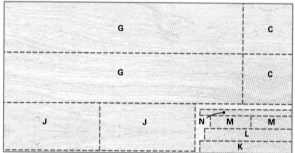

3/4" PLYWOOD

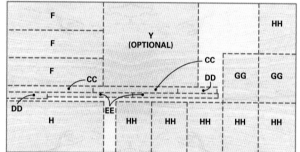

3/4" PLYWOOD

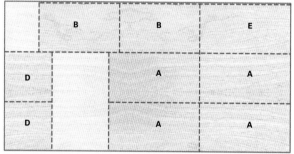

1/2" PLYWOOD

Wire Shelving Made Easier

Wire shelving is popular because of its price, flexibility and ease of installation. Wire shelving can be designed to meet almost any need at a fraction of the cost of a custom built-in system. And while installing wire shelving isn't quite a no-brainer, you don't need to be a master carpenter or own a fully equipped cabinet shop to get it done. We picked the brain of a pro for these tips to help you on your next installation.

MEET THE EXPERT

Over the past 15 years, Tim Bischke has hung wire shelves in thousands of closets. His jobs have ranged from simple one-shelf reach-in closets to elaborate walk-in wardrobe sanctuaries. When you've hung that many shelves, you can't help but know what you're doing.

Buy extra pieces

Even if you're just planning to build one closet shelf, have extra parts on hand. It takes a lot less time to return a few wall clips than it does to stop working to make a special trip to the store for just one. And plans change, so if you or your customer decides to add a section of shelving, you'll be prepared.

Leave the heavy stuff for the garage

Tim primarily works with Closet Maid's standard wire shelving, sold at home centers. Most manufacturers make a heavier-duty product for garage storage, but Tim feels that the regular stuff is plenty strong for the average bedroom or hall closet. However, if your customer's closet is going to store a bowling ball collection, you may want to consider upgrading. The materials for the closet shown here (approximately 22 ft. of shelving and rod) cost about $150 to $200.

CLOSET GAUGE

HEAVY GAUGE

END CAP

BEARING POINT

END BRACKET

BUBBLE STICK

Lay it out with a bubble stick

Tim uses a bubble stick rather than a level. A bubble stick is like a ruler and a level rolled into one. Holding a level against the wall with one hand can be frustrating. Levels are rigid, and they pivot out of place when resting on a stud that's bowed out a bit. A bubble stick has a little flex, so it can ride the imperfections of the wall yet still deliver a straight line. You can get one at hardware stores or online.

Measure an inch short

When cutting the shelf, measure wall to wall, and subtract an inch. This allows for the thickness of the end brackets plus a little wiggle room. It's the top, thinner wire that actually supports the shelf, and one wire per end is enough. Cutting exact lengths will only earn you wall scratches and a trip back to the cutting station.

TEMPLATE

A bolt cutter works best

Cut your shelving with a bolt cutter. It's quick and easy, and it makes a clean cut. To make room for the cutter, Tim uses his feet to hold the shelving off the ground.

Use a template on the end brackets

Tim's first template was nothing more than a 1x3 with a couple of holes drilled in it. He rested a torpedo level on top of the board and marked the end bracket locations with a pencil. The template he's using here has a built-in level and allows him to drill the holes without marking them first. At $190, this is for guys who do lots of closet shelving. But if that's you, it's a great investment. You can order one from your local Closet Maid dealer.

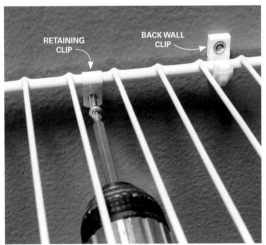
RETAINING CLIP

BACK WALL CLIP

Avoid upheaval

Back wall clips are designed to support the shelf, but if there are a bunch of clothes hanging on the front of the shelf with nothing on top to weigh them down, the back of the shelf can lift. To keep the shelf in place, Tim installs a retaining clip in a stud near the middle of the shelf. One clip toward the middle of an 8-ft. shelf is plenty.

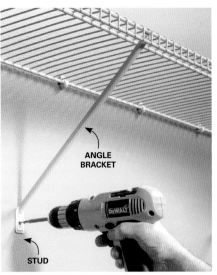
ANGLE BRACKET

STUD

Space the angle brackets evenly

Tim considers aesthetics when installing his angle brackets. If a shelf only needs one bracket, he'll find the stud closest to the center. If two or three brackets are required, he'll try to space them evenly, making sure that at least one bracket toward the center is hitting a stud.

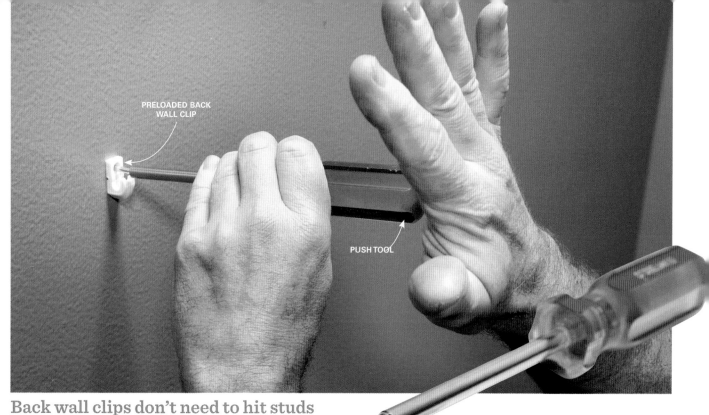

PRELOADED BACK WALL CLIP

PUSH TOOL

RECESSED END

Back wall clips don't need to hit studs

It may go against your every instinct, but hitting a stud when you're installing the back wall clips slows the process down and isn't necessary. After marking their locations, Tim drills a 1/4-in. hole and pops the preloaded pushpin in with a push tool. He loves his push tool. It has a little indentation in the tip that won't slip off the pin when it's being set in the drywall. The occasional wall clips that do land on studs need to be fastened with a screw instead of a pin. You can order a push tool from your local Closet Maid dealer.

Hanger sliding freedom

One common complaint about wire shelving is that it restricts the movement of the hangers because the hangers are stuck between the shelves. That's why Tim always offers the upgrade of a hanger rod. Most manufacturers make some version of one. A hanger rod allows clothes to be slid from one end of the closet to the other, even past an inside corner. This upgrade will add about 30 percent to the cost of the materials on a standard shelf design. Make sure the type of shelving you buy will work with the hanging rod hardware you plan to use.

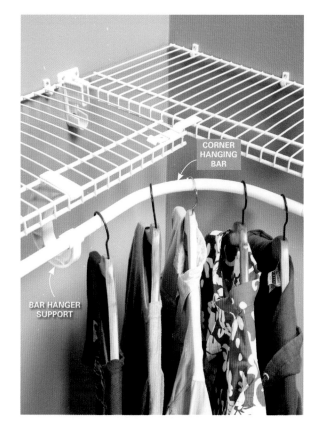

CORNER HANGING BAR

BAR HANGER SUPPORT

Pegboard prevents tipping

When Tim installs wire shelving in pantries, he likes to cap the top of the shelves with white 1/4-in. pegboard. This stops the skinnier items from tipping over. He uses white zip ties to hold the pegboard in place. A 4 x 8-ft. sheet costs less than $20 at most home centers, which makes it an inexpensive option.

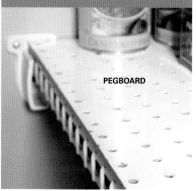

PEGBOARD

Interior Trim Simplified

All the basics–start to finish–plus a clever way to get those miters tight

Installing trim is one of the most rewarding home improvement projects you can do. No matter what style you choose, you'll take pride in the finished product . . . as long as you get all those joints tight.

Fortunately, installing trim isn't all that difficult. With a few basic carpentry tools and a little bit of patience, you can complete a room in less than a weekend.

Here we'll show you the basic steps for installing a wide trim around a door and window, complete with mitered corners. We'll also show you how to put in a built-up baseboard made from a combination of three types of moldings. The key to a good job is two joint techniques: mitering and coping. We'll help you master these techniques for tight and professional-looking joints.

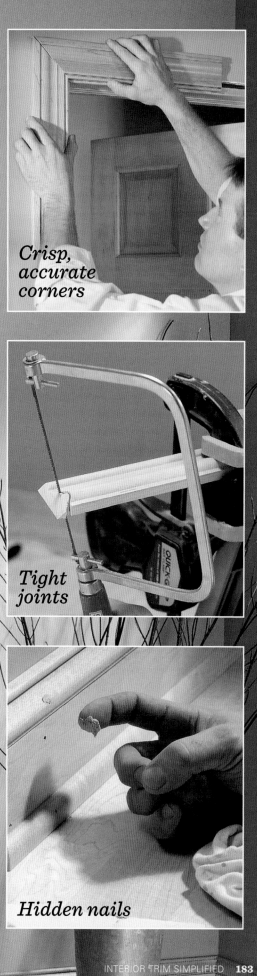

Crisp, accurate corners

Tight joints

Hidden nails

Trim a door

1 Mark a reveal line 3/16 in. from the edge of the jamb with a combination square. Use a sharp pencil and position the marks in the corners and about every foot along the jamb edge.

REVEAL LINE

COMBINATION SQUARE

DOOR JAMB

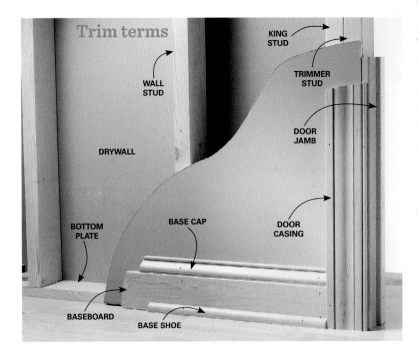

Trim terms

KING STUD

WALL STUD

TRIMMER STUD

DOOR JAMB

DRYWALL

BOTTOM PLATE

BASE CAP

DOOR CASING

BASEBOARD

BASE SHOE

Use a power miter saw for clean angle cuts

A power miter saw (**Photo 2**) vastly simplifies the job because it allows you to make incredibly accurate cuts in a matter of seconds. Even professionals admit they couldn't do the same quality of work without one. If you don't have a power miter saw, you can rent one at most rental stores for about $50 a day. **Tip:** If you're renting a miter saw, cut several scrap pieces to get the feel of the tool before cutting your trim.

> ### CAUTION
> This saw is powerful and loud. Be sure to keep your hands well away from the blade and wear hearing protection and safety glasses when using it.

Buy a good-quality blade for your miter saw

The more teeth a blade has, the crisper the cut. Choose a blade with a minimum of 40 teeth. We prefer a blade with 80 teeth. It leaves a cut that's as smooth as glass, making it well worth the investment.

You'll also need a coping saw

This saw (**Photo 18**) has a narrow blade and tiny teeth that allow you to cut tight curves. **Tip:** Avoid that annoying trip to the hardware store in the middle of your project—pick up a couple of spare blades in case you break one.

The only other tools you'll need are basic carpentry tools: a sharp pencil, a tape measure and a combination square. A wood file also is a must for fine-tuning joints (**Photo 20**). Use a round file, called a rattail file, for fitting tight curved profiles, and a combination flat/half round for all other trim (**Photo 19**).

In this project, we predrilled our nail holes. If you have more than one room to trim, consider using an air-powered finish nailer to speed up the process. It rents for about $75 a day.

Reduce legwork: Set up your saw in the room you're trimming

If sawdust isn't a problem, cut your trim in the room where you plan to install it (**Photo 13**). Set up the miter saw in the middle of the floor with plenty of room on either side. Cover the floor with a tarp to prevent scuff marks and scratches. Use blocks the same height as the miter saw table to support long lengths of trim.

Start with the casing around the doors and windows. The first few times you install casing, we suggest drawing light lines (called "reveal lines") 3/16 in. from the edge of the jamb to align the casing to the door jamb and windows (**Photo 1**). With experience, you'll skip this step and simply "eyeball" the reveal when you put up the trim.

Prefinishing saves a ton of time

Once you get your trim home, sand and stain or paint the trim before you install it. To be perfectly honest, this part of the project isn't much fun. But it's a lot easier to finish trim before

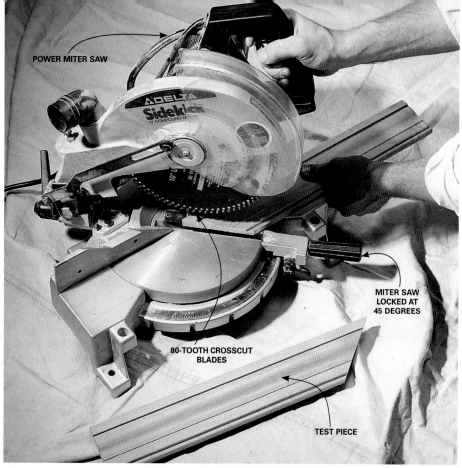

POWER MITER SAW

MITER SAW LOCKED AT 45 DEGREES

80-TOOTH CROSSCUT BLADES

TEST PIECE

2 Cut two 12-in. long test pieces of casing at opposite 45-degree angles on the power miter box to check the fit of your casing on the door jamb.

OPEN GAP

SET TRIM ON REVEAL MARK

TEST PIECE

MOLDING PROFILE

3 Hold the test pieces on the reveal marks to check the fit of the miter in the corner. If the joint is even slightly open at the top or bottom of the miter, adjust the angle on the miter saw slightly, recut both pieces and check the fit again. Take your time—you may be surprised how tight you can get the joint to fit.

ROUGH CUT

SIDE CASING

4 Cut the side casing about 1/2 in. overlong and hold it in place on the door jamb along your reveal marks. Use a sharp pencil to transfer the top reveal mark from the head jamb to the side casing. Then cut the miter at the angle you established with your test pieces.

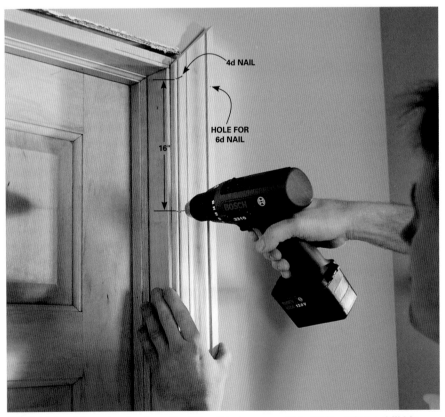

4d NAIL

HOLE FOR 6d NAIL

16"

5 Hold the side casing in place. Predrill nail holes every 12 to 16 in., using a drill bit about 1/32 in. smaller than the nail size. Stay 1 in. away from the ends to avoid splitting. Drive 4d finishing nails into the jamb and 6d finishing nails into the wall.

installation, working on sawhorses, than afterward, lying on the floor with sandpaper and a staining rag. Plus you can do a better job of sanding and finishing the pieces. After you've installed the pieces, be prepared to touch them up a bit. Do all the finish work in a well-ventilated area.

We applied a Salem maple stain to our trim and three coats of low-sheen varnish to protect it.

CAUTION
Dispose of any staining rags carefully to avoid spontaneous combustion: Open up the oil-soaked rags and hang them up until they're completely dry. Then dispose of them in the trash.

The test-piece technique simplifies the toughest part—getting the miters tight.

Check the miters at the corners with two 12-in. sections of casing cut at exactly 45 degrees (**Photo 3**). Even though the corners should be a perfect 90 degrees, often they're not. In addition, if the jamb sticks out or is set back slightly from the wall, a 45-degree miter cut won't fit tight. By holding the test pieces at the corner you can see exactly how your casings will fit. If you see a gap, adjust the saw slightly and cut both pieces at the new angle (**Photo 3**). **Tip:** Make small adjustments. Even one-quarter of a degree makes a big difference.

If the angle of the miter is accurate but a gap still appears along the face, the pieces are probably tipping back against the wall. Cut or file the back side of the miter (back cut). This allows the joint to fit tight on the face of the miter. Don't worry about taking too much off the back; it won't be visible.

Mark and cut the first side casing at the angle you established with your test pieces (**Photo 4**). Always cut the pieces a little long and check the fit; the power miter saw gives you the ability to cut very slight amounts off with a high degree of accuracy. When the inside angle of the miter lines up with the reveal mark on the top of the jamb, tack the casing in place.

Don't split that perfect miter— predrill nail holes

With maple, oak and other dense wood, predrilling your nail holes in the casing is a must (**Photo 5**). Even with a softwood like pine, we prefer to predrill to avoid splitting a perfectly fit piece. Use a 1/16-in. bit for 4d nails, 3/32-in. for 6d nails and 1/8-in. for 8d nails. **Tip:** Use a nail with the head snipped off as a substitute for a drill bit. The same size nail you're driving works best.

Tack the casing into the jamb first, then to the wall. Wait until you've fit all the casings before you drive the nails in completely in case something doesn't fit right and you have to remove the trim to recut it. We used 4d nails for the jamb and 6d nails for

6 Cut the corresponding angle on the top casing, leaving the opposite side at least 1 in. overlong. Check your miter at the second corner with your test pieces, and adjust if necessary to fit tight. Then mark the opposite corner on the top casing, cut it and tack it up.

TOP CASING

PERFECT MITER

BACKWARDS SIDE CASING

7 Cut the second side casing about 1 in. overlong. Then hold the casing backward and parallel to the door jamb. Make a mark where the edge of the side casing intersects the upper edge of the top casing. Cut the side casing about 1/32 in. overlong. Slide the casing into place. Check your fit, and then trim it to its final length. Once the miter fits, nail the casing in place.

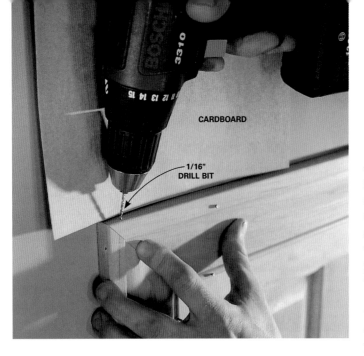

CARDBOARD

1/16" DRILL BIT

8 Align the miters and predrill a 1/16-in. hole for 3d finish nails, one from the top and one from the side. Hold a piece of cardboard against the wall to prevent marring the wall while drilling.

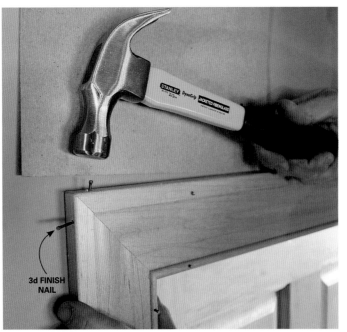

9 Drive the nails into the casing gradually, alternating between the two nails so the miter doesn't slide out of alignment. Use cardboard again between the wall and the hammer to avoid marring the wall.

3d FINISH NAIL

10 Tap the nails just below the surface with a hammer and a nail set.

NAIL SET

walls. If you're using thicker casing, increase your nail size one increment, using 6d nails in the jamb and 8d nails in the wall. Your nails should penetrate the studs and the jamb at least 3/4 in. **Tip:** On wood with a strong grain pattern, place your nails in the dark portion of the grain to make them less noticeable.

With your first corner fit perfectly, set the top casing aside and check the second corner with your test pieces the same way you did the first. Once you have established the angle of the miter, hold your top casing in place and transfer the reveal mark from the side jamb to your top casing (**Photo 6**). Cut the miter, check your fit and tack in place. **Tip:** Match your pieces of wood so the grain pattern and color are similar at the joints.

Then mark and cut the second side casing, leaving an extra 1/32 in. for fitting purposes (**Photo 7**). Slide the casing into place parallel to your reveal marks and check your fit. If the miter is tight and the length is a little long, trim a hair off the bottom at a 90-degree angle until you get a perfect fit.

This pinning technique will hold the miters tight

When your miters fit perfectly, "pin" the corners (**Photos 8** and **9**) to help align the two casings and keep the joint tight. Use your finger to press the casings flush with each other. You may have to slip a small shim behind one of the casings to align them. Next predrill the corners for 3d finishing nails, one from the top and one from the side (**Photo 8**). If your casing is less than 1/2 in. thick, you'll have to predrill the corners before tacking the casing up.

Finally, work around the door, driving the nailheads slightly below the surface with a hammer and a nail set (**Photo 10**). Nail sets are sold in various sizes; choose one that matches the size of the nailhead you're using. Set the nails deep enough to hold nail putty: A good rule of thumb is half the diameter of the nailhead.

Case a window

The trick to 'picture-frame' window trimming is fitting the fourth piece

There are two basic ways to trim a window. One way is to "picture frame" the window, so that all four corners are mitered to 90 degrees. This method is common on most newer homes, especially with casement windows. The second way is to install a stool and apron. Basically, this is a small ledge (a stool) at the bottom of the window with a piece of casing (an apron) under it. This method is normally found in older homes and is more often used on double-hung windows.

Trim a window using the same techniques as with a door. Mark your reveal lines, use test pieces to check your corners, and transfer the reveal lines to the casings for cutting and nailing. When you "picture frame" a window, however, install the top casing first (**Photo 11**), then the two sides, and finally, the bottom. Fitting the bottom is the toughest part, becauseyou have to fit both corners at once (**Photo 12**). But if you use your test pieces and always cut the casing a little long, you shouldn't have any problem. Cutting the piece long allows you to adjust the miters if you have to. Once the miters are tight, gradually trim a small amount off with your miter saw until you have the proper length.

Trim out a window with a stool in the same order as you would a door, but with a few added steps. Install the stool first, then one side, the top and the other side. Install the apron under the stool last.

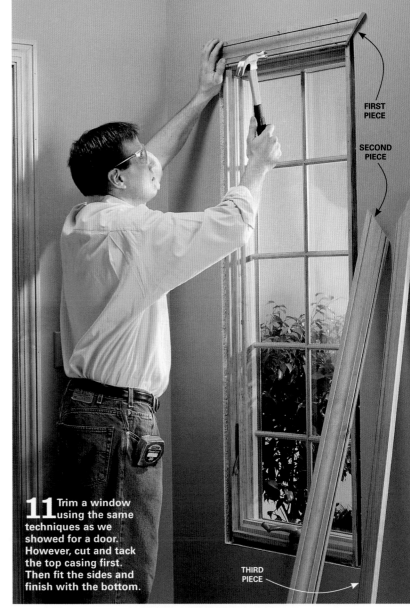

11 Trim a window using the same techniques as we showed for a door. However, cut and tack the top casing first. Then fit the sides and finish with the bottom.

FIRST PIECE

SECOND PIECE

THIRD PIECE

12 Fit one miter on the bottom, then overlap the opposite miter and mark it. Cut the miter 1/8 in. overlong, slide the casing into place and trim it down gradually while checking the fit.

COMPLETED MITER

BOTTOM CASING OVERLAPS SIDE CASING

Install a baseboard

Installing a three-piece base is well worth the extra effort

Begin by using a stud finder to locate the studs, and mark their location on the wall with a narrow piece of painter's tape (**Photo 13**). You can pull the tape off without leaving a mark. Rough-cut the baseboard about 2 in. overlong and lay the pieces along the wall. Install the longest section first and work away from the ends until you reach an opening or door. This ensures that the last cut will be a simple 90-degree cut.

In general, measure and cut each piece about 1/16 in. overlong to ensure a tight fit. If you don't have a piece of baseboard long enough to cover the entire wall, splice two pieces with a "scarf joint" (see **Splice Tip,** p. 191). Bow the casing slightly to fit between the walls and press it into place. This ensures a nice, tight fit. But don't force the piece in. Trim a bit off and try the fit again.

Continue around the room butting the inside corners at 90 degrees. When you come to an outside corner, use test pieces to find exact angles (**Photo 14**).**Tip:** If you're adding a base cap, as we are, overcut the miter slightly, leaving the back side slightly open (**Photo 16**). The front side will be tight and the cap will cover the gap.

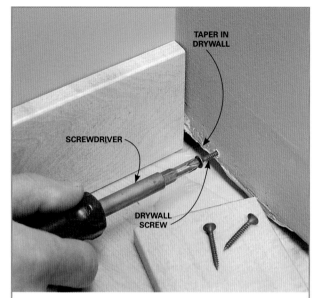

TAPER IN DRYWALL

SCREWDRIVER

DRYWALL SCREW

Screw tip

If the drywall tapers in at the bottom of the wall or stops short of the floor, simply drive a screw at the bottom of the wall and turn it in until the head of the screw is at the same plane as the main wall. The head will prevent the baseboard from tipping in.

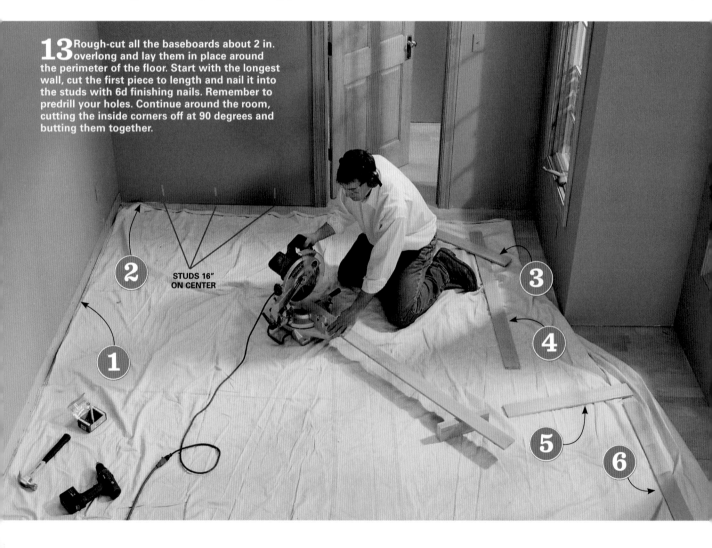

13 Rough-cut all the baseboards about 2 in. overlong and lay them in place around the perimeter of the floor. Start with the longest wall, cut the first piece to length and nail it into the studs with 6d finishing nails. Remember to predrill your holes. Continue around the room, cutting the inside corners off at 90 degrees and butting them together.

STUDS 16" ON CENTER

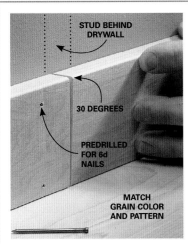

STUD BEHIND
DRYWALL

30 DEGREES

PREDRILLED
FOR 6d
NAILS

MATCH
GRAIN COLOR
AND PATTERN

Splice tip

If possible, purchase your trim in lengths long enough to cover an entire wall. If you have to splice two pieces on a wall, use a "scarf joint." Cut a 30-degree angle on each piece; if the joint opens slightly, this angle will hide the crack. Select pieces with similar grain color and pattern so the joint is less visible. Always locate a splice over a wall stud.

Nail the pieces in place using 6d finishing nails. You can also put a small amount of glue at the miters and cross-nail them with 4d finishing nails. But remember to predrill to avoid splitting the ends (**Photo 16**).

The coping technique simplifies the cap installation

Install the base cap pieces in the same order as the baseboard. However, because base cap has a curved profile, you can't butt the inside corners. Instead, make a "coped joint" by cutting off one piece square and cutting the adjoining piece to match the profile of the molding (**Photo 19**). Just follow the steps in **Photos 17–20** and you'll find it's easier than it looks. (Actually, coping is kind of fun once you get the hang of it.) Practice a few times on scrap pieces to get used to it.

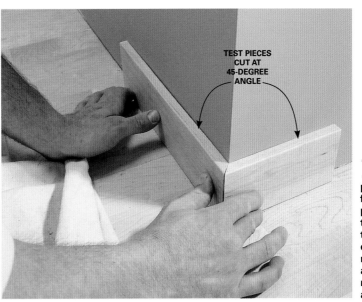

TEST PIECES
CUT AT
45-DEGREE
ANGLE

14 Miter two 1-ft. test pieces about a foot long and press them tightly against the outside corners to determine the correct angle. Adjust the miter saw to get a tight fit.

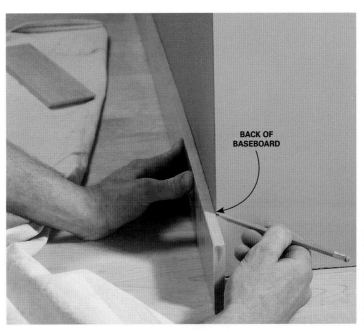

BACK OF
BASEBOARD

15 Hold the baseboard in place and mark the back side at the corner. Now cut the piece to length at the predetermined angle for an exact fit.

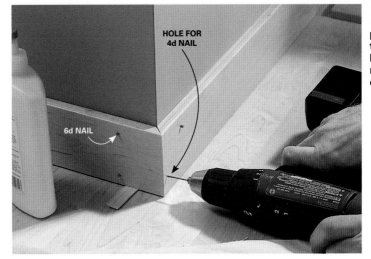

HOLE FOR
4d NAIL

6d NAIL

16 Cut the second piece to length at the same angle. Predrill, glue and nail the outside corner.

INSIDE CORNER

BASE CAP CUT AT 45 DEGREES

17 Run the base cap in the same order as the baseboard. To cope the inside corner of the base cap for a tight fit, first cut one end at a 45-degree angle as if you were cutting an inside miter.

Install the base shoe last. Base shoe is usually used on hard-surface floors to conceal any irregularities or gaps between the floor and the baseboard. Even if your baseboards fit perfectly tight to the floor, you can install the shoe to add another dimension to your trim. Install the shoe the same as the cap, mitering outside corners and coping inside corners (**Photo 21**). Be sure to nail the shoe into the baseboard, not the floor, so it won't pull away from the baseboard when the flooring expands and contracts. Finally, set all your nails and fill them with putty. We couldn't find a putty color to exactly match the stain we chose, so we mixed two shades together (**Photo 22**). **Tip:** With light-colored wood, always mix the color on the light side; darker putty stands out.

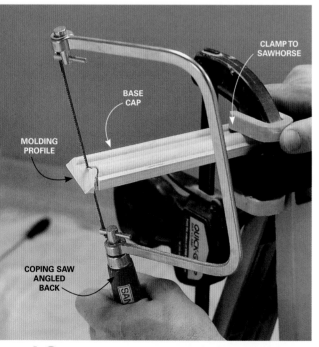

CLAMP TO SAWHORSE

BASE CAP

MOLDING PROFILE

COPING SAW ANGLED BACK

18 Use a coping saw to cut along the profile left by the miter. Angle your coping saw back slightly (back cut) to get a tighter fit on the face of the profile.

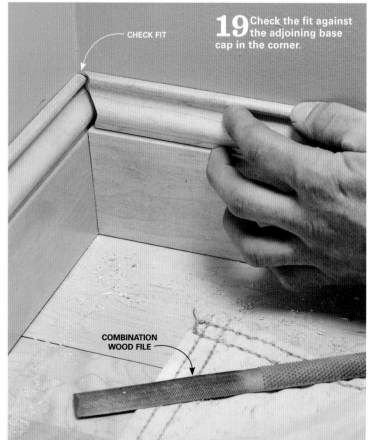

CHECK FIT

19 Check the fit against the adjoining base cap in the corner.

COMBINATION WOOD FILE

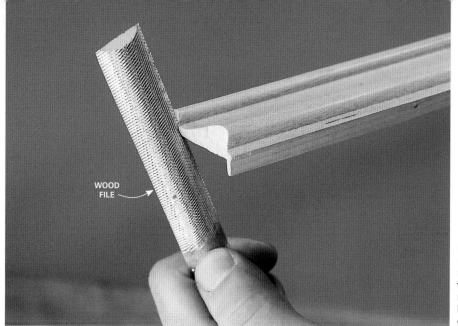

WOOD FILE →

20 Trim with a file as necessary. After fitting the cope, measure the cap for length, cut the other end and nail it up.

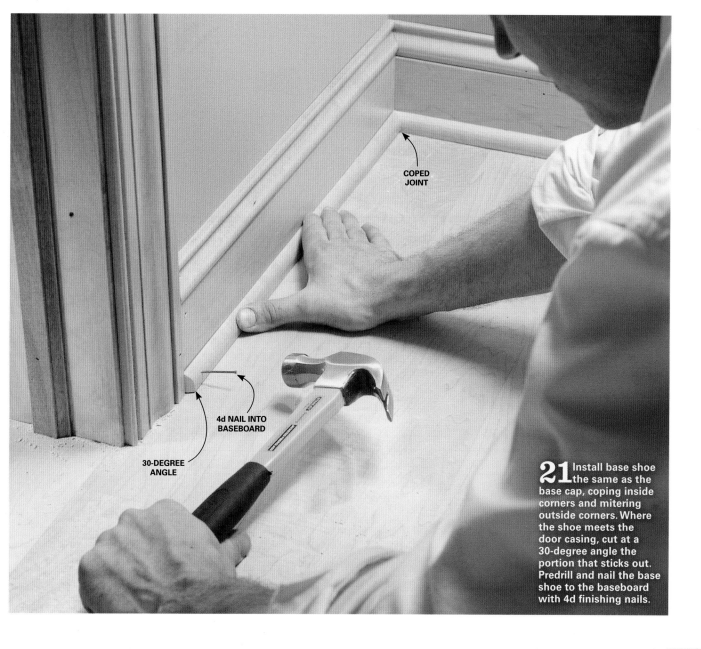

COPED JOINT

4d NAIL INTO BASEBOARD

30-DEGREE ANGLE

21 Install base shoe the same as the base cap, coping inside corners and mitering outside corners. Where the shoe meets the door casing, cut at a 30-degree angle the portion that sticks out. Predrill and nail the base shoe to the baseboard with 4d finishing nails.

GLOB OF PUTTY

COLORED PUTTY

RAG

22 Set the nails and fill the holes with colored putty to match the wood stain. We mixed two shades of putty together to get a good color match. Press the putty into the holes with your finger and wipe the excess off with a cloth.

PUTTY KNIFE

How to shop for trim

Stock trim is available in a wide range of styles from most lumberyards and home centers. We chose a relatively wide (3-1/4 in.) beaded casing to go around our doors and windows. It's 11/16 in. thick. We used three components to create the base: a 1/2-in. x 3-1/4 in. "hook strip," a 9/16-in. x 1-3/8 in. base cap, and a 7/16-in. x 3/4-in. base shoe. Combine other standard trim types to create wider and more detailed shapes.

If you don't find a trim style you like or you're trying to match a molding in an older house, look online for custom millwork shops that produce almost any type of trim from most species of wood. Custom work, however, comes at a price; be prepared to pay as much as three times the cost of stock moldings, plus setup charges of as much as $200. In addition, you may have to wait four to eight weeks.

Most trim is made of solid wood or medium-density fiberboard with a wood veneer. Oak, pine, birch, maple and poplar are the most common types available. We chose maple for our project.

Sometimes you can find trim made of various types of plastic, most often prefinished in white, brown or simulated wood. This trim is far more stable than wood but cuts much the same, if not easier. What it lacks, however, is the warmth and varied grain pattern you can only find in real wood.

Purchase your trim in lengths long enough to cover each wall. If you can't purchase the trim in long enough lengths, don't worry. On p. 191, we show you how to splice two pieces to cover the length of a long wall.

Painting Woodwork

Having trouble getting your paint to look smooth? Welcome to the club. Painting woodwork so it has a flawless, glossy sheen is challenging. Here you'll learn some techniques and tricks that'll produce top-notch results.

For great painted woodwork, good surface preparation and good brushing technique are essential.

Many pros still rely solely on oil-based paints because they dry slowly and allow brush marks to flatten out. But you can achieve similar results with high-quality latex paint. Today's formulations cover and brush out well. You won't have the strong odor of oil that'll drive you out of the house for days. And latex also offers the advantage of fast drying and easy soap and water cleanup.

Latex paint is available in a range of sheens from flat to high gloss. Because you want your wood trim to wear well, use eggshell or semigloss. The downside to these shiny finishes is that every bump and scratch shows through.

1 Remove all loose or cracked paint with a stiff putty knife. Work in various directions to get underneath the loose paint.

HARDENER

FILLER

2 Fill nicks and gouges with a two-part wood filler. Mix it thoroughly (following label directions) with a 2- or 3-in. flexible metal or plastic putty knife.

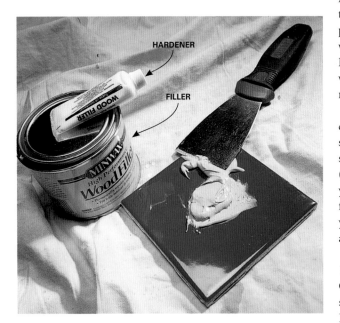

3 Pick up a dab of putty with the knife and apply it to the gouges. Hold the putty knife at an angle and press and smooth the filler into the scraped area. Leave the filler slightly higher than the surrounding surface.

Preparation, preparation

A coat of paint won't fill or hide cracks, chips and other surface defects, and it won't smooth an existing rough surface. You have to fill and smooth the woodwork first.

Wash the woodwork with a TSP solution or TSP substitute, to remove grease and grime. Mix according to the directions on the package and scrub with a sponge or rag. Be sure to rinse well with clear water to remove residues.

> **Tip**
> Stiff putty knives work better for scraping; flexible putty knives work better for filling.

Next examine the surface for loose and cracked paint that'll need scraping. Many scraper types are available, but a 2-in. stiff putty knife works well for small areas (**Photo 1**). When you're done scraping, you'll be left with a rougher surface and a few more scratches and gouges than when you started. Don't worry—you'll fix these areas next.

For dents and chips deeper than about 1/8 in., use a two-part polyester resin. One example is Minwax wood filler. It sticks well, doesn't shrink and sands easily. It's also the best material for rebuilding chipped corners. Auto body fillers also work well.

Scoop out a golf ball–size amount onto a scrap piece of wood, cardboard or tile. Add the correct amount of hardener (follow the directions) and mix thoroughly but quickly (**Photo 2**). The resin only has a 5- to 10-minute working time.

For finer scratches and chips, use spackling compound. (Ready Patch by

> **CAUTION**
> If your home was built before 1979, check the paint for lead before you scrape or sand. For more information, go to epa.gov/lead.

Zinsser is one brand used by many pros.) Don't use a lightweight compound; it doesn't stick to painted wood as well.

"Spot-prime" the filler and any bare wood with a latex primer. This step is worth the effort because it helps you see imperfections. Check your work by holding a bright light (trouble light or flashlight) close to the woodwork (**Photo 5**). Every small bump and scratch will jump out. Circle the defects with a pencil, then go back to the filler and sanding steps. Spot-prime and finish-sand these reworked areas.

Prep work requires patience, especially when you have to go back to an earlier step. What you decide is acceptable here is what you'll get in the finish coat. But keep in mind that the most critical eye will probably be yours.

Finish up the prep work by lightly sanding all areas that haven't been scraped and spot-primed. Use 180-grit paper or the fine sanding sponge. This will smooth out previous brush marks and scuff the surface to help the new coat of paint stick. Then wipe down the whole surface with a damp cloth to remove all the dust.

Caulk

Now that the filling, sanding and priming are done, caulk any long cracks and gaps (**Photo 6**). Use an acrylic latex caulk; it adheres well, remains flexible and cleans up with water. Cut the caulk tube at the very tip to leave a very small hole. You'll have better control of the caulk. Apply a bead of caulk that protrudes slightly above the crack or gap, then wipe it with a damp cloth wrapped around your finger. Wipe excess caulk off the cloth so you don't smear it on either side of the joint. You may have to wipe several times to produce a smooth, clean caulk line.

SANDING SPONGE

4 Sand the filler flush to the painted surface with 100- or 120-grit sandpaper or a medium sanding sponge. Make sure to eliminate all ridges. Then finish-sand with 180-grit sandpaper or a fine sanding sponge. Spot-prime the filler and any bare wood.

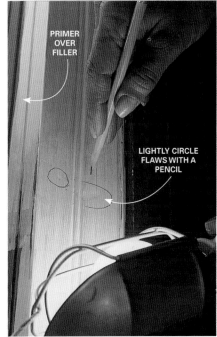

PRIMER OVER FILLER

LIGHTLY CIRCLE FLAWS WITH A PENCIL

5 Hold a utility light close to the surface, and circle any imperfections with a pencil. Fill, sand and spot-prime these areas. Finally, lightly sand the entire surface with the 180-grit paper to ensure that the new paint will stick.

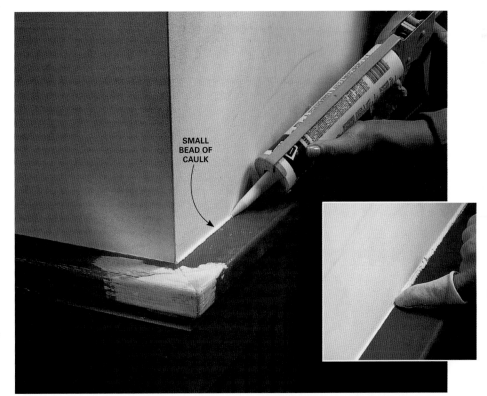

SMALL BEAD OF CAULK

6 Apply a small bead of paintable caulk to the crack between the wood and the wall. Smooth the caulk with a damp rag wrapped around your finger. Wipe the edges to remove any ridges of caulk.

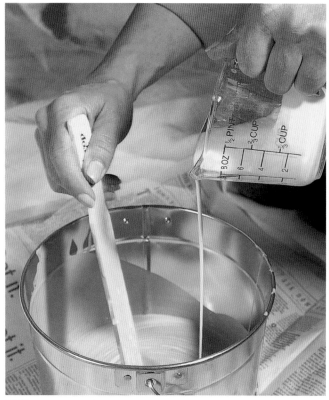

7 Pour a quart of paint into the pail and add a latex additive (such as Floetrol) for smoother results. Follow the label's instructions for the correct amount. Mix thoroughly.

8 Dip the brush bristles 1 to 2 in. into the paint to load the brush. Lightly tap the tip of the brush against the sides of the pail to shake off excess paint.

Choosing a brush

As with paint, buy quality when you shop for brushes. For trim use a 2-1/2-in. straight brush and for detail work and cutting in, a 1-1/2-in. angle brush. Whether to use a straight or an angled brush is an individual choice. For latex, buy a synthetic bristle brush with "exploded" tips. A good brush draws a decent "load" of paint into the bristles and applies it smoothly to the work surface.

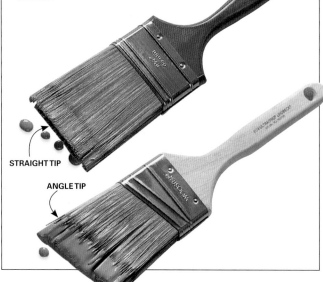

STRAIGHT TIP

ANGLE TIP

The paint and the brush

Don't undermine all the time and effort you've put into the prep work by using cheap brushes and paint. Buy the best. With proper cleaning, a quality brush will last for years. In most cases, you'll find the highest quality paint and tools (and good advice) at specialty paint stores.

Latex paint has one weakness: It dries quickly. The longer the paint remains wet, the better it flows and flattens, leaving a smooth surface. Use an additive that slows down the drying process and helps the paint lie smooth. (Floetrol is one common choice.) Read the directions for the amount to add.

For best results from brushing, don't dip directly from the can. Pour a quart of the paint into a 4- or 5-qt. pail. This is your working paint that will move around with you. Add the measured amount of additive and mix well (**Photo 7**). From this pail you can dip and tap your brush without splattering. Good-quality paints are ready to use out of the can and don't need thinning with water. Be sure to have the paint store shake the can so it's well mixed, then stir the paint occasionally as you use it.

Brushing technique

The sequence in brushing is to quickly coat an area with several brush loads of paint, and then blend and smooth it out by lightly running the unloaded brush tip over it (called "tipping"). See **Photos 9–11, p. 199**. Try to coat a whole board or section, but don't let the paint sit more than a minute before tipping.

The more paint the brush carries, the faster you'll coat the

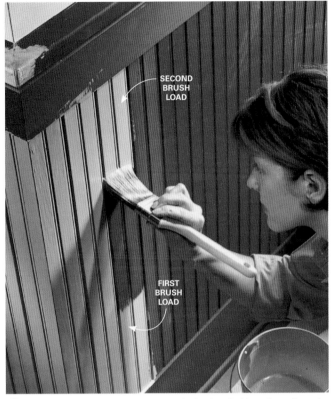

9 Start at the top of the board with the loaded brush and stroke down toward the middle. When the brush begins to drag, stop and reload.

10 "Tip" the wet paint by lightly setting the tip of the brush against the wet paint at the top of the board and lightly stroking down the whole length of the board. Hold the brush almost perpendicular to the surface for this stroke.

woodwork. But you want to avoid dripping. So after dipping, tap the tip of the brush against the pail, like the clapper of a bell (**Photo 8**). For a drier brush, try dragging one side over the edge of the pail.

Hold the brush at about a 45-degree angle, set the tip down where you want to start and pull it gently over the surface with a little downward pressure (**Photo 9**). Here's where the good brush pays off. The paint will flow smoothly onto the surface with little effort on your part. A common mistake is to force paint out of the brush after it becomes too dry. The goal is a uniform thickness but not so thick as to run or sag. With practice, you'll quickly find the ideal thickness. If the new color doesn't hide the old, it's better to apply a second coat than to apply the paint too thick. Continue the next brush load from where the last stroke left off, or work backward, say from an inside corner back into the wet paint.

When "tipping," avoid dabbing small areas as this leaves marks in the paint. Make long strokes. The brush will leave a slight track of parallel ridges, but they'll lie down before the paint begins to skin over (**Photo 11**).

Masking off and cutting in

Often the boards you're painting butt against a different paint color or a wall. There are a couple of ways to leave a sharp, crisp line.

Masking off with tape is one method. Lay painter's tape tight to the line where your new coat of paint will end (**Photo 12**). Push the tape tight against the surface with a putty knife to

11 The fine brushstrokes left after tipping will flow together until the paint begins to skin over.

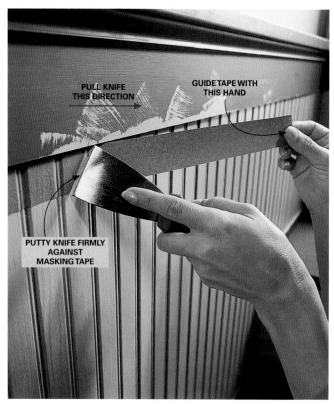

PULL KNIFE
THIS DIRECTION

GUIDE TAPE WITH
THIS HAND

PUTTY KNIFE FIRMLY
AGAINST
MASKING TAPE

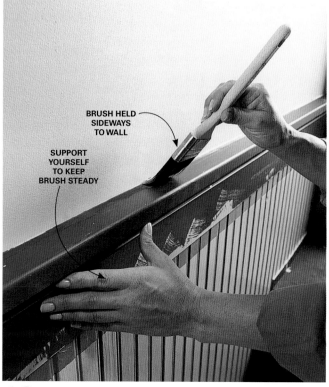

BRUSH HELD
SIDEWAYS
TO WALL

SUPPORT
YOURSELF
TO KEEP
BRUSH STEADY

12 Apply painter's masking tape to protect finished surfaces before brushing on the second color. Carefully position the tape and push it tight against the surface with a putty knife. Be sure the paint underneath has thoroughly dried before taping.

13 Load the 1-1/2-in. brush with paint and drag one side over the edge of the pail. Holding the dry side of the brush toward the wall, carefully set the tip of the brush close to the wall line. Apply a little pressure and pull the brush along the line. Guide the paint up to the line by manipulating the pressure and position of the brush's tip as you pull it along.

Paint brush holder

Soak oil brushes in cleaning solvent without bending the bristles and ruining the brush! Clip a medium or large binder clip around the handle of a brush and spread the arms to span a cleaning container so the brush bristles don't touch the bottom.

BINDER
CLIP

prevent the wet paint from bleeding (running) underneath the tape. Brush the woodwork, letting the paint go partially onto the tape, then tip. Remove the tape when the paint is dry.

The pros usually skip the masking tape and just cut in with a brush; it's faster. With some practice and a steady hand, even an amateur can get very sharp lines. Learn with a smaller brush (1-1/2 in.) and go to a wider brush as you gain control. Dip the brush and scrape one side on the pail. Hold the dry side of the brush toward the wall and slowly draw the brush along (**Photo 13**). Support your arm to steady it, and keep the stroke moving. Use gentle downward pressure; you want the bristles to splay out slightly as you stroke. You'll find you can control the paint line by varying the pressure you apply to the brush.

When the brush is dry, reload and start where the previous stroke ended. Sometimes you'll have to go back over a section where the paint is shy of the wall. Complete cutting in and then coat the rest of the piece.

Finishing up

Whether one coat will suffice depends on the paint used and the color. If the first coat of paint looks streaky or transparent, a second coat is necessary. Let the previous coat of paint dry overnight, then lightly sand with 180- or 220-grit paper or a fine sanding sponge. Wash the dust off the surface with a damp cloth, let dry and brush on another coat.

No Cutting Corners

Tips for tight miters and coped joints

Miters rarely fit on the first try. More often than not, you'll encounter out-of-square corners, walls that aren't plumb and drywall that has bumps. The secret to making tight-fitting miters is knowing how to adjust your cuts for these real-world conditions. We'll show you tricks you can use to cut door and window casing and baseboard joints to fit perfectly, even when you have less-than-perfect walls and jambs.

Shim and shave miters

How many times have you set your miter saw exactly on 45 degrees and cut miters on a pair of moldings, only to discover they don't fit? Well, don't worry. There's nothing wrong with your saw or your technique. Miters almost always have to be shaved to fit perfectly.

One method is to simply adjust the angle slightly on your miter saw and recut both moldings. The trouble is that making tiny adjustments to the cutting angle is difficult on many saws. A quicker and easier method is to place a shim against the miter saw fence to slightly change the angle. Move the shim away from the blade for smaller adjustments and closer for larger ones, or vary the thickness of the shim. Remember, both pieces need the exact same cut to fit precisely.

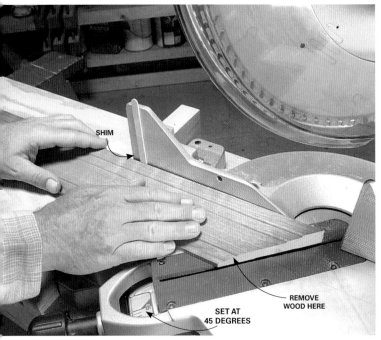

SHIM

SET AT 45 DEGREES

REMOVE WOOD HERE

1 MICRO-ADJUST A MITER. Close a gap on the top of a miter by placing a skinny shim (1/16 in. or less) against the portion of the fence farthest from the blade. Slide the molding tight to the shim and against the fence near the blade. Hold it in this position while you make the cut. To close a gap at the bottom of the miter, place the shim near the blade.

> **CAUTION**
> Keep your fingers at least 6 in. from the path of the blade.

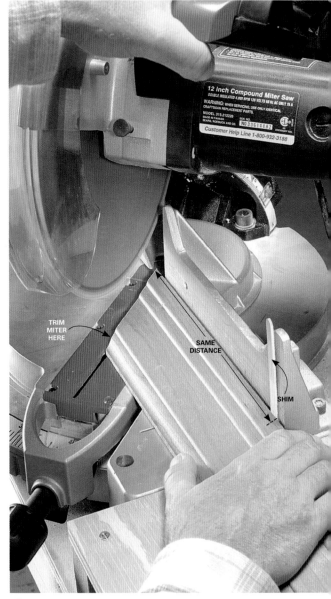

TRIM MITER HERE

SAME DISTANCE

SHIM

2 TREAT BOTH SIDES THE SAME. Trim the other half of the miter using the same technique. Use the same shim and place it the same distance from the blade. Drop the blade slowly through the wood to shave thin slices.

Tilt trim on inset jambs

Occasionally you'll run into a door or window jamb that isn't quite flush with the wall. On a protruding jamb, you can nail the trim to the jamb, slip a shim between the trim and the drywall, and then nail the trim to the wall. Caulk and paint will hide the gap.

An inset jamb demands a different approach. First remove enough drywall so the trim can span the jamb and wall without rocking (**Photo 2**). This solves half the problem. But even now a regular 45-degree miter won't fit because the molding has to tilt down to meet the jamb. Correct this problem by tilting the trim on the bed of the miter box to match the angle at which it rests against the wall. Then make standard 45-degree miter cuts. **Photo 1** shows how to determine the correct thickness for the shim used in **Photo 3** to tilt the molding.

CUT SHIM TO GAP WIDTH

RECESSED DOORJAMB

COMBINATION SQUARE

1 CUSTOM-CUT A SHIM. Cut a shim just thick enough to slip under a straightedge spanning the drywall corner. Use this shim to elevate the outside edge of your molding (Photo 3) before cutting it.

BEVEL THE DRYWALL

UTILITY KNIFE

2 SLICE THE DRYWALL. Trim back the drywall with a sharp utility knife until the molding no longer rocks when it's set in place against the jamb and drywall. Use a hammer to mash and flatten the drywall if necessary.

3 TILT THE TRIM WITH A SHIM. Raise the outside edge of the molding with the shim (right) and cut the 45-degree miter. Repeat the process for the opposite miter. If other small adjustments to the angle are needed, follow the tip in Photo 1.

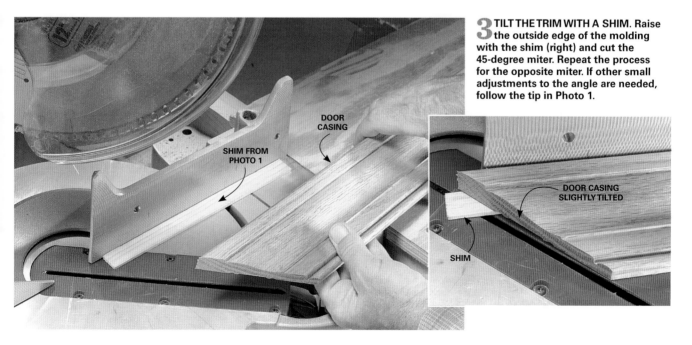

SHIM FROM PHOTO 1

DOOR CASING

DOOR CASING SLIGHTLY TILTED

SHIM

Cope baseboard faster

Coping is better than mitering at inside corners. But on tall baseboards, cutting the long, straight section of the cope with a coping saw is difficult, and the cut is usually wavy. Instead, start the cope as usual (**Photo 1**). Then tip the molding upside down in the miter saw and saw straight down to the profiled section. Finally, complete the cope by sawing out the profile (**Photo 3**).

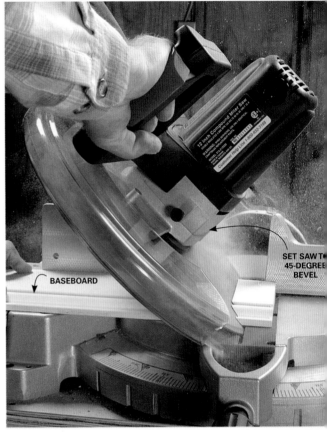

SET SAW TO
45-DEGREE
BEVEL

BASEBOARD

1 START WITH A MITER CUT. As with any coped joint, begin by cutting a 45-degree miter on the baseboard. The miter cut provides a profile to guide your cope cut.

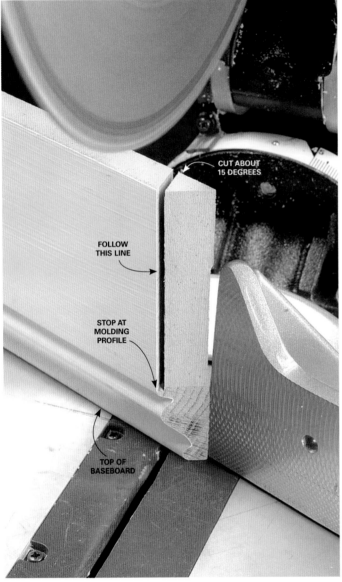

CUT ABOUT
15 DEGREES

FOLLOW
THIS LINE

STOP AT
MOLDING
PROFILE

TOP OF
BASEBOARD

2 MAKE THE STRAIGHT CUT. Turn the mitered baseboard upside down. Adjust the angle to about 15 degrees and saw down along the straight section of the beveled cut. Keep the blade slightly to the outside of the line. Let the blade stop before lifting it from the cut.

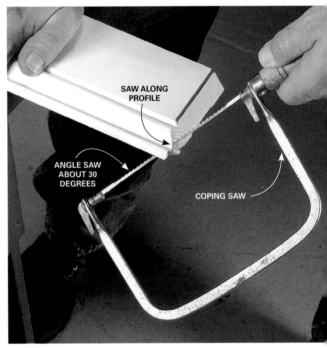

SAW ALONG
PROFILE

ANGLE SAW
ABOUT 30
DEGREES

COPING SAW

3 CUT THE CURVES. Saw out the remaining profiled section with a coping saw. Tilt the saw to at least a 30-degree angle to create a back bevel for easier fitting.

Overcut outside corners

Getting outside corners to fit tight is trickier than it looks. The key is to make accurate marks with the baseboard in place rather than relying on measurements. And then cut the piece a little long so you still have the option to shave a little from the angle if it doesn't fit. Since gaps on the back of the corner are barely noticeable, while gaps on the front are glaring, it's a good idea to start by cutting slightly steeper 45-1/2-degree angles first. Then if there's still a gap in the front, cut a slightly steeper angle on both pieces. You'll need a compound miter saw or sliding compound miter saw to easily cut tight-fitting miters on wide baseboard.

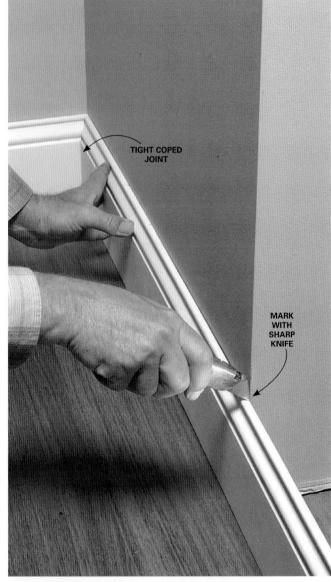

1 MARK WITH A KNIFE. Mark outside corners with a sharp utility knife. It's far more precise than a pencil mark. Repeat the marking process on the opposite baseboard. Cut 45-1/2-degree angles on both boards, leaving each an extra 1/8 in. long.

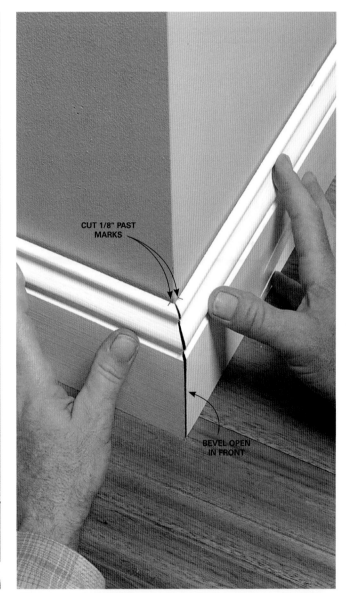

2 CHECK THE FIT. If the miter is open on the front, increase the cutting angle to about 46 degrees and recut both sides. Be careful to remove only a hair's width from each board. Reduce the angle if the cut is open at the back. When the angle is correct, recut each board just to the outside of the marks before nailing them into place.

Close gaps at inside corners

Uneven walls or floors that are out of level can cause even perfectly coped inside corners to look lousy. Check the fit of your cope before you nail in either base molding. That way you'll still have the option to shim out the bottom of the square-cut (uncoped) piece to close a gap at the bottom of the cope (**Photo 2**). **Photo 3** shows marking a cope that's open at the top. You then file or plane to the line.

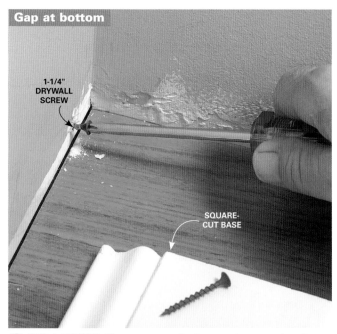

ADD A SCREW. Close a gap at the bottom by removing the square-cut base and driving a drywall screw into the wall about 1/2 in. from the floor. Test the cope and adjust the screw in or out until the cope fits tight.

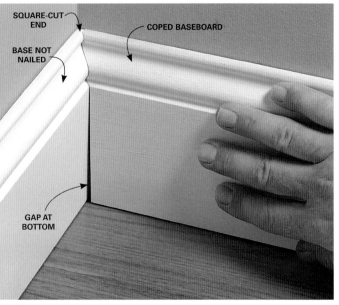

CHECK THE FIT. Check the fit against the square-cut piece of base before nailing either of the two baseboards. The straight sections rarely fit perfectly.

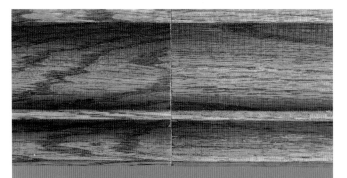

Avoid trim collisions

Here's one of the easiest ways to make your work look better: When sections of trim meet at joints or corners, match the wood tone and grain pattern. It only takes a few seconds, and you'll avoid ugly mismatches like this.

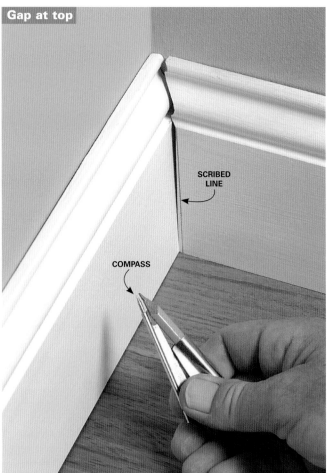

SCRIBE AND TRIM. Close a gap at the top by scribing the gap with a small compass to mark the wood to be removed. Then file to the line.

Ceramic Tile Floor

Whether you're replacing an old shabby floor or installing a new one, you can't beat ceramic or stone tile for durability and appearance. When laid properly, it's virtually a forever floor that requires almost no care and maintenance. And you can select materials from a vast array of colors and textures.

What's equally attractive is that you can lay a first-class tile floor yourself, often in one weekend, and save the $500 to $1,500 cost of hiring a pro.

The key to keeping the job simple is to cover the old vinyl or other flooring with a new thin underlayment that gives you a fresh, clean start. No messy tearout and repair. On the following pages, expert tile installer Edward Read-Morgan of Straight Line Tile and Stone explains how to install a new floor.

This is a two-day project for most bathrooms, even if you don't have any previous tile experience. If you're comfortable using basic hand tools and have the patience to align tiles just right, you can handle this job. The entire cost of this project for a typical bath ranges from $300 to $600.

Assess your floor

The success of any tile job depends on a solid base, that is, a floor that flexes very little as you walk across it. If you have a concrete subfloor, this isn't an issue. You can lay tile directly over the existing vinyl as long as it's well adhered.

If possible, avoid tearing out vinyl flooring. Leaving it in place saves time, of course, but it also reduces asbestos hazard concerns. Asbestos was used in sheet vinyl and vinyl tile until the mid-1980s. By leaving the vinyl undisturbed, you won't risk sending asbestos fibers into the air.

If you have a wood subfloor, there's a good chance that you'll have to install backer board over your vinyl to make the floor thicker and stiff enough for tile. The easiest way to see flooring thickness is to pull off a floor register. Otherwise look for plumbing passageways through the floor. As a last resort, drill through the floor with a 1-in. or larger spade bit (your new floor will cover the hole later). To prevent asbestos dust from becoming airborne, mist the bit with a spray bottle as you drill. In addition to floor thickness, you'll need to determine joist spacing. If there's an unfinished basement or crawlspace below

the floor, simply measure the spacing. If there's a ceiling, probe for joists with a drill bit as described on p. 209.

If the joists are spaced 16 in. apart, the layers of structural flooring beneath the vinyl should add up to at least 1-1/8 in. With joists every 24 in., you need 1-1/2 in. If your floor is too thin for tile, add a thicker layer of tile backer board. If your floor is already thick enough, you can simply prep the vinyl floor (**Photos 1–4**) and skip the backer installation (**Photos 5–8**). Then tile directly over the vinyl, following the same steps used over backer board.

Regardless of the type of subfloor, there are two situations where you can't leave vinyl in place: First, if large areas of the vinyl are loose, don't set tile or backer over it. Small loose spots are acceptable and easy to deal with (**Photo 4**). Second, "cushioned" sheet vinyl must be removed before you can set tile. Cushioned vinyl has a foam backing that makes it noticeably thicker and softer than standard vinyl flooring. It's too spongy to support tile or backer board. Before removing it, call your local health department for instructions on how to check for asbestos and proper procedures if asbestos is present.

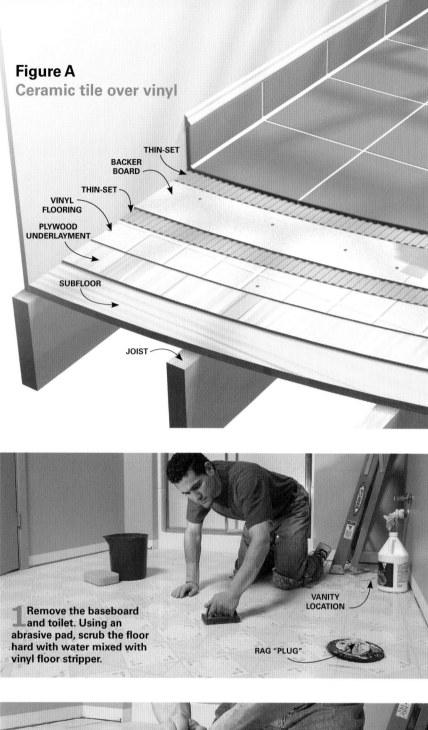

Figure A
Ceramic tile over vinyl

THIN-SET

BACKER BOARD

THIN-SET

VINYL FLOORING

PLYWOOD UNDERLAYMENT

SUBFLOOR

JOIST

1 Remove the baseboard and toilet. Using an abrasive pad, scrub the floor hard with water mixed with vinyl floor stripper.

VANITY LOCATION

RAG "PLUG"

2 Mark the floor joists with chalk lines and drive 2-1/2-in. screws every 8 in. Don't leave any screw heads protruding.

JOIST LOCATION

Estimating the cost of a tile project

The tile itself will be your biggest cost, so start by measuring the square footage of the floor. Then add 10 percent for cutting waste. If you choose a more complex layout than the simple grid pattern shown here, your waste will be greater. Most tile sells for $5 to $15 per square foot, but you can spend as little as $3 or more than $50. If you have to install backer board, add $2 per square foot to the cost of the

Materials list

Everything you need for this project is available at home centers. Most of what you need is also available at tile stores. Here's a list of everything you need:

ITEM

Backer board
1-1/4-in. backer board screws
Alkali-resistant mesh tape
Thin-set
Grout
Acrylic additive
Scouring pad
Toilet extension ring
Wax ring
Silicone caulk
No. 12 x 2-in. stainless steel screws
2-1/2-in. galvanized screws
Transition threshold
Construction adhesive
3/8-in. backer rod
Sanded caulk
Masking tape
Duct tape
1x4 guide boards
Chalk line
T-square or other straightedge
Drywall saw
Scoring knife
Kneepads
Notched trowels
Grout float
Margin trowel
Sponges
Tile spacers
Wedge spacers
Tile cutter
4-in. diamond blade
Angle grinder
Drill mixer
Buckets

tile. Other materials will cost about $90, regardless of bathroom size. The tile tools you'll need (including a tile cutter) will total $60 to $80.

Gather advice while you shop

Home centers carry everything you need for this project, but begin shopping at a tile store, where you're more likely to get expert advice. Snap a photo of your floor plan and jot down all the dimensions. Also take a photo of the floor at the doorway. This will help the tile store staff recommend a "transition" to neatly join the tile to the hallway flooring. Transitions come in different styles to suit any situation. When you choose the tile itself, ask if it requires any special installation steps. Some tile, for example, should be coated with grout release before grouting. Also ask about cutting techniques for the tile. You'll use sanded grout for the floor. Ask if sanded caulk is available in a color that matches your grout for the floor/tub and floor/wall tile joints.

Prepare the room

First, get the toilet out of your way. Stuff a rag in the hole to block sewer gases. If your home only has one toilet, you can leave it in place until you install backer board. Keep a supply of wax rings on hand if you plan to reinstall the toilet at the end of each day.

If you expect to keep your vanity for many years to come, leave it in place and tile around it. But if you think you might replace it, remove it now. When the job's done, you can reinstall the old vanity or put in a new one. Having the vanity out of the way gives you more workspace, and you won't have to cut backer board and tiles to fit around it. This also eliminates the floor repair problem if you install a smaller vanity or pedestal sink in the future.

Pull off the baseboard or plan to add base shoe molding. This leads to a neater-

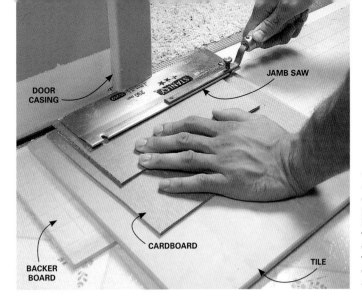

3 Undercut door trim using a jamb saw or handsaw. A piece of backer board, tile and two layers of cardboard raise the saw to the correct height above the floor.

DOOR CASING · JAMB SAW · CARDBOARD · BACKER BOARD · TILE

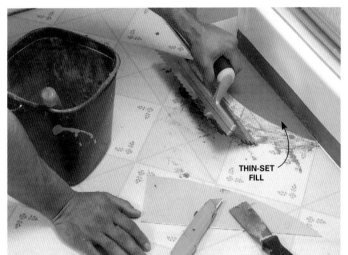

4 Cut out any loose sections of vinyl with a utility knife. Fill the void with thin-set using the flat edge of a notched trowel.

THIN-SET FILL

looking job because the edges of the tile will be covered later—jagged cuts and slight measuring mistakes are hidden. If your baseboard has base shoe molding, remove only the base shoe.

Backer board and tile will raise your floor 3/4 in. or more. So you'll have to remove and undercut the door. To mark the door for cutting, stack backer board, tile and two layers of cardboard on the floor (**Photo 3**). Mark the door 1/2 in. above the stack, remove the door and cut off the bottom.

Scrub, screw and patch the floor

Scrub the floor with a vinyl floor stripper following the manufacturer's instructions. The stripper will dissolve wax and other residue. Scrub hard with an abrasive scouring pad (**Photo 1**). The tiny scratches left by scrubbing help the thin-set bond better.

Next, drive screws through the floor into the joists (**Photo 2**). This ensures that the subfloor and underlayment are securely fastened. **If there's an unfinished basement below the floor, locating the joists is easy:** Go to the basement and drill a couple of 1/4-in. holes up through the floor next to a joist. If you can't locate the joists from below, pick a spot near one wall and drill a hole. If the bit breaks through into hollow space, move over 1 in. and drill another hole. Keep going until you hit a joist. Then go to the opposite wall and find the other end of the joist. Measure at intervals of 16 or 24 in. from the first joist to locate the others.

While you're driving screws, look for any spots where the vinyl has loosened from the floor. Cut out loose spots and fill them (**Photo 4**). If there are any copper pipes that pass through the floor, wrap them with duct tape at floor level. Cement-based thin-set and grout can corrode copper.

CAUTION
Cement products like thin-set and grout draw moisture from skin and can even cause burns that require medical attention. While most pros work bare-handed, wear gloves if you have any skin sensitivity. Also wear eye protection while mixing thin-set and grout.

Install backer board

The backer board is fastened with a combination of screws and thin-set adhesive. Cut and lay out all the pieces before you mix the thin-set (**Photos 5** and **6**). You can run the sheets in any direction, but be sure to stagger the joints so you never have four corners meeting at one point. Leave a 1/8-in. space between the sheets and along the vanity, tub or shower. The gap along walls must be at least 1/8 in. wide, but a wider gap (about 1/2 in.) makes the panels easier to set in place. After cutting and fitting, label the location of each one and set them all aside.

Vacuum the floor and have your drill and screws ready to go before you mix the thin-set. Read the thin-set's label. Spread the thin-set with a 1/4-in. notched trowel. Comb in one direction so air can escape when you embed the backer (**Photo 7**). Drive screws every 6 in. around the perimeter of each piece and every 8 in. "in the field" (across the face of the panel). If the leftover thin-set is still workable, you can immediately embed mesh tape over joints (**Photo 8**). If the thin-set is too stiff or chunky, mix a new batch. Use "alkali-resistant" tape that's meant for backer board. While the tape coat of thin-set hardens, run a putty knife over all the screw heads to scrape off the "mushroom" bulges around screws. Drive in any protruding screw heads you come across.

Careful layout pays off

Too often, tile novices simply start setting tile in a corner and continue along two walls until the floor is covered. Sometimes they get lucky and the floor looks good. But more often this method leads to trouble: They end up with awkward-looking, thin slivers of tile along a prominent wall or at the doorway. And the tile looks even worse when walls are badly out of square or crooked—a straight grout line running too close to a wall emphasizes the wall's imperfections.

5 Cover the floor with backer board. Cut inside corners, circles and curves with a drywall saw. Space pieces 1/8 in. apart and hold each one in place with two temporary screws.

6 Make straight cuts with a scoring knife. Make three or four scoring passes, then snap the backer over a 2x4. When all the pieces have been laid out, label them and set them aside.

7 Comb out a bed of thin-set just large enough for each piece of backer board using a 1/4-in. notched trowel held at a 45-degree angle. Screw the backer down before spreading thin-set for the next piece.

MESH TAPE

8 Press adhesive-backed mesh tape over the joints and skim over the tape with thin-set. When the thin-set is firm but not fully hardened, scrape away any ridges with a putty knife.

Whether you're laying a simple grid pattern as shown here, or a diagonal pattern with a border, the best tile layout usually calls for centering full tiles between walls so the partial tiles along the edges will end up all the same size. Don't rely on your tape measure and mental arithmetic. Rip open a carton of tile, grab a handful of spacers and experiment with your layout on the floor.

To begin, center rows of tile between walls so you have equal spaces along walls that face each other (**Photo 9**). Set the two rows parallel to the two most prominent walls. Then make adjustments, trying to achieve these three goals:

- Use full tiles at doorways and along the bathtub or shower. These are usually the only places where the edges of the floor aren't covered by baseboard. If you use full tiles in these exposed spots, you don't have to worry about making smooth, perfect cuts.
- Minimize cutting and try to avoid difficult cuts. For example: Cutting tile to an L-shape to fit around an outside corner is especially difficult when one arm of the "L" is less than 2 in. wide. The arm tends to break off as you cut.
- Avoid narrow tiles along walls. Ideally, you'll end up with tiles cut to half size or larger. Avoid cutting tile to widths less than 2 in.

Chances are, your layout won't meet all these goals. Because the shower stall was the focal point in this bathroom, it is the No. 1 layout priority. Full tiles are used in front of the shower, leaving 3-in.-wide tiles along the opposite wall, which is less prominent.

Once you determine a layout, establish lines to guide your tile positioning. The usual method is to snap chalk lines on the floor. But chalk lines are hard to see after you've spread thin-set, and one row of tile may slip as you set the next row. Pros use a more reliable guide: Choose straight boards a foot shorter than the length and width of the room. Tape one edge of each board so thin-set won't stick to them. Then screw the boards to the floor at a right angle to form a guide that eliminates guesswork and shifting (**Photo 10**).

Set the tile (finally!)

It's usually easiest—and most efficient—to set tile in two phases: First set all the full "field" tiles (**Photo 11**). Then, when

9 Dry-lay tile to determine the best layout. Start with centered rows, leaving equal spaces at walls. Then reposition rows until you find the optimal layout.

EQUAL SPACES

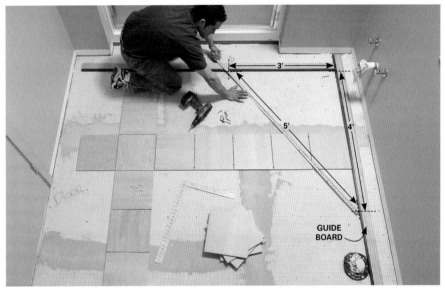

10 Screw guide boards to the floor following your chosen layout. Position the guides so you can lay all the field tiles without moving the guides. Make sure the guides are at right angles by measuring out a 3-4-5 triangle.

GUIDE BOARD

the thin-set has hardened for several hours, cut all the perimeter tiles and set them (**Photo 12**). Here are some tips for both phases of the job:

- The trowel you use for setting tile may be different from the one you used to embed the backer. The thin-set label tells you which notch size to use relative to tile size.
- Dampen the backer board with a sponge just before applying thin-set. This keeps the thin-set from drying out too quickly.
- Comb the thin-set in one direction so air pockets won't be trapped under tile.
- Open three or four cartons and mix the tiles as you set them. Pattern and color vary slightly from one carton to the next.
- Don't just set each tile into place; press down and wiggle the tile to embed

it firmly in the thin-set. Use spacers between tiles.

- Watch for "tipped" corners. When you press a tile in place, it's easy to tilt it slightly so that one corner stands higher or lower than neighboring tiles.
- When you complete a section of tile, inspect it before moving on. Make sure the tiles line up correctly and spacers are in place. Wipe any thin-set off the face of tiles with a damp sponge.
- When the thin-set becomes chunky or too stiff, throw it away and mix more. Never try to extend the life of thin-set or grout by adding water.
- Cut perimeter tile so that caulked joints (at tub) are the same width as grouted joints.

FIELD TILE

SPACERS

11 Comb out a few square feet of thin-set and set tile against the guides. Continue until all the full tiles are in place. Tip: watch for squeeze-out between tiles and get it out with tile spacers.

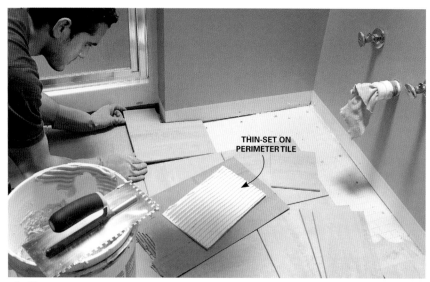

THIN-SET ON PERIMETER TILE

12 Cut and set the perimeter tiles after the thin-set beneath the full tiles has hardened. In spaces too narrow for your trowel, comb thin-set onto the backs of tiles.

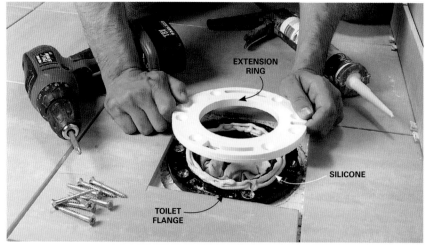

EXTENSION RING

SILICONE

TOILET FLANGE

13 Remove the old screws from the toilet flange and apply a heavy bead of silicone caulk. Fasten the extension ring over the old flange with stainless steel or brass screws.

Prepare the floor for grout

When all the tiles are in place and the thin-set has hardened, remove all the spacers. Next, raise the toilet flange by adding an extension ring or two (**Photo 13**). The extended flange should be flush with or higher than the surrounding tile. When you grout, fill in between the flange and tile. That way, any future leak around the flange will show up on the bathroom floor instead of on the ceiling below.

If you plan to use a glue-down transition, install it now. Remove the old metal strip, then cut your transition strip to fit between the door jambs using a miter saw. Next, add a tack strip to hold adjacent carpet in place. Before gluing the transition to the floor (**Photo 14**), you may have to remove a thin strip of the old vinyl floor.

Grout is too brittle to handle the slight shifting movements that are normal in any room. Keep grout out of joints wherever the floor meets the tub, shower, vanity or walls (**Photo 15**).

Pack the joints with grout

The thin-set directions will tell you how soon you can grout the floor—usually 24 hours. Grouting isn't complex. Just plop a couple of scoops of grout onto the floor in a corner, work the grout into joints (**Photo 16**) and scrape off the excess grout before moving to the next section. In addition:

- Mix the grout to a mashed-potatoes consistency. Adding extra liquid makes grout easier to work with but weakens it.
- Don't just spread the grout over the joints; press hard to pack it into the joints. If you're doing it right, your forearm will get a good workout.
- Whether you're filling joints or scraping off excess grout, always push the float diagonally across the tiles.
- Scrape off the excess to leave tile as clean as you can. The less grout you leave on the tiles, the easier cleanup will be.
- When you're done, cover the grout bucket with a plastic bag and set it in a cool place to slow the hardening process. During cleanup, you may find spots that need a little extra.

Grout cleanup

Clean the surface of the tile when the grout is stiff enough to stay put in the joints but still soft enough to wipe off the tile surface. During hot, dry weather, grout can become difficult to wipe away in just 10 minutes, so get ready for cleanup before you even mix the grout. You'll need two buckets of clean water, two sponges, a synthetic scouring pad and a dry rag.

As soon as you're done grouting, go to the first section you grouted and wipe across a joint with a damp sponge. If the sponge pulls grout out of the joint, wait five minutes and try again. In cool, damp weather, the grout may stay too soft for an hour. When the grout is hard enough, gently wipe the tile with a damp sponge. Rinse the sponge frequently as you wipe the entire floor (**Photo 17**). If you come across tough spots, scrub them with the scouring pad. Be careful where you put your feet and knees—don't mar your perfect grout joints.

Immediately after the first pass, grab the second bucket of clean water and the fresh sponge and make a second, more thorough pass. Then, as the tile surface dries, wipe it with a microfiber cloth. The dry haze should buff off easily. If not, go for fresh water and sponge the floor again.

Finishing up

Let the grout cure overnight before you caulk joints, set the toilet or reinstall baseboard. Grout sealer is a good precaution against staining: Some products can be applied 24 hours after grouting; others require a two- to three-week wait. If you have leftover tile or grout, keep them in case you have to make repairs in the future. Be sure to write down the brand, color and retailer of the tile.

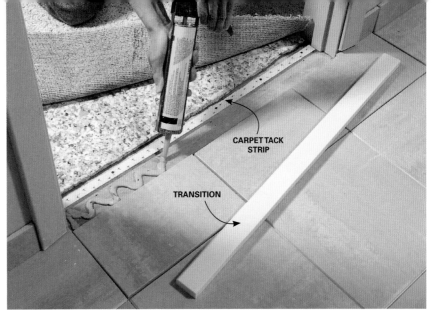

14 Glue the transition into place with construction adhesive. If carpet meets the transition, you may have to add a new tack strip.

CARPET TACK STRIP

TRANSITION

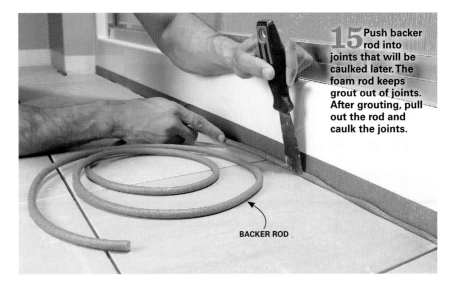

15 Push backer rod into joints that will be caulked later. The foam rod keeps grout out of joints. After grouting, pull out the rod and caulk the joints.

BACKER ROD

16 Work the grout back and forth across the floor, diagonal to the joints and holding the float at a 45-degree angle. Then scrape off the excess grout, holding the float almost upright.

GROUT FLOAT

17 Wipe grout off the tile surface with a damp sponge. Wipe gently on the first pass so you don't pull grout out of the joints. Rise the sponge often.

bench

shelf

Tile a Shower with Panache

Showers used to be simple boxes for fear that any special architectural features could lead to a leak—and expensive repairs. But modern tiling materials, especially spreadable waterproof membranes, can put these fears to rest. Now you can build in a bench or other structure with confidence and make showering more convenient and pleasant.

The following pages show you how to build in three features: a bench, a shelf and an alcove, as described by tiling contractor Dean Sorem of Sorem Tile. Included here are the key planning steps and the waterproofing and special tiling techniques that pros use. This project isn't for a tiling rookie. You should have some hands-on tiling experience before tackling a complex project like this one. But if you have rudimentary framing skills, and have successfully tiled floors, backsplashes or simple shower surrounds, the advanced techniques shown here will enable you to complete a project like this.

Framing, sheathing and tiling a shower like the one shown here will take you about four full days. The tiling alone will take two days. Tile and tiling supplies will cost about $600 if you choose standard tile. If you want fancy glass tile accents like the ones shown, brace yourself. Glass tile starts at $30 per sq. ft. and can cost upward of $100 per sq. ft., so it's wise to think of it as an accent only. It pays to rent or buy a "score and snap" tile cutter if you're using 4 x 4-in. tiles like the ones shown. But if you're using natural stone or larger tiles and your tile layout requires lots of cuts, especially notching, rent a tile saw for a day. You can score and snap glass tile (small mosaic tiles only), but you'll break about every 10th tile—not a big deal if you plan the tile layout well and only have to cut a few.

alcove

Plan the layout

First make sure you have enough space in your shower to add a bench. You'll need to leave at least 3 ft. of shower area so you can still move around.

The key to an exceptional tile job is to plan the shower with the actual tile you intend to use. Use the tile to decide exact dimensions and positions of benches, alcoves and even wall thicknesses so you can use whole tiles as much as possible and minimize cutting.

A foolproof method is to draw a full-scale template of each wall (**Figure A** and **Photo 1**). Be sure the wall drawing includes the thickness of backer board and any plywood that's needed, like on the bench seat. Then mark existing studs that outline alcove positions. Next, lay the tile on the template to decide on the heights, widths and depths of shower features like benches, alcoves and shelves.

Try to end up with full tiles outlining or covering those features whenever possible. Notice that this alcove is surrounded by full tiles. Those tiles determined the final position and size of the alcove. (It's easier to deal with cutting the tiles that cover the back of the alcove than the ones that border it.) Notice also that the exact height of the bench allowed for full tiles around it—no cutting needed.

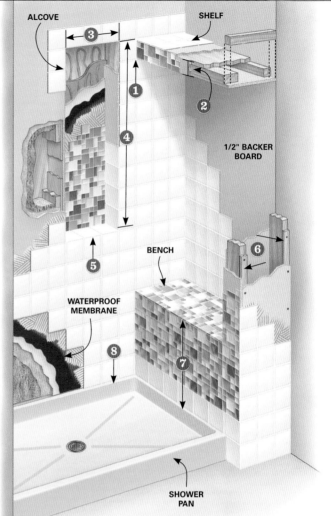

Figure A: Layout objectives

1 Shelf rests on full tile

2 Thickness matches face tile

3 Adjust alcove width for full field tiles

4 Plan height for full field tiles

5 Start alcove at top of tile row

6 Fur out as needed to avoid cutting tiles

7 Full tiles define bench height

8 Start with full tiles at base

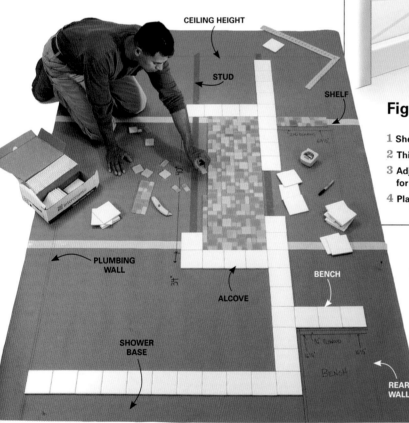

1 Plan the framing and tile layout for each wall on rosin paper cut to match the size of each wall.

Also adjust the thicknesses of walls and ledges for full tiles. If needed, fur out the 2x4 wall with strips of 1/2-in. plywood so the tile will cap the end without any cutting. Choose framing and sheathing thicknesses to achieve the same aim with the shelf edge. If possible, plan the tile for the large wall expanses so that you'll have columns of similar-width tiles at both ends of each wall. (**Figure A.**) You won't be able to avoid all tile cutting, of course. The goal is to simplify the tile work as much as possible. The more effort you put into planning the project, the easier it will be to install the tile. And you'll be rewarded with a first-class tile job.

Frame the shower

If you have a space between the shower base and the wall, start by framing a continuous wall, floor to ceiling, between the base and the wall (**Photo 2**). If there's no framing behind the ceiling for anchoring the wall, just screw it to the drywall and then add a bead of construction adhesive around the ceiling plate. Next, frame in the alcove. Use your template to establish the height of the top and bottom and then add blocking there. Fur out the side(s) if needed to accommodate tile sizes within the alcove and/or surrounding the opening. If your alcove is on an outside wall, glue 1-in.-thick foam insulation against the outside sheathing using special foam adhesive.

Frame the bench with a 1/4-in. slope so water will run off. Cap the bench with 3/4-in. plywood, screwing it with 1-5/8-in. screws. Lastly, add 2x6 blocking to anchor any shelves and any missing blocking at any inside corners.

Cement board tile backer is commonly used for shower walls, but pros use a drywall-type tile backer called DensShield. It's slightly more expensive than cement board but much easier to work with. You score it, snap it and cut it just like drywall.

Whatever material you use, anchor it with 1-1/4-in. cement board screws spaced every 4 in. at seams and every 6 in. everywhere else. If you have a premade shower base, keep the bottom row of backer board just above the lip. The tile will hang down over the lip to direct water into the base.

Next lay a strip of fiberglass mesh tape over all seams and corners. It has adhesive on one side, but many brands don't stick very well or for very long. If you have trouble, use staples to hold it in place. Mix up about a quart of thin-set mortar to the consistency of creamy peanut butter and trowel it over all the seams with a 6-in. putty knife. Try to avoid big buildups, which keep the tile from lying flat.

2 Add blocking to the top and bottom of the alcove, shimming the sides as needed, and fill in the back with foam board. Frame the end wall and then the bench.

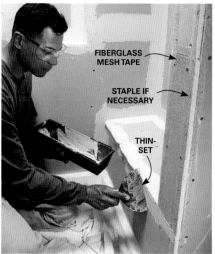

3 Cover all seams and corners with fiberglass mesh tape. Embed the tape with a thin layer of thin-set.

4 Coat water-prone areas with two coats of water-proofing membrane.

Apply waterproofing membrane

Any area that will be exposed to lots of water should be coated with two coats of a brush-on waterproofing membrane; (available at some home centers and all tile stores). Use disposable brushes and let the first coat dry thoroughly before recoating. The RedGard product shown here goes on pink and dries to red when it's ready for a second coat (**Photos 4** and **5**). Focus on areas that will get the lion's share of showerhead water, especially corners and horizontal bench surfaces and recessed alcoves. For extra protection, also coat all of the screw heads in areas that'll get deluged. As with the thin-set, try to avoid big buildups.

WATER-PROOFING MEMBRANE

Tile the alcove wall

Use your template as a guide to snap exact tile layout lines. First establish lines for the rows of tiles surrounding the alcove.

Then dry-stack and measure tiles to get an exact measurement from the bottom of the alcove to the top of the first row of tile. Draw a level line and screw a 1x2 ledger to the wall (**Photo 7**). The ledger will ensure a perfectly straight bottom course of tiles and keep them from sliding down the wall before the adhesive sets. (You'll remove the ledger and add the bottom row of tiles later, cutting them to height if needed.)

5 Spread thin-set on the back of the alcove with a 1/4-in. notched trowel and then embed the mosaic tile into the adhesive.

6 Support sagging mosaic tiles with shims and/or nails until the adhesive sets. Tamp all the tiles level with a grout float as shown in Photo 11.

Mix up about a quart of thin-set at a time (follow directions on the bag). Spread the thin-set onto the back of the alcove with a 1/4-in. notched trowel (**Photo 5**). Then press the mosaic tile sections into the thin-set. Lightly tap the tiles with a grout float to embed each small tile evenly with its neighbors (**Photo 11**). Look carefully for grout that works its way out between the tiles and wipe it off with a damp rag; it's tough to scrape off after it sets.

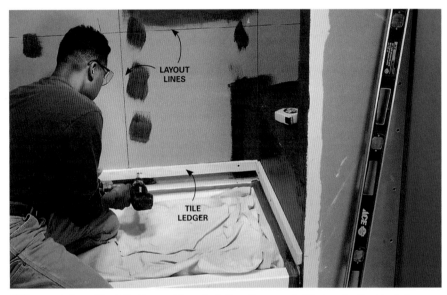

7 Lay out the critical tile lines with a chalk line. Screw a 1x2 ledger to the studs to support the second row of tiles.

Begin setting the field (wall) tile following your layout lines. After you set each tile, give it a little rap with your fist to better embed it. Dip tiles in water before sticking them to the wall so they form a better bond with the thin-set (**Photo 8**). Continually check the rows of tile for straightness. When the thin-set is still fresh, you can even out rows just by pushing a level against several tiles at once (**Photo 12**). Finish tiling the wall, cutting the top row to fit as needed. Leave out the row of tiles where the shelf will rest (**Photo 8**).

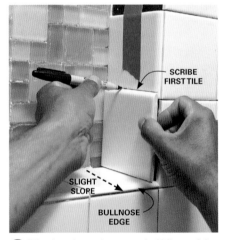

Tile the alcove sill, sides and top. Slightly slope the sill tiles toward the shower for drainage by piling on a little extra thin-set on the back side. Match the slope on the bottom tiles at the side by taping the bottom tile even with the row above it and scribing the angle with a full tile (**Photo 9**).

8 Spread thin-set up to the horizontal layout line and around one corner of the alcove. Set those tiles and then continue tiling the wall, leaving out the row of tiles directly behind the shelf.

9 Tile the alcove bottom shelf first with bullnose-edged tile, sloping it slightly toward the shower. Scribe the bottom side tiles to get the proper angle, and then finish tiling the sides and top.

Tile the bench

Starting at one end, set the tile on the face of the bench. If you're left with a gap at the other end, cut the mosaic into strips and slightly expand the grout lines between rows (**Photo 10**). Small variations in the width of the lines won't be noticeable. Lay tile on the seat to gauge the final grout line width between the seat and the face tile. Then add the seat tile, working from front to back and aligning the grout lines with the face tile. Make sure the seat tile edges align perfectly with the face tile surface— they shouldn't be backset or overhanging. Finish tiling the rest of the field tile above the bench, stopping at the shelf (**Photo 13**).

Mount and tile the shelf

Build the shelf 1/8 in. narrower than the opening so you can tip it into place. Leave off the plywood top but add backer board to the underside. Rest the shelf on the field tile and screw it to the blocking behind the backer board with two 3-in. screws at each side. Then screw the 3/4-in. plywood top to the framing with 1-5/8-in. screws (**Photo 13**) and add the backer board to the top and the front edge.

Tile the edge first, supporting it with a ledger screwed to the shelf underside (**Photo 14**). Remove the ledger after an hour or so, and then finish tiling the underside and top and the field tile above it. Lastly, remove the 1x2 ledgers and add the bottom row of tiles.

TILE FRONT FIRST

10 Tile the front of the bench first. Cut the mosaic tiles into strips if you need to adjust the spacing to get a better fit with less cutting.

GROUT FLOAT

11 Tile the bench and the end of the short wall. Force mosaic tiles evenly into the thin-set with a grout float.

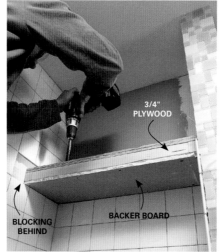

3/4" PLYWOOD

BLOCKING BEHIND

BACKER BOARD

13 Frame the shelf. Sheathe the bottom with backer board, rest it on the tile and screw the sides into the blocking. Add the 3/4-in. plywood and cover the exposed wood with backer board.

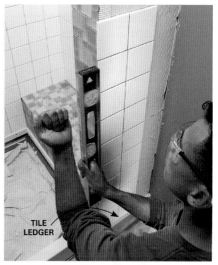

TILE LEDGER

12 Add the rest of the field tile, stopping at the underside of the shelf. Align tile edges at outside corners with a straightedge.

SUPPORT LEDGER

14 Screw a support ledger to the shelf underside to support the lip tile. Then tile the underside, top and the rest of the wall tile. The following day, grout the whole works and caulk all inside corners.

Tile a Backsplash

Nothing packs more style per square inch than mosaic tile. So if your kitchen's got the blahs, give it a quick infusion of pizzazz with a tile backsplash. Because the small tiles are mounted on 12 x 12-in. sheets, installation is fast. You can install the tile on Saturday morning and then grout it on Sunday morning.

Professionals charge about $20 per sq. ft. for installing the tile (plus materials), so you'll save $20 for every sheet you install yourself. The sheets cost $8 to more than $20 each at home centers and tile stores.

The total cost for this backsplash was about $200. The sheets of tile shown cost $10 apiece plus adhesive and grout. For an 8-ft. backsplash, you could save about $45 by using less expensive tile.

Shown here are slate tiles, which sometimes crumble when you cut them. Other types of mosaic tile, especially ceramic tiles, are easier to cut.

Here you'll learn how to install the tile sheets. You'll need basic tile tools, available at home centers and tile stores, including a 3/16-in. trowel and a grout float. You'll also need mastic adhesive, grout and grout sealer. You can rent a wet saw to cut the tiles.

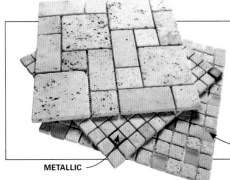

Mosaic tile sheets make it easy to achieve a great backsplash. Layout is a cinch—you can simply cut the mesh backing on the sheets to fit the tile along counters and cabinets. In fact, the hardest part of this or any other tiling project may be choosing the look—the tiles come in a variety of shapes and materials, and many sheets have glass or metallic tiles built in for accents. To add to your options, strips of 4 x 12-in. tiles are available for borders. So you can match the existing look of your kitchen—or try something new!

GLASS

METALLIC

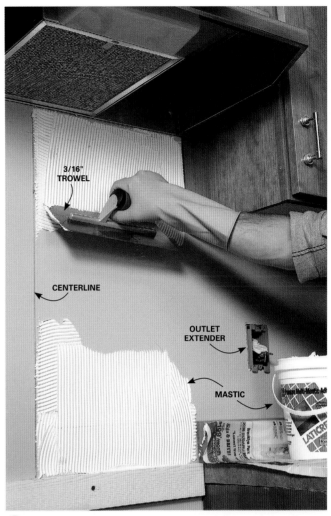

1 Mark a centerline between the upper cabinets so the tiles will be centered under the vent hood. Screw a ledger board to the wall to support the tile.

2 Spread a thin layer of mastic adhesive on the wall, starting at the centerline. Spread just enough adhesive for two or three sheets at a time so the adhesive doesn't dry before you set the tile.

Prepare the walls

Before installing the tile, clean up any grease splatters on the wall (mastic won't adhere to grease). Wipe the stains with a sponge dipped in a mixture of water and mild dishwashing liquid (like Dawn). If you have a lot of stains or they won't come off, wipe on a paint deglosser with a lint-free cloth or abrasive pad so the mastic will adhere. Deglosser is available at paint centers and home centers.

Then mask off the countertops and any upper cabinets that will have tile installed along the side. Leave a 1/4-in. gap between the wall and the tape for the tile (**Photo 1**). Cover the countertops with newspaper or a drop cloth.

Turn off power to the outlets in the wall and remove the cover plates. Make sure the power is off with a noncontact voltage detector (sold at home centers). Place outlet extenders (sold at home centers) in the outlet boxes. The National Electrical Code requires extenders when the boxes are more than 1/4 in. behind the wall surface. It's easier to put in extenders now and cut tile to fit around them than to add them later if the tile opening isn't big enough. Set the extenders in place as a guide for placing the tile. You'll remove them later for grouting.

On the wall that backs your range, measure down from the top of the countertop backsplash a distance that's equal to three or four full rows of tile (to avoid cutting the tile) and make a mark. Screw a scrap piece of wood (the ledger board) to the wall at the mark between the cabinets.

The area between the range and the vent hood is usually the largest space on the wall—and certainly the most seen by the cooks in the house—so it'll serve as your starting point for installing the tile. Make a centerline on the wall halfway between the cabinets and under the vent hood (**Photo 1**). Measure from the centerline to the cabinets. If you'll have to cut tile to fit, move the centerline slightly so you'll only have to cut the mesh backing (at least on one side).

Install and seal the tile

Using a 3/16-in. trowel, scoop some mastic adhesive out of the tub and put it on the wall (no technique involved here!). Spread the mastic along the centerline, cutting in along the ledger board, vent hood and upper cabinets (**Photo 2**). Then use broad strokes to fill in the middle. Hold the trowel at a 45-degree angle to the wall to spread the mastic thin—you should be able to see the layout lines

3 Tap the tile into the mastic with a wood scrap and a rubber mallet. Stand back, look at the tiles and straighten any crooked ones.

4 Cut tile sheets to the nearest full row to fit around outlets, then fill the gaps with tiles cut on a wet saw.

where the points of the trowel touch the wall. Have a water bucket and sponge on hand to keep the trowel clean. Whenever the mastic starts to harden on the trowel, wipe it off with the wet sponge.

Place plastic tile spacers on the ledger board and countertop. This leaves a gap so the tiles don't sit directly on the countertop (you'll caulk the gap later).

Align the first tile sheet with the centerline, directly over the spacers. Press it onto the wall with your hand. If the sheet slides around and mastic comes through the joint lines, you're applying the mastic too thick (remove the sheet, scrape off some mastic and retrowel). Scrape out any mastic in the joints with a utility knife.

Eyeball a 1/16-in. joint between sheets of tile (you don't need spacers). After every two or three installed sheets, tap them into the mastic with a board and rubber mallet (**Photo 3**).

If tiles fall off the sheets, dab a little mastic on the back and stick them right back in place. The sheets aren't perfectly square, so you may need to move individual tiles to keep joints lined up.

Move the tiles with your fingers or by sticking a utility knife blade in the joint and turning the blade. If an entire sheet is crooked, place a grout float over the tile and move the sheet. You'll have about 20 minutes after installing the tile to fine-tune it.

If you're lucky, you can fit the tile sheets under upper cabinets and around outlets by cutting the mesh backing with a utility knife. If not, you'll have to cut the tile with a wet saw. Nippers and grinders cause the slate tiles to shatter or crumble, although you can use these tools on ceramic tile.

Slice the backing to the nearest full row of tile, install the sheet around the outlet or next to the cabinet, then cut tiles with a wet saw to fill the gaps (**Photo 4**). Cut the tiles while they're attached to the sheet. Individual tiles are too small to cut (the blade can send them flying!).

Let the tile sit for at least 30 minutes, then apply a grout sealer if you're using natural stone (like slate) or unglazed quarry tile. The sealer keeps the grout from sticking to the tile (it's not needed for nonporous tiles such as ceramic). Pour the sealer on a sponge, then wipe on just enough to dampen the tiles.

5 Force grout into the joints with a float. Scrape off excess grout by moving the float diagonally across the tile.

DULL SIDE

6 Rake the grout out of the joints at inside corners and along the bottom with a utility knife so you can fill them with caulk. Keep the dull side of the blade along the countertop.

Grout and clean the tile

Wait 24 hours after installing the tile to add the grout. Use a premium grout that has a consistent color and resists stain. Since the backsplash will be subject to splatters and stains from cooking and food prep, spend the extra money for a premium grout. You can find it at home centers or tile stores. Use unsanded grout for tile with gaps of 1/8 in. or less, and sanded grout if the gaps are more than 1/8 in.

Mix the grout with water until it reaches mashed potato consistency, then put some on the wall with a grout float. Work the grout into the joints by moving the float diagonally over the tiles (**Photo 5**). Hold the grout float at a 45-degree angle to the tile. Scrape off excess grout with the float after the joints are filled.

Ten minutes after grouting, wipe the grout off the surface of the tiles with a damp sponge. If the grout pulls out of the joints, wait another 10 minutes for it to harden. Continually rinse the sponge in a bucket of water and wipe the tiles until they're clean.

These slate tiles have a lot of crevices that retain grout. While most of the grout comes off the tiles with the wet sponge, some

won't. Most pro installers leave some grout in slate and other rough-surface tile—it's just part of the deal with some types of natural stone. But if you want the tile completely clean, remove the grout from individual tiles with a toothbrush.

After cleaning the wall, use a utility knife to rake the grout out of the joints along the bottom of the backsplash and in the inside corners (**Photo 6**). These expansion joints allow the wall to move without cracking the grout.

Two hours after grouting, wipe the haze off the tiles with microfiber cloths. Then caulk the expansion joints with latex caulk. Use a colored caulk that closely matches the grout (available at tile stores).

After seven days, sponge on a grout sealer to protect the grout against stains.

That's it! Now every time your family and friends gather in your kitchen, they'll be impressed with your custom backsplash.

Hide-The-Mess Lockers

Build simple boxes and add store-bought doors

In many houses, there's a big coat closet by the front door, but the garage is in the back, so everyone uses the back door.

We designed and built these hide-the-mess lockers with those houses in mind. Each locker is big enough to stash a coat, backpack, boots, hats, and odds and ends that normally wind up on the floor. Since they're modular and space efficient, you can build one for each member of the family—including the dog

(leashes, toys, food, you name it). Now everyone has a personal place for stashing stuff—and the responsibility for keeping it organized.

The louvered door is made from one of a pair of closet bifold doors, which you can buy at almost any home center. Since the doors come in pairs and you can get two locker "boxes" from each sheet of plywood, you'll make the best use of materials by building them in twos. Here's how to do it.

Money, materials and tools

The total materials cost was only around $100 per locker. Since we were planning to paint the lockers, we used inexpensive "AC" plywood. If you plan to stain your lockers, and use hardwood plywood such as oak or birch and hardwood doors, you'll spend more. On a row of lockers, only the outer sides of the end lockers show, so you can use inexpensive plywood for the inner parts and more expensive material for the outer parts. Expect to spend at least a day buying materials, rounding up tools and building a pair of lockers. Set aside another day for finishing.

A table saw is handy for cutting up plywood, but a circular saw with a guide will provide the same results. You'll also need a miter saw to cut the screen molding. A finish nailer will help you work faster, but hand-nailing will work too as long as you drill holes to prevent splitting.

Buy the doors first

There are a variety of bifold doors available. If you need more ventilation, use full louvered doors; if ventilation isn't an issue, use solid doors. The doors you buy may not be exactly the same size as ours, so you may have to alter the dimensions of the boxes you build. Here are two key points to keep in mind as you plan your project:

You want a 1/8-in. gap surrounding the door. So to determine the size of the box opening, add 1/4 in. to the height and width of the door. Since our bifold doors measured 14-3/4 x 78-3/4 in., we made the opening 15 x 79 in.

To determine the depth of the shelves, subtract the door thickness from the width of the sides (including the 1/4-in. screen molding). Our doors were 1-1/8 in. thick, so we made the shelves 10-7/8 in. deep (12 minus 1-1/8 equals 10-7/8 in.). When the doors are closed, they'll rest against the shelves inside and flush with the screen molding outside.

Get building!

Use a table saw or straight-cutting guide to cut the plywood sides (A) and top and bottom (B). The **Cutting List** on p. 227 gives the parts dimensions for the lockers. If you plan to paint or stain the lockers, it's a good idea to prefinish the insides of parts. Once the lockers are assembled, brushing a finish onto the insides is slow and difficult.

Assemble the boxes with 2-in. trim-head screws (**Photo 1**). Trim-head screws have smaller heads than standard screws and are easier to hide with filler. Cut the 1/4-in. plywood back (C) to size. Make certain the box is square by taking diagonal

1 BUILD A SIMPLE BOX. Cut the plywood parts and assemble them with trim-head screws. Make sure the box opening is 1/4-in. taller and wider than the door itself.

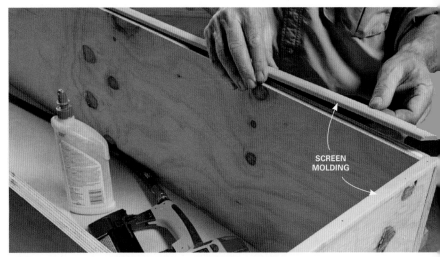

2 SQUARE IT UP. Take diagonal corner-to-corner measurements, then adjust the box until the measurements are equal and the box is square. Install the back, using one edge of the back to straighten the box side as you fasten it. Check once again for squareness, then secure the other edges of the back.

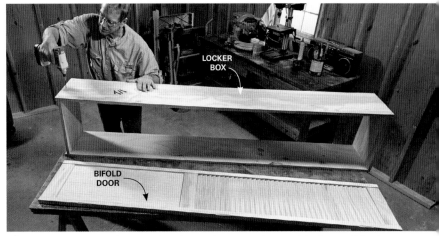

3 COVER THE PLYWOOD EDGES. Install screen molding over the front edges of the box. Apply wood glue lightly and use just enough nails to "clamp" the molding in place while the glue dries.

4 BUILD SLATTED SHELVES. Plywood shelves would work fine, but slatted shelves allow better ventilation so wet clothes and shoes can dry. Space the slats with wood scraps.

5 INSTALL THE SHELVES. Stand your locker up and position the shelves to suit the stuff that will go in it. Mark the shelf locations, lay the locker on its back and screw the shelves into place. Make sure the shelves are inset far enough to allow for the door.

6 MOUNT THE HINGES. Remove the hinges from the doors (they'll be pointed the wrong way) and reinstall them on the door based on the direction you want it to swing. Prop up the door alongside the box and align the door so there will be a 1/8-in. gap at the top and bottom of the box. Then screw the hinges to the box.

measurements (they should be equal; see **Photo 2**), and then secure the back using 1-in. nails. Use the edges of the back as a guide to straighten the edges of the box as you nail the back into place.

Cut 1/4 x 3/4-in. screen molding and use glue and 1-in. finish nails or brads to secure it to the exposed front edges of the plywood (**Photo 3**). Cut the shelf front and back (D), sides (E) and slats (F) to length, then assemble the three slatted shelf units (**Photo 4**). With the locker box standing upright, position the shelves and hold them temporarily in place with clamps or a couple of screws. Adjust the shelf spacing based on the height of the locker's user and the stuff that will go inside. Once you have a suitable arrangement, lay the locker on its back and screw the shelves into place (**Photo 5**). The shelves are easy to reposition in the future as needs change.

Add the hardware and finish, and then install

Remove the hinges that hold the bifold doors to each other. Determine which way you want the door to swing, then mount the hinges onto the door accordingly. (**Note:** You'll need to buy another set of hinges if you're building two lockers.) Remember, you want the louvers to point downward on the outside! With the locker on its back, position the door and secure the hinges to the plywood side (**Photo 6**). Install door handles and magnetic catches to hold them closed.

Remove the doors (but don't finish them yet!) and install the locker boxes. Your lockers can stand against baseboard, leaving a small gap between the backs of the lockers and the wall. Or—if you remove the baseboard—they can stand tight against the wall. Either way, installing them is a lot like installing cabinets: Fasten all the boxes together by driving 1-1/4-in. screws through the side of one locker into the next. Then screw the entire assembly to wall studs.

Install the unfinished doors to make sure they all fit properly, then remove them again. This may seem like a waste of time, but there's a good reason for it: Your locker boxes may have shifted a little during installation, and the doors may not fit properly. If a door or two need some edge sanding, you want to do that before finishing.

When you've checked the fit of all the doors, remove them one last time for finishing. Whether you're using paint or a natural finish, louvered doors are a real pain. If your plans include a clear coat, consider polyurethane or lacquer in spray cans: You'll get better results in far less time, though you'll spend a bit extra. After finishing, install the doors and load up those lockers!

Figure A
Locker construction

Overall Dimensions:
16-1/2" wide x 81" tall x 12-1/4" deep

Materials list (for two lockers)

Because bifold doors are sold in pairs, and one sheet of 3/4-in. plywood yields two lockers, you can make the best use of materials by building an even number of lockers.

ITEM	QTY.
30" bifold door pack (2 doors)	1
3/4" x 4' x 8' plywood	1
1/4" x 4' x 8' plywood	1
1/4" x 3/4" x 8' screen molding	5
3/4" x 1-1/2" x 8' solid wood	9

2" trim-head screws, 1-1/4" screws, 1" nails, 1-1/2" nails, wood glue, no-mortise hinges, door handles and magnetic catches.

Cutting list (for one locker)

These locker parts suit a door measuring 14-3/4 x 78-3/4 in. Verify the exact size of your doors before building.

KEY	QTY.	SIZE & DESCRIPTION
A	2	11-3/4" x 80-7/8" sides (3/4" plywood)
B	2	11-3/4" x 15" top/bottom (3/4" plywood)
C	1	16-1/2" x 80-1/2" back (1/4" plywood)
D	2	3/4" x 1-1/2" x 15" shelf front/back (solid wood)
E	2	3/4" x 1-1/2" x 9-3/8" shelf sides (solid wood)
F	6	3/4" x 1-1/2" x 15" shelf slats (solid wood)

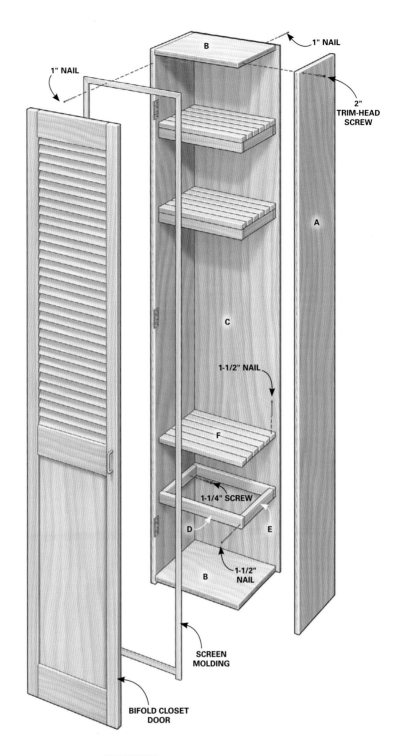

1" NAIL

1" NAIL

2" TRIM-HEAD SCREW

1-1/2" NAIL

1-1/4" SCREW

1-1/2" NAIL

SCREEN MOLDING

BIFOLD CLOSET DOOR

Figure B
Cutting diagrams

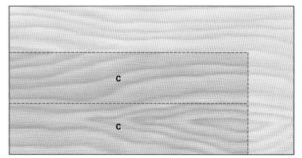

3/4" PLYWOOD

1/4" PLYWOOD

Entry Organizer

Cure back-door chaos!

If you would love to have a mudroom but just don't have the space, this compact bench and shoe shelf may be exactly what you need. Mount it near the garage service door and you'll have a convenient spot to remove and store your shoes or boots before going inside. There's even a hollow bench with a flip-up lid to store your hats and gloves.

All of the parts for this project are cut from standard pine boards, so you don't need to haul big sheets of plywood home or worry about finishing exposed plywood edges. You do need to choose your lumber carefully, though. The wide pine planks tend to cup and warp, so look for boards that are flat and straight. And plan to build the project soon after buying the lumber. If you leave the lumber sitting around for weeks, it may begin to warp or twist.

Cut out the parts

Start by choosing the four straightest, best-looking 1x12s for the shelf sides. Cut these to 72 in. Then use the **Cutting List** on p. 231 to cut the remaining parts (**Photo 1**). If you're lucky enough to own a sliding miter saw, you can use it to cut the parts to length. Otherwise a circular saw will work fine. The boards for three sides of the bench and one of the bench bottoms have to be ripped a little narrower. You can use a circular saw or table saw for this. After cutting the lumber, sand it with 100-grit sandpaper to remove any marks and smooth out any ripples left from the milling process. A random orbital sander works great for this, but you could hand-sand if you don't own a power sander.

MEET THE EXPERT

Jeff Gorton took advantage of his nearly two decades of experience building projects for *Family Handyman* to design this simple shoe and boot storage project.

A seat with storage

A hinged lid provides easy access to the compartment under the seat. It's a perfect place to store hats, gloves and all kinds of other small stuff.

1 CUT THE PARTS. Cut the boards to length, following the Cutting List on p. 231. Running your circular saw along a large square ensures straight, square cuts. Parts F, G and N also have to be ripped to width. You can do this with your circular saw or on a table saw.

2 MARK THE SCREW LOCATIONS. On the inside of the shelf sides, mark the middle shelf location. On the outside, make light pencil lines at the center and 3/8 in. from both ends. These light marks will help you position the screws. Drill 1/8-in. pilot holes at the screw locations to avoid splitting the boards.

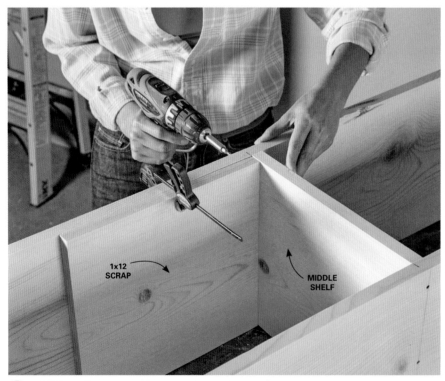

1x12 SCRAP

MIDDLE SHELF

3 ASSEMBLE THE SHELVES. Arrange the parts on a flat surface and clamp them together. Clamp a scrap along the centerline to help you position the middle shelf. Then drive trim-head screws through your pilot holes to connect the parts. If you want to fill the screw holes later, recess the screws slightly.

Assemble the parts with screws

We joined the parts with 2-in. trim-head screws, recessing them slightly to make room for the wood filler. But you can substitute regular screws if you don't mind the look of screw heads. Even though our screws had self-drilling tips, for extra insurance against splitting the wood we drilled 1/8-in. pilot holes for the screws.

Clamping the parts together before you drive in the screws makes it easier to keep the parts aligned. And if the wood is a little twisted or cupped, you can flatten it with clamps before driving the screws. We also added three cleats to the bottom of the seat board to hold it flat. Spread wood glue on these cleats and attach them with 1-1/4-in. screws.

We chose a continuous hinge for the lid. Cut the hinge to 35-5/8 in. with a hacksaw. Since you'll also have to cut all the metal shelf standards to fit, buy a sharp, new 32-tooth blade. **Photo 6** shows how to attach the hinge. Finish up the assembly by cutting and attaching the metal shelf standards (**Photo 7**).

Hang the project on the wall

First, locate the wall studs. An electronic stud finder makes it easy. Mark the stud locations with strips of masking tape. Now choose a position for the project that will allow you to attach each of the 12-in.-wide shelf units to at least one stud. Next, screw the temporary 1x2 ledger to the studs, making sure it's level and the top is located 7-1/2 in. from the floor (**Photo 8**). The ledger supports the shelf units and bench while you attach them to the wall. **Photos 9 – 13** show the installation steps. Finish up by choosing the locations for the adjustable shelves and installing them with the shelf clips. We prefinished the project with Behr Semi-Transparent Waterproofing Wood Stain.

Figure A

Entry organizer

Overall dimensions:
63" wide x 72" tall x 15-3/4" deep

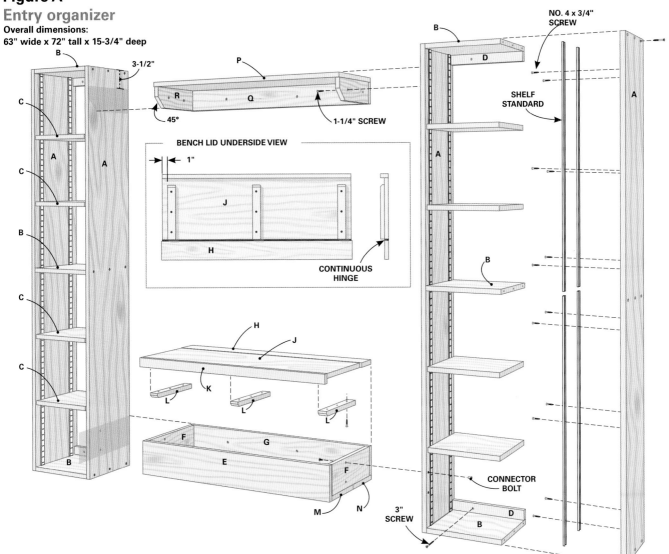

Materials list

ITEM	QTY.
1x12 x 8' standard pine boards	6
1x8 x 6' standard pine boards	1
1x6 x 10' standard pine boards	1
1x4 x 8' standard pine boards	1
1x2 x 10' standard pine boards	1
Hardware	
2" trim-head screws	100
1-1/4" screws	14
3" cabinet screws	10
No. 4 x 3/4" screws (for shelf standards)	Sm. box
1-1/2" connector bolts	4
1-1/2" x 36" continuous hinge	1
72" shelf standards	8
Shelf clips	32
Coat hooks	
Wood filler and 100-grit sandpaper	

Cutting list

KEY	DIMENSIONS	QTY.	NAME
A	3/4" x 11-1/4" x 72"	4	Sides
B	3/4" x 11-1/4" x 12"	6	Top, bottom, middle shelf
C	3/4" x 11-1/4" x 11-5/8"	8	Shelves
D	3/4" x 1-1/2" x 12"	4	Hanging strips
E	3/4" x 5-1/2" x 36"	1	Bench front
F	3/4" x 4-3/4" x 13-1/4"	2	Bench sides
G	3/4" x 4-3/4" x 36"	1	Bench back
H	3/4" x 3-1/2" x 36"	1	Bench top (back)
J	3/4" x 11-1/4" x 35-5/8"	1	Bench top lid
K	3/4" x 1-1/2" x 35-5/8"	1	Bench lid nosing
L	3/4" x 1-1/2" x 10"	3	Bench seat cleats
M	3/4" x 7-1/4" x 36"	1	Bench bottom
N	3/4" x 6-3/4" x 36"	1	Bench bottom
P	3/4" x 11-1/4" x 36"	1	Top shelf
Q	3/4" x 3-1/2" x 36"	1	Top shelf back rail
R	3/4" x 3-1/2" x 10-1/4"	2	Top shelf side rail

4 BUILD THE BENCH FRAME. Drill pilot holes in the sides of the bench frame and clamp the parts together. The wide part (E) is the front of the bench, so face the best-looking side out.

BENCH FRONT

5 ATTACH THE BENCH BOTTOM. To make sure the bench frame is square, measure diagonally from opposite corners. Adjust the frame until the two diagonal measurements are equal. Then screw the bottom boards to the frame.

BENCH BOTTOM

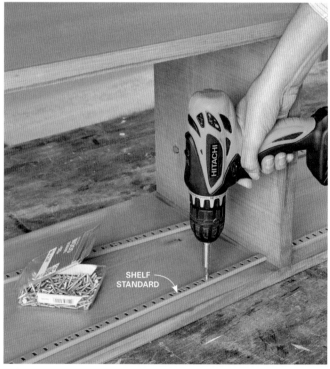

6 MOUNT THE SEAT HINGE. Clamp the lid and the back rail together as shown. Center the hinge on the two lid parts and attach it with four screws, two on each end. Then drill 5/64-in. pilot holes and drive in the remaining screws.

CONTINUOUS HINGE

7 INSTALL THE SHELF STANDARDS. Cut each of the 72-in. shelf standards into two 34-3/4 in. pieces using a hacksaw. Measure from the ends to the centers to retain factory ends on each piece. We spray-painted the standards to match the finish.

SHELF STANDARD

8 INSTALL TEMPORARY SUPPORT. Locate the wall studs with a stud finder and mark them with strips of masking tape. Install a 1x2 ledger with the top edge 7-1/2 in. above the floor to support the shelves and seat while you install them.

STUD LOCATION

LEDGER

HANGING STRIP

9 INSTALL THE FIRST SHELF UNIT. Rest the shelf on the ledger. Drive a screw through the top hanging strip into a stud. Then use a level to make sure the sides of the shelf unit are plumb. If necessary, push the bottom one way or the other to plumb the sides. Drive a screw through the lower hanging strip into a stud to secure the shelf unit.

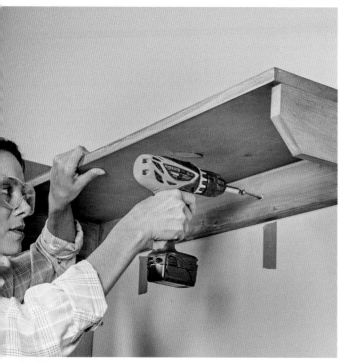

10 INSTALL THE COAT-HOOK SHELF. Screw the coat-hook shelf to the studs, making sure it's level. Then level the shelf from front to back and attach it to the side of the tall shelf with 1-1/4-in. screws. Attach the opposite side after you've installed the second shelf unit.

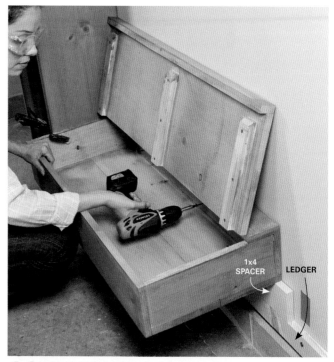

1x4 SPACER

LEDGER

11 MOUNT THE BENCH. Rest a scrap of 1x4 spacer on top of the temporary ledger to elevate the bench to the correct height. Set the bench on the spacer. Then drive screws through the back of the bench into the studs.

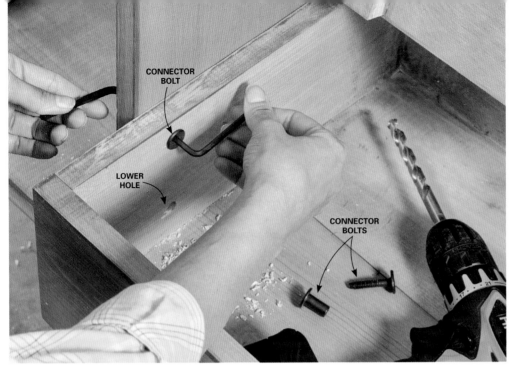

LOWER
HOLE

CONNECTOR
BOLT

CONNECTOR
BOLTS

12 CONNECT THE BENCH AND SHELF.

Use two-part connector bolts to connect the front of the bench to the shelves on each side (connect the second side later after the second shelf is mounted). These bolts provide more support than screws to ensure the bench will be safe to sit on. The bolts we used required two Allen wrenches to tighten.

13 FINISH UP WITH THE SECOND TALL SHELF.

Rest the second shelf unit on the ledger and tip it up into place. Attach it to the wall by driving 3-in. screws through the top and bottom hanging strips and into the stud. Then connect the bench with the connector bolts and attach the other side of the upper shelf with 1-1/4-in. screws.

WHAT IT TAKES

TIME: One weekend

Cost: $150

SKILL: Beginner

TOOLS: Tape measure, large square, level, cordless drill, drill bits, circular saw, hacksaw, clamps.

Chapter Three

BIG IMPACT FIXES

Cures for Top 5 Lawn Problems.................236
Concrete Cover–up......................................242
Recap Concrete Steps................................246
Fixing Cracks in Concrete...........................249

Recoat a Driveway.......................................256
Seal Attic Air Leaks.....................................260
Replace a Storm Door.................................266
Replace a Toilet...271

Cures For Top 5 Lawn Problems

Even the best lawns could use a little therapeutic attention now and again. To help you make your lawn the best on the block, the following pages offer the most effective remedies for the most common turf maladies.

Problem:

Dog spots on grass

Symptoms: Dog spots are round patches about 4 to 8 in. in diameter with dead grass in the middle, encircled by dark green grass. They're most apparent in the early spring when dormant grass first begins to turn green again.

Cause: Dog urine contains high concentrations of acids, salts and nitrogen, which burn (dry out) the grass roots and kill them. As rain washes the area, the urine is diluted and the nitrogen spreads, causing the grass surrounding the spot to grow faster and turn greener.

Remedy: You have to replant your grass; it won't come back on its own. But first you have to dilute or remove the caustic urine from the soil (**Photo 1**). Thoroughly soak the area with lots of water. Let the hose run for at least three minutes. Then you can start the replanting process (**Photo 2**). Add a half inch of new soil to help absorb any remaining urine (**Photo 3**). Then you can spread new seed, or use a commercial yard patch mixture (available at most nurseries or home centers) or even sod. The secret of good germination is keeping the seed moist. Keep the area moist until the new grass is about 3 in. high.

Recovery time: Four to six weeks.

> **Tip**
> When you're watering new seed, moisten the soil daily and keep it damp—but don't soak it. Over-watering is a common mistake.

An ounce of prevention

- Soak your pet's favorite areas in your lawn to get the salts out of the root zone before they kill the grass.
- Fertilize your lawn in the spring to boost the overall color and mask the darker green dog spots.
- Train your pet to urinate in a designated area. Replace or repair the grass in this area annually or cover it with mulch.
- Keep your pet well hydrated to make its urine less concentrated.

1 Soak the patch until the grass is sopping wet to dilute the urine acids and salts and wash them deeper into the soil, beyond the grass roots.

2 Scrape up the dead grass with a hand rake and remove it. Rough up the area to loosen the soil 1/2 in. deep. Seeds germinate better in soft soil.

3 Sprinkle on a 1/2-in.-thick layer of topsoil, then pepper it with grass seed. Cover with a thin layer of new soil. Keep the area moist until the new grass is about 3 in. high.

Problem:
Thatch

Symptoms: If your grass feels soft and spongy when you walk on it, your lawn may have a thatch buildup. Thatch is a fibrous mat of dead stalks and roots that settles between the lawn's green leaves and the soil (**photo right**). When this mat becomes greater than 3/4 in. thick, it can cause your lawn to suffer from heat and drought. Affected lawns will rapidly wilt and turn blue-green, indicating they're hot and dry.

Cause: Cutting off too much at each mowing (letting the grass get too long) and cutting too low. Both will produce more dead grass tissue than microbes and earthworms can recycle. Thatch can develop in any soil but is most often associated with high clay content. Other causes are overfertilization and frequent, light watering, which encourage a shallow root system.

Remedy: Slice open a section of your lawn (**Photo 1**). If your grass shows 3/4 in. or more of thatch, it's time to rent an aerator. An aerator is a heavy machine that opens the soil by pulling up finger-size soil cores. The lawn will absorb more oxygen and water, which will encourage healthy microbe growth and give worms some wiggle room.

Aerate in the spring or fall when the grass is growing but the weather is not too hot to stress the plants (**Photo 2**). If the machine isn't pulling plugs, your lawn may be too dry. To avoid this problem, water thoroughly the day before you aerate. You can also rake in topsoil (**Photo 3**) to increase the healthy microorganisms that aid thatch's natural decomposition. Topsoil is available at any garden center.

Recovery time: You can expect the thatch layer to decrease by about 1/4 in. per year, about the same rate at which it forms.

> **CAUTION**
> Call 811 or visit call811.com to mark your underground utility lines before you aerate.

An ounce of prevention

- Mow often and cut no more than one-third of the grass height.
- Water your lawn less often but for longer periods to prevent shallow root systems.
- Reduce the amount of fertilizer you spread at any one time.
- Reduce the use of pesticides. This will help keep the worm and microorganism populations healthy.
- Aerate at least once every year if your lawn is prone to thatch.

1 Slice the turf grass with a shovel and pry it back. If the thatch depth measures more than 3/4 in., aerate at least 3 in. deep.

2 Make two or three passes with an aerator until you've made 3-in.-deep holes 2 in. apart throughout your yard.

3 Spread 1/4 in. of topsoil on the yard's most thatchy areas and then rake vigorously to fill the holes with loose soil.

Problem:

Fairy rings

Symptoms: Fairy rings are circles approximately 3 to 8 ft. wide that consist of a dark green and fast-growing area of grass surrounding an inner area of partially dead or thin grass. Some rings also produce mushrooms.

Cause: Fairy rings are caused by fungi that live in the soil. As the fungi feed on organic matter, they release nitrogen, causing the grass to turn dark green. As the colony grows, it disturbs the flow of needed water to the turf roots, creating thin or dead spots. Fairy rings often begin with the decomposition of organic matter, such as an old tree stump buried under the lawn.

Remedy: By bringing up the color in the rest of your lawn with a nitrogen fertilizer, you can mask much of the overgreening of the fairy ring (**Photo 1**). Hand-aerating the ring will break up the fungus and allow the flow of water and other nutrients to the grass roots (**Photo 2**).

Recovery time: Generally fairy rings can be masked with the application of fertilizer, with results in 10 to 14 days. The grass within the ring will thicken up with aeration in about two to three weeks.

An ounce of prevention

Aeration will help with fairy rings, but maintaining a healthy lawn with a balanced fertilization program is essential. Apply three doses:

- ■ Apply 1/2 lb. per 1,000 sq. ft. in late April or early May to give the overwintering grass roots a bit of a boost.
- ■ Add no more than 1/2 lb. per 1,000 sq. ft. at the end of June or in early July when temperatures are not at their peak. Stimulating growth during a heat wave will stress the plants.
- ■ Spread 1 lb. per 1,000 sq. ft. at the end of October. The best root growth takes place when the soil temps are between 58 and 65 degrees F. The roots store energy over the winter, making the entire lawn healthier the following spring.

DO NOT FERTILIZE THE RING ITSELF

1 Spread 1/2 lb. of nitrogen fertilizer per 1,000 sq. ft. to green up your lawn, but skip the fairy ring zone. This masks the lush green of the fairy ring by blending it into the rest of your yard.

CORE PLUGS

2 Break up the fungi with a hand aerator (available at home centers and garden stores). Punch holes every 2 to 4 in. throughout the ring and 2 ft. beyond.

DECAYING WOOD

3 Go "treasure" hunting if you see no improvement in three weeks. Dig out rotting stumps, roots, construction debris or other organic materials under your lawn.

Problem:

Grubs

Symptoms: Grub-chewed turf has patchy areas that wilt and die. You can easily pull up the affected turf if you tug on it. Another indicator of grubs may be increased raccoon, bird or mole activity. They like to dig up and eat the grubs at night. While this may sound good, the moles will kill the grass as they forage for grubs.

Cause: Lawn grubs are the larval stage of moths and beetles. The grubs eat the roots of grass, setting them up to die by dehydration.

Remedy: Be vigilant. Are beetles swarming around your porch light? In the next month, keep an eye out for patches of grass that wilt or are blue-green on hot days. They may be larvae infested. Turn over some turf (**Photo 1**). If you count six to 10 grubs (white

wormlike larvae with black heads) under a 1-ft.-square area of sod, consider using a grub insecticide (available at home centers and nurseries). Or talk to a professional (search online for "grass service") about treating your yard. They will be familiar with the grub problems in your region and the most suitable treatment methods.

If you spot the grubs but your count is lower than six per square foot, baby your lawn to strengthen its natural defenses. Mow on a higher blade setting and water thoroughly but infrequently to encourage the grass to grow new, deep roots. Do not cut off more than one-third of the grass height at each mowing, to avoid stressing the plant.

An ounce of prevention
Inspect your turf periodically by pulling on patches that look unhealthy, or have a professional inspect your lawn if you suspect a problem.

GRUBS

1 Pierce the lawn with a shovel in a u-shape. Peel back the lawn (as though rolling up a rug) and count the white grubs in a 1-sq.-ft. area.

2 Treat your lawn with an insecticide if the count is six to 10 grubs in a square foot. Follow the manufacturer's directions carefully. Or consult with a yard service.

Problem:

Shade

Symptoms: Shaded grass will look thin and patchy. Some types of grass actually produce wider blades as the plant attempts to catch more rays. But they also produce far fewer blades, lending a spindly appearance to the lawn. The cold truth is, if your lawn gets less than six to eight hours of sun daily, you are unlikely to sustain lush grass.

Cause: Trees, buildings and bushes.

Remedy: You can increase the sunlight as much as possible by trimming trees and shrubs. Also try starting areas in shade with sod instead of seed. The sod will adjust to the lower level of light. Although all seed varieties have their shade limitations, try overseeding your thin area with a shady grass mix.

Or throw in the towel, grab your trowel and plant a shade-tolerant ground cover. Many will thrive where your turf withered. Lamium (dead nettle) and ajuga (bugleweed) collaborate nicely in providing lovely blooms and an enthusiastic, but not invasive, carpet. This pair fares well, with a hearty tolerance spanning zones 3 to 8, and can be planted right up to your grass. They are fairly low growers and won't get more than a few nicks from a lawn mower.

Also, mulching between the ground cover plants will help retain moisture. This is especially wise if your new "shade garden" is on a slope; mulch will help prevent your fledgling plants from washing out in a hard rain.

Recovery time: The plants and mulch will immediately boost the appearance of an area that was once thin grass. It'll take a couple of seasons for the ground cover to become fully established.

An ounce of prevention

Avoid the frustration of sun-starved grass by starting a shade garden or ground cover in any area that doesn't receive six to eight hours of good light per day.

Using a garden hoe, work up the shady area to remove any struggling grass. Plant ground cover or a shade garden.

Concrete Patio Cover-up

No need to tear out an ugly slab—just hide it!

Figure A
Pavers over a concrete slab

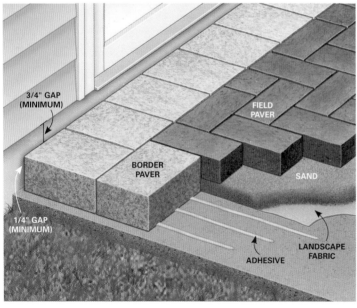

3/4" GAP (MINIMUM)

FIELD PAVER

BORDER PAVER

SAND

1/4" GAP (MINIMUM)

ADHESIVE

LANDSCAPE FABRIC

A concrete patio is made for practicality—not beauty. It starts out looking plain and goes downhill from there. As craters, cracks and stains accumulate, it can go from dull to downright ugly in just a few years. But there's a simple solution, whether you want to dress up a bland patio or hide an aging one. Covering concrete with paver bricks is much easier than pouring new concrete or laying pavers the traditional way. It requires less skill and less time, and it's a whole lot easier on your back.

Assess your slab

This project will work with most patios. Surface damage like flaking, chips and craters is no problem. But a few conditions make this method a no-go:

■ A too-low threshold. Door thresholds have to be high enough above the existing patio to allow for the thickness of the border pavers, plus an extra 3/4 in. to allow for "frost heave"—rising of the slab when the soil freezes.

Before

After

■ **Expanding cracks.** This method will work over most cracks—which grow and shrink with seasonal ground movement. But if you have a crack that has noticeably grown in recent years, this method is risky. The crack may eventually "telegraph" through the pavers, creating a hump or gaps.

Money and materials

The materials for this 12 x 14-ft. patio cost approximately $7 per sq. ft. Using less expensive pavers, you could cut the cost by almost half. Most landscape suppliers and home centers stock all the materials, but you may have to do a little hunting for the

right combination of pavers. The pavers used for the border must be at least 3/4 in. thicker than the "field" pavers, which cover the area between the borders. That thickness difference will allow for a bed of sand under the field. A difference of more than 3/4 in. is fine; you'll just need a little more sand. If you can't find thick pavers you like, consider retaining wall cap blocks for the border. We used cement pavers for the border and clay pavers for the field.

To estimate how much sand you'll need, first determine the square footage of the sand bed (length x width). Then divide that number by 12 for a 1-in. bed or 18 for a 3/4-in. bed. That will

Standard Patio = CONCRETE AND SOIL REMOVAL GRAVEL SAND PAVERS

Patio Cover-up SAND PAVERS

SAVE 12 TONS OF TOIL. A standard paver patio rests on a thick base of compacted gravel. This patio cover-up will save you the cost of that gravel. More important, it eliminates the backbreaking drudgery of breaking up concrete, digging up soil, hauling it all away and hauling in gravel. On this 12 x 14-ft. patio, a patio tear-out and new gravel base would have meant more than 12 extra tons of wheelbarrow work.

1 SCRUB THE PERIMETER. Clean the edges of the patio where you'll later glue down the border pavers. Clean concrete means a stronger glue bond.

Figure B
Border layout

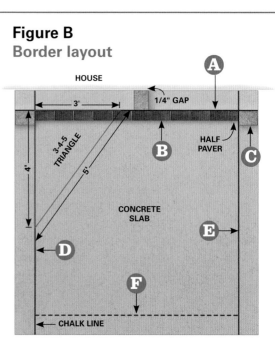

HOUSE

3'

1/4" GAP

A

B

HALF PAVER

C

4'

3-4-5 TRIANGLE

5'

CONCRETE SLAB

E

D

F

CHALK LINE

A Snap a chalk line parallel to the house to mark the location of the border pavers. Remember to leave a gap of at least 1/4 in. between the border pavers and the house.

B Lay out field pavers to locate the side borders. A simple row of pavers will work even if you plan to lay them later in a "herring-bone" pattern as we did. The goal is to establish a field width that allows each course to end with a full or half paver, but not smaller pieces. That means less cutting, less waste and a neater look.

C Position the border pavers and mark their locations. It's OK if the border pavers don't quite reach the edge of the patio, but don't let them overhang. Nudge one border outward by 1/4 in. to allow a little extra space for the field pavers.

D Snap a chalk line to mark one side border. To make this line square with the line along the house, use the 3-4-5 method.

E Mark the other side border. Measure from the first side to make sure the two sides are parallel.

F Leave the final border unmarked and install the border after the field is complete. That open end makes screeding off the excess sand easier and lets you position the final border perfectly.

BORDER PAVER

CHALK LINE

2 GLUE DOWN THE BORDER PAVERS. After setting each paver, run a bead of construction adhesive up the side of it. That will keep the sand from washing out between pavers.

determine you how many cubic feet of sand to get. You can have a load of sand delivered or save the delivery fee by picking up a load with a truck or trailer. Most home centers also sell bagged sand.

Lay the border first

To get started, scrub the border area (**Photo 1**) with a concrete cleaner or muriatic acid mixed with water (check the label for mixing and safety instructions). Any stiff brush will do, but a deck stripping brush on a broom handle makes

it easier. Hose down the patio when you're done scrubbing the border.

While the concrete is drying, grab a tape measure and a chalk line and carefully plan the locations of the borders (**see Figure B**). Using the chalk lines as a guide, glue down the border pavers along the house and two sides of the patio (**Photo 2**). We used polyurethane construction adhesive for a strong, long-lasting bond. If adhesive squishes up between pavers, don't try to wipe it off. Just let it harden, then trim it off with a utility knife.

A flat bed of sand

If the field area is more than 10 ft. wide, you'll need a screed pipe in the center of the patio (**Photo 3**). A 10-ft. section of black or galvanized steel plumbing pipe works best. For a 1-in. bed, use 3/4-in. pipe; for a 3/4-in. bed, use 1/2-in. pipe. Keep in mind that each pipe size is listed by its inner diameter, but the outer diameter is what matters here: 3/4-in. pipe has an outer diameter of about 1-1/8 in.; 1/2-in. pipe, about 5/8 in. In both cases, you'll get an extra 1/8 in. of sand bed thickness and the field pavers

3 SPREAD FABRIC, THEN SAND. Lay down landscape fabric to keep the sand from washing down into cracks. Then position the screed pipe and spread the sand.

SCREED PIPE
LANDSCAPE FABRIC

SCREED PIPE
NOTCH

4 FLATTEN THE SAND. Notch one end of a 2x6 to match the depth of the field pavers. The other end rides on the screed pipe. Screed both halves of the field, moving your screed pipe as you go.

5 LAY THE PAVERS. Cover the sand with field pavers. When the field is complete, glue down the final border pavers. Then tamp the field with a plate compactor and sweep sand over the pavers to fill in the gaps.

will stand about 1/8 in. above the border pavers. Then, when you "tamp" the field with a plate compactor, the sand will compact and the field pavers will settle flush with the border.

"Screed" the sand flat with a notched 2x6 (**Photo 4**). The depth of the notch should be 1/8 in. less than the thickness of the field pavers. If the field is less than 10 ft. wide, notch both ends of the screed

board and skip the pipe. Screeding is hard work and it's best to have a helper.

Lay the pavers and finish the border

From here on out, this is mostly a standard paver job. Lay the field pavers as you would on any paver patio. Scrape away the excess sand and cut off the excess landscape fabric with a utility knife. Glue down the last

border. Let the glue dry for a few hours before you tamp the field pavers and sweep sand across the patio to fill the joints.

Q&A

Q: Why not skip the sand and glue down all the pavers?
A: You could do that. But gluing down hundreds of pavers will add a few hours to the job and you'll spend at least $100 on adhesive.

Q: I want a bigger patio. Can the pavers extend beyond the current footprint?
A: The pavers could continue onto a standard gravel base. But the gravel base and the existing slab might shift in different ways, creating a gap or hump where they meet. So it's best to keep them separate. If you want to add a grilling area, for example, separate it from the main patio and set a steppingstone or two between the two paved areas.

Q: Can I glue pavers over the steps?
A: Yes. If your patio includes steps, you must cover the treads in order to maintain the height of the steps. Or you can completely cover the steps if you like. Just be sure to leave a gap of at least 1/2 in. between the pavers on the steps and those on the patio to allow for movement.

Q: Do I have to use paver bricks?
A: You can cover the field with any type of paving product: natural or manufactured flagstone, pavers of any size or shape. But paver bricks are best for the border because they provide a flat, even surface for screeding (**see Photo 4**).

Materials list

Aside from pavers and sand, you'll need one 10-oz. tube of adhesive for every 8 ft. of border, concrete cleaner or muriatic acid, landscape fabric, a 2x6 and a screed pipe. To tamp the pavers, you'll need to rent a plate compactor.

Recap Concrete Steps

Rebuild damaged edges and corners to make your steps look like new

Concrete steps break up, especially in northern climates. Water soaks into the concrete, freezes and breaks off the outside corners. Once that starts, the damage spreads along the front edge of the step, eventually turning the step into a ramp. That's not only ugly but mighty dangerous.

The best repair for severe corner and front edge breakage—short of completely replacing the steps—is to "recap" them. You break away the damaged areas, rebuild them with new concrete and then coat your entire steps to give them a uniform look. It takes about two days altogether to complete this project.

Bust off the old surface

Start by rigging up your circular saw and grinder with water supply lines (**Photo 1**). All it takes is a few bucks' worth of sprinkler system parts from any home center to fabricate a water-cooling and dust-reduction system. Secure the assembly to the saw with hook-and-loop tape. Build another spray unit (with only one nozzle) for your angle grinder.

Set the circular saw blade to full depth and adjust the water flow. Then don your safety gear (goggles, hearing protection, knee pads and leather gloves) and connect your saw/ grinder to a GFCI extension cord. Cut a grid pattern into the steps (**Photo 2**) and bust off the surface (**Photo 3**). You must remove at least 3/4 in. of concrete (3/4 in. is the minimum thickness for a cap). But a thicker cap is stronger, so try to remove 1-1/2 in. of concrete or more.

Switch to the angle grinder to cut the remaining concrete where the stair tread meets

Repair or replace?

The very best way to fix concrete steps is to demolish the old ones and pour new ones. No repair lasts forever. And replacement is the only real fix for steps that are sinking or have deep cracks. But if your steps are level and have only the usual damage that goes a few inches deep, you can save yourself a ton of money and/or labor by patching or recapping them.

Patching works well for small, shallow chips and cracks (less than 1/4 in. deep). Simply fill them with premixed concrete patching material. To patch cracked corners, chisel them out to a depth of at least 3/4 in. Then drill holes and drive in concrete screws as anchors, apply a bonding adhesive and fill with crack-resistant concrete. The patch won't match the color or texture of the steps, so you may want to recoat all the steps with concrete resurfacer for a uniform look.

If the cracks or voids extend over large areas of your steps, forget about patching. Go ahead and cap the steps following the procedure shown here.

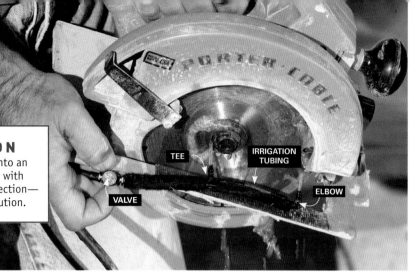

1 TURN YOUR SAW INTO A WET SAW. Rig up a water line using irrigation system parts. Water keeps the blade cool and eliminates dust. In addition to the parts shown here, you'll need an adapter to connect the tubing to a garden hose.

2 SLICE UP THE DAMAGED AREA. Cut the stair tread into a 4- to 5-in. grid pattern. Sawing concrete is no fun, but the more cuts you make, the easier it will be to break off the step's surface.

3 BREAK OUT THE BLOCKS. Aim the chisel at the same depth as the saw cuts and whack away. The squares of concrete created by your saw cuts will pop off neatly (well, usually).

the riser (**Photo 4**). Once you've removed the entire stair tread, run the circular saw lengthwise down the front and side edges of the step. Break off the faces with the maul and chisel.

Pour a new cap

Hose down the steps and let them dry. Then coat the chipped-out areas with concrete bonding adhesive.

Build a concrete form to match the original height of the step. Locate the front of the form about 1 in. out from the old face of the step. If that extra inch will cause the step to overhang the sidewalk, place a strip of 1/2-in.-thick foam under the form to create a gap between the step and the sidewalk. The gap will allow the sidewalk to rise during a freeze.

Next, mix the crack-resistant concrete and fill the form (**Photo 5**). Then finish the concrete (**Photo 6**). Remove the form after 24 hours.

Wait a week and then apply the resurfacer. Mix it in small batches. Then wet all the steps with a water spray bottle and apply the resurfacer (**Photo 7**).

5 FILL THE FORM. Work the concrete into the front form with your shovel or a stick. When the form is completely full, screed off the excess concrete.

4 CUT INTO THE CORNER. Your saw can't reach into the corner where the stair tread and riser meet. So cut with a grinder and chisel out the concrete. Add a spray system to your grinder similar to the one on your saw.

RISER

STAIR TREAD

6 FINISH THE CONCRETE. Skim the surface with a wood float. When the mix hardens a little, round the edges with a concrete edger and smooth it with a steel trowel. Don't overwork the concrete or you'll weaken the surface.

WOOD FLOAT

7 RESURFACE THE WHOLE THING. Resurfacer hides the mismatch between old and new concrete and masks small imperfections. Pour it on and spread it with a masonry brush.

Fixing Cracks in Concrete

Long sleeves and a dust mask are required!

If your concrete driveway and steps look like a scene from a post-apocalypse movie, it's time to strap on your dust mask, arm yourself with a chisel and a trowel and fight back. Don't let that broken corner, hairline crack or crumbling surface ruin the look of your home.

REMEMBER TO
CLOSE NEARBY
WINDOWS!

SHOULDER
CUTS

MASONRY
BLADE

1 Cut a 3/8-in. to 1/2-in.-deep "shoulder" around the edge of the spalled area with a saw and masonry blade. Move the saw slowly as you cut. Make sure you cut back into solid concrete to ensure a strong bonding surface.

Tip
You'll raise an impressive dust cloud when sawing, so close up nearby windows and doors. Otherwise, you'll be housecleaning, too!

("Spalling" is the mason's term for concrete that's pitted or chipped.)

We won't deal with the other common problem, cracks. You can repair them exactly as we show here, but they'll most likely return unless you can stabilize the concrete slab to prevent the movement that caused the cracks in the first place.

Concrete is hard stuff, but don't let that intimidate you. With the proper tools and techniques we show in our photo series, even a novice can make a durable patch, first try. Sawing concrete with a special masonry blade (**Photo 1**) may be new to you, but if you've handled a circular saw, you'll quickly get the hang of it. It's less hazardous than sawing wood. However, the blade kicks up an incredibly thick cloud of abrasive dust, so be sure to wear goggles to protect your eyes, ear protection, gloves and a dust mask, as well as old clothes.

Size up the job first

Before beginning any repair, assess the general condition of the concrete slab. (See "Patch or Replace?" on p. 251.) Sometimes the best strategy is to break out an entire section and repour it with new concrete rather than patch it. Patching works best for local damage in otherwise sound concrete.

If this is your first concrete repair project, allow about a half day to pick up materials and complete two to three patches. It took us about four hours from start to finish to complete the two repairs we show here.

Complete the job during comfortable working conditions, ideally in dry weather with a temperature between 50 and 80 degrees F. Both you and fresh concrete happen to agree on this one. Fresh concrete is easiest to handle and hardens best (a process technically called "setting" and "curing") in this temperature range. Colder weather lengthens the setting time; freezing temperatures can ruin the concrete. Hotter weather causes faster setting and drying; the slab may harden before you can smooth it. Or the surface can dry too fast and not harden properly, eventually causing it to spall. In hot weather, work in the cooler mornings or in the shade.

Tip
Spend $20 to repair the damage yourself or pay hundreds of dollars to replace this simple slab.

2-LB. MAUL

MASON'S COLD CHISEL

2 Break out all weak and loose concrete with a maul and cold chisel. Sharp concrete chips will come flying out, so wear safety goggles.

Repair spalled areas

The key to a lasting repair is to make a saw cut around the perimeter of the damaged area, cutting back to solid concrete. The cut should be at least 3/8 in. deep: Most repairs that fail do so because the patch is too thin at the edges and breaks off. Set a masonry blade at a 5-degree angle so the cutout is slightly wider at the bottom than at the top. This helps "lock in" the patch (**Photo 1**). Slowly guide the saw through the concrete. The masonry blade grinds a groove, so don't put a lot of pressure on the saw; let the blade do the work. Cut about 1/4 in. on each pass.

A diamond grit blade can cut the concrete about five times faster than a masonry blade, and it won't wear out as fast. But it also costs more ($35 vs. $3). The extra cost is worth it if you have more than about 10 ft. of concrete to cut.

3 Clean the chips and dust from the repair area with a broom or shop vacuum. Be thorough. Then mix the patching material.

Patch or replace?

Should you patch your old concrete or completely tear it out and repour it? While there's no hard and fast rule, here are some tips to guide your decision:

1. ASSESS THE SEVERITY OF THE DAMAGE. If your driveway is full of spalled areas and broken edges, the surface is probably severely weakened. It'll continue to deteriorate, and chances are the patches won't last.

Contact a concrete contractor to help you assess the situation and ask for a price on complete replacement. But, keep in mind that contractors are in the business of selling concrete. With their labor costs, it's usually cheaper for them to replace than repair. We had trouble finding a contractor who would even do patching.

2. IS APPEARANCE IMPORTANT? A patch will be lighter-colored than the old concrete. Even after weathering for a few years, the new patch will probably still stand out. One way to hide the patch is to stain the entire surface to blend the old with the new. But you'll have to renew the stain periodically.

3. HOW MUCH ARE YOU WILLING TO SPEND? We spent $20 in materials to repair the damaged areas shown in this story. Pros would have charged $300 to $400 to replace this simple 6 x 6-ft. porch slab.

A $3 corundum masonry blade grinds through concrete slowly. A diamond blade ($35) cuts much faster.

SPONGE

WOOD FLOAT

PATCH MIX

4 Moisten the patch area with a wet sponge. Then pack in the patch mix with a wood float. Leave the mix slightly higher than the surface of the old concrete.

> **CAUTION**
> Wet concrete is highly alkaline and can cause severe burns to bare skin. Immediately wash off any that gets on your skin with cool water.

SCREED BOARD

5 Screed off the excess material by sliding a board side to side in a sawing motion while pushing it forward. if you find low spots, pack in more mix and screed off again.

Once you've cut and thoroughly cleaned loose concrete from the repair area (**Photos 2** and **3**), moisten the area with a wet sponge before packing in the concrete mix. Don't leave standing water in the patch area; use just enough to dampen the old concrete and help it bond to the new.

The recipe for a strong patching mix

For your patching mix, use either a prepackaged sand mix or concrete mix, depending on the depth of the patch. (See "Use the Correct Patching Mix," p. 253.) Each 60-lb. bag makes about 1/2 cu. ft. of concrete, enough for a 2-in. thick patch about 1 ft. wide by 3 ft. long. Estimate the volume of patching material by multiplying approximate length, width and thickness (in feet) to arrive at cubic feet, and buy a bit more than you think you'll need. At only $5 per bag, it's cheap enough to buy extra. Better to have too much than to fall a few scoops short!

Mix it with water and acrylic fortifier, following the mixing directions on the package. The fortifier strengthens the new concrete and helps it bond better to the old concrete. The mix should be just wet enough to hold together when it's troweled into the repair. Don't add too much water. It'll result in weaker concrete.

We used a normal sand mix, which sets hard enough to walk on in about a day or two. It continues to cure and harden for weeks. If you have to use the area right away, you can buy a special fast-setting concrete, which hardens in about an hour. It costs about twice as much and you won't have as long to spread and smooth it, so stick to the regular mix when possible. Most building supply dealers that carry regular concrete also carry the fast-setting type.

Pack the repair mix firmly

After mixing the concrete, pack it firmly into the repair area using a wood float (**Photo 4**), the tighter the better. Mound the mix so it's slightly higher than the old concrete. Then immediately level it even with the old concrete using a screed board (**Photo 5**).

Use the correct patching mix

IN A NUTSHELL: Use a sand mix for repairs less than 2 in. deep. Use a concrete mix for repairs deeper than 2 in.

 CONCRETE MIX consists of sand, gravel and Portland cement. The gravel reduces shrinkage, so it won't crack as readily when laid in thick. However it may not bond well in thin layers. Replace 50 to 80 percent of the water with the acrylic fortifier in either mix to improve the patch's bonding strength.

B **SAND MIX** (sometimes called topping mix) consists of sand and Portland cement. It's easier to trowel in thinner layers (to about 1/4 in. minimum) for thinner patches or patches with thinner edges. However, if you apply it thicker than 2 in., its natural shrinkage might cause it to crack or break the bond with the old concrete.

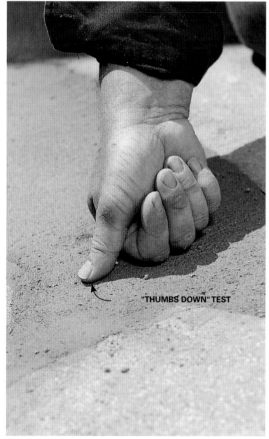

"THUMBS DOWN" TEST

SPONGE FLOAT

6 Test the firmness of the patch by lightly pressing your thumb on the surface. When your thumb no longer leaves an indentation, go ahead and finish the surface.

7 Match the texture of the old, rough concrete by rubbing the surface of the patch with a sponge float. Use a steel trowel for a smooth finish or a stiff bristle broom for a lightly grooved finish.

FORM BOARD
FOR STEP

8 Cover the patch with plastic to retain the moisture. Weight down the edges to keep the plastic from blowing off. Concrete requires moisture to cure properly.

Finish the patch to match the old surface

Begin finish trowel work when the surface moisture starts to evaporate and the patch begins to harden. It may only be 10 minutes on a warm day or perhaps an hour on a cool day. One sign of evaporation is the loss of some of the surface gloss. When the patch appears to be getting stiff, test it with your thumb (**Photo 6**). Once the surface is about as stiff as the skin of a grapefruit, begin the finish work.

We used a sponge float (**Photo 7**) to match the slightly rough texture of the old concrete. A sponge float has a rough rubber surface. If you want a smooth surface, use a steel trowel; for a lightly grooved appearance, drag a stiff-bristle broom across the surface.

Cover the patch to retain the water

After using a float on the surface, cover the patch with plastic for two days. The plastic helps the concrete retain the moisture, which the concrete needs to cure and strengthen (**Photo 8**).

Tip

Coat the wood form with motor oil or WD-40 to keep the concrete from sticking to the wood.

MASONRY
BLADE

CUT LEDGE

1x6 FORM

9 Square off the edges of the broken step with a masonry blade. Chip out loose and weak concrete with a cold chisel.

Restore broken step corners

Use the same basic patching technique for a broken corner as for spalled areas, but add three key steps.

1 Create a ledge for the patch to make a stronger bond with the old concrete (**Photos 9** and **10**). Don't be afraid to make the cutout well beyond the edges of the original damaged area. Smaller patches simply won't hold as well as larger ones.

2 Prop a wood form tightly against the vertical portion of the step to hold the concrete patch in place (**Photo 10**). Block the form against the step with bricks or other heavy objects.

3 When the concrete begins to set, use the edging tool to create a slightly rounded edge to match the step (**Photo 11**). Then remove the form board (carefully, because the concrete is still soft) and finish all exposed surfaces with a float or trowel to match the texture of the old concrete. Cover the patch with plastic and let it cure for at least two days before walking on it.

Materials list

- Sand or concrete mix; $5 per 60-lb. bag
- Concrete acrylic fortifier; $15 per gallon

Tools list

- Circular saw with masonry blade
- 2-lb. maul; (a regular hammer is slower, but OK)
- Mason's cold chisel; (**Photo 2**)
- Wood float; (**Photo 4**)
- Sponge float, to match texture of rough concrete; (**Photo 7**)
- Corner edging tool; (**Photo 11**)
- Shop vacuum and broom
- Release agent for wood forms (light oil, WD-40)
- Gloves, dust mask, goggles and hearing protection

PATCH AREA

WOOD FORM

10 Anchor a form board against the side of the step, moisten the area and pack in the repair mix. Screed off the excess patching material.

EDGING TOOL

ROUND EDGE

11 Slide an edging tool along the step edge to round it. Use the edging tool only if the old step portion has a rounded edge.

Recoat the Driveway

A fresh coat of driveway sealer helps your home look well cared for

An asphalt driveway can last almost 30 years. But you can't achieve that long life span unless the driveway was installed properly and you perform regular maintenance, like filling cracks annually and applying sealer when needed. Here, we'll show you how to clean and prepare the driveway so you get the longest life and best protection from driveway sealer.

Preparation can take a full day (including drying time), and it's tedious. The application phase is much faster, taking only a few hours per coat for a typical driveway. Most sealer manufacturers recommend two coats with a minimum drying time of eight hours between coats, so this project will fill an entire weekend.

The materials cost about $100, but you'll save about $200 in labor over a professional job. A power washer speeds the cleaning process, but you can do the job without it. In addition to a squeegee or application brush, you'll need a broom, drill, mixing paddle, duct tape, dashing brush and poly sheeting to protect painted surfaces.

Avoid these common driveway-sealing mistakes

- Depending on the sealer to fill cracks. It won't. Fill them properly before applying sealer.
- Failure to clean and prep the driveway before applying the sealer. If you don't want to spend time cleaning the driveway, you may as well skip the sealer too, because it won't stick to a dirty driveway.
- Failure to stir properly. Don't depend on a stir stick. It simply won't blend the water and solids enough to get a consistent mixture.
- Use of the wrong applicator. Using a brush when the manufacturer specifies a squeegee (or vice versa) will cause premature sealer failure.
- Applying sealer too often. Too much sealer will flake off. Wait until you begin to see asphalt aggregate before you apply a new coat of sealer.

Buying the right materials

Driveway sealer is available in various grades and price ranges, from as little as $15 per 5-gallon pail to about $35 per pail for a premium product. Some bargain products contain almost 50 percent water and have lower coverage rates and a correspondingly shorter guarantee, so they're not the most cost-effective solution over the long term. Use one of them if you're trying to spiff up the driveway before selling your home. Premium products, on the other hand, are made with higher-quality resins and UV stabilizers and contain filler and elastomeric material, so they last longer and carry a longer guarantee.

Manufacturers also make different formulas for different driveway conditions: one formula for newer driveways in good condition and another formula for older driveways that haven't been well maintained. The two formulas also vary in their coverage, so read the labels carefully and choose the correct sealer and quantity for your particular driveway. Follow the manufacturer's directions for the type of applicator to use (brush or squeegee). Using the wrong one can cause premature failure.

You'll also need liquid driveway cleaner/degreaser to remove oil and tree sap. If your driveway has visible oil stains, pick up a bottle of oil spot primer.

Check the weather before you start

You'll need at least two days of dry weather to seal your driveway. Temperatures must be above 50 degrees F during application and throughout the night. And, it's best to avoid scorching-hot sunny days (the sealer may dry too fast). If you ignore the weather forecast, you may see $100 worth of sealer wash away in a heavy rain.

Start with cleaning and priming

Even if you think your driveway is clean, trust us, it isn't. Exhaust gas contains combustion byproducts that deposit a light, sometimes oily film on your driveway. That film, along with dirt and tree sap, must come off if you want the sealer to stick. So clean the driveway first (**Photo 1**).

1 SOAP AND SCRUB. Use the soap nozzle on your power washer or a garden hose applicator to apply the driveway cleaner. Then scrub the entire driveway with a stiff-bristle push broom.

40-DEGREE NOZZLE SETTING

2 RINSE WITH A STRONG STREAM. Flush the soap and dirt residue with a 40-degree power washer nozzle or a strong stream of water from your garden hose.

3 PRETREAT THE OIL STAINS. Pour the oil spot primer on the damaged areas and brush it into the pores with a disposable chip brush. Apply a second coat to heavier stains. Let the primer dry fully before applying the driveway sealer.

Next, rinse the driveway with clear water (**Photo 2**). Let the driveway dry completely before applying the sealer. Then perform a final sweep with a push broom. Treat any oil stains with an oil spot primer (**Photo 3**).

Mask, stir and trim

Driveway sealer will splash onto your garage door and sidewalks as you pour it. And it'll get all over your shoes and clothes. It's very difficult (often impossible) to remove later, so wear old work clothes and shoes. Mask the garage door with poly sheeting and apply strips of duct tape to concrete walks where it butts up to the asphalt.

Choose an area on the driveway for mixing and cover it with poly sheeting to protect against spills (dried spills will show through the sealer). Remove the pail lids and cut a small hole in the center of one lid. Use that lid to prevent splashing during mixing. Stir until the mixture is smooth (**Photo 4**).

Next, cut in all four edges of the driveway with a large dashing brush (**Photo 5**). Clean the brush with soap and water as soon as you're done cutting in the edges—you'll need it again the following day. Then stage the pails equally down the driveway (**Photo 6**).

Pour and spread

Pour the sealer onto the driveway (**Photo 7**). Then spread the puddle with a squeegee or broom, depending on the manufacturer's directions (**Photo 8**). Pour enough sealer to maintain a puddle in front of the applicator tool.

When you reach the bottom of the driveway, cap the remaining pails and clean the squeegee or brush. Set the empty pails along the curb to prevent cars from ruining the job. Then let the sealer dry overnight.

Repeat the sealer application the next day. Let the sealer dry for 48 hours before driving on it (better safe than sorry). Don't ask how we learned that lesson.

4 MIX THE SEALER. Start the mixing paddle near the top of the pail and slowly lower it into the contents settled at the bottom. Cycle the mixing paddle up and down while it spins to combine the water and solids into a smooth consistency.

5 CUT IN THE EDGES. Dip the dashing brush into the sealer and apply a liberal coating to all four edges of the driveway. Don't spread it too thin; you want it to fill in all the pores.

POLY SHEETING TO MASK DOOR

STAGED PAILS

6 STAGE THE PAILS. Guesstimate the coverage of each pail and stage each additional pail along the driveway. That saves time and reduces the need to walk through wet sealer to get the next pail.

7 POUR ONTO THE DRIVEWAY. Start at the top left or right edge of the driveway and pour the sealer in an upside-down U-shape pattern.

8 SPREAD THE SEALER. Start at one leg of the upside-down "U" and apply even pressure to spread the puddle across the driveway and down along the opposite leg. Then pick up the excess sealer on the down leg and start the next row.

Driveway sealers: Real protection or just black paint?

Some asphalt driveway companies tell their customers that driveway sealer is a waste of money, that it's cosmetic and doesn't do anything to extend the life of the asphalt.

It's true that driveway sealer can't replace the liquid asphalt (oil/tar) that oxidizes and bakes out of the mixture from heat and sun exposure. But a high-quality sealer can dramatically reduce future heat and UV damage. Plus, it seals the pores to prevent breakup damage caused by water penetration, freeze/thaw cycles and chemicals. So it really does extend the life of the driveway.

Seal Attic Air Leaks

Chances are, your ceiling has the equivalent of a 2-ft.-square hole that's acting like a chimney, drafting expensive heated air into your attic and sucking cold air in around your windows and doors. You can't see the hole because it's the sum of many smaller openings. These gaps around plumbing pipes, light fixtures, chimneys and other attic bypasses are hidden under your insulation.

For around $100 in materials and a day's labor, you can save lots of money on heating every year by sealing these holes. On the following pages, Peter Krych of the building and remodeling company Northwind Winterization shows you where to find the bypasses in your attic and simple techniques for plugging and sealing them.

You'll find everything you need at any full-service hardware store, home center or lumberyard. If you can't find the reflective foil insulation (**Photo 3**), substitute drywall or pieces cut from 4 x 8-ft. sheets of rigid foil-faced insulation. Fitting rigid material requires more precise measuring, but the result is the same.

1 Get your bearings from below

Before you crawl into the attic, make a quick sketch of the floor plan. Make note of dropped soffits over kitchen cabinets or bath vanities, slanted ceilings over stairways, and any other dropped-ceiling areas. These areas usually have open stud cavities leading directly into the attic that are huge sources of air leaks (**Photos 1 – 3**). Locate the main plumbing stack, furnace flue or chimney and note this on your sketch for a reference point once you get into the attic.

Figure A
Common attic air leaks

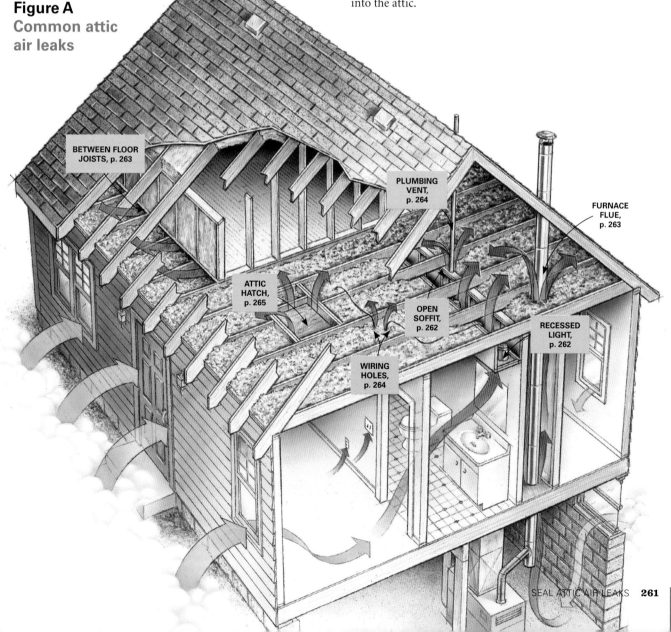

BETWEEN FLOOR JOISTS, p. 263

PLUMBING VENT, p. 264

FURNACE FLUE, p. 263

ATTIC HATCH, p. 265

OPEN SOFFIT, p. 262

RECESSED LIGHT, p. 262

WIRING HOLES, p. 264

Pressurize your house

Before you crawl into the attic, place a box fan in a window so it's blowing air into the house and close all the remaining windows and doors. Tape cardboard around the fan to cover large gaps. When you turn the fan on high, the house will be pressurized, like an inflated balloon. And just as you can feel the air from a leaky balloon, you'll be able to confirm leaks in the attic by feeling the draft with your hand. You may even be able to locate bypasses visually by looking for insulation being blown about. Close the attic access door or hatch behind you to maximize the effect.

Gather your supplies (see Materials List on p. 264) and suit up. Attics are miserable places to work. Be sure to read the tips on p. 264 before you start.

③ Plug the big holes first

It's tempting to grab a can of expanding foam and squirt it into all the little holes, but your biggest savings will come from plugging the large holes. Find the plumbing stack or flue for a reference point. Then use your sketch to locate the soffits, stairwells or other dropped-ceiling areas. You'll probably have to dig around in the insulation to uncover them. Soffits may be filled with insulation or covered with cardboard or fiberglass batts. Push back the insulation and scoop it out of the soffits. Now plug the open stud spaces (**Photos 1** and **2**) and seal the top of the cavities with reflective foil (**Photo 3**). Cover the area with insulation again when you're done.

CAUTION

Some attics have vermiculite insulation, which may contain asbestos, a health hazard. Vermiculite is a lightweight, pea-size, flaky gray mineral. Don't disturb vermiculite insulation unless you've had it tested by an approved lab to be sure it doesn't contain asbestos. Contact your local health department for the name of an approved lab.

1 Cut a 16-in.-long piece from a batt of unfaced fiberglass insulation and fold it at the bottom of a 13-gallon plastic garbage bag.

2 Fold the bag over once and stuff it into the open stud cavity. Make sure there's enough insulation in the bag to form a tight fit in the cavity.

3 With scissors, cut a length of foil insulation about 6 in. longer than the opening to be covered. Apply a bead of latex caulk around the opening. Embed the foil in the caulk and staple it in place.

④ Stuffed bags seal joist spaces, too

Heated rooms built into attics often have open cavities in the floor framing under the walls. Even though insulation may be piled against or stuffed into these spaces, they can still leak air. **Photo 4** shows how to stuff these spaces with the same type of garbage-bag plug used to seal stud cavities.

4 Plug all open joist spaces under insulated side walls. Cut a 24-in.-long piece from a batt of fiberglass insulation and place it at the bottom of a 13-gallon plastic garbage bag. Fold the bag over and stuff it into the joist space under the wall.

KNEE WALL

24" BATT ROLLED INSIDE GARBAGE BAG

OPEN JOIST CAVITY

FIBERGLASS BATT

13-GALLON PLASTIC GARBAGE BAGS

⑤ Furnace flues require special techniques

The opening around a furnace or water heater flue is a major source of warm air into the attic (**Photo 5**). Because the pipe gets hot, building codes require 1 in. of clearance from Class B flues (2 in. from masonry chimneys) to any combustible material, including insulation. **Photos 5** and **6** show how to seal this gap with lightweight aluminum flashing and special high-temperature silicone caulk. Before you push the insulation back into place, build a metal dam (**Photo 7**) to keep it away from the pipe. Use this same technique for masonry chimneys.

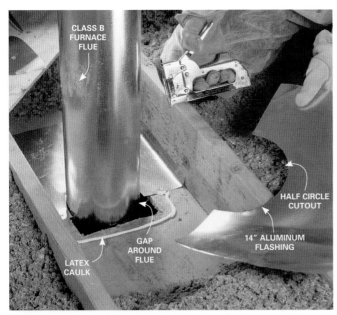

CLASS B FURNACE FLUE

HALF CIRCLE CUTOUT

GAP AROUND FLUE

14" ALUMINUM FLASHING

LATEX CAULK

5 Cut aluminum flashing to fit around the flue. For round flues like this, cut half circles out of two pieces so they overlap about 3 in. in the middle. Press the flashing metal into a bead of latex caulk and staple it into place. If there's no wood, staple it right to the drywall.

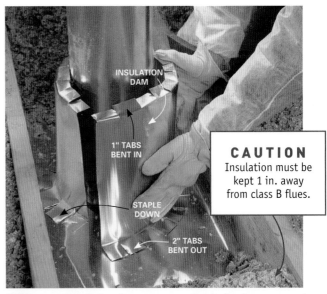

INSULATION DAM

1" TABS BENT IN

STAPLE DOWN

2" TABS BENT OUT

CAUTION
Insulation must be kept 1 in. away from class B flues.

HIGH-TEMP SILICONE CAULK

6 Seal the gap between the flue and metal flashing with special high-temperature silicone caulk. Don't use spray foam here.

7 Form an insulation dam to prevent insulation from contacting the flue pipe. Cut enough aluminum from the coil to wrap around the flue plus 6 in. cut slots 1 in. deep and a few inches apart along the top and bend the tabs in. Cut slots about 2 in. deep along the bottom and bend out the tabs. Wrap the dam around the flue and secure the bottom by stapling through the tabs.

Use foam and caulk to seal small holes

Seal openings around plumbing vents and electrical wires with expanding foam (**Photos 8** and **9**). Be careful though; this stuff is super sticky and almost impossible to get off your clothes and skin. Wear disposable gloves and eye protection. Seal around electrical boxes with caulk (**Photo 9**).

Tip

TELLTALE SIGNS—FINDING ATTIC BYPASSES

Even though most of the gaps allowing warm air into your attic are buried in insulation, you'll still see evidence of the escaping air. While in your attic, look for areas where the insulation is darkened (see photo), a result of filtering dusty air from the house. In cold weather, you may see frosty areas in the insulation caused by warm, moist air condensing and freezing as it hits the cold attic air. In warmer weather, you'll find water staining in these same areas. If you pressurize the house with a window fan (see "Pressurize your house," p. 262), you may be able to feel the leaks with your hand as the air finds its way into the attic.

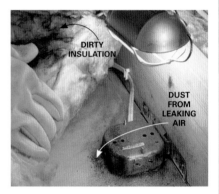

DIRTY INSULATION

DUST FROM LEAKING AIR

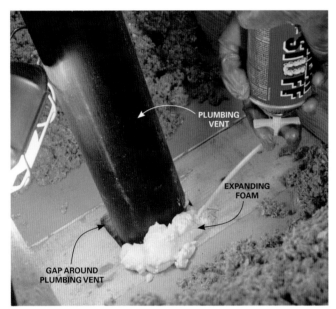

PLUMBING VENT

EXPANDING FOAM

GAP AROUND PLUMBING VENT

8 Stuff a small piece of fiberglass batt insulation into the space around the plumbing vent pipe as a backer for the expanding foam. Then follow the directions on the can to fill the space around the pipe with expanding foam insulation.

Materials list

- Roll of reflective foil insulation
- Bundle or roll of unfaced fiberglass batt insulation
- Acrylic latex caulk
- Special high-temperature silicone caulk
- Roll of 14-in.-wide aluminum flashing
- Roll of 13-gallon plastic garbage bags
- Can of expanding spray foam insulation

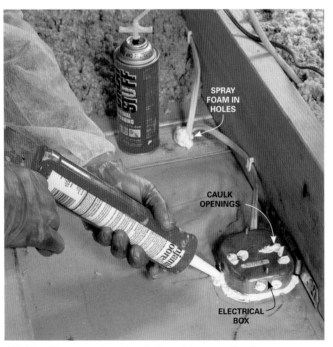

SPRAY FOAM IN HOLES

CAULK OPENINGS

ELECTRICAL BOX

9 Fill wiring and plumbing holes with expanding foam. Caulk around electrical junction boxes and fill holes in the box with caulk.

Tips for working in the attic

- Start in the morning when it's cool. Pick a cool, cloudy day if possible. Don't spend more than 15 or 20 minutes in a hot attic.
- Wear a lightweight disposable coverall (available in paint departments), gloves and a hat to keep itchy insulation off your clothes and skin.
- Always wear a double-strap dust mask or an OSHA-approved particulate respirator.
- Wear knee pads if you have them. Crawling around on joists gets painful. Use scraps of plywood to kneel on and as a platform for your supplies.
- Buy a rough-service lightbulb and a clamp-on light, both available at hardware stores. Have a flashlight handy just in case.
- Minimize trips in and out of the attic by collecting all of your tools and supplies and placing them in the attic before you go up.
- Watch where you step. You must walk on ceiling joists or truss chords and carry a small piece of plywood to work from. Don't step on the ceiling drywall.

⑦ Complete the job by sealing the hatch

When you're done sealing your attic bypasses, push the insulation back into place with an old broom handle or stick as you back out of the attic. Then finish up by sealing the access hatch with self-sticking foam weatherstrip (**Photos 10** and **11**). If your hatch rests directly on the moldings like this one did, add 2-1/2-in.-wide stops around the opening. The stops provide a wider surface for attaching the weatherstrip and a space to mount hook-and-eye fasteners. Position the screw eyes so the weatherstrip is slightly compressed when the hooks are latched.

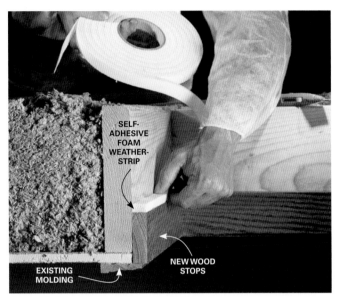

SELF-ADHESIVE FOAM WEATHER-STRIP

EXISTING MOLDING

NEW WOOD STOPS

10 Weatherstrip the attic access hatch or door. Cut 1x3 boards to fit the perimeter of the opening and nail them on with 6d finish nails. Apply self-adhesive foam weatherstrip tape to the top edge of the stop.

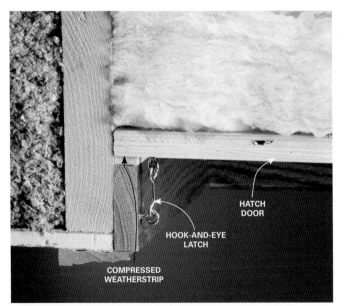

HATCH DOOR

HOOK-AND-EYE LATCH

COMPRESSED WEATHERSTRIP

11 Attach hook-and-eye fasteners to the door and stops. Position the eyes so that the weatherstrip is compressed when you latch the hooks.

Stop a draft in 60 seconds

In exterior walls, electrical boxes that hold switches or outlets can let in a lot of cold air. Worse, they can let warm, moist indoor air into walls, causing problems like wood rot or peeling exterior paint. One way to stop the airflow is to seal the gaps around them and the holes inside them with caulk—messy and time consuming. But there's a much easier way: With foam gaskets, all you have to do is unscrew the cover plate, stick the gasket in place and put the plate back on. A pack of a dozen gaskets costs about $3 at home centers and hardware stores.

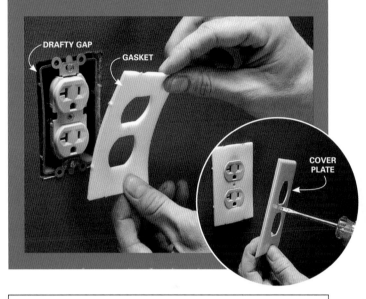

DRAFTY GAP

GASKET

COVER PLATE

Check for backdrafting

Whenever you make energy improvements—like sealing attic bypasses—that result in a tighter house, install carbon monoxide (CO) alarms if you don't already have them. Allow one per floor. Also have a pro check your combustion appliances for backdrafting at the next servicing.

Recessed can lights— no easy solution

Cut a 6-in. hole in your ceiling and add a 100-watt bulb—enough heat to bake cookies—and you have a recipe for huge heat loss as well as a major contributor to ice dams. That's what a recessed light does. Here are the solutions pros recommend if you have recessed can lights protruding into your attic:

- Replace incandescent bulbs with cooler-operating LED bulbs.
- Replace your old recessed lights with new airtight models available at some home centers and lighting stores. This is the best solution for those with electrical skills. New cans are relatively inexpensive—about $20 apiece plus decorative trim and bulb—and can usually be installed in a few hours each.

Replace a Storm Door

Our seasoned pro shows you how to make a perfect installation even in less-than-perfect situations

If you live where storm doors are a must and yours is in bad shape, replace it.

Replacing a storm door is easier than you might think. Manufacturers have made installation more DIY friendly by providing standard sizes that'll fit almost any door opening and simpler installation kits. Still, you'll find some sticking points. The following step-by-step directions walk you through some tricks and techniques you won't find in any instruction manual.

If you have a hacksaw, screw gun, a short level and a pair of side cutters and two to three hours, you're on your way to saving the cost of a professional installation.

Replacing an old storm door or installing a new one is a perfect Saturday morning project, even if you have limited carpentry skills. Be sure to choose a storm door that complements the style of your home.

1 Pick a flat area near the entry door, lay the box flat on the ground, fold it open and check to make sure you have all the parts.

Selecting the door

To find the size of the storm door you need, simply measure the height and width of the main door. Most front entry doors are 36 in. wide and require a 36-in. storm door.

Here, we chose a "full-view" storm door. The one we show has removable screen and glass panels that you interchange each season. The other common type, a "ventilating" storm door, has glass panels that slide open or closed over the screen, much like a double-hung window.

Tip

If your entry door trim needs paint, do it now. It's a pain in the neck painting around a new door, and you'll have a crisper-looking job.

Nearly every storm door sold is reversible. That is, you can install it with the hinge on either side. The manufacturer's directions tell you how to do it. When you buy it, you don't have to specify which way the door must swing.

You typically mount storm doors to the exterior door trim using "Z-bars." The hinge-side Z-bar may already be screwed to the door (ours was), or you may have to mount it once you determine the door swing direction. On some doors, you'll also have to drill holes for the latch.

Getting started

Begin the project by folding open the box and removing the glass storm panel. Set it and the screen panel in a safe place out of the wind. Then check for damaged or missing parts by comparing the contents with the parts list in the instruction manual. (Ours had been returned, repackaged and sold as new. One of the

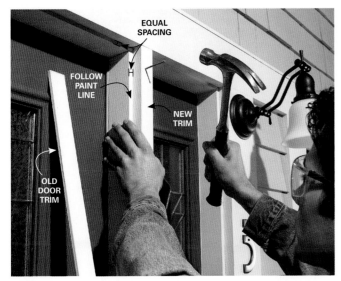

2 Add a trim extension if needed to doors with sidelights. Prime and paint the new trim, position it with a reveal equal to the other trim and then nail it into place.

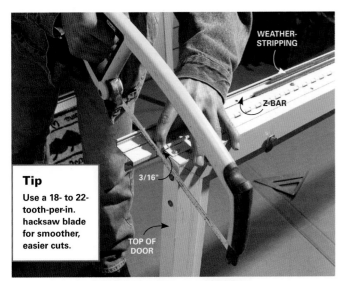

Tip

Use a 18- to 22-tooth-per-in. hacksaw blade for smoother, easier cuts.

3 Confirm the door swing direction and fasten the hinge-side Z-bar to the correct side (if necessary). Mark a cutting line on the Z-bar 3/16 in. above the top of the door with a square. Slide the weatherstripping aside and cut the Z-bar with a hacksaw.

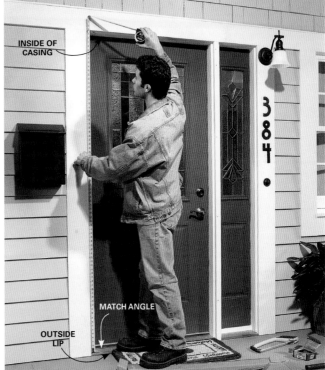

4 Measure from the outside lip of the threshold to the top door casing. Transfer the measurement to the bottom of the hinge-side Z-bar and cut it to length, matching the angle on the threshold.

parts had already been cut to length and the mounting screws were missing.) Use the cardboard as a work surface to prevent scratching the parts while you work. Then determine the door swing. In general, hinge the storm door on the same side as the main door. However, consider these exceptions:

- **ADJOINING WALLS.** If there's an adjoining wall or rail, it's best to have the door swing against it; otherwise entry can be awkward, especially if you're carrying groceries.
- **ELECTRICAL.** Will the door open against any light fixtures? Will the doorbell or light switch wind up on the latch side where they belong?
- **WIND.** If there's a strong prevailing wind, it's best to have the door hinge side face the wind direction. That way, sudden gusts can't fling it open and break it.

Why a storm door

A traditional storm door was a real workhorse. It protected the handsome but vulnerable wooden main door from harsh weather and helped to insulate it.

Today's better insulated and protected main doors have little need for a storm door and are often eliminated from new homes, showing off fancy front doors. However, the "full-view" storm door (like the one we're installing here) still showcases the main door and, when screened, allows you to take advantage of those cool summer breezes too.

7 Lift the door into the opening and pry it against the hinge-side casing with a twist from rubber-handled pliers on the latch side. Screw the hinge Z-bar into the door casing side.

LATCH-SIDE CASING

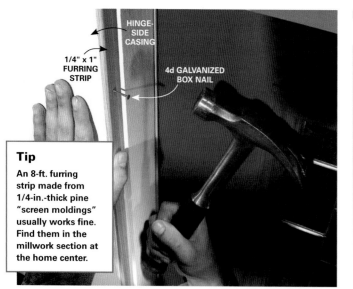

5 Center the weatherstripping in the Z-bar, then snip off the ends, leaving it 1/2 in. extra long at each end.

1/2"

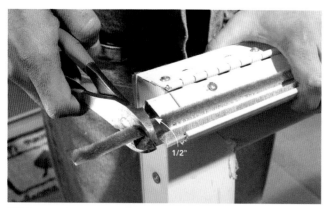

HINGE-SIDE CASING

1/4" x 1" FURRING STRIP

4d GALVANIZED BOX NAIL

Tip

An 8-ft. furring strip made from 1/4-in.-thick pine "screen moldings" usually works fine. Find them in the millwork section at the home center.

6 Measure the opening width and determine the furring strip thickness (**see text**). Cut a furring strip to length, then nail it to the inside edge of the hinge-side casing with four evenly spaced 4d galvanized box nails.

TOP-SIDE Z-BAR

TOP CASING

POWER-PLUS

8 Swing the door open, slip the top-side Z-bar into place and close the door to hold it. Adjust the gap between the Z-bar and the top of the door until it's even and screw it into the top casing.

LATCH MARKS

PROTECTIVE FILM

Tip

Your door may come with a protective plastic film. Only peel off those areas needed for installing hardware during installation (Photos 9 and 13). That way the door will be protected from scratches. After installation is complete, peel away the plastic.

9 Mount the latch mechanism, then mark the position of the top and bottom of the latch on the door casing. If the space between the door and the casing is over 5/8 in., nail two 1/4-in.-thick furring strips to the inside of the casing, one above and one below the marks (see Photo 11).

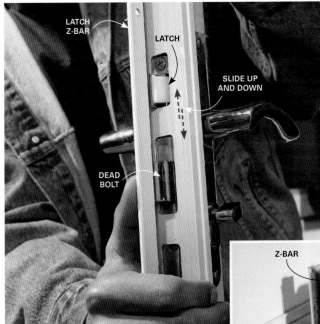

LATCH Z-BAR

LATCH

SLIDE UP AND DOWN

DEAD BOLT

Z-BAR

MARK TOP

10 Hold the latch-side Z-bar against the open door and center the holes on the latches. Then push the door and Z-bar against the door frame and mark and cut the bottom at the angle of the threshold. Then mark the top (inset) and cut it.

Out with the old storm door

Taking off an old aluminum door is usually just a case of unscrewing the mounting screws on the door, closer and safety chain. But sometimes there's caulk around the frame. You can usually cut through the caulk with a utility knife. But worse yet, you could find old caulk between the frame and the door casing. If so, you'll have to pry the frame away with an old chisel and scrape the trim surfaces clean. A heat gun may help soften the caulk. If you don't know what to do with the old door, put a free sign on it or post in on the Craigslist free stuff page.

Wooden storm doors generally have hinges that are mortised (notched into the wood) and screwed to the door casing. Don't worry about the hinge or latch recesses. When you install your new storm door, they'll be hidden behind the new door frame.

Prep the opening

Storm doors hang from the door trim, technically called "exterior casing." If the door has never had a storm door (as in our situation), you may have to extend the trim between the door and a sidelight (**Photo 2**). This is the most difficult situation you're likely to encounter. You have to rip a new trim piece to match the thickness of the other trim (usually 1-1/8 in. thick).

Manufacturers make storm doors a bit narrower than standard openings to make sure they'll fit. If your opening is typical, you'll have to "fur out" the sides to center the storm door in the opening. You'll nearly always need to install at least one 1/4-in. furring strip on the hinge side (**Photo 6**) and possibly even have to add another one to the latch side (**Photo 11**). To figure this out, measure the exact width of the opening, that is, the distance between the inside edges of the trim. (Measure at the middle, top and bottom.) The manufacturer's instructions will usually list the minimum width required. Subtract that width from your measurement and make the furring strip thickness along the hinge side about half the difference.

It's important to mount the door tightly to the hinge-side trim. Pry against the latch side to make sure it snugs up tight (**Photo 7**).

Follow the photos with your instructions for the rest of the installation steps. Door latch and Z-bar systems vary. Cutting the latch-side Z-bar is a bit fussy. The idea is to center it on the latch and lock (**Photo 10**). Observe where it strikes the sill and cut the bottom at an angle that matches the sill. Then cut the top so it fits against the top Z-bar. Don't worry if the latch and lock bolt end up a bit off-center, as long as they work smoothly.

You may need to chisel out the latch or deadbolt pocket as we show (**Photo 11**). It all depends on the door latch style.

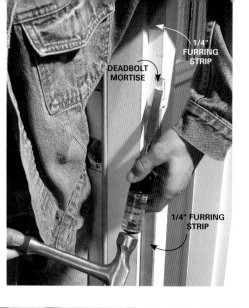

11 Close the door against the casing with the dead bolt extended and chisel out the wood where the deadbolt hits. Slip the latch-side Z-bar into place, close the door against it and screw it to the casing, keeping a consistent 1/8-in. gap with the door.

DEADBOLT MORTISE

1/4" FURRING STRIP

1/4" FURRING STRIP

After installing the door sweep and closers, adjust the closer tension. Begin with the window panel rather than the screen in place. The closers should be set with the door at its heaviest. You may want to reset a gentler setting for the screen panel.

Finally, it's a good idea to save the boxes for the window and screen panel for off-season storage. Under a bed is a great safe storage location.

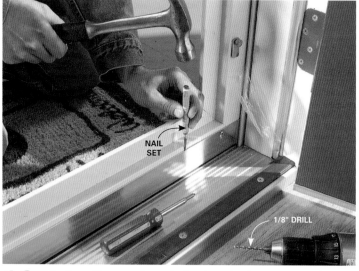

NAIL SET

1/8" DRILL

12 Slide the rubber weatherstripping into the door sweep and crimp the ends. Slide the sweep over the door bottom and tap it down to snug it to the threshold. Drill 1/8-in. holes through the adjustment slots and add the screws.

Dealing with a warped storm door

Storm doors often appear to be warped because they don't rest evenly against the weatherstripping at all corners. However, it's usually the entry door trim that's a bit out of whack. Small gaps may disappear when you install the door closers, especially if your door comes with one for the top and one for the bottom. If that doesn't do the trick, try prying out the Z-bar slightly and slip in a shim (photo below) that should close the gap.

Bigger gaps call for more drastic measures. First loosen all the Z-bar screws and remove the screws at opposite corners of the door. Then slip a shim behind the corner screws, opposite the gap. Tighten the corner screws to see if the gap closes. Try varying sizes of shims until the door closes well. Then slip in progressively smaller shims behind the rest of the screws as you tighten them to taper the gap between the Z-bar and the door casing. Cut off the shims, then caulk the gap and paint it to match.

DOOR JAMB

CLOSER

BRACKET

13 Position the closer bracket and screw it to the jamb. Attach the closer, level it and mark the screw positions on the door. Drill 1/8-in. pilot holes and screw the closer to the door. Repeat for the top closer.

Replace a Toilet

Tips for a fast, trouble-free, leak-free installation

Whether you're installing a better-flushing toilet or resetting the old one after repairs or remodeling, these tips will help you do it faster and with fewer problems. The job can take less than an hour, but set aside a whole morning in case you run into trouble. Everything you'll need is available at home centers and hardware stores.

Hiring a plumber to replace a toilet typically costs $100 to $200. If there are hidden problems, such as a broken floor flange, that cost can easily double.

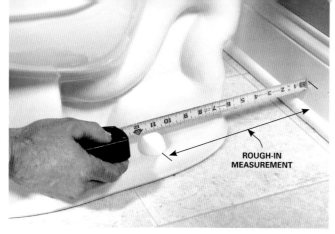

ROUGH-IN
MEASUREMENT

Check the "rough-in"

If you're buying a new toilet, you need to know the "rough-in" measurement of the old one. For the vast majority of toilets, the waste pipe is centered about 12 in. from the wall. But with a few models, that measurement is 10 in. or 14 in. To check the rough-in, just measure from the wall to the toilet's hold-down bolts. If that measurement (plus the thickness of the baseboard) isn't approximately 12 in., toilet shopping will be a bit harder. Most home centers carry only one or two 10-in. models and no 14-in. models. If you have to special-order a toilet, be prepared to spend much more.

If there's a door near the toilet, also measure how far the bowl protrudes from the wall. If you replace a standard bowl with an "elongated" model, the door may not close.

Brass bolts are best

Some metal toilet bolts have a yellowish zinc coating that makes them look like brass. So check the label and make sure you're getting brass bolts and nuts. They won't rust away and they're easier to cut off later. If you need to re-anchor the toilet flange, buy stainless steel screws. They won't corrode like steel or break off like brass while you're driving them.

Cut hold-down bolts

Don't be surprised if the old nuts that hold the toilet in place won't budge. Years of corrosion can weld them to their bolts. In that case, a hacksaw blade is the solution. You can buy a "close quarters" blade holder at home centers and hardware stores, or just wrap a bare blade with a rag or duct tape. Most toilet bolts and nuts are brass, so they're easy to cut. If the bolt spins, grab it with locking pliers as you cut.

EXTRA NUT
AND WASHER

Lock down the bolts

Setting a toilet onto the new bolts can be the most frustrating part of the whole installation. The bolts slip and tip as you're straining to align them with the holes in the toilet. And each time you miss, you risk crushing or shifting the wax ring. The plastic slip-on washers sometimes included with bolts help, but they still allow the bolts to move. The best approach is to buy a second set of nuts and washers so you can lock the bolts in place before you set the toilet. To make sure they're in the correct position, set the toilet and check its height and position. Then lift it off and add the wax ring. To make the bolts easier to find, mark their locations with masking tape.

Flange fixes

A rock-solid toilet flange is the key to a leak-free toilet. The flange is the only thing anchoring the toilet to the floor. If the flange is loose or damaged, the toilet will rock. And a rocking toilet will distort the wax ring and cause leaks. So be sure to scrape off the old wax ring and inspect the flange. Here are some solutions for broken, corroded or loose flanges:

Ear-type ring

Loose flanges are usually the result of wood rot. The flange screws simply won't hold in the soft, decayed subfloor. The best solution depends on the extent of the rot. If the rot is only under the flange, use an ear-type repair ring. The ears let you drive screws into firm wood farther away from the flange. Before you install this kind of ring, hold it up to the drain horn on the underside of the toilet. You may have to cut off a couple of ears to make it work with your toilet. If the rot extends well beyond the flange, you'll have to replace a section of the subfloor.

Repair ring

Plastic flanges often bend or break, but that's an easy fix. Just screw a stainless steel repair ring over the plastic flange with at least four 1-1/2-in. stainless steel screws. Consider doing this even if the plastic flange is in good shape—it's cheap insurance against future trouble. The repair ring raises the flange by about 1/4 in., so before you install the ring, set it on the flange and set your toilet over it to make sure it fits.

Two-part repair ring

Steel flanges attached to plastic hubs can rust away. The easiest solution is a two-part ring that locks onto the plastic just like the old one. To cut away the old flange, use a hacksaw blade or an angle grinder with a metal-cutting wheel. The repair flange is available at some Lowe's stores. To buy online, search for "bay flange" or go to quickfixplumbingproducts.com.

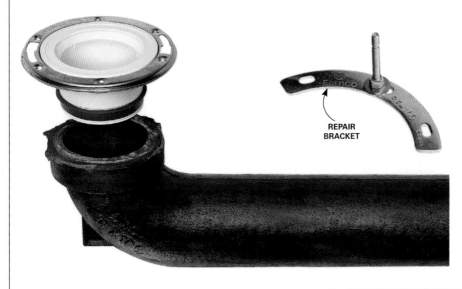

REPAIR
BRACKET

Repair flange

Cast iron flanges can break or corrode. If only the bolt slot is damaged, slip a repair bracket under the flange. If the flange is in bad shape, you can add a brass repair ring similar to the stainless steel ring shown here or install a plastic flange that slips inside. If necessary, break away the cast iron flange with a cold chisel. Home centers carry one or two slip-in flanges. For a wider variety, search online for "replacement toilet flange."

Cut the bolts last

To make positioning a toilet easier, new toilet bolts are extra long. That means you have to cut off the protruding ends later with a hacksaw. But first connect the water line, flush the toilet a couple of times and check for leaks. Leaving the bolts uncut until you've done these final checks lets you easily remove and reset the toilet if you find any problems.

After cutting, double-check the bolts for tightness. Cutting often loosens the nuts a bit.

Eliminate rocking with shims

A toilet that rocks on an uneven floor will eventually break the wax ring seal and leak. So check for wobbles after you've set the toilet in place and loosely tightened the nuts. For slight wobbles, slip coins or stainless steel washers into the gaps under the toilet. Don't use regular steel washers, which might rust and stain the floor. For larger gaps, use shims. There are plastic shims made especially for toilets, but plastic construction shims like the ones shown here work just as well. When you've eliminated the wobble, tighten the nuts, cut off the shims and caulk around the toilet base. A toilet set on thick vinyl flooring can loosen as the vinyl compresses. In that case, just retighten the nuts a few days after installation.

Don't overtighten the water connections

Do yourself a favor and buy a flexible water supply line. They're a lot easier to install than stiff metal or plastic tubing. Be sure to get one that's covered with stainless steel mesh. For a good seal, hold the hose so it aims straight into the shutoff or fill valve while you're screwing on the connectors. Make them hand-tight, then add another quarter turn with pliers. Connections that are too tight can actually cause leaks or spin the fill valve inside the tank. Check for leaks and tighten a bit more if needed.

Squish the wax ring with your own weight

When you set the toilet in place, you have to squish the wax ring until the toilet settles to the floor. DON'T force the toilet down by tightening the nuts on the toilet bolts—that might crack the porcelain base. Instead, sit on the toilet backward with your weight centered over the wax ring. Then wiggle your bottom like a belly dancer until the toilet reaches the floor. But don't over-do it. You want to drive the toilet straight down with minimal twisting or shifting of it from side to side. When the toilet reaches the floor, snug down the toilet bolt nuts.

Special Section

OUR MOST POPULAR WORKBENCHES

Super-Simple Workbench............................ 276
Classic Workbench 280
Best Workbench Upgrades 284

Super-Simple Workbench

*Got two hours on your hands and 50 bucks in your pocket?
Do we have a workbench for you!*

This sturdy 30-in. x 6-ft.-long workbench is the ultimate in simplicity. It's made from only fifteen 8-ft.-long 2x4s and one sheet of 1/2-in. plywood. Follow the cutting diagrams to cut the parts: **Figure B** to cut the plywood tops, then **Figure C** to cut all the framing. Use the lengths provided in the **Cutting List**. You can either screw the framing together with 3-in. screws or hand- or power-nail it together with 3-in. nails. Screw the plywood down with 1-5/8-in. screws.

To make these project plans even easier to follow, we tinted the parts that get added at each step.

Accessorize it!

Lighting

Good light is mandatory for any workbench. Buy a 4-ft. shop light and screw it right to the underside of the top shelf.

Power strip

Forget extension cords. Mount a power strip to one of the legs and you'll have all the power you need for tools and chargers. Use its switch to control the light.

Pegboard

Whether you cover the whole back or just the lower half, keep down the bench clutter by stowing all of those tools you use every day within easy reach.

Bench vise

Yes, it'll cost as much as or more than the bench, but what workbench would be complete without one?

Figure A
Main workbench parts

WORK SURFACE

LEGS

LOWER SHELF

Watch it being assembled
If you want to see how quickly and easily this bench goes together, you can watch a video of it being built at familyhandyman.com/workbench.

1 Assemble the frames for the work surface and lower shelf

WORK SURFACE

LOWER SHELF

2 Screw the legs to the work surface frame

Tip

Use paint cans to support the lower shelf frame when you're attaching it to the main workbench legs.

3 Flip over the bench and attach the lower shelf frame

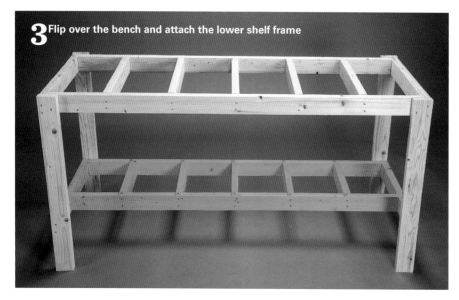

Cutting list

KEY	QTY.	SIZE & DESCRIPTION
A	9	71-7/8" (backer boards, upper shelf legs and rims)
B	4	68-7/8" (work surface and lower shelf rim)
C	4	35-1/2" (legs)
D	4	27" (end rims)
E	5	24" (work surface joists)

Figure B
Plywood cutting diagram

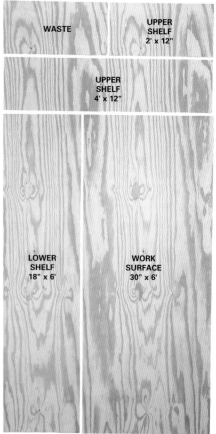

WASTE

UPPER SHELF 2' x 12"

UPPER SHELF 4' x 12"

LOWER SHELF 18" x 6'

WORK SURFACE 30" x 6'

4 Screw the plywood to the frames

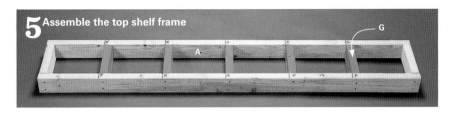

5 Assemble the top shelf frame

G
A

6 Add the plywood

7 Attach the top shelf legs upside down

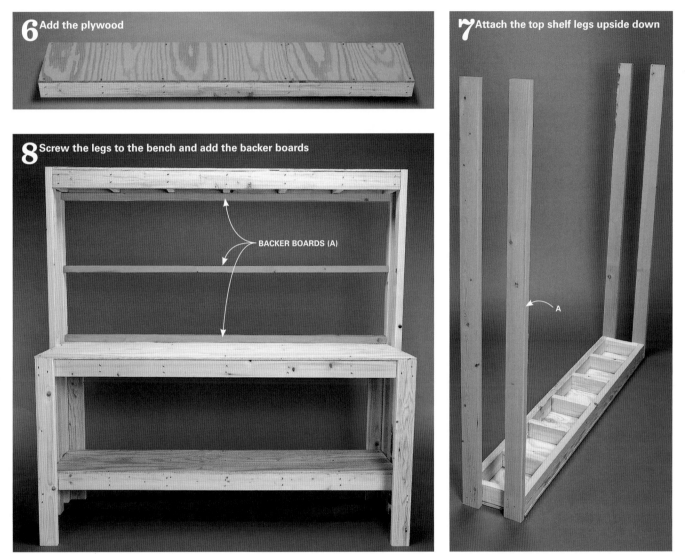

8 Screw the legs to the bench and add the backer boards

BACKER BOARDS (A)

A

Figure C
2x4 usage diagram

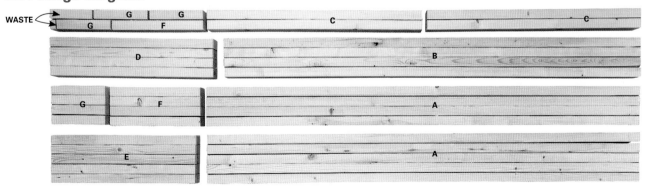

WASTE →

G   G   G
G   F   C   C

D   B

G   F   A

E   A

Classic Workbench

A timeless design that's simple and strong

WHAT IT TAKES

TIME: One day

COST: $85

SKILL: Beginner

TOOLS: Circular saw, drill, No. 6 countersink bit

1 **BUILD THE FRAMES.** Use 3-in. screws to assemble the frames that support the top and the shelf. To avoid splitting the 2x4s, either drill pilot holes or use self-drilling screws. Build both frames and set the top frame aside.

If this workbench looks familiar, it's probably because you've seen one a lot like it in your father's or grandfather's shop. Variations of this design have been around for decades, and for good reason: The bench is strong, practical and super easy to build. You can run to the lumberyard in the morning, grab a few boards, and by noon you'll have a perfectly functional workbench.

The workbench isn't fancy—it's built from standard construction lumber. But you can easily customize it with drawers or other features now or later. To see some of the improvements you can make, search for "workbench upgrade" at familyhandyman.com.

If you can cut a board, you can build this bench. And you don't need any fancy tools either. In addition to a small square and a tape measure, you'll need a circular saw to cut the parts and a drill to drive the screws.

Getting started

You'll find all the materials at a lumberyard or home center (see **Materials List**). Choose lumber that's straight and flat, and that doesn't have too many gouges, slivers or cracks. We used Torx-head screws with self-drilling tips. But you can substitute any construction screw. If you're not using screws with self-drilling tips, drill pilot holes to avoid splitting the wood.

> **Tip**
> If your car is too small for the long boards, you can ask to have the boards cut to length. Just remember to take the Cutting List with you to the store.

Cut the parts according to the **Cutting List** on p. 283. We used a miter saw, but a circular saw will work fine. Mark the 2x4s with a Speed square or combination square. Then carefully cut the boards to length. If you plan to stain or paint the bench, now is the time to sand the parts. And to really simplify your job, you could also stain or paint the parts before you assemble the bench.

Start by building the top and shelf frames

We used an old door propped up on saw-horses as a work surface, but the floor will work too. Lay the 2x4s for the front and back of the top and shelf on the work surface and mark the centers. Remember, if you're not using self-drilling screws, drill pilot holes for the screws. **Photo 1** shows how to assemble the frames. Set the top frame aside and screw the shelf boards to the shelf frame (**Photo 2**).

2 **ATTACH THE SHELF BOARDS.** Attach the outside boards first. Then position the two remaining boards to create equal spaces between them and screw them to the frame. Before driving screws, drill pilot holes with a countersink bit.

3 **ASSEMBLE THE LEGS.** Drill five holes about 2 in. from the edge of the pegboard with the countersinking bit. Spread a bead of construction adhesive on the legs and attach the pegboard with 1-1/4-in. screws. If glue oozes through the holes, wait for it to dry. Then shave it off with a sharp chisel.

TOP FRAME

4 SCREW THE LEGS TO THE TOP FRAME. Apply construction adhesive where the legs contact the top frame. Then attach the legs with screws.

SHELF

BOTTOM OF PEGBOARD

5 ADD THE SHELF. Rest the bench on one end. Slide the shelf between the legs and line it up with the bottom of the pegboard. Screw through the shelf into the legs.

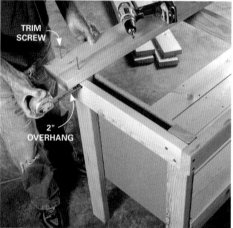

TRIM SCREW

2" OVERHANG

6 MOUNT THE TOP BOARDS. Starting at the back, align the first 2x6 flush to the back and measure for the 2-in. overhang on the side. Attach the 2x6 with trim screws. Attach the rest of the boards the same way. The front 2x6 will overhang the frame about 2 in.

7 INSTALL THE BACKBOARD. Attach the 1x4 shelf to the 1x10 backboard. Then add a 2x4 block at each end. Rest the backboard assembly on the workbench and drive screws through the back to hold it in place.

Build and attach the leg assemblies

Photo 3 shows how to build the leg assemblies. You'll notice that the leg assemblies are 1/8 in. narrower than the inside dimension of the top. That's so you can install the legs without binding, which would cause the pegboard to bow. Also, if the only pegboard you can find is thinner than the 1/4-in. pegboard specified, add the difference to the front and back of the shelf frame (C). For example, if you buy 1/8-in. pegboard, add 1/4 in. to parts C.

The pegboard is useful for hanging tools, but its real function is to stabilize the workbench as a brace. We added the construction adhesive to make sure the assemblies stayed strong and rigid. Be aware, though, that some of the adhesive will be visible through the holes.

The pegboard holes are a little too big to use as screw holes, so use a No. 6 countersink bit to drill pilot holes and make countersinks for the screws. Secure five evenly spaced 1-1/4-in. screws into each leg.

The next step is to attach the legs to the top frame. Apply construction adhesive to the top 3 in. of the legs. Then attach the leg assemblies with 3-in. screws (**Photo 4**).

Add the shelf and top

Stand the workbench on one end. Then it's simple to slide the shelf into place and line it up with the pegboard (**Photo 5**). Drive 3-in. screws through the shelf frame into the legs to support the shelf.

The top of this bench is 2x6s, placed tight together. The boards overhang the frame 2 in. on the sides and front. The overhang makes it easier to use clamps on the edges of the workbench. **Photo 6** shows how to get started. We attached the 2x6s with trim screws, but you could substitute 16d casing nails.

Attach the back brace and backboard

The 1x10 back brace keeps things from falling off the back of the shelf, but it also stiffens the bench to prevent side-to-side rocking. Apply construction adhesive before attaching the brace with 2-in. screws.

The backboard is a 1x10 with a 1x4 shelf attached. On the side of the 1x10 you want facing out, draw a line the length of the board, 1-3/4 in. down from the top. This is where you'll align the bottom of the 1x4.

Figure A
Classic workbench

Overall dimensions:
60" wide x 28-1/4" deep x 36" tall plus a 7-3/4" backboard

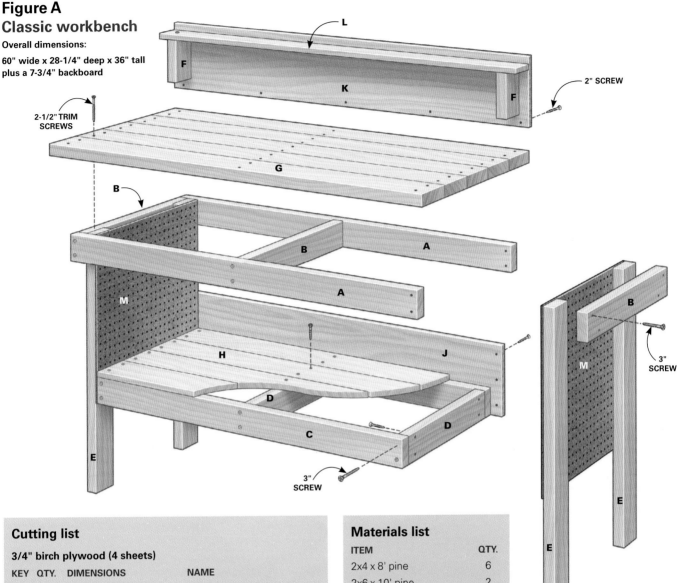

2-1/2" TRIM SCREWS

2" SCREW

3" SCREW

3" SCREW

Cutting list

3/4" birch plywood (4 sheets)

KEY	QTY.	DIMENSIONS	NAME
A	2	1-1/2" x 3-1/2" x 56"	Top frame front and back
B	3	1-1/2" x 3-1/2" x 22-1/2"	Top frame crosspieces
C	2	1-1/2" x 3-1/2" x 49-1/2"	Shelf frame front and back
D	3	1-1/2" x 3-1/2" x 19-1/2"	Shelf crosspieces
E	4	1-1/2" x 3-1/2" x 34-1/2"	Legs
F	2	1-1/2" x 3-1/2" x 6"	Back shelf supports
G	5	1-1/2" x 5-1/2" x 60"	Top boards
H	4	3/4" x 5-1/2" x 49-1/2"	Shelf boards
J	1	3/4" x 9-1/4" x 53"	Back brace
K	1	3/4" x 9-1/4" x 60"	Backboard
L	1	3/4" x 3-1/2" x 60"	Backboard shelf
M	2	22-3/8" x 22-3/8" x 1/4"	Pegboard leg braces

Materials list

ITEM	QTY.
2x4 x 8' pine	6
2x6 x 10' pine	2
2x6 x 8' pine	1
1x10 x 10' pine	1
1x6 x 10' pine	2
1x4 x 6' pine	1
2' x 4' x 1/4" pegboard	1
3" self-drilling screws	42
2" self-drilling screws	50
1-1/4" self-drilling screws	20
2-1/2" trim screws	30
Construction adhesive	1 tube

Draw a second line 1-3/8 in. from the top. Drill pilot holes with the countersink bit every 8 in. along this line. Now ask a helper to hold the 1x4 on the line while you drive 2-in. screws into the shelf through the pilot holes. After the shelf and 2x4 blocks at each end are attached, screw the backboard to the workbench (**Photo 7**).

You can modify your bench to fit your space and work style. We mounted an inexpensive woodworking vise on the front of the workbench and drilled holes in the 1x4 shelf to hold screwdrivers. If you've got a pint-size carpenter in the family, check out the mini version of the bench at familyhandyman.com (search "mini workbench"). It's a great project to build with your kids or grandkids.

Best Workbench Upgrades

Our favorite ways to add storage, convenience and handy features to any workbench

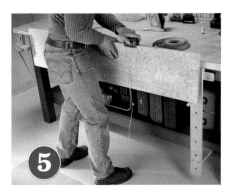

To find the best ideas for simple workbench upgrades, we sampled the workbenches of our staff and pro friends. No matter what kind of workbench you have, you can add one or all of these improvements to make your bench more functional and fun to use.

The largest project here, the three roll-out drawers, only requires one sheet of 3/4-in. plywood and less than a day to build. The rest of the projects require even less time and materials. You could build any of these projects with basic carpentry tools and a circular saw, drill and jigsaw. But a table saw will simplify the process by adding speed and accuracy. And, of course, a pneumatic trim nailer would be handy for building the shallow drawers and for tacking together the roll-out drawers before you strengthen them with screws.

① Easiest add-on drawers

These roll-out drawers are easy—you don't even have to mount them to the bench. They're just sturdy boxes that ride on 2-in. casters. Measure from the floor to the bottom shelf of your workbench and subtract 3-1/4 in. to figure the height of the boxes. Then subtract 3/4 in. from this measurement to determine the height of the drawer front, back and sides. Next, decide how many drawers you want and calculate the widths. Allow for a 1/2-in. space between drawers.

Cut the parts and screw them together. Then measure the width and length of the box and cut the bottom. Screw on the bottom and cut a handhold in the front of the drawer with a jigsaw. Finish up by screwing 2-in. fixed (not swiveling!) casters to the bottom of the drawer, as shown.

Build basic plywood boxes and screw on the casters. Carefully align the casters parallel to the box sides so the drawers roll smooth and straight.

❷ Our favorite convenience feature

Every bench needs easy-access storage for all the odds and ends that would otherwise clutter the benchtop. These shallow drawers, which mount directly under the benchtop, fit the bill perfectly.

There's no fancy joinery on these drawers. And the special pencil drawer slides simplify mounting. We used 22-in.-deep drawer slides and built the drawers 22 in. deep to match. The drawer slides (No. KV8250; $24 a pair) are available from wwhardware.com.

You can build the drawers up to about 30 in. wide, but remember to allow a few inches of space on each side for the mounting hardware. Rip strips of 3/4-in. plywood or solid lumber to 3-1/4 in. wide for the front, sides and back. Cut the sides 22 in. long and the front and back pieces 1-1/2 in. less than the desired width of the drawer. Glue and nail the sides to the front and back. Then measure the width and length of the drawer and cut a bottom from 1/4-in. plywood. Glue and nail the bottom to the assembled frame. If you're careful to cut the bottom piece perfectly square, your drawer will be square. Or you can hold one side and the drawer front

against a framing square while you nail on the bottom.

Photo 1 shows how to attach the drawer slide. Line up the bottom of the slide with the seam between the drawer bottom and drawer side. If you don't have 2x4 crosspieces under your bench, add them in the location of the drawer hardware. Then prop up the drawer in the right spot and screw through the brackets into the crosspieces (**Photo 2**). Finish by cutting drawer fronts that are 1-1/2 in.

longer and 1/2 in. taller than the drawer. Attach the drawer front from the back with 1-1/4-in. screws driven through the front of the drawer box.

PENCIL DRAWER SLIDE

1 Mount the drawers with special "pencil drawer" slides. These slides include hanger brackets, so you don't have to build extra parts just to attach drawer slides.

ADDED CROSSPIECE

TEMPORARY SUPPORT

2 Prop up the drawer and screw it to the underside of the workbench. Add crosspieces if there's nothing to screw into.

❸ Best benchtop space-saver

When you want to use the whole top of your workbench, a permanently mounted vise or grinder just gets in the way. Free up space by mounting your grinder and vise to a double-thick piece of 3/4-in. plywood and hanging them on the end of your workbench until they're needed.

Cut four 20-in.-long x 12-in.-wide pieces of 3/4-in. plywood. Glue and nail them together in pairs to make two 1-1/2-in.-thick slabs. Transfer the location of the mounting holes on your vise and grinder to the plywood. Use a 1-in. spade bit to drill a 1/2-in.-deep recess at each hole location. Then drill through the plywood with a 3/8-in. bit and mount the tools with 3/8-in. bolts, washers and nuts. Position the recess on the side of the plywood opposite the tool to ensure a flush surface.

We screwed a double-thick piece of 3/4-in. plywood to the end of the workbench to make a sturdy mounting plate, but your workbench may not need this. Any strong, flat surface will work. Drill two 1/2-in. holes into each tool holder and mark matching hole locations on the mounting plate. Drill 3/8-in. holes at the marks and attach 3/8-in. bolts with nuts and washers. We recessed the nuts in the mounting plate so the tool holders would sit flush, but this isn't necessary.

1/2" HOLE

3/8" BOLT

❹ Our favorite 15-minute workbench accessory

This tool tray is so simple to build that you can have it mounted in about 15 minutes, start to finish. It's a great place to keep small, commonly used tools handy but off the benchtop. And it keeps pencils and other small tools from rolling or getting knocked off the bench and landing on the floor where you can't find them.

Building the tray couldn't be simpler. Just cut a 1x4 and two 1x3s 24 in. long and nail the 1x3s to the sides of the 1x4. Cut two pieces of 1x3 5 in. long and nail them to the ends to complete the tray. Screw the tray to the end of your workbench and you'll never waste time searching for a pencil again.

⑤ Simplest support for long boards

Have you ever needed to hold a long board or door on edge to work on it but struggled to find a good method? If you have a woodworker's vise, adding this board jack is an easy solution. The board jack shown hooks onto the beveled support strip and slides along it to adjust for the length of the workpiece. The 3/4-in. dowel adjusts up and down to accommodate different widths.

Start by ripping a 45-degree angle on a 1x3 board or strip of plywood. Screw the strip to the front of your workbench. Then build a board jack like the one shown. Drill 3/4-in. holes every 6 in. and insert a 4-in. dowel in the hole to support your work. Adjust the length of the standoff to hold the board jack plumb on your workbench.

3/4" DOWEL

3/4" HOLE

BOARD JACK

STANDOFF

Mount a board jack to the front of your workbench and use it with your vise to support your work. Screw a beveled strip to the front of your workbench. Then build the board jack and hook it over the top to support your work.